The Swedish Monarchy and the Copper Trade

Entanglements, Interactions, and Economies in the Early Modern World

The books published in this series pursue particular historical themes that illuminate the interactive and interconnected dimensions of the early modern world, roughly periodized from 1400 to 1800. These studies either take a comparative approach to commensurate historical developments in various parts of the world or examine trans-regional patterns and forces that affected local societies. The series places emphasis on intellectual, cultural, religious, and economic analyses on topics such as migration streams and diasporas, empire-building and colonialism, epidemiological patterns and environmental changes, long-distance trade and commercial networking, and missionary programs and spiritual encounters. Authors working on these and related topics connect the global phenomena to local peoples in their nations, cities, villages, tribes, and families. Thus, this series explores the reciprocity between global processes and local affairs, which illustrate the unfolding human condition in specific historical moments.

Series editors
Charles H. Parker, Saint Louis University, USA
Ulrike Strasser, University of California San Diego, USA

The Swedish Monarchy and the Copper Trade

The Copper Company, the Deposit System, and the
Amsterdam Market, 1600–1640

Lawrence Stryker

Amsterdam University Press

Cover illustration: Cornelius Arendtz (1610–1640), *King Gustav II Adolf*, c. 1625. Current location of painting unknown; source, Wikimedia Commons.

Cover design: Coördesign, Leiden
Lay-out: Crius Group, Hulshout

ISBN	978 90 4856 081 3
e-ISBN	978 90 4856 082 0
DOI	10.5117/9789048560813
NUR	685

Printed and bound by CPI Group (UK) Ltd, Croydon, CR0 4YY

Table of Contents

List of Illustrations

Preliminary Notes

In order to approach the great exchange of raw materials and financial resources that took place between Sweden and the United Provinces we must consider several mundane, but essential, problems. First, the reader will encounter prices in three different currencies: Swedish *dalers* (SD), *riksdaler* (RD), and Dutch guilders (DG). The Swedish *daler* and Dutch guilder are self-explanatory. The *riksdaler* was used in the Holy Roman Empire and was the reserve currency of its day. The exchange rate was as follows: RD 1 = DG 2.5 and RD 1 = SD 1.624. All three were silver based currencies, and because they were minted coins the relative values remained stable during the period we will consider.

In Sweden and northern Germany copper was traded in *skeppund* or literally, ship pounds. To complicate matters, a *skeppund* at the mine weighed more than a *skeppund* at the port. According to Eli F. Heckscher, one of the more important Swedish economic historians we shall encounter, a *skeppund* in Stockholm weighed 136 modern kilograms.[1] Our key for the various weights is a balance sheet that the Amsterdam merchant, Louis de Geer, drew up in 1626. He was shipping copper ingot and plate from Stockholm to Amsterdam. He had to convert the Stockholm *skeppund* into Dutch hundredweight denominations. From this conversion I was able to derive the following ratios in Amsterdam pounds:[2]

1 *skeppund* mine weight = 302.53 Amsterdam pounds.
1 *skeppund* Stockholm weight = 274.3 Amsterdam pounds.
1 *skeppund* Amsterdam weight = 317.24 Amsterdam pounds.

As a practical matter, the Stockholm *skeppund* denomination was used extensively, and the other two used only rarely. Unless otherwise specified, all *skeppund* are Stockholm weight.

1   Eli F. Heckscher, *Sveriges economiska historia från Gustav Vasa*, 2 vols. (Stockholm, 1936), I, 603. (A kilogram weighs 2.2046 American pounds.)
2   Riksarkivet. Leufsta arkiv. *Cooper Platen Debit Ano 1625* Amsterdam # 22, *Garcooper Debit Ano 1626* Amsterdam # 25, *Rouwcoper Debit Ano 1626* # 27.

Stryker, L., *The Swedish Monarchy and the Copper Trade: The Copper Company, the Deposit System, and the Amsterdam Market, 1600–1640*. Amsterdam: Amsterdam University Press, 2024
DOI 10.5117/9789048560813_PRE

Regarding sources, I have used two collections of published letters extensively. The first is the collected correspondence of Axel Oxenstierna, the king of Sweden's highly capable chancellor. The Swedish Royal Academy began publishing this collection in 1888; to date, they have published sixteen volumes of letters written by the chancellor and thirteen volumes of letters written to the chancellor. The letters are mostly from the extensive collection in the *Riksarkiv* in Stockholm. In citing this source, I have followed the example of Swedish historians and used the abbreviation AOSB for *Axel Oxenstiernas skriften och brefvexling* (Axel Oxenstierna's Writings and Letters). The other collection is the correspondence of Louis de Geer published by his biographer E.W. Dahlgren in 1934. Again, taking the example of Swedish scholars, I have abbreviated this as LDGBOA for *Louis de Geer brev och affärshandlingar 1614–1652* (Louis de Geer's Letters and Business Correspondence).

I also cite unpublished letters and accounting records. The Riksarkiv in Stockholm offers a large variety of scanned documents over the internet. Most of these documents interest genealogists. The *Riksarchiv*, however, has also scanned thousands of letters from the copybooks of Karl IX and Gustav II Adolf.

One final bit of information is necessary—the bill of exchange. This was a complex financial instrument that first appeared in Renaissance Italy. Its purpose was to allow merchants, and later banks, to exchange goods for money without the necessity of transporting large quantities of coins over distances. To use an example from the copper trade, let us assume that the king of Sweden, Gustav Adolf, had borrowed RD 100,000 from the States General of the United Provinces in the Netherlands to pay for military necessities. To repay interest and some principal the king might send a bill of exchange to Elias Trip, a prominent merchant in Amsterdam. In the bill the king could instruct Elias Trip to pay RD 10,000 to the States General on his behalf. Naturally, the king knew that Elias Trip had the resources to cover the payment. If Trip accepted the bill, he would sign it and pay the RD 10,000 to the States General. Trip now had a promise from the king of Sweden to pay the bearer of the bill RD 10,000 when the bill was presented in Stockholm. In practice, however, Trip would not travel to Stockholm to receive payment. Let us assume that the following month the king sold copper to Elias Trip for delivery in Amsterdam. The copper had a value of RD 20,000. Trip would then send the endorsed bill of exchange to the king in payment for the copper. He would also draw up a new bill of exchange to his factor in Stockholm instructing him to pay the balance of RD 10,000 to the king.

On the other hand, let us suppose that Trip had no further business with the king. How would he collect the RD 10,000 owed to him without making the journey? Trip would contact his brother-in-law, Louis de Geer, another merchant with business in Sweden. Perhaps, de Geer had just purchased bronze cannon from a foundry in Sweden, and he needed to pay the foundry RD 10,000 locally. Trip would sell the bill of exchange to de Geer for RD 10,000 plus a small commission. This would reimburse Trip for his original outlay of RD 10,000. De Geer would then forward the endorsed bill of exchange to the foundry in Sweden. The foundry, in turn, would present the bill to the king and receive the RD 10,000 that de Geer owed to them.

The following is an example of a bill of exchange drawn up by Chancellor Axel Oxenstierna in favor of Louis de Geer:

> 1632. From 12 October in Nuremberg. 6,301, and 3/8 Guilder and 73 *Groschen*. Earnest and discrete Herr, good friend. Please pay this my first bill of exchange to Jeronimo Hesters, Guilder six thousand, three hundred one and three eights and seventy-three *Groschen*. This value in the king's treasury was properly approved by Herren Hainrich and Hannss Mülleg. Signed by Axel Oxenstierna.[3]

At this stage de Geer was in Amsterdam. If he did not have further business with the Swedish crown, he would sell this bill to a merchant in Amsterdam who needed to make a payment in Stockholm.[4]

The vast majority of long-distance payments were made by bills of exchange. They had, however, an inherent weakness. Payment by bills of exchange was slow and awkward. Sufficient business between two destinations was necessary for the method to work, and it could take time for offsetting business to occur. The king and chancellor calculated at least a seven-month delay between shipping copper and receiving payment from Amsterdam. We shall see that it often took longer. That was between two busy ports. It would take much longer between less active ports. This issue of time will be a major factor in our arguments regarding the king's decision to issue a copper currency in order to pay his army.

---

3   AOSB, I, 8, 598, Till Louis de Geer. Nürnberg, October 12, 1632.
4   For further information see: Thomas Max Safley, "Commerce and Markets," in *Europe 1450 to 1789, Encyclopedia of the Early Modern World*, ed. Jonathan Dewald (New York, 2004), II, 16.

Introduction

Abstract

In 1611, the seventeen-year-old prince, Gustav Adolf, (1594-1632) ascended to the throne of Sweden. This marked the beginning of the time in Swedish history known as "the period of greatness." A visionary king, Gustav II Adolf began his reign by settling disputes with the domestic nobility and organizing the payment of a ransom to redeem the fortress at Älvsborg from Danish occupiers. These were key elements in the crown's efforts to develop an administrative state. The young Gustav II Adolf then turned his attention to the major asset his country offered, the Stora Kopparberg copper mine. With the help of capable administrators, the king reorganized the mine to increase the revenue flow. He used the funds to help finance wars in the Baltic region, and later in northern Germany.

Keywords: Gustav II Adolf, state formation, wars in Poland, Trace Italienne, copper

> "The first loss is the best loss."
> Old trader saying

Background

The first half of the seventeenth century was a period of extraordinary development for the Swedish monarchy and the country it ruled. Sweden, with a population of fewer than one and one-half million souls, had remained for centuries a remote rural outpost with a short growing season and limited economic prospects. That changed dramatically between 1611 and 1632, during the reign of the ambitious young King Gustav II Adolf who substantially expanded the Swedish Empire and its sphere of influence.

Even as heir to the throne of Sweden, Gustav Adolf was a war-like prince. In 1611, while he was still only sixteen years old, his father, Karl IX (1550–1611),

Stryker, L., *The Swedish Monarchy and the Copper Trade: The Copper Company, the Deposit System, and the Amsterdam Market, 1600–1640.* Amsterdam: Amsterdam University Press, 2024
DOI 10.5117/9789048560813_INTRO

gave him the command of a small army in East Gotland during a war with Denmark. His role was defensive; in no time, however, the eager young prince assembled a militia and began raiding across the border into Danish Skåne. Learning of the Swedish incursion, the commander of the border fortress of Kristianopel sent a message to the king of Denmark, Kristian IV (1577–1648), requesting reinforcements in the form of Danish cavalry. Gustav Adolf's pickets, however, captured the messenger. Understanding the possibilities this message provided, Gustav Adolf assembled his cavalry and disguised them as Danish troopers. They appeared at night before the gates of Kristianopel. Assuming this was their relieving forces, the fortress opened its gates to allow the troopers to enter. After a brief struggle the fortress was taken, and the young heir provided his father with a surprise victory in an otherwise disastrous war. A few weeks later the ailing Karl IX was dead. Within months, Gustav Adolf turned seventeen and was crowned king of Sweden.[1]

As a mature king, Gustav Adolf's most ambitious project was leading his armies in the Thirty Years War to challenge the Catholic Habsburg dynasty in the struggle for the political and religious future of Germany. During the conflict, Gustav Adolf succeeded in extending the Swedish Empire to encompass large sections of Polish Livonia and northern Germany. How did this northern backwater muster the resources to enable this active and ambitious king? Part of the answer was that Sweden possessed the largest copper mine in Europe and had the means to exploit and distribute its bounty.

The mine was the Stora Kopparberg (Great Copper Mountain) located in Dalarna, a central province of Sweden. It is a curious fact that historians of the present century have tended to deemphasize the importance of the mine in the development of Sweden as a proto-modern administrative state. Compare, for example, a description of the copper from the Kopparberg penned by the king's able chancellor, Axel Oxenstierna (1583–1654):

> Copper is the noblest commodity that the Swedish crown produces and can boast of, wherein also a great part of the crown's welfare stands; and therefore, it is most reasonable that we address ourselves to exploit that mine and to raise and maintain the price of copper, so that the might and riches of our country, and the revenue of the crown may be strengthened and increased.[2]

---

1   Lunde, *A Warrior*, 36. Nils Ahnlund, the Swedish biographer of Gustav Adolf, is skeptical of this story. See Ahnlund, *Gustav Adolf*, 44. He, nevertheless, reports another example of the young prince's penchant for direct action. At the age of five Gustav Adolf was with his father in a field near Nyköping. Some locals warned him not to go into the bushes because of snakes that inhabited the area. Instead of heeding the warning he requested a stick so he could annihilate the serpents.
2   Axel Oxenstiernas, *Skrifter och brevväxling* (AOSB) I.1. 344 (Translation by Michael Roberts).

Portrait 1.   Michiel Jansz. van Mierevelt (1566–1641), *Axel Oxenstierna af Södermöre, 1583–1654, Count, Councillor of the Realm and Lord High Chancellor*, c. 1635. Nationalmuseum Stockholm.

Compare this to the following bland description from Jan Glete, a highly respected modern scholar: "Sweden had the natural resources (iron and copper ores, forests, waterpower) to produce iron and copper for weapons."[3] The reader will observe that the argument of this work rests firmly on the relationship between the mine and the monarchy. It is my contention that not only was the Stora Kopparberg the most lucrative source of income for

3   Glete, *War and the State*, 180.

the crown until the end of the 1620s, but that the mine was also the crucible for reform. We will observe that the king and his chancellor successfully applied the lessons learned in reforming the mine to the larger task of reforming the realm as well.

For the most part Sweden avoided the debilitating political rivalries common between early modern monarchs and their national diets. This was partly, at least, because of the young king's personality. We will observe repeatedly that Gustav Adolf had the ability to assert his authority at just the right time for decisive results. He persuaded his subjects, for example, that the best way to protect the realm against invasion was to support the army and fund his offensive wars against Russia and Poland. Neither his predecessor, Karl IX, nor his successor, Queen Kristina (1626–1669), were as skilled as Gustav Adolf negotiating with the *Riksdag*, the Swedish diet.[4] And King Kristian IV, Gustav Adolf's nemesis in Denmark, was notorious for battling with his *Riksdag* in Copenhagen. Despite being chronically short of cash the Swedish crown was not forced to impose overly burdensome taxes on the population: "The common European type of paralyzing conflicts between estates and princes, where the estates demanded redress of grievances before taxes would be granted, was not important in Sweden."[5] It was not necessary for the crown to demand an excess of unpopular taxes from the Swedish diet, because revenue from the Stora Kopparberg contributed to the routine costs of running the state.

Sweden Emerges

Gustav Adolf's early military conquests were modest. He captured the port of Pernau in Polish Livonia in 1617 and his general on the Russian front, Jacob de le Gardie, captured Novgorod in 1611. The tempo changed, however, in 1621 when Gustav Adolf led 17,850 soldiers into Livonia and marched on the important Polish trading port of Riga. He met stiff resistance, but he outnumbered the defenders significantly and the city surrendered in September 1621 after a brief siege.[6]

Riga had about 30,000 inhabitants and was a prosperous port. The capture of the city signaled Sweden's emergence as a regional military power. By the middle of the decade, Sweden had forced the Polish army out of Livonia

---

4   Glete, *War and the State*, 193.
5   Glete, *War and the State*, 193.
6   Frost, *The Northern Wars*, 103.

Portrait 2.   Cornelius Arendtz (1610–1640), *King Gustav II Adolf*, c. 1625.

as part of an ongoing war. In 1626 Gustav Adolf attacked and occupied Prussia including the prosperous northern coast. This gave the Swedes access to the revenue from the lucrative Prussian river tolls. The campaign also included capturing the port city of Elbing, the future headquarters of Swedish Germany.[7]

In 1629 Poland was forced by her contemporary rivals to sign a humiliating six-year truce with Sweden. Gustav Adolf took advantage of neutralized Poland to invade Germany. He landed his army at the north German port of Peenemunde in 1630 and proceeded to join the Protestant side of the Thirty

7   Frost, *The Northern Wars*, 103.

Years War. His motives have been the source of debate ever since. The most compelling arguments are related to Swedish security. Already in 1627, the Holy Roman Emperor, Ferdinand II (1578–1637), was considering moving troops into the northern German trading cities of Danzig and Lübeck. There was even talk that the leading Imperial general, Count Wallenstein (1585–1634), was to be named Imperial Admiral over the Baltic Seas. Such a move would paralyze seaborne trade in the area.[8] Another possible explanation was religion. Michael Roberts has written that "It is futile to deny the importance of religious motive in shaping Gustav Adolf's policy."[9] According to Roberts, the German Catholic princes and electors thought the Swedish incursion would be limited to restoring the Protestant dukes to the Duchy of Mecklenburg. They then expected Gustav Adolf to return to his frozen homeland.[10] In fact, the Swedish army remained in Germany for the next eighteen years. Roberts wrote that Gustav Adolf certainly believed that he was invading Germany to protect the "remanent" of German Protestantism, but equally he was concerned for the long-term safety of his realm. If he had to fight a war to protect Sweden, it was preferable to fight such a war far from Swedish shores.[11]

The sudden presence in Germany of the Protestant Swedish army profoundly affected the course to the Thirty Years War, then already twelve years old. At first the king's Protestant allies were taken aback by his appearance. If Gustav Adolf expected his co-religionists immediately to join his ranks, he was disappointed. Only the small port city of Stralsund pledged unreserved support. As Gustav Adolf delivered one decisive victory after another, however, the German Protestant princes began to realize that they were now in the presence of new, competent leadership.

Demand for Copper and Mining Reform

The administrative reforms at the mine began in the last decades of the sixteenth century when King Karl IX expanded and modernized production. Perhaps his most critical move was to import experienced German technicians to build a contemporary pumping system. This, and the addition of an up-to-date hoisting complex, again engineered by German

8   Ringmar, *Identity*, 112.
9   Roberts, *Gustavus Adolphus*, 2, 419.
10   Roberts, *Gustavus Adolphus*, 2, 420.
11   Roberts, *Gustavus Adolphus*, 2, 424.

experts, greatly increased output at the mine. Fortunately for the Swedish crown, these improvements coincided with sharp price increases in copper, spurred by the growing demand for copper across Europe. Various factors were at work, some immediate and some long-term. Beginning in the last quarter of the sixteenth century Castile adopted a copper standard and began purchasing large quantities of copper ingot on the open market. By the beginning of Gustav Adolf's reign, Castile was the leading European consumer of Swedish copper.[12] In addition, the increased use of bronze cannon for military applications, caused by the artillery arms race across Europe, led to a structural change in demand. Smaller field cannon could be cast from iron, but large cannon, designed for mounting a major siege or for defending towns and fortresses, were made of bronze.

Demand for the larger cannon began in the first decades of the sixteenth century with the development of a new type of fortification, the *trace Italienne,* designed to resist a besieging foe armed with artillery. Unlike its predecessor, the curtain wall castle, the *trace Italienne* fortress presented lower, sloping walls with protruding bastions that insured defensive fields of fire in forward and side directions. In a properly designed *trace Italienne,* fortress besiegers could not fire cannon from a blind side, nor could they approach the fortress with sappers to undermine the walls. Niccolò Machiavelli (1469–1527) first described this type of fortress in his 1521 book, *The Art of War.* Its use spread north during the sixteenth century to Germany, France, England, and most particularly to the Netherlands. In fact, such fortresses were a powerful advantage for both sides in the Netherlands during the eighty-year war of independence from Spain. In 1572, for example, when hostilities began between the Spanish monarchy and her Dutch-speaking subjects, there was only one *trace Italienne* in the Netherlands. By 1648, the year the revolt formally ended, there were twenty-eight in the Spanish Netherlands and thirteen in the United Provinces.[13]

Geoffrey Parker labeled these new types of defensive works "artillery fortresses" because they bristled with large-bore cannon made of bronze. The development of the artillery fortress led inevitably to an increase in the size of siege guns, and an increase in the number needed to mount a serious siege. In 1601, for instance, the Dutch rebels mounted an unsuccessful siege of Spanish held Hertogenbosch with only twenty-two large-bore siege guns. They initiated a successful attempt in 1627, however, with eighty large-bore

---

12 Heckscher, *historia,* 1, 450: "Spain had a great need of copper for its mint; by Gustav Adolf's time there is no doubt that Spain was the most important end market for Swedish copper."

13 Parker, *The Army of Flanders,* 14–15.

Figure 1   Copper Production at the Stora Kopparberg and Copper Prices in Amsterdam

guns.[14] This artillery arms race continued across Europe during the first half of the seventeenth century. The result was an increase in demand for copper, a demand that was met, in part, by the production increases at the Stora Kopparberg.

From 1624 forward, Swedish copper prices in Amsterdam were published in the "Price Currents." These were lists of commodities traded in Amsterdam, from Alicante anise to whale oil, along with current price information. These "Price Currents" were collected and published by the twentieth-century Dutch historian, N.W. Posthumus.[15]

Still other sources indicate that the price of copper rose steadily throughout Europe from the last years of the sixteenth century to 1625. In 1626 Spain dropped the copper standard and left the market because the large quantity of copper currency in circulation was causing inflation.[16] This changed the supply and demand balance sufficiently to soften prices for the next several years. To demonstrate this trend, in 1625 the average yearly price was Dutch Guilder (hereafter DG) 64.55 per hundredweight (as reported in the "Price Currents") or *riksdaler* (hereafter RD) 71 per *skeppund* (hereafter skd). In 1650, however, the price on the Amsterdam market was the equivalent of RD 57.1 per skd. There were many ups and downs in between (see figure 1).[17]

14   Parker, *The Army of Flanders*, 14–15.
15   Posthumus, *Prices*, 1, 373.
16   Hamilton, *American Treasure*, 92–94.
17   For prices in Amsterdam see Posthumus, *Prices*, 1, 371-73. For copper production figures see Lindroth, *Gruvbrytning*, 2, 389–90.

Prices rose in 1632, before King Gustav Adolf's death in November of that year. But they fell again in 1635 and copper continued to trade in a narrow band at lower levels until the end of our period. Despite this lackluster price performance for copper after 1626, the Stora Kopparberg made great strides in production levels. In 1600, the Stora Kopparberg produced 2,400 skd of copper. From 1643 through 1648, the mine produced between 12,000 and 12,225 skd per year. In 1649 and 1650 production jumped to 14,323 skd and 20,323 skd respectively. After 1650 production gradually fell back to earlier levels. Needless to say, the increase in production meant greater revenue for the crown.

The Älvsborg Ransom

Why did production at the Stora Kopparberg increase so precipitously during a period of relative price stability? Did the increased production influence the price in Amsterdam? The answers determined the fortunes of the young Swedish king. From the beginning of his reign, King Gustav Adolf faced financial problems inherited from his father, Karl IX. While mitigated by revenue from the Stora Kopparberg, the unfortunate War of Kalmar with Denmark (1611–1613), threatened the royal treasury. During that conflict, the Danes captured the fortress of Älvsborg, which protected Göteborg and the southwestern coast of Sweden. In January 1613, slightly over one year into his reign, the young king agreed to an onerous treaty, the Peace of Knäred. The terms of the peace negotiated by Gustav Adolf included a ransom of one million *riksdaler* payable over four years, beginning in 1616. This was such an unrealistically high price the king of Denmark, Kristian IV, probably assumed that the Swedish crown would forfeit the fortress and leave the small, but strategic, Göteborg area vulnerable to future Danish incursion.

To understand just how vulnerable the area was, and why Gustav Adolf agreed to pay the ransom, one must be aware of the geographical boundaries of southern Sweden when the Peace of Knäred was negotiated. At the time, most of the coast facing the Kattegatt and the Skagerack was controlled by Denmark and the Danish possession, Norway. Only a small band of land north of Danish Halland was Swedish territory. The Swedish crown originally built the fortress of Älvsborg in the fourteenth century to protect the small Atlantic port of Lödöse, and later the new port of Göteborg. The crown rebuilt and reinforced the fortress many times before the reign of Gustav Adolf.

As we shall soon see, the fortress was critical for the protection of Göteborg and the future of Sweden. Göteborg was the only Swedish port with open access to the North Sea and the Atlantic, and it permitted merchant vessels from Sweden and the West to avoid passing through the Danish Sound, which was located just south of the narrows between the two Danish fortress towns of Hälsingör and Hälsingborg. At the time, Denmark controlled all possible routes from the Baltic to the Atlantic. The passage through the Danish Sound between Hälsingör and Hälsingborg, however, was by far the most navigable route, and therefore, the most widely used. During the Middle Ages, the Danish crown began to impose a toll on all ships moving through the Sound. It jealously guarded this right because it was the Danish crown's largest source of revenue.[18] The Sound was only four kilometers across and relatively easy to patrol, which gave the Danish king the ability to impose a boycott on deliveries to Sweden from the West in times of war.

To mitigate the problem, Karl IX of Sweden began renovating Göteborg in 1607. In addition to opening trade with Western Europe, he also successfully recruited Dutch merchants to settle in the new trading town. Four years later, Karl IX sought a land route to the North Sea through Lapland, north of populated Danish Norway. His goal was to establish another alternative to the Danish-controlled Sound. To facilitate this, he declared himself the "King of the Lapps." In response, King Kristian IV of Denmark declared war on Sweden in 1611. Recognizing the advantage that would accrue to Sweden were the settlement at Göteborg to continue, King Kristian used the war to justify razing the town and occupying the Älvsborg fortress. As long as he controlled the fortress, he reasoned, any vessels sailing between Sweden and the West would be forced to continue using the Sound and paying the toll.[19]

Legitimacy

Perhaps an equally serious problem facing the young Gustav Adolf was legitimacy. While still the heir apparent of Sweden, Prince Sigismund (1566–1632), was elected king of the Polish-Lithuanian Commonwealth in 1587. He then inherited the throne of Sweden at the death of his father, King Johan III (1537–1592). It was Sigismund's intention to rule Sweden by uniting it with the Polish-Lithuanian Commonwealth. As a Counter-Reformation Catholic, however, Sigismund was not popular in Lutheran Sweden. In 1599 his uncle and regent, Duke Karl, staged a coup and overthrew the absentee

18   Glete, *War and the State*, 112.
19   Roberts, *Gustavus Adophus*, 2, 273.

king. With the compliance of the *Riksdag*, Karl proclaimed himself King Karl IX in 1604.

Sigismund did not, however, quietly give up his Swedish claims. He was, after all, a Vasa, and the lawful ruler. He waged intermittent warfare against Karl between 1600 and 1611, a period called the Swedish-Polish War. Because of his religion Sigismund received little support from his former subjects in Sweden, but there was a discontented minority.

Thus, when Gustav Adolf came to the throne in 1611, he did not inherit a solidly united kingdom. The new king's age, moreover, added to the problem. As mentioned earlier, Gustav Adolf was just sixteen when King Karl died; the law of the land, the Succession Agreement, dictated that no heir under the age of 25 could occupy the throne. It took considerable parliamentary maneuvering on the part of Axel Oxenstierna, Gustav Adolf's future chancellor, to push through an exemption to the agreement.[20]

Yet another dilemma the young monarch faced was the division of his kingdom. Two duchies, within Sweden proper, were nearly autonomous from the crown. Gustav Adolf's cousin, Johann, was the duke of Östergötland and Karl Philip, King Gustav's younger brother, was duke of the rich provinces of Söndermanland, Västmanland, and Närke. Not Surprisingly, the two dukes refused to accept new burdens when the crown sought tax increases to pay the Älvsborg ransom. The queen mother, Kristina of Holstein, a fierce and determined woman, made the situation considerably worse. She acted as regent for Karl Philip, and thoroughly dominated him. She flatly refused to contribute to the war effort, and frequently acted in direct contradiction to Gustav Adolf's political and military interests. We will encounter this robustly independent dowager again shortly.[21]

Given the above threats to stability, the Stora Kopparberg's importance as a source of revenue was critical. We will trace the crown's successful efforts to gain control over the production and marketing of this valuable commodity. This allowed the crown to use copper as the primary income stream for funding its ambitious military and political policy. The king's program, to negotiate a monopoly on copper distribution, ran parallel to his consolidation of power in the kingdom and paying the Älvsborg ransom. During this same period the king won over political dissenters, strengthened his hand with the *Riksdag*, and oversaw multiple successes on the battlefield.[22]

---

20 Roberts, *Gustavus Adolphus*, 1, 57-59
21 Heckscher, *historia*, 1, 442.
22 Glete, *War and the State*, 210.

The Chancellor

The success of the monarchy during and after the life of Gustav Adolf was also due, in large part, to the talents of Axel Oxenstierna, the king's friend and chancellor. Oxenstierna was born into one of the more important noble families, who for years had served both the crown and the church. Like many of his contemporaries in the Swedish higher nobility Oxenstierna was educated in the safely Lutheran universities of Rostock, Wittenberg, and Jena. He remained a convinced aristocrat and was never fully comfortable with new men on the rise.

After university, Oxenstierna was offered a post in the government of Gustav Adolf's father, Karl IX. He was already a member of the *Kammar-Råd* (privy council) when Gustav Adolf succeeded to the throne in 1611. We alluded earlier to the fact that the existing charters forbad the crowning of a new king before he reached the age of 25. Oxenstierna adroitly handled this problem. The result was a negotiated agreement between the king's supporters and the nobility known as the Charter or the King's Declaration. This document allowed Gustav Adolf to claim the throne at the age of 17; in return it confirmed a series of privileges to the nobility, including a monopoly on higher offices, an appropriate wage for government or military service, and protection from arbitrary dismissal. The agreement was a springboard for the bureaucratization of the government and members of both the higher and the lower nobility competed for appointments.[23]

In return for his handling of the succession issue Gustav Adolf appointed Oxenstierna chancellor in 1613. He was a tireless administrator and supervisor. In the letters between the two there was seldom a note of resentment or impatience. The chancellor understood his subordinate position to the king; yet in this role, he rose to become the second most important person in Sweden. After the king's death in 1632, he served Queen Kristina, Gustav Adolf's successor, until her abdication in 1654. In addition, the chancellor was well regarded outside of Sweden, especially for his success as the ruler of the Swedish territories in Germany. He was often favorably compared to his two powerful contemporaries, the Count Duke of Olivares in Spain and Cardinal de Richelieu in France.[24]

An excellent example of the chancellor's efforts to transform the semi-feudal, realm into a nascent, tax paying, fiscal state was his revision of the city charter for Falun, home of the Stora Kopparberg, written in 1618. The new charter streamlined Karl IX's older, medieval, self-governing organization

---

23   Rystad, *The King*, 62.
24   Wetterberg. *Kanslern*, II, 9.

and established closer crown control over mining activities. There was to be a *bergmästare*, who was chosen by the more prominent *bergsmän*[25] of the city. He was assisted by a *gruvfogte*, or mining bailiff, and the *sexmän* (six men), a unique organization whose members were nominated from the ranks of the *bergsmän*. The crown insisted on appointing one of the *sexmän* but allowed the *bergsmän* to elect the other five. Along with the *gruvfogte*, the six men oversaw all aspects of the day-to-day work at the mine. This was an important step for the crown because, despite being chosen by the *bergsmän*, the *bergmästare* and the *gruvfogte* were crown officials. A *bergsmän* with a complaint about the allocation of mining areas, for example, would first go to the six men. If not satisfied with the result, he would apply to the *gruvfogte* for redress.[26] This meant that, for the first time in the mine's history, the crown had the final authority over the allocation of mining areas, which was key to governing the mine.[27] The mine consisted of many different sections, some with rich ore and some with less rich ore. The owner of mining rights shared in the rich ore, but also in the lesser ore. The lower the copper content, the higher the cost to extract the metal. The power to decide who mined where, therefore, was an important source of influence. The chancellor also dictated the qualifications for governing positions at the mine in the new city charter for Falun: "Hereafter all 'six men' and mining accountants must be members of the burgher class. The only exceptions are the officials that we will appoint to oversee mining and smelting activities."[28] This was more than a symbolic exercise of power; it was the crown setting the rules for membership in the governing councils for local *bergsmän*, but specifically exempting its own officials from these qualifications. In other words, the crown could bring officials from the outside to govern the mine.

One of the more sinister expansions of the crown's authority as part of the 1618 charter involved the collection of taxes in Falun. Upon demand, the municipality was subject to arbitrary taxes to be collected by the *bergmästare*, the bailiff and the town council. Further, it was the *bergmästare*'s duty to record every year, on Walpurges Eve, the incomes of each member of the burgher class and

---

25 Michael Roberts used the term *bergsmän*, meaning people who worked at the mine, because the term miner is too narrow. In addition to the men who went into the mine and dug up the ore, there were charcoal burners, ore carriers, pump workers and so on. A *bergsmän* might control a certain section of the mine and hire laborers to do the work, or he might be digging himself. It is an inclusive term.

26 Boëthius, *Gruvornas*, 152.

27 AOSB, I, 1, 287.

28 AOSB, I, 1, 288.

the administrators, so the tax could be collected quickly if necessary. It is hard to imagine a better example of the expansion of royal influence and power.[29]

Overall copper production at the Stora Kopparberg was overseen by the governor of Darlarna province, Carl Bonde. In many ways Bonde was typical of the new breed of bureaucrats who, under Gustav Adolf, were now inhabiting the more important governmental posts. This trend was, of course, one of the results of the King's Declaration of 1611, mentioned earlier. Bonde was a member of the upper nobility, with a list of titles including Baron of Laihela. He spent two years studying in France and returned to a couple minor posts until Gustav Adolf appointed him governor of Dalarna. As governor, he oversaw the critical royal reforms at the Stora Kopparberg and represented the crown in major disputes with the *bergsmän*.[30]

The crown recruited educated talent for service in foreign territories as well. After the invasion of the Prussian coastline, in 1626, Sweden took possession of the lucrative tolls on river traffic including ports from the Neva to the Vistula plus the dominant port of Danzig.[31] In some years, towards the end of the Gustav Adolf's reign, the revenue from the river tolls exceeded even the income from copper.[32] To administer this cash cow, Oxenstierna appointed a Dutch accountant, Pieter Spierinck. Not surprisingly, he fitted nicely into the category of educated expert, "a man of energy and ability."[33] Upon taking office Spierinck hired his own brothers, who apparently matched him for zeal and honesty. In 1627 Oxenstierna sent brother Issac Spierinck to Amsterdam as part of an attempt to audit a large shipment of copper mortgaged to the Trip family. He was largely ignored by the Trips and returned to Elbing, the seat of administration for the overseas empire, recommending that business with Trip family be discontinued immediately. The Spierinck brothers are just one more example of the administrative specialists that were now inhabiting the mine, the mainland, and the overseas empire.[34]

State Formation

In an influential book published in 2002, *War and the State in Early Modern Europe*, the Swedish maritime historian, Jan Glete, explored the military side

29   AOSB, I, 1, 290.
30   Svenski Biografiskt Lexikon Band 04 (1924) sida 325.
31   Roberts, *Gustavus Adolphus*, 2, 82.
32   Roberts, *Gustavus Adolphus*, 2, 82–84.
33   Roberts, *Gustavus Adolpohus*, 2 82–84.
34   Roberts, *Gustavus Adolpohus*, 2, 82–84.

of modern state formation. It was his contention that the development of a navy, although very limited, gave the young king a strategic advantage over his neighbors without a maritime force. This enabled, for example, Gustav Adolf to compete with Poland and Russia with fewer, but more concentrated resources. In the conclusion we will explore the disadvantages of a smaller navy. For Glete, however, the military presence was "protection selling"[35] and it allowed Gustav Adolf to maintain a "monopoly of violence"[36] both at sea and on land. This monopoly was the first step in the formation of the military "fiscal state." Earlier, the dynasty had gained control over the domestic Swedish military resources such as fortresses, the small navy, and local militias. A classic example of "protection selling" was Gustav Adolf's decision to keep his army in Germany during his participation in the Thirty Years War. He was, thereby, certain that his well-trained forces remained active, while supported by local German resources. It also allowed him to maintain his occupation of the north German coastline.[37]

While he does not mention his name, Glete's comments also fit Kristian IV's collection of Sound tolls. The Danish king sold protection to the Baltic Sea lanes and, as we saw earlier, he was prepared to go to war to defend this right. He raised both an army and a navy, which, in turn, required administrative control. Whether conscious or not, Kristian had taken the first steps toward nation building, as he now assumed the costs of maintaining a strong military.

Jan Glete was not alone among contemporary historians to observe Sweden's trend toward military statehood. Robert Frost published *The Great Northern Wars 1558–1721* in 2000. The author acknowledges the importance of copper from the Stora Kopparberg in financing Gustav Adolf's military campaigns in the 1620s and describes the problem facing the crown when Spain suddenly left the marketplace: "... the abrupt Spanish decision to suspend the minting of *vellón* coinage in May 1526 had knocked the bottom out of the lucrative copper market, which provided Sweden with vital foreign exchange."[38] Similarity, David Parrott in the insightful *The Business of War, Military Enterprise, and Military Revolution in Early Modern Europe*, describes Gustav Adolf's army and the hiring of mercenaries. The king's goal was to supplement the diminished numbers of native Swedish and Finish troops

---

35 Glete borrowed the term "protection selling" from the American economic historian Frederick C. Lane. It means simply that protection is a commodity that the developing state sells to its citizens or subjects.

36 A phrase coined by Max Weber.

37 Glete, *War and the State*, 187.

38 Frost, *The Northern Wars*, 115.

in the period after 1625: "Much of this hiring was sustained on the basis of unprecedented opening up of Swedish copper and iron mines …"

Sweden also enjoyed a distinct advantage over its rivals in the rush to form military nation states. The kingdom had a long tradition of conscription. This had several advantages. First, trained native troops formed a loyal cadre for otherwise mercenary armies. It also led to an important innovation. Conscription had to be organized. This inevitably led to the local clergy organizing the flow of recruits. There was, therefore, in every village a member of the royal bureaucracy at the grass root level. Other countries had state supported clergy, but none that were so intimately involved in feeding the war machine.

The Royal Copper Monopoly

Gustav Adolf's first step towards controlling the revenue from the Stora Kopparberg was to negotiate a partial purchasing monopoly with the *bergsmän*. This was not yet a full crown monopoly; that came only in 1619. In addition, the king and his chancellor directed investments to improve the smelting, refining, minting, and manufacturing facilities at the mine. Their goal was to increase production and improve the quality of the exported copper. Both understood that exporting semi-finished products added value and was preferable to exporting raw materials. It also allowed the king to sell copper to foreign markets in exchange for *riksdalers*, which he needed to pay the ransom. This connection made the Stora Kopparberg as important to Gustav Adolf as the Potosi silver mines in Spanish Peru were to the kings of Spain.[39]

As the king entered the 1620s, however, his aggressive military and political policies required that copper be turned into cash quickly and efficiently. Floating substantial loans, with copper as collateral was not possible in Sweden because it lacked credit facilities. On the other hand, sophisticated banking houses were already well established in other major capitals of Europe. The kings of Spain, for example, had access to banking facilities in Genoa and in Flanders. France and England both had prosperous merchant classes, with access to credit. Sweden, however, was financially immature.[40]

39   The comparison is one sided. The Potosi mine in colonial Peru helped the Spanish crown finance its military and imperial endeavors, and the Stora Kopparberg did the same for Sweden. The comparison breaks down, however, on the position of the domestic miners. The *bergsmän* were respected members of the burgher class. The miners at Potosi were brutally exploited native peoples. Dewald, ed., *Europe*, 5, 47.

40   See Heckscher, *historia*, 1.2, 370–73 for a discussion the lack of credit facilities.

Her political allies in Amsterdam and in The Hague had helped to fund the
Älvsborg ransom. But the United Provinces were under constant threat
from the Spanish armies to the south and the west, and they had their own
defense to consider. It was only after the Älvsborg ransom was fully paid in
1620, that the king looked for more willing sources of credit. His solution
was to form the Swedish Trading Company, which he loosely based on the
Dutch East India Company. He granted the company a true monopoly on
purchasing copper from the *bergsmän* at the Stora Kopparberg, expecting
the company to do three things: first, to maintain a reasonably tight hold
on copper marketing and administration under his personal supervision;
second, to push production at the mine and invest in smelting capacity;
and third, to become a more reliable source of credit than the Dutch States
General. The company, in existence from 1620 to 1628, oversaw a steady
increase in production at the mine, as it monopolized the purchase of copper
(see figure 1). The company was, in fact, the agent of royal policy and during
its existence the king increased his influence at the mine and at the various
processing facilities. Unfortunately for the company's future, however, the
king borrowed heavily from it.

While the crown had other means for turning copper into cash, one
option the king did not enjoy was leaving the copper in the ground. Even
during 1626, when the price began to retreat after a decade of growth,[41] the
crown had no choice but to mine and refine as much copper as possible. As
the king's able chancellor, Axel Oxenstierna, remarked: "While there was
general agreement that copper was undervalued, and would soon recover,
the crown was financially weak; it could not afford to let copper lie [unsold],
as it would have preferred."[42]

As we have seen, the king's need for income meant that the mine produced
copper at full capacity regardless of demand. That tended to keep prices
down throughout Europe. There was another corollary to this action. Other
mines, such as the copper mine at Schwaz in the Tyrol, were reducing output
during this period. This may have been because of declining mineral reserves,
but it was probably also dictated by the Swedish king's need to produce
copper—regardless of price. As a result, between 1600 and 1640, production of
copper at the Stora Kopparberg increased nearly fourfold. By 1640, therefore,
the Stora Kopparberg completely dominated the European market for copper
ingot and semi-finished products, such as copper sheet, wire, and plate.[43]

41   Heckscher, *historia*, 1.2, 450.
42   AOSB, I, 1, 345.
43   Boëthius and Heckscher, *Svensk Handelsstatistik*, 632–36.

The Sources

We now turn our discussion to the existing literature on the Swedish copper industry and crown policy. Not surprisingly, Swedish historians have been active. I will mention only the most important and helpful commentators, starting with a towering figure from the last century, Eli F. Heckscher. It is fair to say that Heckscher was the most influential of a long line of twentieth-century Swedish economic historians. He was prolific on many related subjects, but one of his most enduring contributions was his survey of late medieval and early modern Swedish economic history, *Sveriges ekonomiska historia från Gustav Vasa* (*Swedish Economic History from the Time of Gustav Vasa*). This is a sweeping account of the subject and is still most helpful more than seventy years after publication. Heckscher believed that history should be underpinned by economic theory and principles. By theory, Heckscher meant classic free market economics, for he was largely untouched by the Keynesian revolution, and had a pronounced preference for *laissez-faire* government policy toward business and trade.

Using statistical resources, Heckscher provided an account of the relationship between the Stora Kopparberg and crown finances. He concluded that the crown clearly understood the potential for increasing revenue from the mine. Without mentioning Gustav Adolf by name, Heckscher stated that by 1613 the crown had begun efforts to improve efficiencies at the site. This resulted in better conditions for the *bergsmän* and increased production. Between 1613 and 1619, output from the property increased considerably. During these years the mine's total output was 25,500 skd.[44] If the crown had managed to capture all the profit from the sale of this production, it could have paid down the Älvsborg ransom from this source alone.[45] Additionally, Heckscher wrote disapprovingly that Gustav Adolf used revenue from the mine to finance the wars in Poland and Germany. Finally, Heckscher points out that without the Stora Kopparberg, Sweden could never have financed participation in the Thirty Years War in later years.

Heckscher was also convinced of the essential role that copper played in financing the crown during the "great power age." Without copper revenue Sweden could never have financed the Älvsborg ransom or participated in the wars against Poland and Catholic states in the Holy Roman Empire. In Heckscher's eyes, copper was a "treasure house"[46] and the mainstay of war

---

44 Heckscher, *historia*, 1.2 443.
45 Heckscher, *historia*, 1.2 443.
46 *Kopparfyndigheter.*

financing during the reign of Gustav Adolf.[47] As indicated earlier, in 1619 the king founded a monopoly company to sell copper abroad, called the Copper Company. Like many economists, Heckscher's interests spilled over into politics. He was politically liberal on greater European questions, but he was a true believer in an unhampered free market, and he was involved in the politics of this cause. In the introduction to Heckscher's *An Economic History of Sweden*, Alexander Gerschenkron calls Heckscher "a staunch supporter of laissez-faire policies." In line with this view, Heckscher opposed any Swedish government stimulus programs during the Great Depression because he considered the prospect of a larger, more influential, government to be a greater threat to the economy than severe unemployment. One should not be surprised then, that Heckscher's description of Gustav Adolf's Swedish Copper Company was negative. He considered the idea an attempt to copy the Dutch example, and therefore, not suitable for commerce in Sweden. He further accused Gustav Adolf of using the company for his own narrow fiscal concerns and ignoring the interests of the shareholders.[48]

Heckscher's vehemence on the subject merits some comment. He was writing his great survey of Swedish economic history in the early to mid 1930s. In other words, he was writing at precisely the time that Hitler had come to power and was rearming Germany. As a Jewish scholar in neutral Sweden, he naturally considered Nazi Germany a growing menace, and a perfect example of the evil that could flow from a government monopoly of resources. Heckscher disapproved of Gustav Adolf's economic policy, and one can certainly understand his views, given the era in which he worked.

Returning now to the Copper Company, George Wittrock, the most widely cited authority on the subject, provides an important perspective on the crown's intervention in business. Wittrock's *Svenska handelskompaniet och kopparhandeln under Gustaf II Adolf (The Swedish Trading Company and Copper Trading under Gustaf II Adolf)*, published in 1919, is a short work based entirely on archival research and published letters. Surprisingly, there are no subsequent works that deal exclusively with the Copper Company, although recent writers on related subjects quote Wittrock extensively. Wittrock was not completely unsympathetic towards the king's efforts to form a monopoly, as he recognized the financial necessity that some of his fellow countrymen tend to overlook. He was, however, negative on the overall success of the company. Voicing his own opinion, Wittrock described Gustav Adolf's business acumen as follows: "Despite a vivid interest and

47   Heckscher, *historia*, 1.2, 274.
48   Heckscher, *historia*, 1.2. 456–58.

diligent consideration, clearly the king was in unfamiliar territory when he got involved in financial matters. There was much he could not fathom."[49]

Regrettably, there is little written on the Swedish crown's copper policy in English. The one exception is the English-language world's undisputed expert on early modern Sweden, Michael Roberts. While he wrote on a wide variety of Swedish topics, he is perhaps best known for his biography of the king, *Gustavus Adolphus, A History of Sweden 1611–1632* (1957). When he touched on financial and economic issues, however, he tended to follow Heckscher's lead. It is not surprising, therefore, that Roberts thought the idea of the Copper Company was misguided. He described the decision as the result of four goals: to extract as much revenue as possible from the mine, to have a dependable source of revenue for the future, to transfer trading risks from the crown to the Copper Company, and to simplify the collection of relevant taxes. Roberts believed that the king designed the company not to benefit its shareholders, but to help subsidize the crown; further, he believed the king capable of intervening to falsify the company's balance sheets.[50] Regarding copper policy in general, Roberts concluded that: "Gustav Adolf was at the mercy of economic forces, which he could not control, and only dimly appreciated."[51]

Whether or not one agrees with Robert's negative assessment, one must allow that the crown's economic policy and particularly the crown's copper policy was dictated by economic necessity. As already emphasized, from the first days of his reign, Gustav Adolf had little room to maneuver. He had to pay the Älvsborg ransom and mobilized revenue from the mine to do so. That meant that he subordinated economic concerns to political concerns; he paid the ransom, and at the same time, fielded armies against Poland. Later, he led his armies into Germany to fight against the Hapsburg coalition. All this left the crown short of cash and dependent on revenue from the Kopparberg. We should not judge the crown's fiscal and copper policy in terms of modern economic theory, but rather in terms of mobilizing resources to meet political and military goals. In short, the crown's priority was to pay the ransom and feed his army and navy. When considered from this perspective, I think that Roberts's summaries of the king's economic limitations are unjustified.

The story of Swedish copper does not end with the mines and smelters of Sweden. The Dutch and their markets are another vital piece of the

49   Wittrock, *handelscompaniet*, 161.
50   Roberts, *Gustavus Adolphus*, 2, 92–94.
51   Roberts, *Gustavus Adolphus*, 2, 98.

picture. The first half of the seventeenth century was a period of massive expansion for the Dutch markets in almost every direction. If we use copper as an example, we can begin to understand the growing dominance of Amsterdam in European trade. In 1585, for instance, the Stora Kopparberg produced 3,892 skd of raw copper. In that same year, 3,411 skd of copper were exported from Stockholm to Lübeck. Conversely, only 230 skd, or less than 6 percent of the mine's output, passed from the Baltic to the North Sea through the Danish toll station. By 1642, however, when the Kopparberg produced 13,245 skd of copper, 7,138 skd, or 54 percent of the mine's output, went through the Sound to Amsterdam.[52] This shift from exporting copper to the old Baltic ports of the Hanseatic League, in favor of Amsterdam, occurred for countless other commodities as well.

The Amsterdam Market

The close cooperation between the Swedish crown and the merchants of Amsterdam, not surprisingly, grew out of the Swedish crown's financial difficulty. As mentioned earlier, when Gustav Adolf needed to raise money, he approached his Protestant brethren at the States General in The Hague. The States General floated loans, in Dutch Guilders, and specified that security be supplied in the form of copper. Once the copper began to arrive in Amsterdam, merchants understood the potential for profitable trade; soon, they were dealing directly with the Swedish crown. These relationships developed into important trading links between the two parties; Sweden exported copper to Amsterdam and imported credit and vast quantities of weapons for wars in Poland and Germany.[53]

Two individuals dominated the copper trade between Stockholm and Amsterdam during the first part of the seventeenth century: Louis de Geer and Elias Trip. De Geer was originally from Liège but moved to Dordrecht to avoid religious persecution in the Spanish controlled southern provinces. There he met the Trip family. The de Geer sisters, Maria and Marguerite, married Elias Trip and Jacob Trip, the two brothers who co-founded the family fortunes. In fact, a portrait of Marguerite de Geer by Rembrandt now hangs in London's National Gallery next to the same artist's portrait of her husband, Jacob Trip. Two of their sons also married de Geers, further deepening the families' relationship. The Trips amassed their fortunes

---

52 Kumlien, Staat, *Kupfererzeugung*, 415–16.
53 Van Dillen, *Van Rijkdom en Regenten*, 310–26.

Portrait 3.   Unknown artist after David Beck (1621–1656), *Louis De Geer (1587–1652)*, n.d. National-museum Stockholm.

trading in weapons, saltpeter, coal, iron, and copper. They bought and sold in Sweden and eventually followed de Geer there building warehouses and factories.

The fortunes of the Trip family were chronicled by P.W. Klein in his *De Trippen in de 17e Eeuw, een Studie over het Ondernemersgedrag op de Hollandse Stapelmarkt (The Trip Family in the 17th Century: A Study of the Behavior of an Entrepreneur on the Dutch Staple Market)*. His goal was to explore Joseph A. Schumpeter's theoretical views on monopolies using the Trip family as an early modern case study: "Contrary to the general opinion, I want to claim that the monopolistic practices of the Dutch merchants of the seventeenth century—whatever their moral merits—also promoted economic growth ..."[54]

In Klein's view, early modern merchants sought monopolies to reduce risk. There were so many variables in trade, such as "wars, official or unofficial privateering, shipwrecks, and the manifold breaches of contract, practiced by governments and private firms alike."[55] Removing risk by having the power to set prices, or guaranteeing supply, were essential. Of course, the best-known example of a monopoly from the seventeenth century was the Dutch East India Company. It was formed from several smaller companies doing business in Asia. Because of fierce competition none could make a profit. The solution was to band together, obtain a monopoly charter for trade in Asia from the States General, and begin trading without internal competition. One could argue that the result was higher prices for the company's commodities sold in Amsterdam. Klein would retort that the alternative would be cessation of trade with the East.

To summarize, there is no question that Gustav Adolf's innovative approach to the copper monopoly made a significant difference. I have already explained that immediately upon coming to the throne, he set about to reform and improve organization at the mine. These changes upset the *bergsmän* and the local merchants, which may have been the king's intention. His approach was unique; first, he gradually gained a purchasing monopoly at the mine. Next, he established the Copper Company, which revolutionized the marketing of Swedish copper. Still not satisfied, he began to mint copper currency. Finally, he arranged strategic alliances with the more important merchants in Amsterdam. At each step, his goal was the exploitation of copper resources to obtain credit and money to strengthen the army and the administration that served the state.

Original Sources

I have made extensive use of the collection of Axel Oxenstierna's correspondence published in thirty volumes by *Utgifna af Kongl. Vitterhets Historie och Antikvitets Akademien* (*The Royal Literary, Historical, and Antiquities Academy*). This remarkable treasure trove includes letters to and from the king, prominent statesmen, foreign princes, important merchants, and other

54 Klein, *De Trippen*, 475.
55 Klein, *De Trippen*, 475.

luminaries. In addition, I was fortunate to spend time at the Riksarkiv in Stockholm which contains collections of correspondence related to the Stora Kopparberg, the Älvsborg ransom, the Copper Company, and trade between Germany and Holland. This collection also includes the *Leufsta arkiv*, the surviving letters and financial records of the de Geer family.

Side by side with correspondence, the Riksarkiv is rich in balance sheets and journal entries; I found them the most helpful and revealing part of the archives. One learns in Accounting 101 that accounting is "the language of business;" that was certainly as true in the seventeenth century as it is today. For reasons that escape me, these resources were ignored by the commentators of the last century. Even those whose work was centered on archival research did not make use of the balance sheets and commercial journals of the Copper Company or the individual merchants doing business with the crown. The balance sheets will allow us to analyze the inner workings of the commercial entities that we will soon encounter.

The work is divided into six chapters and is presented chronologically. The first chapter describes the delicate relationship between the crown and the mine. It is largely the story of a competent administrator, Carl Bonde, and his efforts to establish royal control. Karl IX and Gustav Adolf gradually dominated the Stora Kopparberg mine, and under Carl Bonde's tutelage, transformed the *bergsmän* from an archaic work force, owing days of labor to their feudal lords, to market sensitive burghers. They were, moreover, shielded from the worst excesses of a market economy by the king's policy of paying them a fixed price for a guaranteed yearly minimum quantity of copper.

Chapter two is, on the surface, the story of the crown's frantic efforts to pay a one million *riksdaler* ransoms to the king of Denmark to return the Älvsborg fortress to the Swedish crown. It is also, however, the story of the young king's efforts to establish relationships with the prominent merchants of Amsterdam. He needed weapons and credit, and the center of northern European finance seemed a logical source. We learn in this chapter how the king arranged for both weapons and credit thanks to his agents' involvement in political intrigue in Amsterdam and The Hague.

Chapter two, moreover, examines the Swedish administrative state at the local level. Sweden raised her domestic army by conscription. As mentioned earlier, this had implications far beyond supplying troops to the state. Such an administrative apparatus meant that agents of the monarchy were operating locally to collect and distribute tax revenue as well as representing the central government.[56]

---

56   Glete, *War and the State*, 176.

All of the above should have provided the necessary background for Sweden to develop into a functioning military state. The Swedish monarchy, however, was not united. As mentioned earlier Gustav Adolf shared power with his cousin, Duke Johan of Östergötland, and Gustav Adolf's younger brother, Duke Karl Philip. As a practical matter both dutchies were politically independent and categorically refused to pay taxes, even for the ransom, outside of their respective realms.[57]

The birth of the Copper Company is the main feature of chapter three. Despite dissent among his closest advisors, the king forged ahead and oversaw the funding of the new entity. The company charter, which we shall later examine in detail, contained a feature that was probably among the most important economic decision of Gustav Adolf's reign. The king granted the new company a full monopoly on purchases from the mine at a fixed price of SD 50 (RD 30.7 mine weight).[58] Persuading the *bergsmän* to accept a fixed sales price and the purchasing monopoly was a stunning victory for the king. The price was adequate to keep the *bergsmän* satisfied, while, at the same time, allowing the crown to sell at a profit on the world market. The profits, in turn, helped propelled the Copper Company to several years of successful trading and growth. Of course, growing companies need competent, well-educated employees. The Copper Company, combined with the Stora Kopparberg would have required mining engineers, administrators, accountants, sales representatives, and other specialists.

The euphoria over the company's early success, however, did not last. In chapter four we examine the decline of the company's fortunes. Beginning in 1625 the king demanded a series of loans from the company. At first the king's requests were moderate. During the latter part of the year, however, as the king was preparing to campaign in Prussia, his demand for loans from the company increased. In this chapter we ask the important question: "Did Gustav Adolf mis-manage the Copper Company." If he had allowed the company to function without political interference, could it have developed into a reliable source of revenue in its own right? Luckily the accounting records for the company survive in the Stockholm's Riksarkiv and we can do a proper analysis of the company's prospects.

Chapter five is noteworthy because it shows what can go wrong in a fiscal state when the administrators involved are confronted with problems they cannot easily remedy. Since he was unhappy with the Copper Company's ability to make loans, the king searched for an alternative strategy. In 1627,

---

57 Roberts, *Gustavus Adolphus*, I, 129.
58 Stiernman, *Samling*, IV, 726.

during a visit to Sweden Louis de Geer and the king developed a plan to send copper to Amsterdam and mortgage it.[59] The resultant funds were directed to theaters of war in Germany and Poland to pay and feed mercenary troops.

While the plan appeared solid, it was poorly executed. The Swedish administrators in Stockholm and Elbing trusted the Dutch merchants to transfer the funds in a timely manner. The merchants in Amsterdam, however, simply neglected to make the transfers and sat on the funds over the winter earning interest. Meanwhile the troops in northern Germany either starved or raided local villages. Once the king and the chancellor discovered the problem, they were able to order the payments to be made, but not in time to avoid major dislocations.[60]

Chapter five also examines the representatives the crown employed in Amsterdam. The king's ambassadors and commissioners in Amsterdam were competent men with experience in law and administration. They were not, however, capable of overseeing or even fully understanding the complex world of buying and selling commodities in Amsterdam. The trading and financial experts, like Elias Trip and Louis de Geer simply ran circles around the king's administrators. The results were repeated financial setbacks for the crown.

Finally, chapter five recounts the attempt of Louis de Geer, one of the king's closest financial advisors, to mislead the king and the chancellor. De Geer made a series of false claims, asserting that he could manipulate the copper market in Amsterdam. His goal was to convince the king to name him the exclusive agent for the sale of Swedish copper in continental Europe. The plan showed every sigh of success but was derailed by the king's death on the battlefield of Lützen in November of 1632.[61]

We confront the king's death in chapter six. This was inevitably a serious blow to the power of the monarchy and consequently to the move toward statehood. The reins of power, to no one's surprise, fell to the chancellor, who led the army in Germany while still influencing events in the home country. By 1633 he enjoyed the power and prestige normally reserved for crowned monarchs: "Armed with plenipotentiary powers which were almost regal, treating petty princes as equals, he stood covered before kings."[62]

Regretfully this position did not last. A few years later Oxenstierna's policies in Germany were failing and his influence in Sweden was overshadowed by the regency council and the *Riks-Råd*. While he was seeking the

59   Louis de Geers, *Brev och affärshandlingar* (LDGBOA), 120.
60   ASOB, I, 4, 70–73.
61   Dahlgren, *Louis de Geer*, I, 168.
62   Roberts, *Oxenstierna*, 61.

opportunity to return to Sweden, he encountered a humiliating experience; a group of mutinous officers held him captive and forced him to make impossible promises regarding pay and supplies in return for his freedom.[63]

In chapter six we also witness the outcome of a dispute between the Trip family and the Swedish government. In abbreviated terms, in 1632 the Swedish government owed the Trip family RD 836,000 plus an annual interest bill of RD 58,500.[64] The sum was crippling and there was no chance of a conventional settlement. The chancellor made several attempts to pass oversight responsibility to the *Riks-Råd* without success. Over the next couple of years, the crown carried out a desultory negotiation with the Tripp Family, but it ended in harsh recrimination on both sides. Finally, the crown lost patience and defaulted on its loans from the Trip family. The resulting legal suits were finally settled in 1873.[65]

Bibliography

Printed Primary Sources

Dahlgren, Erik Wilhelm, ed. *Louis de Geers brev och affärshandlingar 1614–1652*. Stockholm: P.A. Norstedt & Söner, 1934.

Oxenstierna, Axel. *Rikskansleren Axel Oxenstierna skriften och brefvexling*, Series I, 16 vols. Stockholm: P.A. Norstedt & Söner, 1888–Present.

Oxenstierna, Axel. *Rikskansleren Axel Oxenstierna skriften och brefvexling*, Series II, 14 vols. Stockholm: P.A. Norstedt & Söner, 1888–Present.

Stiernman, Anton von, ed. *Samling utaf kongl. brev, stadgar och förordordningar i angående Sweriges Rikes*, 4 vols. Stockholm: Kongl. Tryckeriet, 1747.

Van Dillen, Johannes Gerard, ed. "Amsterdamsche Notarieele Acten Betreffende den Koperhandel en de Uitoefening van Mijnbouw en Metaalindustrie in Zweden." In *Bijdragen en mededeelingen van het Historisch Genootschap* 58. Utrecht: 1937.

Secondary Sources

Ahnlund, Nils. *Gustav Adolf the Great*. Translated by Michael Roberts. Cambridge: Cambridge University Press, 1940.

Boëthius, Bertil. *Gruvornas, hyttornas och hamrarnas folk, berghanteringes arbetare fran medeltiden till Gustavianska tiden*. Stockholm, Tiden Fölag, 1951.

---

63 Roberts, *Oxenstierna*, 62.
64 Stryker, *The King's Currency*, 66.
65 Dahlgren, *Louis de Geer*, 1, 250.

Dahlgren, Erik Wilhelm. *Louis de Geer, 1587–1652, hans lif och verk*, 2 vols. Uppsala: Almqvist & Wiksells, 1923.

Frost, Robert I. *The Northern Wars: War, State, and Society in Northeastern Europe 1558–1721*. London: Routledge, 2014.

Glete, Jan. *War and the State in Early Modern Europe, Spain, the Dutch Republic, and Sweden as Fiscal–Military States, 1500–1660*. London: Routledge, 2002.

Hamilton, Earl J. *American Treasure and the Price Revolution in Spain, 1501–1650*, Cambridge, Ma: McGill–Queen's University Press, 1934.

Heckscher, Eli Filip. *Sveriges economiska historia från Gustav Vasa*, 2 vols. Stockholm: Albert Bonniers, 1936

Klein, Peter Wolfgang. *De Trippen in de 17e Eeuw, een Studie over het Ondernemersgedrag op de Hollandse Stapelmarkt*. Rotterdam: Assen, 1965.

Kumlien, Kjell. "Staat, Kupfererzeugung und Kupferausfuhr in Schweden 1500–1650." In *Schwerpunkte der Kupferproduktion und des Kupferhandels in Europa 1500–1650*, edited by H. Kellenbenz, 241–59. Cologne: Böhlau Verlag, 1977.

Lindroth, Sven. *Gruvbrytning och kopparhantering vid Stora Kopparberg intill 1800 talets början*, 2 vols. Uppsala: Almqvist & Wiksells, 1955.

Lunde, Henrik O. *A Warrior Dynasty, the Rise and Fall of Sweden as a Military Superpower, 1611–1721*. Oxford: Casemate, 2013.

North, Michael. *The Baltic, a History*. Translated by Kenneth Kronenberg. Cambridge, Ma: Harvard University Press, 2017.

Oredsson, Sverker. *Gustav Adolf: Sverige och Trettioåriga kriget*. Lund: Wahlström & Widstrand, 1992.

Parker, Geoffrey. *The Army of Flanders and the Spanish Road 1567–1659*. Cambridge: Cambridge University Press, 1974.

Posthumus, Nicolaas Wilhelmus. *Inquiry into the History of Prices in Holland*, 2 vols. Leiden: E.J. Brill, 1946.

Ringmar, Erik. *Identity, Interest and Action: A Cultural Explanation of Sweden's Intervention in the Thirty Years War*. Cambridge: Cambridge University Press, 1996.

Roberts, Michael. *Gustavus Adolphus, a History of Sweden 1611–1632*, 2 vols. London: Longmans, Green and Co., 1957.

Rystad, Göran. "The King, the Nobility, and the Growth of Bureaucracy in 17th Century Sweden." In *Europe and Scandinavia, Aspects of the Process of Integration in the 17th Century*, edited by Göran Rystad, 59–70. Lund: 1983.

Rystad, Göran, and Klaus-R Böhme. *In Quest of Trade and Security: The Baltic in Power Politics, 1500–1890*, 2 vols. Lund: Lund University Press, 1994.

Safley, Thomas Max. "Commerce and Markets." In *Europe 1450. to 1789, Encyclopedia of the Early Modern World*, 6 vols, edited by Jonathan Dewald, 2, 11–19. New York: 2004.

Schumpeter, Joseph A. *The Theory of Economic Development, An Inquiry into Profts, Capital, Credit, Interest, and the Business Cycle*. Translated by Redvers Opie. New Brunswick: Transaction Publishers, 2008.

Svenski Biografiskt Lexikon Band 04 (1924) sida 325.

Tjaden, Anja. "The Dutch in the Baltic, 1544–1721." In *The Baltic in Power Politics 1500–1990*, edited by Göran Rystad, Klaus-R Böhme, William M. Carlgren, 1, 61–137. Lund: Lund University Press, 1994.

Utterström, Gustav. "Eli Heckscher, Bertil Boëthius och Sveriges economiska historia från Gustav Vasa." *Meddelande från institutionen för ekonomisk historia*, Umea Universitet, nr. 2 (1982): 1–33.

Van Dillen, Johannas Gerard. *Van Rijkdom en Regenten. Handboek tot de Economische en Sociale Geschiednis van Nederland tijdens de Republiek*. The Hague: Martinus Nijhoff, 1970.

Wetterberg, Gunnar. *Kansler Axel Oxenstierna*, 2 vols. Stockholm: Atlantis, 2002.

Wingquist, S. "Om det gamla koppar–compagneit och kopparmyntningen under Gustav II Adolfs tid." In *Skandia IV*. Lund: 1834, 5–68.

Wittrock, Georg. *Svenska handelscompaniet och kopparhandeln under Gustav II Adolf*. Uppsala: Almqvist & Wikesell, 1919.

Wolontis, Josef. *Kopparmyntning i Sverige 1624–1714*. Helsingfors: 1936.

1.   The Stora Kopparberg

Abstract

The first chapter describes the delicate relationship between the crown and the mine. It is largely the story of a competent administrator, Carl Bonde, (1581-1652) and his efforts to establish royal control at the mine. Karl IX (1550-1611), Gustav Adolf's father and predecessor, began the reforms by hiring German mining experts to modernize the mine. The new young king, under Carl Bonde's tutelage, transformed the role of the mine workers, (called *bergsmän*). Under the young king's supervision they evolved from an archaic work force, owing days of labor to the crown, to market sensitive burghers. They were, moreover, shielded from the worst excesses of a market economy by the king's policy of paying them a fixed price for a guaranteed yearly minimum quantity of copper.

Keywords: Karl IX, Carl Bonde, *Bergsmän,* German mining technology, Christoffer Klem

"The bulls have their day, the bears have their day, the pigs get slaughtered."

Let us move to the dark and damp world of the Stora Kopparberg, once the largest copper mine in Europe. The Stora Kopparberg is located in Falun, a town in the province of Darlarna, about 120 miles northwest of Stockholm. Karl IX and his son King Gustav Adolf substantially increased production at the mine during their reigns, simultaneously centralized governance, and moved toward a royal monopoly for the purchase of copper from the mine. Karl began the effort by making expensive investments in the mine's infrastructure. These investments were a prerequisite for the increases in production at the mine during the reign of his son, Gustav Adolf. Copper from the Stora Kopparberg was the basis for the crown's war-time finances at least until the death of the king in 1632.

Transforming Sweden from a primitive backwater to a European power required reform at all levels of Swedish society. The program of expanding

Stryker, L., *The Swedish Monarchy and the Copper Trade: The Copper Company, the Deposit System, and the Amsterdam Market, 1600–1640.* Amsterdam: Amsterdam University Press, 2024
DOI 10.5117/9789048560813_CH01

royal power and influence at the mine was paralleled with similar efforts in the financial and military sectors. The crown had no choice. If it were to meet domestic security obligations, and pursue an aggressive military and political agenda, it was necessary that the Stora Kopparberg be exploited in an efficient manner. That meant investment in new mining technology and organization "... as the Swedish historian Jan Glete reminds us, in early modern Europe 'Wars were not decided by the existence of resources, but how these resources were organized.'"[1] The key to improved organization, Glete argues, was a fiscal-military state dedicated to extracting, centralizing, and redistributing resources to finance the use of violence. And Geoffrey Parker has written: "Only its superior ability to organize available resources enabled Sweden, with scarcely one million inhabitances, to hold 20 million to ransom during and after the Thirty Years War."[2] This brief statement summarizes the role of the Stora Kopparberg in Sweden's future. A future that included the financing of a war effort that lasted for the next twenty years. This is the story of the king's successful effort to bring the mine under royal control. But how does one persuade the *bergsmän* to accept contemporary practice and innovation without threatening their traditional rights and privileges?

The crown could not simply dictate changes to the *bergsmän*. Like most medieval and early modern corporate groups, the *bergsmän* enjoyed protections, which had been negotiated with the crown over generations. Karl IX and his son Gustav Adolf were able to increase output and gradually gain control over the purchasing of finished copper by using various sources of leverage. Ironically, it was the crown's willingness to invest in the mine that gave it influence over the miners. The crown repeatedly forced concessions from the *bergsmän* by threatening to abandon its ownership rights in the mine and, therefore, cease further investment in the infrastructure.[3] We will also consider the status of the *bergsmän* and their level of prosperity. We will learn that they were commercially sophisticated and fully aware of their role in the Stora Kopparberg's future.

In addition to the *bergsmän* other barriers stood in the way of expansion and control. First, we shall examine a series of questions related to logistics. How, for example, did the copper get to market? What were the normal shipping routes? Was the marketing of copper logical and efficient, or was it still based on medieval barter trade? The mining and smelting operations

---

1   Glete, *War and the State*, 214. Also cited by Parker, *Global Crisis*, 35.
2   Parker, *Global Crisis*, 35
3   Boëthius, *Karl IX*, 32.

had an insatiable appetite for wood and charcoal. Carl Bonde (1577–1648), the able governor of Darlarna during the reign of Karl IX and during the early years of Gustav Adolf's reign was responsible for locating and transporting vast quantities of wood and charcoal. How did Carl Bonde and the crown solve these issues? Little work has been done on these critical subjects. But there are letters (published and unpublished) between Carl Bonde and the crown that will help us to answer these questions.

A modern visitor to the Stora Kopparberg sees only a large crater that looks more like an abandoned open pit mine than a busy underground complex of tunnels, shafts, and large underground chambers. Until 1687 there was a small mountain on the site of this crater that contained a hard-rock copper mine. By 1687, however, the mine was being exploited to the limit of the mining technology of the day; at the time it resembled a giant Swiss cheese because of the maze of mining tunnels crossing above and below one another.[4] This obviously presented a safety problem. In fact, the authorities suspected that trouble was imminent when fissures appeared in several shaft walls in 1682 and 1683. A royal commission headed by a mining expert named Fabian Wrede, visited the mine and made a detailed report to the crown explaining that the mine was in danger of collapse. He received little local cooperation despite frequent rock falls in the tunnels.[5] Then in January 1687, the ceiling in one of the major chambers collapsed killing three *bergsmän*. This was only a warning. On 24 June, 1687 the entire mountain collapsed leaving the crater that one sees today; by mere chance it was Midsummer Day, a holiday for the *bergsmän*, so there were no casualties. The mine was back in production within months.[6]

The Stora Kopparberg mine was a large outcropping of pyrite ore. It was not necessary for early modern miners to follow seams of ore because the entire mountain was copper ore, in varying degrees of concentration. By 1600 there were three large underground chambers: the Bondotötarna, the Blankstötarna, and the Skepstötarna, plus an infinite number of tunnels and smaller rooms.[7] The actual mining technique had not changed from the early medieval period. At the conclusion of the working day, the *bergsmän* tossed logs down the shafts and hauled them into the mining areas. The *bergsmän* then piled the logs against the wall that they planned to mine the

---

4   Comments made by Mats Nilsson, the last managing director of the active copper mine at Stora Kopparberg, October 2007.
5   Lindroth, *Gruvbrytning*, 1, 235.
6   Lindroth, *Gruvbrytning*, 1, 237.
7   Lindroth, *Gruvbrytning*, 1, 223.

next day. They lit the logs and allowed them to burn overnight; this made the rock brittle and workable. The following day the *bergsmän* would work the rock wall with hammers and chisels.[8]

Like all deep, hard-rock mines, the Stora Kopparberg had water problems. From the middle of the sixteenth century, the deeper mining areas were periodically flooded. At first, the miners tried to address the problem using small hand pumps, but it soon became clear that major investment was required for a proper system. Installing an efficient system of pumps was well beyond local means so it was necessary for the crown to finance the capital expenditure. Gustav Vasa—Gustav Adolf's grandfather (1496–1560)—began this effort by importing German technicians familiar with the German ball-and-pipe technique. The system employed a long circular chain with leather balls attached. The balls were pulled through vertical wooden pipes. Since the balls were the same diameter as the pipes, the water could be lifted through the pipe to a height of eleven meters. Initially, horses moving in a circle supplied the power; later innovations included wind power, and finally, waterpower.[9]

Despite the investment, flooding continued to hamper production during wet periods. In 1594 Duke Karl (later Karl IX) hired a German mining engineer, Christoffer Klem, as the technical director of the Kopparberg. Klem recruited German building masters, carpenters, and laborers. He then oversaw the construction of an effective pumping system throughout the mine that kept the entire facility dry year-round. He accomplished this by constructing a *"seriekopplade pumpwerk,"* or a series of linked pumps.[10] This technology was known in Germany by the mid 1500s. Georgius Agricola mentioned the linked-pump technique in his classic work on mining and metallurgy, *De Re Metallica*, first published in 1556. As noted, each individual pump could only operate efficiently to a maximum height of eleven meters. Klem addressed the problem by stacking the pumps—one upon the other—from the lowest mining area to the very top of the mine.[11]

Water was not the only problem. When Christoffer Klem arrived at the Stora Kopparberg, the only means of lifting ore above ground, was hauling it through a series of tunnels to a central vertical shaft, and then raising the ore by horse-drawn winches. Klem constructed water-wheel-based hoists, and increased the number of vertical shafts, which greatly increased the

---

8   Rydberg, *The Great Copper Mountain*, 77.
9   Lindroth, *Gruvbrytning*, 1, 137.
10   Lindroth, *Gruvbrytning*, 1, 136.
11   Lindroth, *Gruvbrytning*, 1, 136-37.

capacity for removing ore from the mine. This technique also reduced the cost of production considerably and allowed the *bergsmän* to exploit lower-grade deposits.[12] Without these improvements, the *bergsmän* could never have removed the large quantities of ore they needed by the next century.

Once the copper ore was on the surface processing could begin. The first step in refining was "cold roasting." This is a misnomer because the ore was roasted at above 600 degrees Fahrenheit.[13] The ore from the Kopparberg contained high levels of sulfur, an undesirable impurity in copper, and this initial roasting removed most of it. The roasting lasted several weeks and was performed at the mine. Next, the *bergsmän* transported the roasted ore to one of the local smelting furnaces. There were several near the mine, but some were as far as fifteen miles away. The main requirement for a smelting furnace was a moving stream to supply water to the wheels that powered the bellows, and water for washing the ore. In 1540, Gustav Vasa built several smelters on the royal estate of Born, which was close to the mine.[14]

Once it arrived at the smelter, the ore was placed in a hearth and heated with bellows to above 1,400 degrees Fahrenheit. The non-metallic minerals came off in the form of slag. The resulting material was called copper matte and would normally contain about 20 percent copper. The third stage was called "turn roasting" and was designed to remove most of the remaining sulfur and other non-metallic impurities. The matte was roasted in the smelter at well above 1,000 degrees Fahrenheit for several weeks and constantly raked to ensure the maximum surface area was exposed to the heat. The finished product was *"råkoppar"* (raw copper) with a copper content of about 90 percent.[15]

To understand Karl IX's willingness to make substantial capital investments in the mining operation we must first understand the complex relationship that existed between the *bergsmän* and the crown. Many of the *bergsmän* active during the reigns of Karl IX and his successors were comfortable businessmen who owned mining rights. Other *bergsmän* were subsistence laborers. Michael Roberts has colorfully stated, "the *bergsmän* was a miner in the summer, a forge man in the autumn and spring, and a charcoal burner in the winter."[16] He further clarified: "The miners were for

---

12 Rydberg, "Stora Kopparberget", 5.
13 Conversation on 7 July, 2011 with Craig Hafner, a chemist, and CEO of DBlock Metals, Gastonia, NC. None of these temperatures appear in the literature. Craig Hafner calculated the temperature based on the chemical process it was intended to perform.
14 Rydberg, *Stora Kopparberget*, 7.
15 Rydberg, "Stora Kopparbeg", 7.
16 Roberts, *Gustavus Adolphus*, 2, 31.

the most part no better off than the more prosperous of the peasantry; they won the ore by their personal exertions, for the number of hired laborers was still small ..."[17]

This description tends to underplay the specialized trades within the mine, all of which fall under the general category of *bergsmän*. In a letter to Chancellor Axel Oxenstierna, written in April 1614, Carl Bonde reported an accident in the mine. After a description of the repairs, he mentioned some complaints from other workers and wrote, "... the men who mine the ore (*mallmän*), thank God, are not giving me trouble."[18] In a second letter, written two years later, Bonde asked the chancellor to inform the king that he had sent the smelter (*smeltare*), two ore miners (*mallmbrytare*), and the machinery mechanic (*konsteknekt*) requested by the king, to Botued Lakie in Västerås.[19] The fact that the governor mentioned these subclasses of *bergsmän* by name indicated that they were active in specialized areas. In his description of the crown's mining area in 1619, Bertil Boethius listed the crown's employees as the foreman (*konststigare*), mining baliff (*gruvfogde*), and bookkeeper (*gruvskrivare*), all of whom would be on the management side. He also listed several categories of *bergsmän*, including thirteen carpenters (*timmermän*), two master smiths (*mästersmeder*), four regular smiths (*andra smeder*), four bellows workers (*vindvaktare*), five machinery mechanics (*konsteknektar*), nine generalist hands (*styrare*), six carriers, and thirteen ore and wood movers.[20]

Also, there is a problem with Roberts's numbers. In support of his image of the yeoman mine worker, exploiting his own ore deposit and acting as his own charcoal burner, he wrote, "the number of hired laborers was still small." He thereby implied that the bulk of the work was done by the *bergsmän* themselves. In a footnote to that point, Roberts quoted Tom Söderberg, stating that there were only fifty hired laborers in 1550.[21] Söderberg, however, was referring to the number of active *bergsmän* in 1550, not hired laborers. In any case, in 1550 the Stora Kopperberg produced a total of 500 skd of copper. Roberts was writing about the situation in 1611. In that year the mine produced 6,300 skd of copper.[22]

Thanks to Bertil Boëthius we also have an example of a successful *bergsmän*. In the 1630s Johan Trotzig, "the rich," established a cannon foundry

17   Roberts, *Gustavus Adolphus*, 2, 34.
18   Axel Oxenstiernas, *Skrifter och brevväxling* (AOSB), II, 11, 16.
19   AOSB, II, 11, 23.
20   Boëthius, *Gruvornas*, 87.
21   Roberts, *Gustavus Adolphus*, 2, 34 n.
22   Boëthius estimated that 500 bergmän were active in 1620. Boëthius, *Gruvornas*, 105.

in Falun. Trotzig was vertically integrated; he also owned substantial mining rights and, therefore, had access to copper ore. He had the ore smelted locally and used it to make bronze cannon. He employed up to 100 local people.[23] Through ownership of mining rights, Trotzig was certainly a *bergsmän*, but he neatly defied Robert's contention that the *bergsmän* "certainly ... had no capital resources adequate to the introduction of new techniques and expensive machinery ... none were capitalists."[24]

Finally, a random remark in 1619 from Carl Bonde in a letter to the chancellor bears close attention. The letter concerned the theft of ore from a warehouse. After a description of the crime, Bonde changed the subject to support the application of Christopher Noret for a coat of arms (*Sköldebrev*). Christopher was a *bergsmän*. Bonde went on to say that many of the old *bergsmän* already had coats of arms and Christopher deserved his own because of his service to the crown.[25] The kind of *bergsmän* that Roberts described would not be applying for coats of arms. Some of the *bergsmän*, at least, were successful businessmen who did not fit his description "no better off than the more prosperous of the peasantry." If we accept Roberts's description of the *bergsmän*, we will have difficulty understanding the complicated relationship that existed between the *bergsmän* and the crown. The *bergsmän* were a diverse group of craftsmen, specialists, entrepreneurs, and capitalists who populated all levels of Falun society, from the moderately poor, to the rich and successful. These were not docile peasants; the king could not simply order them about. We will see later in this chapter that each change the king wanted to make in his relationship with the *bergsmän* was the subject of delicate and protracted negotiation.[26]

The basic unit of ownership was the "*par*."[27] Since the mine was owned by the crown one must regard ownership of a *par* much like owning the right to farm on crown-owned land. The *bergsmän* owned the *pars* "of" the king. When new *pars* were created, the *bergsmän* paid the king a fee to purchase them. Thus, it is important to understand that the *bergsmän* did not own the mine, or any part of it. They owned solely the right to mine ore and smelt copper. The *par* was normally divided into quarters; a miner could

---

23   Boëthius, *Gruvornas*, 88.
24   Roberts, *Gustavus Adolphus*, 2 34–35.
25   AOSB, II, 11, 28.
26   AOSB, II, 11, 16.
27   The term *par* comes from the decree of 1360. King Magnus Eriksson specified that each of the smelters should have a pair of bellows. Since he combined the ownership of shares in the smelting works with the mining interests the term "pair" was used for mining shares as well. Söderberg, *Stora Kopparberg*, 497.

own a whole quarter or any part of one. The contract of 1587 specified the existence of twenty-seven *pars* or one hundred and eight quarters. Then, in 1593, during the regency of Duke Karl, the crown and *bergsmän* agreed to increase the number of *pars* to thirty; this resulted in one hundred and twenty quarters. In 1598 thirteen *bergsmän* held whole quarters, one hundred and thirty-eight had half quarters, and one hundred and forty owned some smaller portion of a quarter. There was also a discernable trend toward growth in the number of owners during the end of the sixteenth and the beginning of the seventeenth century. In 1570, for example, there were one hundred and eighty owners, in 1598 the number was up to two hundred and ninety-eight, and by 1617 there were six hundred owners.[28]

The crown's motive for increasing the number of *pars* was simple. The *bergsmän* paid fixed taxes per *par*, so more *pars* meant greater revenue. Perhaps more important, more *pars* meant more copper mined and sold. This was less of an advantage to the crown before the purchasing monopoly, but once King Gustav Adolf began to enforce the monopoly in 1617 and 1618, greater production meant larger profits for the crown.

Previously, during the reign of Gustav Vasa (1523 to 1560), the yearly tax per quarter was set at one *skeppund* copper.[29] Bertil Boëthius stated that the king judged that normal production of copper should be about 10 skd per quarter per year, so the tax amounted to a tithe. *Bergsmän* producing more than 10 skd per year also paid 10 percent on the overproductions. *Bergsmän* producing fewer than 10 skd, however, still paid the minimum one *skeppund*. This system remained intact until 1592. In that year Duke Karl, the reformer, assumed the regency and began the series of changes that laid the groundwork for the expansion of production in the following century.[30]

In addition to the *avrad*, as the mining tax was known, the miners owed workdays and charcoal to the king. When he came to power in 1592, Karl began negotiations with the miners on the whole issue, as the system was awkward and outdated. When Duke Karl began the discussions with the *bergsmän*, they each owed the king 11 "*stigar*" of charcoal per quarter per year.[31] It took between 10 and 15 *stigar* of charcoal to smelt one *skeppund* of copper (depending, of course on the quality of the ore). Then for each quarter the miners owed days working in the crown's smelting works, days on the pumps removing water from the main mining areas, days working on the

---

28   Boëthius, *Karl IX*, 2.
29   As a reminder, *skeppund, a unit of weight abbreviated as "skd."*
30   Boëthius, *Karl IX*, 5–6.
31   One *stigar* of charcoal was equal to 12 metric tons.

cold-roasting hearth in the crown's mining area, and days for construction and transport. Altogether the *bergsmän* owed a total of about seventy-five days per year.[32] Duke Karl understood that the days the *bergsmän* spent working in crown areas of the mine meant fewer days of productive work on their own areas, hence less tax revenue. Karl's reforms, therefore, greatly reduced the labor obligations, and by the beginning of the new century the *bergsmän* owed only sufficient labor to keep the crown mining areas running.[33]

To understand the complex relationship between the crown and the *bergsmän* one must also understand the difference between the crown's copper and the *bergsmän's* copper. The crown had traditionally claimed a portion of the ore mined at the Stora Kopparberg as a tax. During the early years of his reign, Gustav Vasa developed the smelting works at Born, the royal estate near the Stora Kopparberg. This soon became the administrative center of the crown's activities in the area. The crown's bailiff was resident in Born, and the crown's scales were next to the ore-storage area. Born, a late-medieval industrial center, had areas for cold roasting, smelters with bellows, and water-driven hammer mills. At this time the *bergsmän* were paying the tithe in ore, but Gustav soon realized that he was not getting sufficient raw material from the *bergsmän*, and what he was receiving was poor quality. His solution was to devote crown resources to increase mining capacity at the largest of the mining areas, Blankstöten, and to develop the nearby areas of Blötmalmsgruvan and Drottninggruva. The new mining areas were the exclusive property of the crown, and although the *bergsmän* worked these areas while performing obligatory workdays, the ore belonged to the crown. Ore from the crown's new mining areas was sent to Born for processing.[34]

This distinction between crown mining areas and *bergsmän* mining areas remained in force throughout the reign of Karl IX. It was a distinction, however, with some flexibility, and Karl allowed the *bergsmän* to mine in crown areas in return for other concessions in his efforts to reform an outdated system. Karl strove for much greater regulation of the *bergsmän's* activities than any previous monarch had attempted.[35] At the same time he increased oversight, however, he also attempted to withdraw from ownership positions. In the negotiations of 1593, Karl turned over large sections of the crown's mining concessions in the Bondestöten area, and the *bergsmän*, in

---

32 Boëthius, *Karl IX*, 5–6.
33 Boëthius, *Karl IX*, 5–6.
34 Lindroth, Gruvbrytning, 1, 44-47
35 Boëthius, *Karl IX*, 3-5.

turn, agreed to increase the number of *pars* to thirty (one-hundred-twenty quarters). In 1595 when some of the *bergsmän* working in the Bondestöten encountered sections of low-grade ore in their allotted mining area, Karl turned over further concessions of rich-ore sections to the *bergsmän*. It is useful to keep in mind that in most cases the *bergsmän*'s interests coincided with Karl's interests. After all, crown revenue from the mine depended on prosperous *bergsmän*.[36]

We noted earlier that Karl IX was responsible for recruiting German technicians and mining experts who built modern pumping and hoisting systems, bringing the Stora Kopparberg up to seventeenth-century continental standards. Because each *bergsmän* at the Stora Kopparberg operated as an independent profit center, these innovations could not be financed without the crown's participation. Equally obvious, the expansion that occurred during the first half of the seventeenth century would not have occurred without the capital expenditure made in the 1590s through the first decade of the next century. Technical development alone, however, would not have been sufficient.[37] Karl IX also had to introduce flexibility into the system so that the crown could expand production by adding more *pars* when necessary. Under the then current system, he could only expand the number of *bergsmän* through difficult negotiations with the members, who were wary of any attempt to dilute their rights and earning power. His solution was the introduction of the "*nya bergsmän*" or the new miners.[38]

The crown's works suffered from a lack of good ore during the years 1603 to 1605. This was primarily the result of collapsed walls in the crown's mining areas and generally poor-quality ore available in reachable areas. During those years the *bergsmän* produced 14,172 barrows of ore, of which only about one third came from the crown's mining areas. This, of course, affected the royal income, and provoked the king into real action on the question of new *pars*. Already in 1599, he had announced to the *bergsmän* that he wanted to increase the number of *pars*. In 1607 he negotiated an increase in *pars* from thirty-three to sixty-five. He sold the new *pars* to *nya bergsmän*, or new miners. At first *nya bergsmän* were restricted to mining in abandoned areas. They were not allowed, for example, to work in the mining rooms used by the "*gamla bergsmän*" or old miners. Before long, however, the *nya bergsmän* were working the major mining areas as well.[39]

36   Boëthius, *Karl IX*, 6.
37   Boëthius, *Karl IX*, 6.
38   Boëthius, *Karl IX*, 13–14.
39   Boëthius, *Karl IX*, 13–14.

The *nya bergsmän* paid a different tax. They were free from the *avrad* or the one *skeppund* per quarter. However, they paid a full tithe on their entire production. On the other hand, the *gamla bergsmän* paid the *avrad* plus a tithe on all copper they produced over 10 skd. In practice the difference amounted to little. There was, however, some enduring resentment; Mats Jöransson, the king's bailiff, reported in a 1614 letter that the "rich" *gamla bergsmän* were trying to eliminate the "poorer" *nya bergsmän* by forcing inferior allotments of mining areas on them. He also stated that some of the new miners had become as prosperous as some of the old miners.[40]

The king timed the introduction of the new work force well. The local price went from 120 marks (SD 30 or RD 15.5) per skd to 160 marks (SD 40 or RD 24.5) per skd during the first decade of the century, because demand was strong and remained so throughout the next decade.[41] During the last decade of the sixteenth century, the Stora Kopparberg produced an average of 2,000 skd per year. By 1606 the mine was producing 5,500 skd per year of which 4,400 skd were produced by the *bergsmän* for their own account while the balance came from crown properties.[42]

Karl IX, however, gradually became disillusioned with his role as a miner and processor using a semi-feudal labor force. In addition, his share of the overall output of the mine had diminished markedly; in 1590 the crown properties produced 55 percent of the total copper output, but by 1606 they produced only 20 percent of the output.[43] In light of his smaller share of production, Karl IX decided he would prefer to transfer all crown mining rights to the *bergsmän*, and benefit from the increased tax base, rather than producing and selling copper. This would also transfer market risk from the crown to the *bergsmän*, in the event of a price drop. Despite the apparent benefits to themselves, the *bergsmän* were wary of this possibility. They feared that if the crown withdrew from active participation, it would no longer be willing to make the capital investment necessary to build and maintain pumping facilities and hauling machinery. In the end, the *bergsmän* and the crown reached a compromise. The king kept one mining area, the Tolvmansrummet, as an exclusive crown preserve. In addition, the king would own one quarter of every *par*. Thus, the crown became partners with each *bergsmän*, both new and old.[44] This guaranteed the

40 Boëthius, *Karl IX*, 13–14.
41 As a reminder, currencies are abbreviated as follows: SD for Swedish *dalers*, RD for *riksdaler*, and DG for Dutch Guilders. The exchange rate was RD 1=DG 2.5 and RD 1= SD 1.624.
42 Lindroth, *Gruvbrytning*, 1, 73.
43 Lindroth, *Gruvbrytning*, 2, 389.
44 Boëthius, *Karl IX*, 27.

crown's continued participation in the various mining activities, but it
had one disadvantage for the miners. The crown did not contribute to the
avrad, and as each quarter owed an annual *avrad* of two *skeppund*, the
other owners had to make up for the king's share. Thus, the *avrad* for each
bergsmän-owned quarter jumped from two *skeppund* per quarter to two
and two-thirds *skeppund*.[45]

Another part of the agreement for 1607 was a new tax on the *bergsmän*.
The fear of losing the crown's support for the maintenance of the equipment
was so strong, that the *bergsmän* agreed to an additional 5 percent tax called
the "*konstavgiften*" or literally machinery fee. In 1611 this was transformed
into a fixed fee of four *skeppund* per *par*. Like the *avrad*, the *konstavgift* was
collected when the *par* weighed their 100 skd (more or less). The *bergsmän*
were not allowed to sell any copper to merchants before they paid the *avrad*
and the *konstavgiften*. Nor were they allowed to sell ore to one another to
avoid crown taxes. It was also intended to prevent smuggling. For obvious
reasons, the crown did not want copper sold before it was taxed.[46]

One can see a pattern in Karl IX's approach to the Stora Kopparberg.
He wanted to receive maximum revenue but was also willing to step back
and allow the *bergsmän* to do their specialized work. He would tax the
production, and the greater the production, the greater the tax revenue. The
king's attempt to turn crown mining areas and rights over to the *bergsmän*
probably demonstrated his realization that the *bergsmän* were less motivated
when performing feudal labor obligations than they were when working their
own areas. Turning the crown mining areas over to the *bergsmän* would, in
the long run, boost production. This demonstrated an enlightened, common
sense understanding of human behavior. It should certainly not be taken
for lack of interest. Karl IX was known as a keen observer of the mining
and processing techniques at the mine, and, at every turn, he attempted to
exert greater crown control over everyday mining activities. The *bergsmän*,
for their part, wanted the king to share their risks so he would continue to
have a strong stake in improving the mining and processing infrastructure.

In summarizing Karl's impact on the Stora Kopparberg, we may conclude
that he made important contributions to the enterprise, and he laid the
foundations for the growth in production during his son's reign. His own
record was certainly positive on the production issue. As mentioned earlier,
when he became regent in 1592, the mine was producing an average of 2,000
skd per year. In the year before his death, 1610, the mine produced almost

45   Boëthius, *Karl IX*, 27.
46   Boëthius, *Karl IX*, 28.

6,500 skd. In that same year, the crown succeeded in raising the *avrad* to 12 skp per *par*, and in 1613 the *avrad* and *konstavgift* were combined for a total of 16 skd per *par*. Of course, the crown did not pay taxes so the 16 skd were split among the other three owners of the quarters.[47] More important, however, was Karl's effort to improve the infrastructure, a prerequisite for the growth of the next four decades. We will soon see that while Gustav Adolf was active in adding refining capacity, it was not necessary for him to make large investments in the mine. Once the mine was operating to seventeenth-century standards, Karl's successors were able to increase production simply by maintaining the equipment and adding *pars*, which they did continuously during the next twenty years.[48] Perhaps Karl IX's most important contribution was pressuring the *bergsmän* to be cooperative and flexible. This was an absolute requirement for the future. If the *bergsmän* had been intransigent on the issuing of more *pars*, expansion would have been difficult if not impossible.

Since the crown's income from mining was based on a series of confusing, and constantly changing taxes and leases, a clearer picture will emerge by taking one year and examining the actual results (see figure 2). Since Karl had increased the number of *pars* to sixty-five for 1607, he expected the miners to produce of 6,500 skd. The *avrad* that year was still only 8 skd per *par*. This would mean a total anticipated *avrad* of 65 x 8 skd or 520 skd, plus the *konstavgift* of 5 percent or 325 skd, totaling 845 skd. Also, as the owner of one quarter in each *par*, the crown could expect 25 percent of the output, after deducting the *avrad* and *konstavgift*. In addition, the king would also have revenue from his residual mining properties referred to as the "*kronobruk*," or the crown's works.

This is an oversimplification, because, in practice, the king would also have collected some minor amounts of copper for use of the crown smelters, and there was a small variation between the tax paid by the *gamla bergsmän* versus the *nya bergmän*. It is, nonetheless, a workable approximation of crown revenue from copper for the year. In fact, 1607 must have been a disappointing year for the crown. According to Boëthius, the ore mined that year was poorer than expected.[49] The actual *bergmän* production was 4,500 skd, while the crown's works produced 1,024 skd;[50] both were less than the king had anticipated.

---

47   Boëthius, *Karl IX*, 28.
48   AOSB, II, 11, 149.
49   Boëthius, *Karl IX*, 29.
50   Lindroth, *Gruvbrytning*, 2, 389.

Figure 2.   Calculation of Expected versus Actual Crown Revenue from Copper

	Expected Revenue based on Miner's production of 6,500 skd In skd of copper	Actual Revenue based on Miner's production of 4,500 skd In skd of copper
Avrad	520	520
Konstavgiften based of 5 percent	325	225
The king's one quarter share	1,414	939
Crown's works	1,024	1,024
Total Crown Copper	3,283	2,709

The mundane details of running the mine were just as important as the organization and ownership of the mine. Not one *skeppund* of copper would have reached Amsterdam without a system of accurate scales, a method of quality control, and an adequate supply of raw materials, especially wood and charcoal. Since the crown's revenue depended on the output of the miners, the crown was concerned that all copper produced was weighed on official scales. Initially all the crown's copper was weighed at the Born works, and the *bergsmän*'s copper was weighed at the central marketplace in Falun.[51] The weights were duly recorded in the *"vågbok"* (book of weights) at the site. This book was kept daily from the time of Gustav Vasa until well into the eighteenth century. Before a finished ingot could be weighed, it had to bear the owner's mark, and the mark of the smelter, called the *"bomärke."*[52] Apparently this was not easy to enforce; there was considerable correspondence from the crown to royal officials requesting strict observance of these rules. Gustav Adolf expended serious effort to tighten up this system, especially once he had a full monopoly for purchasing all the copper at the mine. Even as late as 1630, he was instructing his bailiffs to be vigilant on the issue of proper weighing and marking.[53] Before the age of analysis certificates, which accompany every shipment of copper ingots today, the owner's mark and the smelter's mark were a guarantee of quality. If a shipment that ended up at the mint in Säter was

---

51   Kristiansson, *Falu*, 19.
52   Kristiansson, *Falu*, 20.
53   Riksarkivet. SE/RA/1112.1/B # 65, Kungl. brev till Peder Nilsson och Erik Eriksson. 14 February, 1630.

high in impurities, the mint master could trace it back to a specific source. No doubt, certain smelter's marks meant that the quality was assured, and others might mean the opposite. If the owners were planning to sell the copper outside the legal channels, a commonplace as the crown sought ever closer control of the trade, they would have preferred that the copper ingot remain as anonymous as possible.[54]

If the copper bore the correct *bomärke*, the crown-appointed weighing master would consent to weigh the copper ingot and enter it into the book. In addition to the weighing master, the crown officials present in Falun included the crown's tax inspector (*kronoavradsinspektoren*) and his assistant, the tax recorder (*avradsskrivaren*). These three officials were servants of the crown with full authority (*fullmakt*). Their role was to ensure that all copper produced was weighed and recorded, and to collect the appropriate taxes.[55]

Of course, the purpose of accurate scales was not only to collect taxes for the crown. The scales were an indispensable element of trade. Since the miners sold their copper to visiting merchants, having accurate weights was necessary for the merchants to be certain that they were paying only for full weight received. When a shipment was destined for export, it was weighed again in Stockholm. Once the copper was received at a customer's warehouse it was normally "weighed in" before payment. To demonstrate just how sacred accurate weights were to all participants, in February 1639 the Falun *bergsmän* of the Kopparberg petitioned Chancellor Oxenstierna complaining about the behavior of the mint master at the royal mint in Säter. They expressed outrage that the mint master had rejected Falun's weights on a shipment of copper that arrived at Säter. They said that both the scales at Falun and the scales at Säter were manned by "oath sworn" weighing masters, so how could the mint master at Säter reject Falun's weights out of hand, and blame the *bergsmän* of Falun for the discrepancy? If their weights were questioned, they could not do business with the crown, or with merchants.[56] Weight discrepancies remain to this day a major annoyance for producers and merchants.

Another critical element in the cost structure of copper was transport. What is the value of a copper ingot in Falun without any means of transport? Almost nothing. Without a network of roads and lakes providing access to seaports the Great Copper Mountain could never have contributed the vast

---

54   Kristiansson, *Falu*, 21.
55   Kristiansson, *Falu*, 21.
56   AOSB II, 11, 364–65.

sums that the crown needed to fuel its worldly ambitions. From the Middle Ages until quite recently, the Stora Kopperberg was a transportation hub.[57]

The traditional shipping route for copper ingot destined for the continental market began by crossing the Runn Lake, near Falun, by boat in the summer or by sled in the winter. Then the ingots were taken by wagon overland via Hedemora to Västerås, on the banks of Lake Malar. The copper then went by boat or sled over the lake to Stockholm. An established alternative route was to cross the Svärdsjö (a lake), travel overland to the port of Gävle, and sail down the coast to Stockholm. These were not the only routes. We will see later that copper made its way to many cities in the course of trading and exchange, but these two routes were primary. In the late Middle Ages, the roads to Västerås were appalling. Gustav Vasa devoted considerable resources to eliminating trees and removing boulders from the road. For transport on the larger inland lakes the local sailors used large flat-bottom sailboats. The overland route to Göteborg was expensive and time consuming. It was used only when the Danes threatened to close Swedish traffic through the Sound. The western routes through Norway were seldom used because of the mountainous terrain. They were, however, ideal for smuggling.[58]

The local peasant labor force performed the transportation, which provided supplemental income. We do not have accurate cost figures for the seventeenth century, but we have some indications for the very end of the sixteenth century. The peasant workers received between four and six marks (one Swedish *daler* to one and one-half Swedish *daler*) per wagon from the Kopparberg area to Västerås. In the winter each wagon could hold two *skeppund* because of the frozen ground. In summer, however, the wagons could haul only one and one-half *skeppund*.[59]

After paying the Älvsborg ransom to the king of Denmark, Gustav Adolf decided to reform the distribution of copper. His first step was to negotiate a purchasing monopoly with the *bergmän*. This was a prerequisite for the formation of the Copper Company, and it meant that the *bergmän* were obligated to sell only to the crown. One way to measure the effectiveness of this new purchasing monopoly is to compare the size of the average purchase both before and after the reforms. The Stora Kopparberg *vågbok* for the years 1608 to 1610 lists the merchants who received copper and their locations. In preparation for his work on the city of Falun during the middle of the seventeenth century, Karl-Gustav Hilderbrandt analyzed the

57 Kristiansson, *Falu*, 21.
58 Kristiansson, *Falu*, 59.
59 Odén, *Kopparhandel*, 326–28.

shipping information.[60] The result was a helpful profile of the pre-monopoly trade patterns. Between 1608 and 1610, some 8,370 skd were weighed and shipped from the mine. From the data we learn that no merchant or group of merchants dominated the business, and that the individual shipments were small. For example, no merchant purchased more than 175 skd in any one year, and some bought as few as 15 skd. Any merchant buying more than 100 skd per year was significant. In 1610, Knut Kråka purchased 144 skd, which made him the leading buyer for the year.[61]

Looking at the merchants by city, those based in Stockholm, the center of the export trade, received about one-third of all copper shipped. Merchants based in Västerås were second, receiving about 20 percent of the copper. Most of that copper, however, would eventually be shipped to Stockholm for export. The two smaller northern ports of Gävle and Hudiksvall together took 11.5 percent. Merchants there took noticeably smaller lots. The portion purchased by merchants from Gävle was divided between sixty different individuals. These were poor rural areas specializing in agricultural goods, and the copper was almost certainly exchanged for agricultural products, a common feature of copper distribution before the monopoly period. The same was true for merchants from Uppsala and Enköping, who took only 8 percent of the mine's output in return for corn. The towns of Jönköpping and Växjö took a total of 2 percent and supplied oxen in return.[62]

By comparison, during the period of the Copper Company (after 1619), the crown seldom shipped fewer than 500 to 1,000 skd at one time from the Kopparberg. Again, we are seeing the dramatic changes that the crown realized after paying off the Älvsborg ransom in 1619. Under the medieval system the bergsmän exchanged small amounts of copper with merchants in return for food, supplies of wood, and charcoal for use in the mine. The copper would gradually migrate to a port of export, perhaps passing through several more hands along the way. This was expensive and inefficient. To streamline the process, Gustav Adolf purchased copper directly from the bergsmän and bypassed the local merchants. He could then make larger shipments and increase his profits. As we shall see, however, he only gradually overcame the inefficiencies of the traditional medieval barter economy.[63]

As mentioned, supplying the mine and the smelting works with wood and charcoal was a major task, and it became increasingly complicated

---

60   Hilderbrand, *Falu*, 32.
61   Hilderbrand, *Falu*, 32–34.
62   Hilderbrand, *Falu*, 32–33.
63   Hilderbrand, *Falu*, 34.

as the output at the mine increased. During the years we are examining, tremendous quantities of wood and charcoal were consumed. One estimate is that during the period 1625 to 1650 the Stora Koppperberg consumed an average of 400,000 cubic meters of wood in the mine and as charcoal in the smelters per year.[64] Since the nearby forests were long since denuded, the wood had to come from ever-greater distances.

There were other factors that would make the problem even greater. In the coming chapters we will document the production of refined copper for the overseas market and for the mint. Refining furnaces would consume even more wood. Clearly Sweden was thrice blessed. She had a large copper deposit, abundant wood for making charcoal, and rivers and lakes for transport. The crown would never have been able to exploit the Stora Kopparberg without the abundant forests growing in northern Sweden and the waterways necessary for the movement of goods. The largely successful effort to supply the mine with wood and charcoal was a testament to the crown's ability to marshal resources in its determination to exploit the mine to meet its political and military goals.[65]

Perhaps an even greater hindrance to the crown's quest to gain control over the production at the Stora Kopparberg was smuggling. It was a tradition going back much further than the years we are considering. Even during periods when the *bergsmän* were encouraged to trade freely with local merchants, they would still prefer to avoid paying the *avrad*. Karl IX demonstrated his awareness of the problem in a letter dated March 1593. Apparently, Norwegians were accustomed to visit the *bergsmän* secretly at the Stora Kopparberg to buy copper from them before taxes had been paid. They somehow carted the metal across the border and exported it to the continent. Karl specified new rules to prevent this illegal trade, the first being "sell only to native Swedes."[66] In addition he cautioned the local bailiff, Lars Bagge, that the *bergsmän* should not be permitted to remove copper from the public areas until it was properly weighed.[67]

Another common technique for avoiding the *avrad* was the so called *gårdshandel* or yard trade. Instead of conducting business with merchants in the marketplace, as specified by law, the *bergsmän* would meet a merchant in his private yard, or place of business. In 1606 Karl IX forbade the sale of

---

64 Rydberg, "Stora Kopparberget," 9.
65 Rydberg, "Stora Kopparberget," 9–10.
66 *"av svenske män."*
67 Riksarkivet, SE/RA/1112.1/B 1593 # 75, Kungl. brev. om handelen wed Kopparberget, October 28, 1593.

copper anywhere other than in the public market, and only after it had been weighed, stamped, and recorded.[68] In 1611 the king again complained of the yard trade and set up additional safeguards. In this later letter he repeated the ban on trade at the *bergsmän*'s yards and stipulated that all "wares" should change hands in the public marketplace. No copper could leave the marketplace unless it was weighed and bore the appropriate *bomärke*. This time the crown put some teeth into the proclamation. The king gave the local bailiff, Nils Byrielsson, full authority (*fullmakten*) to confiscate any copper located outside the marketplace not bearing the *bomärke*, regardless of whether in the possession of a *bergsmän* or a merchant.[69]

The crown's complaints about *bergsmän* privately selling copper, however, missed an important point. We observed earlier the importance of scales in any copper transaction. The only reliable scales at the Stora Kopparberg were the crown's scales near the mine, and the scales at the Born works. Merchants could not accept a *bergsmän*'s word for the weight of the copper he was trading and vice versa. Otherwise, the merchant would transport his smuggled cargo to Gävle for export only to find that he paid for 50 *lispund* and received only 40 *lispund*. There must have been some unofficial complicity allowing access to the scales for smuggling to be such a widespread problem.

The most compelling reason for the perceived growth in smuggling was the king's new copper policy begun while the Älvsborg ransom payments were still due. The financial obligations that accompanied the ransom forced Gustav Adolf to explore new sources of revenue; he immediately focused on the Stora Kopparberg. At first, beginning in 1615, he attempted to buy copper at the Kopparberg in competition with the merchants. When this proved unfruitful, he sought to impose a crown monopoly on all purchases of copper at the mine. Johan III (reigned 1568 to 1592) had made a half-hearted effort to impose a purchasing monopoly in the 1580s, but it proved unworkable. Gustav Adolf also had difficulty; there is no evidence of an effective crown monopoly on purchases until 1619, when the king established the Copper Company. Once the crown began to enforce the Copper Company's monopoly, however, smuggling became epidemic, and one wagonload after the other headed for Norway or for the northern port cities of Gävle and Hudviksvall. The king's purchase price of SD 50 per skd was not the only reason for smuggling. The terms of the agreement between the crown and the *bergsmän* called for payment in cash (*reda pengar*). Predictably, the crown

68 Kristiansson, *Kopparsmugglingen*, 58.
69 Kristiansson, *Kopparsmugglingen*, 58.

immediately fell behind and payments were late, which led to difficulties for the *bergsmän* and threatened to disrupt production at the mine. Naturally smuggling became an attractive alternative.[70]

Smugglers do not keep scrupulous records, so we gauge the extent of the problem by the official reaction. In 1615 Gustav Adolf appointed Peder Pedersson and Peder Jonsson with full authority to search and recover all unreported copper. In addition, he appointed Mats Jöransson bailiff (mentioned by Carl Bonde above) and sent Peder Eriksson to be the crown buyer with authority to buy copper produced at the mine for the crown's account. This new team wasted no time in attempting to purchase copper. Unfortunately, they were not equipped with ready cash. When the *bergsmän* realized that they would be selling for credit, rather than cash, they rioted and refused any further sales to the crown.[71] In response the king issued a proclamation to the *Kammar-Råd* (privy council) ordering that cash be kept in reserve at the mine to pay the *bergsmän*. He assumed that if he paid cash to the *bergsmän* they would prefer dealing with him rather than selling to merchants.[72]

In June 1616, the king wrote directly to the *bergsmän* warning them not to remove copper from the smelting area until it was weighed and the *avrad* paid. He threatened confiscation by local crown officials from either the *bergsmän*, or from the equally guilty merchants. This time the *bergsmän* replied directly to the king, complaining that crown copper buyers had no cash, and every sale was for credit. This is the reason they sold to merchants rather than to the crown's agents. The *bergsmän* were in debt to the merchants for food and supplies, such as charcoal and wood, and had to repay them. The king then responded in a conciliatory tone. He found the *bergsmän*'s complaints valid.[73] The king was not amused, however, at the *bergsmän*'s suggestion that he end his request for a purchasing monopoly. He called their position "mere lack of cooperation" with the established order. On the issue of the *bergsmän*'s indebtedness, he was particularly dismissive stating that it was not his concern.[74]

The struggle between the crown and the *bergsmän* dragged on and the *bergsmän* continued selling the majority of their copper to merchants with whom they had done business for years. After 1617, however, there is evidence

---

70   Kristiansson, *Kopparsmugglingen*, 59.
71   Riksarkivet. SE/RA/1112.1/B # 182, Kungl. brev March 16, 1616 met fullmakt för Mats Jöransson.
72   Riksarkivet. SE/RA/1112.1/B # 176, Kungl. brev October 26, 1615. med resolution för kammarrådet.
73   Kristiansson, *Kopparsmugglingen*, 59.
74   Riksarkivet. SE/RA/1112.1/B # 351, Kungl. brev. til kopparbergsmännen July 27, 1616 med svar på deras skrivelse av den 7 July.

that the king was at least making a serious effort to discourage smuggling. In 1619, the king sent a new copper buyer, Erik Eriksson, with the authority to confiscate any copper sold illegally at the Stora Kopparberg, or in any other part of the country. He specifically instructed Eriksson to search the cities that were normal transit points for copper, including Västerås, Tälje, Enköping, Norrköping, Arboga, Köping, Gävle, and Hudiksvall. In addition, the king granted Eriksson the right to keep one third of all illegal copper that he recovered.[75] There is other evidence, as well, that the crown was now serious. Carl Bonde wrote to Chancellor Oxenstierna, in August 1618, informing him that he would be shipping the copper confiscated from an unfortunate merchant named Lasse Abrahamson to the crown.[76] In a later letter he confirmed to the chancellor that additional newly confiscated illegal copper was being delivered to the local cathedral.[77] (Copper was commonly used as roofing material for large buildings).

Avoiding crown's taxes was not the only reason the *bergsmän* continued to trade with local merchants. Over the centuries they had developed a pattern of interdependence. We saw earlier that in 1618 Chancellor Oxenstierna issued a proposal for new town privileges at Falun.[78] In this document he stated that the merchants should have the freedom to buy copper from the *bergsmän*, but only for "ready money." Again, this suggests that a crown monopoly was not yet in effect. It was also unworkable at the time because there was very little "ready money" available at Falun, or any other provincial city before the advent of the copper currency; payment in "ready money" was entirely impractical. Between the local merchants and the *bergsmän*, however, there existed a long-standing and mutually beneficial relationship based on credit. The *bergsmän* needed tools, and, as we have seen, vast quantities of wood and charcoal to make copper. They also needed food and other domestic supplies. Merchants, for their part, wanted copper to sell in Stockholm and the other port cities. The merchants would furnish the necessary monetary advances to the *bergsmän* who could then purchase raw materials, in exchange for future deliveries of copper, credit was the invisible connection that made production of copper possible. The crown-imposed monopoly interfered with these traditional connections. Before the monopoly, most of the business conducted between merchants and *bergsmän* took place in Köping at the Feast of St. Olaf on July 29, and in

---

75   Riksarkivet. SE/RA/1112.1/b # 146 and 147, Kungl. brev. August 5, 1619.
76   AOSB, II, 11, 27.
77   AOSB, II, 11, 37.
78   AOSB, I, 1, 287-89.

Västerås at the Feast of St. Martin on November 11, during market fairs. The merchants would buy copper for delivery the following summer, and they would provide credit in advance. The *bergsmän* would then use the credit to purchase the supplies they needed. The merchants involved were not just local players. Some of the more prominent Swedish merchants of the day were involved in this trade. Peter Kruse and Knut Kråha together lost the value of 100 skd of copper because they purchased copper in advance in return for credit; the *bergsmän* used the credit but never delivered the copper.[79] The local merchants, merchants from Stockholm, and as the century progressed, merchants from overseas, would meet the *bergsmän* at the fairs and negotiate for future deliveries.[80]

Let us assume that Peter Kruse and Knut Kråha had financed a reliable trading partner, and they were confident that they would receive 100 skd of copper in one year at RD 38 per skd in return for the credit that they had advanced to the *bergsmän*. As soon as they concluded the transaction and advanced the credit, they could contact their customers in Lübeck or Amsterdam and offer copper for delivery in one year at RD 48 per skd. If they sold at that level, they would be assured a profit of RD 10 per skd, less the freight, with no market risk. However, if they decided not to sell forward and the market fell, they might be receiving copper in one year at RD 38 per skd and sell at a loss. This appears to have been a fully developed futures market.

In summary, during the first decade of his reign, Gustav Adolf was increasingly active at the Stora Kopparberg directly and through his governor, Carl Bonde. He had his father to thank for the investments in infrastructure and technology. Thereafter, it was a question of negotiating with the *bergsmän* for more *pars* to increase production. His record was impressive. In the year 1600 the mine produced a total of 2,405 skd. In 1611, when the king assumed the throne, the mine's output was 5,665 skd; in 1620, the production was 8,637 skd.[81] This increase indicated that the crown was learning to cope with the myriad of complications that we explored in this chapter, including the intransigence of the *bergsmän*, the problems of transportation in a country with few roads, and the ever-growing need for copper ore, wood, and charcoal. Much of the credit for the impressive record must go to Carl Bonde, the king's able administrator in Darlarna. His correspondence with the king and the chancellor was filled with the details of running the mine and the difficulties he successfully overcame.

79   Hilderbrand, *Falu*, 32.
80   Hilderbrand, *Falu*, 32.
81   Lindroth, *Gruvbrytning*, 2, 389.

Despite impediments, the trend was clear. The crown was preparing to enforce a full monopoly. These reforms were fundamentally important and enabled the king to finance his political and military policies for the balance of his reign. Gaining control over this resource was one of the major achievements of the young monarch. In the face of this accomplishment, Heckscher asserted that the expansion of the mine was driven by high prices during the first two decades of the century. Further, he criticized the king for not devoting 100 percent of the mine's output toward paying the Älvsborg ransom.[82] Certainly, the king was fallible, but one cannot ignore the crown's single-minded approach to reforming the governance of the mine, working toward a full purchasing monopoly, and expanding production.

The development of the military fiscal state requires substantial revenue. Sweden, a poor country with a threadbare nobility and a limited burgher class had no possibility of developing into a military powerhouse without the contribution of the Stora Kopparberg. Her political and military rivals had the advantage of longer growing seasons, more developed urban elites, and generally more potential to extract revenue simply because there was more revenue to tax. Before plunder from the German wars began to arrive, Sweden struggled for its place on the Baltic northern coast. Denmark had the Sound Tolls, Poland had vast steppes growing grain for export to the West. Sweden had only the mine and she had to make the best of it.

The crown's success at the mine was a major step towards funding the state. The mine was by far the king's most important source of revenue during his lifetime. In 1629, the year before Sweden entered the Thirty Years War, the mine contributed SD 1.6 million (or RD 991,000) to the national budget.[83] The second largest contributor, the sale of grain gathered as tax revenue, came to only RD 441,000.

Bibliography

Archival Sources

Riksarkivet. SE/RA/1112.1/B # 65, Kungl. brev till Peder Nilsson och Erik Eriksson. February 14, 1630.
Riksarkivet. SE/RA/1112.1/B 1593 # 75, Kungl. brev. om handelen wed Kopparberget. October 28, 1593.

---

82 Heckscher, *historia*, 1, 443–44.
83 AOSB, I, 1, 455–57.

Printed Primary Sources

Dahlgren, Erik Wilhelm, ed. *Louis de Geers brev och affärshandlingar 1614–1652.* Stockholm: P.A. Norstedt & Söner, 1934.

Oxenstierna, Axel. *Rikskansleren Axel Oxenstierna skriften och brefvexling*, Series I, 16 vols. Stockholm: P.A. Norstedt & Söner, 1888–Present.

Oxenstierna, Axel. *Rikskansleren Axel Oxenstierna skriften och brefvexling*, Series II, 14 vols. Stockholm: P.A. Norstedt & Söner, 1888–Present.

Secondary Sources

Boëthius, Bertil. *Karl IX och driftsorganisationen vid Stora Kopparberget.* Stockholm: Hugo Löjdquist, 1957.

Glete, Jan. *War and the State in Early Modern Europe, Spain, the Dutch Republic, and Sweden as Fiscal-Military States, 1500–1660.* London: Routledge 2002.

Hilderbrand, Karl-Gustav. *Falu stads historia 1641–1687.* Falun: Falu nya boktryckeri, 1946.

Kristiansson, Sture. *Falu kopparvåg 1546–1873, historiska inblickar i en institution och livet kring denna.* Filipstad: Bronells Tryckeri AB 1993.

Kristiansson, Sture. "Kopparsmugglingen vid Stora Kopparberg 1580–1638," *Bergslagsarchiv: årsbok för historia och kulturhistoria I bergslagen*, 4. Karlstad: 1992, 52–64.

Lindroth, Sven. *Gruvbrytning och kopparhantering vid Stora Kopparberg intill 1800 talets början*, 2 vols. Uppsala: Almqvist & Wiksells, 1955.

Odén, Brigitta. *Kopparhandel och statsmonopol*, studier I svensk handelshistoria under senare 1500-talet. Stockholm: Almqvist & Wiksells, 1960.

Parker, Geoffrey. *Global Crisis, War, Climate Change, and Catastrophe in the Seventeenth Century.* New Haven: Yale University Press, 2014.

Roberts, Michael. *Gustavus Adolphus, a History of Sweden 1611–1632*, 2 vols. London: Longmans, Green and Co., 1957.

Rydberg, Sven. *The Great Copper Mountain, the Stora Kopparberg Story.* Hedemora: Gidlunds Publishers, 1988.

Rydberg, Sven. "Stora Kopparberget: The Great Copper Mountain." Copy of a paper presented at the Science Museum, London, October 12, 1988.

Söderberg, Tom. *Stora Kopparberg under medeltiden och Gustav Vasa.* Stockholm: Tryckt hos Victor Pettersons, 1932.

2.   The Älvsborg Ransom

Abstract

Chapter two is, on the surface, the story of the crown's frantic efforts to pay a one million *riksdaler* ransoms to the king of Denmark to return the Älvsborg fortress to the Swedish crown. It is also, however, the story of the young king's efforts to establish relationships with the prominent merchants of Amsterdam. He needed weapons and credit, and the center of northern European finance seemed a logical source. We learn in this chapter how the king arranged to purchase weapons and obtain credit thanks to his agents' involvement in political intrigue in Amsterdam and in The Hague. Chapter two, moreover, examines the Swedish administrative state at the local level. Sweden raised her domestic army by conscription, and this had implications beyond supplying troops to the state.

Keywords: Axel Oxenstierna, Göteborg, Kristina of Holstein, Johan Skytte, States General in The Hague

> "Always be the first to panic."
> Old trader saying

The period of the Älvsborg ransom began with the signing of the Peace of Knäred in 1613. The amount of the ransom was one million *riksdalers*, payable over four years beginning in January 1616.[1] Subsequent payments were due in January 1617, 1618, and 1619. The Danish king probably specified payment in *riksdalers* because he believed the Swedish crown would have difficulty accumulating enough of the imperial German currency. To put the amount in perspective, a regiment of mercenary foot soldiers cost the crown about RD 90,000 per year, and a company of German cavalry cost

---

1   As a reminder, currencies are abbreviated as follows: SD for Swedish *dalers*, RD for *riksdaler*, and DG for Dutch Guilders. The exchange rate was RD 1=DG 2.5 and RD 1= SD 1.624.

Stryker, L., *The Swedish Monarchy and the Copper Trade: The Copper Company, the Deposit System, and the Amsterdam Market, 1600–1640.* Amsterdam: Amsterdam University Press, 2024
DOI 10.5117/9789048560813_CH02

about RD 25,000 per year. While the amount of the ransom would be a strain on crown finances, it should not have been insurmountable. The new king began preparing to finance the ransom immediately after he signed the treaty. As explained earlier, it was critical for Gustav Adolf to regain the fortress from the Danes so he could defend the new port city of Göteborg.

The focus of this chapter is on the king's early attempt to harness revenue and use it to pay the ransom, while simultaneously funding armies in the field. A central theme, therefore, is the king's attempts to turn copper into cash. The other issues facing the crown, while serious, were subordinated to raising money. We will see how the king's financial challenges affected his approach to problems at home. For example, the commoners and the aristocracy were united in resisting new taxes, and the crown had not yet succeeded in subduing Sweden's "over-mighty subjects," especially the king's mother, his cousin, and his younger brother. By the terms of Karl IX's will, Gustav Adolf's younger brother, Karl Filip, was given a generous duchy consisting of Södermanland, Västergötland, and Närke (a medieval province located in south central Sweden and part of present day Svealand), while the Queen Mother, Kristina of Holstein, was named regent for Karl Filip. The will also confirmed that Duke Johan, Gustav Adolf's cousin, would remain in possession of Östergötland and Dalsland. The Queen Mother and Duke Johan ruled their respective duchies as independent entities within the larger kingdom. The Queen Mother's political independence, moreover, had profound implications for the king's copper policy. Integrating these disparate centers of power and revenue was a prerequisite for the development of a nation state.

These domestic issues help to explain the king's willingness to pay the ransom. A bellicose king like Gustav Adolf might have renewed the war with Denmark and retaken the fortress at Älvsborg by force. And indeed, if he had been surrounded by friendly powers, the king might have done just that. In addition to problems at home, however, there were threats from abroad. The king had dual rivals in the Baltic area, Kristian IV, the Protestant king of Denmark, and Sigismund III, the Catholic king of Poland. Just to remind the reader, the Polish nobility had elected Gustav Adolf's cousin, Sigismund Vasa, king of Poland in 1587. He was also the absentee king of Sweden between 1592 and 1604, although as a pious Catholic he was never popular in Lutheran Sweden. Gustav Adolf's father, Karl IX, deposed Sigismund in 1604. Sigismund, nevertheless, remained king of Poland, and continued to claim the throne of Sweden. Because Gustav Adolf's father had deposed Sigismund from the throne, Gustav Adolf also had a "legitimacy" problem. He was only the second sovereign from his branch of the Vasa family to rule Sweden; Sigismund's claim to be the legitimate ruler of Sweden caused much concern in Stockholm, and it helps to explain the series of wars the king fought in the eastern Baltic. After all, Karl IX was able to depose Sigismund, at least in part, because Sigismund was Catholic. In addition, Catholic Poland was a center for discontents, Swedish Jesuits, and intriguers of many stripes.[2]

In summary, one should not underestimate the role of religion in the king's calculations. The religious Reformation in the previous century was a key element in Gustav Adolf's branch of the Vasa family's claim to legitimate sovereignty in Lutheran Sweden. Whether valid on not, Gustav Adolf perceived the claims of his Counter-Reformation rival as an impediment to the religious stability of his kingdom. The Polish threat was also a convenient excuse for the king to mobilize resources.[3]

Although the king considered his wars in Russia and Livonia necessary to keep Poland's territorial ambitions in check, they were not helpful in his efforts to fund the Älvsborg ransom. Financing these wars was only possible by diverting copper from the ransom payments. Furthermore, by pursuing these wars, the king jeopardized Sweden's only access to North Sea ports, avoiding the Danish tolls. Perhaps as important, his closest allies in the Protestant camp, the States General considered him unreliable. They had a valid interest in helping the king to retain the Älvsborg fortress, but no interest in seeing their money diverted to wars in the eastern Baltic region. In summary, the king's policy of spending copper revenue on wars against Sigismund of Poland and relying on loans from the States General to make up the difference was a delicate balancing act. It was, of course, made necessary by the king's conviction that the king of Poland was a major threat to Sweden's security.

The details of the king's relationship with the Swedish nobility, the merchant class, and the States General are also critical to understanding the basic facts of crown finances. The young king struggled and made mistakes as he learned the harsh realities of funding wars in Russia and Poland while attempting to pay the ransom. It will soon be apparent that funding the Älvsborg ransom was the first step in the king's efforts to pay for what he considered to be his security obligations. After the ransom was paid, the king embarked on a series of wars in Poland and in northern Germany that required putting the Swedish economy on a permanent war footing. One may disagree with the king's warlike efforts; yet allow that in his own

2   Foster, *The Northern Wars*, 117.
3   Roberts, *Gustavus Adolphus*, 1, 143.

mind the king was defending Sweden's interests, especially against Poland. In other words, one can be critical of the king's military adventures, but sympathize with his reasons for them and with his struggle to pay for them.

The king had no possibility to finance the ransom or the wars in Russia and Poland with revenue from Sweden alone. At this early stage in his attempt to pay the ransom he had already nearly exhausted local sources. Sweden was a backward economy and most of the king's domestic revenue was in kind. He could not, for example, pay armies or ransoms with timber or charcoal. Among the merchant classes there was not sufficient liquid capital in Sweden for a true banking system to develop. Therefore, the king had to look towards the money-centers of continental Europe. As the fastest growing Protestant merchant economy, the United Provinces was the king's natural choice to seek funding. In the meantime, however, we must consider the details of the king's struggle to fund the ransom (while fighting in Russia and Poland) to grasp the importance for him to establish a monopoly on purchasing copper at the mine, and to complete his struggle to gain control of revenue from copper.

Gustav Adolf also anticipated problems with the Danish king, Kristian IV. He was duplicitous. In 1617, he sent envoys to The Hague advocating a Protestant alliance that would include Sweden. Kristian was, however, simultaneously negotiating with Catholic Spain and with the imperial court in Vienna. Finally, Kristian IV had an "understanding" with the Catholic king of Poland that worried Sweden.[4]

The king understood that real peace with his cousin, Sigismund III, was not possible. Sigismund was not only allied with the Holy Roman Empire, but still claimed the Swedish throne. On the other hand, the king of Denmark was a Protestant, although support for co-religionists was hardly his first concern. In fact, the issues that separated Sweden from Denmark were mainly commercial. The king of Denmark wanted to deprive Sweden of Göteborg, so that all trade between Sweden and the Netherlands would pass though the Danish Sound and be subject to tolls (which constituted about 60 percent of Danish crown revenues). In the meantime, Oxenstierna counseled peace with Denmark and Gustav Adolf wisely took his advice and attempted to appease Kristian IV.[5] In essence, the king believed that he must accept a wary alliance with Kristian of Denmark, because he knew there was no possibility of a long-term peace with Poland. He, therefore, chose to negotiate with Kristian rather than to march against him.

4   Roberts, *Gustavus Adolphus*, 1, 147-51.
5   Roberts, *Gustavus Adolphus*, 1, 169-71.

These threats from abroad help to explain the king's continuing efforts to consolidate power at home while he pursued ambitious foreign military goals. Again, the king's copper policy was a fitting metaphor for his gradual progress towards a centralized government. Above all, we will follow his use of copper, his main financial resource in pursuit of domestic harmony and his foreign political and military goals. The previous chapter described the king's gradual success in consolidating power at the Stora Kopparberg. The flow of copper, however, could not pay for all the king's obligations, and he was forced to seek financial support from his Protestant ally, the fledgling United Provinces of the Northern Netherlands. Because Sweden had limited credit facilities at home, the king turned to Amsterdam and The Hague for financial assistance. We will examine the king's success in obtaining financial support from the States General, the ruling diet of the United Provinces, and consider how well he managed this relationship.

First, however, we will examine the crown's progress in established a purchasing monopoly during the time the Älvsborg ransom. The traditional view is that the crown established a monopoly at the Stora Kopparberg after signing the Peace of Knäred in 1613, and allegedly the terms of the monopoly forced the *bergsmän* to sell all the copper they produced at a low price to the crown. In his classic work on Swedish economic history, E.H. Heckscher explains that the crown was "lord over copper" and could compel the *bergsmän* to sell all their copper to the king's representatives at the mine. The crown would then sell the copper to prominent merchants who exported it to Germany and the Netherlands.[6]

Heckscher was critical of the crown's action, however, because he thought the crown mismanaged the revenue. He wrote that from 1613 to 1619, the Kopparberg produced more than enough copper to pay off the ransom. According to Heckscher the king used much of the revenue elsewhere, especially to pay his troops in the field. This forced the king to borrow from the States General of the United Provinces to make up the difference.

This was possible only because of two major developments. First, Heckscher noted that the crown succeeded in increasing production at the mine from the years 1613 to 1619. According to Heckscher, the second achievement which made possible an increase in revenue from copper, was the crown's ability to enter the international market. Before the Älvsborg ransom agreement, Sweden sold most of its copper in northern Germany. Then, in 1614, the crown began sending copper to Amsterdam as collateral for loans from the States General. This enlarged the distribution network

6   Heckscher, *historia*, 1, 272–73 and 1, 443–44.

and increased the quantity that Sweden could export without causing local disruptions at the destination. Through Amsterdam and the cities of northern Germany, Sweden could reach "all of middle Europe, including Hamburg, Lübeck, Frankfurt-am-Main, and Nuremberg."[7]

Heckscher's views on the copper monopoly were, perhaps, based on his larger overview. If one looks closely, Gustav Adolf did consolidate his position at the Stora Kopparberg, but to call him the "lord over copper" implies complete control, which he never achieved. The relationship between the crown and the *bergsmän* was certainly one-sided in favor of the crown, but the crown had to negotiate in good faith with the *bergsmän*. We will also see that the purchasing monopoly during the Älvsborg ransom period was not straight forward. In fact, there is no evidence in the sources that the king was able to enforce even a partial monopoly until the founding of the Copper Company in 1619.

On this subject, Michael Roberts writes: "The payment of the Älvsborg ransom was effected mainly by the sale of copper ... the king ... exercised a right of pre-emption over all the copper produced by the mine; and the effect was that the whole copper trade passed for a time into the hands of the crown."[8] To prove this assertion Roberts cites G. Wittrock's *Svenska handelskompaniet och kopparhandeln*. If we turn to that work, however, the picture is quite murky compared to Roberts's crisp description. Wittrock quotes a historian from the early nineteenth century, S. Winquist, who wrote that beginning in 1615 all copper sold by the *bergsmän* must be sold to the king.[9] On inspection, however, Winquist's article does not refer to the years of the Älvsborg ransom installments at all; it refers to the period of the Copper Company in the next decade when the monopoly was well established. In a separate section, Wittrock described the agreement made between the crown and the *bergsmän* in 1613, which stipulated that the *bergsmän* had agreed to sell only a portion of their output to the crown.[10] They already owed the crown the *avrad* and the *konstavgift*, plus in the case of the *nya bergsmän*, the tithe. In the new agreement, the *bergsmän* accepted selling the king two additional *skeppund*, (here after skd) per quarter, one at a price of SD 44 per skd and the other for 30 barrels of grain. There was no formal agreement superseding the extra two *skeppund* per

7   Heckscher, *historia*,1.2, 275.
8   Roberts, *Gustavus Adolphus*, 2, 90.
9   Wingquist, *Om det gamla Koppar-Compagneit*, 8.
10   Riksarkivet, RA/SE/RA 1112.1/B120 (1613) Contract meds kopparbergz. Datum kopparberg, November 10, 1613.

quarter. The crown was still receiving only a small portion of the *bergsmän*'s annual production.

Part of Wittrock's argument for an early monopoly was the crown's appointment of the previously mentioned representatives, Peder Pedersson and Peder Jonsson, with full authority to purchase copper on the crown's behalf. Their appointment was announced in a letter on February 24, 1615.[11] The letter, however, does not mention a crown monopoly, or even royal supervision of purchases. One can conclude that by 1615, the crown was present at the mine and was buying copper, but little more.

The limited nature of crown purchases before 1617 is supported by the chancellor's proposed Älvsborg ransom budget for the years 1615 and 1616.[12] In this budget the chancellor describes the king's efforts to raise money for the first installment due in January 1616. He expected crown copper and *avrad* in the amount of only 1,000 skd copper, and he hoped to buy another 2,000 skd from the *bergsmän*. During 1614 and 1615 the mine produced a total of 13,798 skd mine weight of copper, but the king was expecting to have control over only 3,000 skd. This was hardly a monopoly. Two years later, in October 1617, Johan Skytte arrived in Lübeck to supervise the sale of 3,416 skd of the king's copper.[13] While Skytte was in London, over Christmas, another 2,000 skd arrived in Amsterdam. This meant that the crown shipped a total of 5,416 skd of copper in 1617. That year the mine produced a total of 5,684 skd mine weight,[14] meaning that the crown had gained control of virtually the entire year's officially recorded output. This was still nothing like the strict monopoly that Heckscher describes as beginning in 1613. We do have evidence, as mentioned earlier, that as early as March 1615 the king instructed his bailiff at the mine, Mats Jöransson, to purchase all the copper that came to the scales and the Älvsborg commissioners would arrange payment. He did not mention a purchase price.[15] It is now clear, however, that the king's instructions were only partially heeded as late as 1617. It is probable that the crown officials found that implementing a full monopoly before 1619 was just not possible.

Before the king's monopoly, the movement of copper from the mine to the Baltic ports was costly and inefficient. A *bergsmän* would buy charcoal

---

11   Riksarkivet. SA/RA/1112.1/B/125 (1615) # 134, Fullmakt för Peder Pederson och Peder Jonsson. February 1615.

12   Axel Oxenstiernas, *Skrifter och brevväxling* (AOSB) I, 1, 442.

13   ASOB, II, 10, 192–94.

14   Lindroth, *Gruvbrytning*, 2, 389.

15   Riksarkivet, SE/RA/1112.1/B/125 (1615) Letter from Gustav Adolf to Mats Jöransson. March 3, 1615.

and pay for it with copper. The charcoal seller would use the copper to buy vegetables. Finally, a merchant would purchase the copper from the vegetable seller and move it to a port for export. Of course, some of the copper went directly from the *bergsmän* to the merchant. At each step, however, the middlemen made a profit. It appears that only after 1619 was the king able to monopolize the sale of copper by purchasing nearly all the copper officially produced. His decision to impose a monopoly on purchases and export to Amsterdam or Lübeck removed at least one layer of middlemen. In other words, he made the distribution system faster by centralizing control, and he reaped the profits derived from the new efficiencies. The king had finally gained control over the purchasing of copper.

The new monopoly provided another advantage for the crown; it restricted competition at the mine and gave the king control over his costs.[16] If other merchants had been permitted to compete, the king would not have been able to keep his purchasing costs relatively low and stable. This advantage will be more evident in the next chapter when we look at the Copper Company. It could be argued that this system was unfair to the *bergsmän* because it deprived them of the opportunity to bargain for a higher price; that was certainly true. Once again, however, I argue that the purpose of the crown monopoly was not to create a balanced commercial market at the mine. The purpose of the monopoly was to enable the crown to exploit copper as a resource to advance the crown's political and military ambitions. It is worth emphasizing that if the *bergsmän* could not earn a profit on the fixed price the crown was paying, copper production at the Stora Kopparberg would have ended abruptly.

Besides relying on copper to finance the ransom, Gustav Adolf attempted to exact contributions from the nobility, including his close relatives, toward the ransom. His first move was to appoint a four-man commission, called the Älvsborg Commission, which included Johan Skytte, a member of the *Kammar-Råd* (privy council). He was also the king's former tutor. And it also included Brod Andersson, a merchant and influential member of the king's inner circle. It was the commission's task to manage the special revenue streams that were set up to fund the ransom payments, including revenue from the sale of copper.[17] Gustav Adolf's next move was to summon the *Riksdag*, an assembly of representatives from the four estates, including the nobility, the clergy, the burghers, and the peasants, to ask for a special universal tax. Faced with a desperate situation, the *Riksdag* agreed to the tax;

---

16   The reader will recall that the crown bought from the mine at a fixed price of SD 50 (RD 30.7).
17   Roberts, *Gustavus Adolphus*, 1, 123-29.

only the Queen Mother was exempted, probably because of her privileged position within the monarchy. The king and Duke Johan both promised to contribute 32 percent of their incomes (which neither did in the end), and the nobility agreed to forego their privilege of exemption from taxes.[18]

The following year the crown clarified the obligations to be imposed on the merchant class. In a letter to the *Kammar-Råd*, Oxenstierana mentioned that the crown would "allow" the merchant class to bear the lion's share of the first installment due at the beginning of 1616. Each merchant was to be taxed based on their personal wealth. Anticipating obvious questions, he explained that the crown's definition of wealth included all goods and possessions, even jewels and silverware. He wrote that the merchant class was known to be both prosperous and loyal to the crown, so their cooperation was expected.[19] Probably because the Queen Mother, despite her royal position, was a prominent and successful businessperson, the chancellor mentioned that she had agreed to pledge between RD 10,000 and RD 12,000 for the first payment. There is no record of actual payment, however.

In the case of the Queen Mother, the king faced a dual challenge; she threatened his copper policy and his domestic stability because she was notably independent and uncooperative. She was also an active and successful copper trader with excellent connections at the mine and abroad; she did not intend to relinquish her lucrative trade to make way for her son's new copper policy. In fact, she fought him at every turn.

Kristina of Holstein was a remarkable member of the royal inner circle. She was strong willed and influential, and a fierce defender of what she considered her rights and privileges; she was especially concerned that her younger son, Karl Filip, should receive an appropriate share of land and income. Her behavior, however, went beyond maternal protection. She challenged the king constantly and notwithstanding pledges to the contrary, she avoided taxes and contributions to the crown.

Despite the political friction between the Queen Mother and Gustav Adolf, the chancellor was on favorable terms with her, and the two corresponded frequently. Unfortunately, only the letters from the chancellor have survived. Oxenstierna made a point of keeping the Queen Mother abreast of developments overseas, and occasionally informed her of commercial possibilities. The chancellor continued to write to the Queen Mother until her death in 1625. And he obviously realized her importance to the crown. The Queen Mother had extensive lands of her own, and she acted as regent to her

18   Roberts, *Gustavus Adolphus*, 1, 125.
19   Roberts, *Gustavus Adolphus*, 1, 125.

youngest son, Karl Filip, whose duchy included large holdings, as mentioned earlier. In these lands he had sovereign powers including minting coins and appointing judges.[20]

The Queen Mother fought against any issue that might affect the prosperity of her regency. When Karl Filip died in 1622, the Queen Mother quietly took over his dukedom.[21] Under these conditions, the king had to address the problem of the Queen Mother's kingdom within a kingdom, and her attempts to sabotage the royal copper policy.

When the chancellor had problems to pursue with the Queen Mother, he often consulted her secretary, Dr. Nils Chesnecopherus. In a letter of March 24, 1614, to the secretary, the chancellor mentioned that the ice had receded at the Stockholm harbor, and it was now possible for the Queen Mother to make a shipment of grain that she owed in taxes to the army.[22] Since the army on the Russian border was, at this time, in great need of grain, and since the shipment was months late, the chancellor asked that she make the shipment promptly. In the same letter, however, he wrote that the *Riks-Råd*[23] was requesting a full investigation of grain trades carried out between the Queen Mother, her stepdaughter, fröken Catherine, and Catherine's fiancé, John Casimir of Pfalz-Zweibrücken-Kleeburg. Catherine had been with John Casimir in Germany the previous autumn when the trades took place. The obvious conclusion was that the Queen Mother had diverted the grain that she owed to the crown and sold it for a profit through her stepdaughter in Germany, while the Swedish army was starving on the Russian border.[24] Yet, this was a mere peccadillo compared to the next scandal.

On April 22, 1616 the king wrote to the chancellor from Finland in obvious surprise over a letter from the *Räntekammar*.[25] It informed him about a transaction involving the Queen Mother: "I just received a letter from the *Räntekammar* describing a copper trade made by my dear sweet Fru Mother, the Queen Mother. The proceeds will, no doubt, be contributed to the payment of the second installment of the Älvsborg ransom."[26] We understand from the chancellor's reply, however, that this was a more complicated story,

20 Roberts, *Gustavus Adolphus*, 1, 125.

21 Roberts, *Gustavus Adolphus*, 1, 131.

22 AOSB, I, 2, 159. AOSB, I, 2, 264

23 The *Riks-Råd* was a traditional medieval council consisting of noblemen and high clergy.

24 AOSB, I, 2, 159. ASOB, I, 2 186-87. ASOB, I, 2. 197. AOSB, I, 2, 264.

25 The *Räntekammar* was part of the Treasury. It collected taxes and oversaw the collection of money and copper for the Älvsborg ransom. Bro Andersson, mentioned above, was the head of this department.

26 AOSB, II, 1, 90.

and that none of the proceeds would go toward the ransom. According to the chancellor, the Queen Mother had quietly purchased 3,000 skd of copper at the Stora Kopparberg, without the knowledge of officials in Stockholm. She was now planning to sell it in Europe. That would be possible because Karl Filip's duchy included the two northern ports of Gävle and Hudiksvall from which she could export directly to northern Germany. Further, her purchase represented 45 percent of the copper produced that year.[27] One wonders how she could have accumulated such a large percentage of the mine's output without any local officials taking notice. The king's copper buyers, Peder Pedersson and Peder Jonsson, were present in Falun representing the crown's interests and buying copper for the ransom. It is improbable that the Queen Mother's agents could have purchased 45 percent of the annual output without Pedersson and Jonsson noticing the competition, so their silence was suspicious.[28] Her action, moreover, was a serious transgression because it jeopardized the payment of the ransom. There is no suggestion in the correspondence that the Queen Mother was politically motivated, although she was on good terms with Denmark's King Kristian IV; he was one of her traditional customers for copper.[29]

The king found himself in a difficult situation. If he wanted to control the mine's output, he would have to confront the Queen Mother. The chancellor advised the king to insist that the Queen Mother abandon the purchase and leave the copper for the ransom. We do not have the details of the confrontation, but in the end, the king forced the Queen Mother to turn over the copper to the crown. The crown exported the 3,000 plus *skeppund* to Lübeck in 1617 to be sold by two of the crown's agents on the continent, Lorentz Kruse and Lars Bengtsson. The chancellor included the proceeds in his budget for the January 1618 payment.[30] The king may have gained the day, but the Queen Mother was not so easily excluded from involvement in copper, regardless of the consequences to the crown's domestic and foreign policy.

By September the king and the Queen Mother were reconciled, and Gustav Adolf described his relationship with his mother as "comfortable" to the chancellor.[31] What is most noteworthy in this correspondence, however, is a passing remark from the king about another case of pilfered copper. Apparently, the Queen Mother had a shipment of copper at her port of

27 Lindroth, *Gruvbrytning*, 2, 388. Full production for the year 1615 was 6,071 skd.
28 AOSB, I, 2, 264-65.
29 AOSB, I, 2, 264-65.
30 AOSB, I, 1, 446.
31 ASOB, II, 1, 106.

Gävle ready for export, and it had been stolen. The king wanted to appoint a commission headed by Carl Bonde to investigate; he was suspicious, and he hoped that the burghers of Gävle could be encouraged to tell what they knew about the affair. The incident also proved that the Queen Mother could continue to buy copper after the tumult of the previous April. Now, however, the king and the chancellor knew for certain that the Queen Mother had copper hidden in Gävle.[32]

In October of 1617 Johan Skytte was in Lübeck on a crucial mission for the crown. He was to oversee the sale of 3,416 skd of "Älvsborg ransom" copper that had just arrived from Sweden. This was to be sold "on commission" by Lars Bengtsson and Lorentz Kruse, the crown's continental agents mentioned earlier. The parcel was the copper recovered from the Queen Mother's secret purchases the year before. This was a large quantity to ship at one time to a city like Lübeck. In fact, the amount would have been a significant percentage of European consumption for the year; the delivery could cause a sharp decline in the local prices. Bengtsson and Kruse were respected merchants with the interests of the crown in mind. They would have understood the ramifications and would have been careful to make offers in small lots. As they were to be compensated with a small percentage of the final sales price, they were motivated to prevent any price decline. Just when they were ready to begin selling, however, they discovered a nasty surprise.[33]

Skytte previously had reported that the price of copper in Lübeck was well above 114 *marks* Lübeck currency per *skeppund*. But then prices began to fall and soon copper was selling at below 110 *marks* per *skeppund*. Skytte also learned that hundreds of tons of copper were arriving from both Gävle and Hudiksvall but nobody seemed to know who was behind the shipments. Skytte informed the chancellor that this was not the time to sell the "Älvsborg copper."[34]

Johan Skytte may or may not have known who was responsible for shipping quantities of copper from the ports of Gävle and Hudiksvall. He did know, however, that the mysterious seller drove down the price in Lübeck at precisely the time the crown was attempting to sell. Of course, the king and the chancellor certainly knew who was quietly selling the copper because they had already formed a commission to investigate the theft of the Queen Mother's copper from a warehouse in Gävle. The shipper from Gävle was certainly the Queen Mother herself; the two ports involved were part of the duchy she ruled as regent for her younger son. One could speculate that the

32   AOSB, I, 1, 446.
33   AOSB, II, 10, 193–96.
34   AOSB, II, 10, 193–96.

Queen Mother had learned that a large shipment of copper was going to Lübeck from her merchant contacts or her contacts at the mine. She acted on this information and sold a series of small lots ahead of the king's large shipment, which she realized would depress the local market in Lübeck.

What could the king do now to contain his mother? It was apparent that the Queen Mother's actions were not just designed to protect her interests, but also to circumvent the king's copper policy. The king suggested to the chancellor that drastic action was now necessary. Apparently, the Queen Mother had an extensive collection of silver with "costly gilt work" that the king could melt down to strike *riksdalers*. He mused, "I trust that I can endure the injury that I will suffer to obtain it."[35] The same applied to the silver at the Queen Mother's mint, some of which was already fully minted *riksdalers*. The king proposed to negotiate with his mother to obtain the silver. If, however, he was not successful, he wanted the chancellor's opinion on whether he had a legal right to seize the silver by force. Once it was confiscated, he could exchange the silver for *riksdalers* or mint new *riksdalers*.[36] The thought that the king would confiscate silver and plate from the Queen Mother must have horrified the chancellor, because he replied the same day cautioning against any precipitous action that would cause "perplexity."[37]

Gustav Adolf also thought better of the plan and tried another tactic. He bribed her. Realizing that he could not prevent her from working against his copper policy, he reached an agreement with his mother that satisfied both parties. The Queen Mother agreed to accept limited copper purchases in return for generous terms on a new loan. The Queen Mother agreed to lend the crown RD 100,000 to be used toward the third ransom payment. The crown agreed to pay her 8 percent interest per year. The Queen Mother was to deliver the money in March 1617. In addition, the crown agreed to give her an option to buy 200 skd copper per year at the fixed price of SD 70 per skd.[38] This was a coup for the Queen Mother. If the price of copper went up by say SD 10 per skd, she would exercise the option to buy at SD 70 and immediately sell at SD 80. If the price dropped below SD 70, she would simply not buy.[39] She had the potential for profit with no risk.

35 ASOB, II, 1, 108.
36 AOSB, II, 1, 108.
37 AOSB, I, 2, 305-06.
38 AOSB, II, 1, 98-99.
39 It is noteworthy that the king wrote on October 17 to the chancellor with additional details about the loan. At that time the copper option had been increased to 221 skd. The Queen Mother never stopped negotiating. See AOSB, II, 1, 98.

This incident also speaks to a fundamental reality for King Gustav Adolf and Chancellor Axel Oxenstierna. Despite all the difficulty created by the independent and cantankerous Queen Mother, she was an extremely wealthy women and the crown needed to remain on reasonably good terms with her. Stockholm was not Antwerp or Amsterdam. There was no great accumulation of wealth that could be tapped to finance wars and ransoms. The Queen Mother was an important resource to the kingdom, and the king's recognition of this fact forced him to ignore her challenges to his authority. The above agreement with the Queen Mother did not solve the issue of her maintaining a semi-independent realm within Sweden or her failure to pay taxes. It did limit, however, her participation in the copper market. This was essential before the king could proceed to monopolize purchases at the mine.

Regretfully, not even the wealthy Queen Mother could muster resources sufficient to fund the Älvsborg ransom, and in 1614 the king sent Lorenz Kruse to the Netherlands via Lübeck to begin discussions with the crown's Protestant ally about loans to help finance the ransom with copper as collateral. This would be the model for future loans from this source. In addition to the Älvsborg ransom the king had inherited an interminable war in Russia that he chose to pursue until the 1617 Peace of Stolbova. After years of military expenses in Russia, the Swedish crown gained the province of Ingria, on the border of Estonia, and its population of 15,000. Without doubt, the monarchy was now financially overextended.[40]

Meanwhile, Gustav Adolf was with his army in Helsinki, near the border with Russia. He joined General Jakob de la Gardie, who for two years had been fighting a war of succession in Russia. This was the "Time of Troubles" in Russia, following the deaths of Tsar Boris Godunov and his Polish backed successor, the False Dmitri. The immediate goal was to take advantage of the chaos in Russia, to install Gustav Adolf's younger brother, Karl Filip, on the Russian throne. The larger picture, however, related to the king's valid concern to prevent his cousin and bitter enemy, Sigismund of Poland, from establishing a protectorate in Russia, and threatening Swedish Estonia. The king wrote to the chancellor that he had already spent SD 15,000 (RD 24,360) on maintaining the army. This, of course, was revenue that had been designated for the first installment of the Älvsborg ransom. He complained that "every man has his hands out" to receive payment; also, he would need additional grain, so he expected to spend another SD 5,000 (RD 8,120). He referred to 500 skd of copper that had been designated for shipment to

40   Roberts, *Gustavus Adolphus*, 1, 87–92.

Holland as collateral for a loan.[41] The king now wanted to sell it for cash to support the war effort in Russia. The king asked the chancellor if any members of the *Riks-Råd* (the old medieval council) had copper in their possession, or whether any of the port cities had inventory. He directed the chancellor to search and sell anything that he found then send the cash to Helsinki. This letter is unique because it portrays an uncharacteristic anxiety on the part of the king. He was concerned about the crown's cash flow, the looming payment for the ransom, and Lorenz Kruse's mission to the Netherlands; he was more dependent than ever on Kruse getting the advance he promised. The king concludes by saying he must find money to feed and pay his soldiers or they would surely become "discontent." We can assume that discontented soldiers were more of a threat than discontented miners or merchants.[42]

It's clear that the king was living beyond his means. By selling copper that was designated to pay the ransom, he was also putting the future of the Älvsborg fortress in jeopardy, meaning that if he defaulted on the ransom, Göteborg would be undefended against Danish aggression. He would certainly have explained the war in Russia in terms of the continuing threat from Poland. The same day the king wrote the above letter to the chancellor, he posted another, but this letter went to the chancellor plus Johan Skytte, and Bro Anderson. All three were members of the *Kammar-Råd* and were also on the Älvsborg ransom commission. This was a more measured letter in which he told his advisers about the course of the military action in Russia and complained about the quality of troops and officers.[43] He also mentioned that he was pleased the purchase of copper for the Älvsborg ransom was going well for the *Räntekammar*. Obviously concerned, he urged them to remain diligent in buying as much copper as possible, and repeated, for the second time on the same day, the importance of Lorenz Kruse's success in the United Provinces: "Lorenz Kruse's attempt to get an advance [against copper] must be pursued with the utmost diligence and placed first in priority."[44]

Later in July, the king was still fretting over lack of concrete news from Lorenz Kruse. He instructed the chancellor to inform Kruse that in addition to the RD 30,000 that he wanted to borrow from the States General against future copper deliveries, he wanted Kruse to ask for another unsecured loan

---

41   AOSB, II, 1, 43–44.
42   AOSB, II, 1, 43–44.
43   AOSB, II, 1, 44–45.
44   AOSB, II, 1, 46.

of RD 20,000. The *Kammer-Råd* was to apply the RD 30,000 to the ransom and use the RD 20,000 to pay the *bergsmän* at the Kopparberg.[45] This request neatly demonstrates the precarious position of the crown. The king was not yet sure that he would get a secured loan from the States General, and RD 30,000 was an unrealistic amount to expect for 500 skd collateral. It was pure fantasy for the king to request another RD 20,000 without collateral. In the meantime, the *bergsmän* would go unpaid, which meant less production.

When the long sought-after money from Holland finally arrived, it was a disappointment all around. The king was still on the Russian border and in great need. The chancellor wrote the king an apologetic letter; the *Kammar-Råd* sent money as requested, but it was not enough to satisfy the king's requirement: "We have sent, as God will witness, all that was possible, and more will follow as Your Majesty has ordered."[46] The chancellor related the unfortunate news from the Netherlands; the States General had sent only a fraction of what was needed for the ransom. The chancellor did not even inform the king of the amount, only that it was insufficient. However, he would send the king SD 25,173 (RD 40,881) by sea with an exceptionally trustworthy messenger, Nijls Jörenson. From the letter's tone, it is clear the chancellor expected the king to be disappointed and angry.[47]

Finally, there was another "military adventure" from the period that cannot be omitted because it had the unpleasant consequence of tarnishing the king's image in Europe, and it underlined the king's obsession with striking a blow against his cousin the king of Poland. We should recall that Johan Skytte was in Lübeck in October 1617 to oversee the sale of copper that the crown had recovered from the Queen Mother. While there, he carefully gathered intelligence and dutifully passed it on to the king and the chancellor. The most important bit of news came from an unlikely source. Skytte related that while preparing legal documents for the acceptance of the king's bill of exchange, he used the services of a local attorney named Dr. Johannes Witte. Apparently, Witte was well informed because he warned Skytte that the Swedish crown and the Duke of Kurland should not trust a well-known adventurer, named Wolmar von Farensbach, and urged Skytte to write to the king with this information.[48] The Duchy of Kurland was independent and located north of Poland on the Baltic. The incumbent duke, William, had arrested and executed two of the King of Poland's envoys. In

45   AOSB, II, 1, 68.
46   AOSB, I, 2, 218.
47   AOSB, I, 2, 218.
48   AOSB, II, 10, 199.

retaliation, the Polish king sent troops to occupy Kurland and William fled to Sweden to seek the protection of the Swedish crown. In his letter to the king Skytte mentioned that the Poles entrusted the fortress at Dünamünde to Wolmar von Farensbach. Michael Roberts provides additional details about Farensbach: "He was a braggart and a brute, he had an immense conceit of himself, he was utterly devoid of scruples or honor ..."[49]

In 1615 Wolmar von Farensbach contacted Gustav Adolf secretly and offered to turn traitor. If the Swedes wanted to invade Polish Livonia and restore William as duke of Kurland, he would surrender the Dünamünde fortress thus allowing Gustav Adolf's forces to sail up the Düna River and land. Naturally Farensbach expected to be rewarded with land and favors. Gustav Adolf resisted because he was, at that moment, negotiating an extension of the current truce with the King of Poland, and he did not trust the adventurer Farensbach. However, a couple of years later the landscape had changed. Duke William was still in Stockholm asking to be reinstated in his duchy, the peace talks with the King of Poland had collapsed, and Sigismund was massing troops. Gustav Adolf could resist no longer.

In June of 1617, a small contingent of the Swedish army landed near the fortress and Farensbach immediately turned it over to the Swedish commander, Nils Stiernsköld. The fortress of Dünamünde was once again a possession of the Duke of Kurland. Fortunately for the invaders, the Polish army was elsewhere, and the Swedes, together with Farenbach's soldiers, marched to the Livonian port of Pernau and captured the town. Meanwhile, it occurred to Farensbach that he and his soldiers were now more valuable than ever to his old employer, the King of Poland. He promptly changed sides, once again bringing his troops with him. Because of Farenbach's second defection, the Swedish troops were now outnumbered and withdrew, except for a small garrison that remained in possession of Pernau. This was an expensive venture that coincided with the crown's attempt to assemble the third payment of the ransom due in January 1618.

To make matters worse, Johan Skytte was traveling to The Hague to negotiate a new loan for the third ransom payment. Unfortunately for his efforts, the news of the debacle in Livonia preceded him, and the delegates to the States General were upset.[50] The diet publicly repudiated the invasion because it had signed a mutual assistance treaty with Sweden and Lübeck in 1614, and the Estates General did not want to be drawn into a war far away in the Baltic. Skytte wrote to the king: "Let me be bold, Your Royal

49   Roberts, *Gustavus Adolphus*, 1, 160.
50   AOSB, II, 10, 217.

Majesty, the timing was poor and now the States say you tried your luck with a hasty invasion while they have a mutual obligations contract with you."[51] He further explained that this action would certainly hurt his efforts to get immediate assistance with the ransom, and it would make future military alliances more difficult.

During this same trip, Skytte met members of the House of Orange, including Count William of Nassau and Maurice, Prince of Orange. Both were leaders of the ongoing rebellion against the Spanish Habsburgs. The Prince of Orange asked Skytte about the Farensbach affair. It was rumored in The Hague that Farensbach's original intention was to lure Gustav Adolf to the fortress of Dünamünde on the border between Kurland and Livonia and there take him prisoner.[52]

Although brief, this last military adventure may have done more damage to the crown's efforts to obtain support from the States General than the war in Russia. The fact that a known rascal had outmaneuvered the king of Sweden, and hurt his military reputation, caused the States General delegates and their leaders to question his judgment. Why would they support a monarch willing to spend money on an ill-considered scheme when the futures of the Älvsborg fortress and the trading city of Göteborg were in danger? One should not forget that Göteborg was important to the Dutch as well. They wanted access to a Swedish port without the necessity of paying the Danish tolls as much as Sweden wanted access to Amsterdam without Danish interference. Not surprisingly, Skytte was not successful in his bid for a new loan to help Sweden make the third payment.[53]

Although the king considered his wars in Russia and Livonia necessary to keep Poland's territorial ambitions in check, they were not helpful in his efforts to fund the Älvsborg ransom. Financing these wars was only possible by diverting copper from the ransom payments. Perhaps as important, his closest allies in the Protestant camp, the United Provinces, now considered him unreliable. They had a valid interest in helping the king to retain the Älvsborg fortress, but no interest in seeing their money diverted to wars in the eastern Baltic region. In summary, the king's policy of spending copper revenue on wars against Sigismund of Poland and relying on loans from the States General to make up the difference when the payments on the ransom came due, was a delicate balancing act. It was, of course, made necessary by the king's conviction that the king of Poland was a major threat to Sweden's security.

---

51   AOSB, II, 10, 217.
52   AOSB, II, 10, 209.
53   AOSB II, 10, 219–20.

Unfortunately for the king, the States General would not fully cooperate. It demanded that he remain current with interest payments, and it balked at making new loans while the crown was irresponsible about shipping copper to repay old loans. Most importantly, help from the States General became highly politicized; one faction in The Hague supported such loans, and another condemned them. In the long run the king learned that he could not depend on the States General. The details of the king's experience with his nobility, his merchants, and the United Provinces informed him that he needed a stronger, more dependable source of revenue.[54] He needed an efficient method of exploiting his main resource, copper. Eventually, he began moving toward a new solution, which we will explore in the next chapter.

The central financial problem facing the king during the ransom period, was turning commodities, such as iron and copper, into a fungible currency that would be accepted by both his armies abroad and by the Danish king in payment for the ransom. The king of Sweden had three choices. He could borrow from the States General in The Hague and send copper to pay interest and principal. This was difficult and time consuming. Another alternative was to sell copper through merchants and use the resulting cash to pay either the ransom or the armies. This was also time consuming as the crown had to ship the copper to Lübeck or Amsterdam, sell it, and then wait for bills of exchange; all of which took months. Finally, the crown could simply pay creditors by sending copper as payment. We will now examine the king's various strategies for turning copper into cash.

Before beginning, however, it is important to examine the king's agreement at the mine, so we can understand the dependability of his supply lines. While we saw several indications from the king that the *Räntekammar* should continue to purchase as much copper as possible from the *bergsmän*, he had not yet mentioned a monopoly. Without evidence to the contrary, one must assume the crown was still operating under the official agreement made in late 1613, allowing the crown to purchase two extra *skeppund* of copper from each quarter, one at SD 44 per skd (RD 27) and the other for thirty barrels of grain. This was in addition to the normal *avrad* and *konstavgift*,[55] and it meant that the crown had not completed its work at the mine to exploit the resource to full advantage.

To turn copper into cash for ransom payments, the king would send copper to representatives, like Lorentz Kruse, who were stationed on the continent.

---

54   ASOB, II, 10, 219–20.
55   Riksarkivet, SVAR/RA/SE/RA1112.1/B120 (1613) #392 Contract meds kopparbergz. Datum kopparbergz, November 10, 1613.

The merchants were instructed to sell it at the best price obtainable. They would take a commission on the sale and send the proceeds back to the *Räntekammar* for the ransom fund. The problem with this procedure was that it allowed room for fraud; the *Räntekammar* remained in Stockholm, while the king was often far afield in Russia. He was too far away to monitor transactions taking place in Lübeck or Amsterdam. As an example, if the copper market in Lübeck was equivalent to RD 45 per skd, the merchant representing the crown could sell to another merchant at RD 40 and split the five *riksdalers* between them. To avoid this type of "unethical practice," the chancellor suggested that in the future all sales of copper should be made through the Älvsborg commission. The commission members would make it their business to know the markets; merchants would have to check with commission members before making a sale; and commission members would also have the power to direct copper shipments either to Lübeck or to Amsterdam, depending on local prices. In October 1615 the king was about to release 400 skd of copper into the market, and the chancellor suggested that the Älvsborg commission oversee this shipment.[56] We do not have a reply from the king, but the chancellor's suggestion was sound. Unregulated merchants invariably take advantage of such a situation for their own benefit, and the chancellor's advice points out an obvious failing in the copper distribution method. Allowing merchants to determine sales prices on their own was poor business practice. The crown was not yet in full control of purchases at the mine, and the method of distribution was inadequately supervised. Apparently, the king agreed with the chancellor and made changes. In October 1617, when the king sent the copper recovered from the Queen Mother to Lübeck to be sold on a commission basis by Lars Bengtsson and Lorentz Kruse, he also sent Johan Skytte, a member of the Älvsborg commission, to supervise the sales.[57]

Another strategy the crown employed to turn copper into goods and services was to simply ship copper as payment. It is worth exploring several examples that demonstrate the link between the crown's finances and its copper policy. Jacob de la Gardie, one of the king's generals, commanded troops in the Russian wars during most of 1613 and 1615. In September 1613 de la Gardie occupied Novgorod. He wrote to the chancellor complaining of the disorder within Russia caused by marauding Cossacks, who were backing Michael Romanov, a local rival to Karl Filip. He had just hired a regiment of German mercenaries under the command of one Reinholt Taube. The troops

---

56   AOSB, I, 2, 243–45.
57   AOSB, II, 10, 193.

were in poor shape, but he sorely needed them to help against the Cossacks; the upfront cost was RD 4,000, which de la Gardie had distributed to Taube and his soldiers from his own resources. Now he asked the chancellor to intercede with the king to grant him a yearly shipment of 25 skd copper to cover interest on the RD 4,000, and to pay for the mercenaries' wages.[58] With this amount he could also make payments to his other local creditors. A brief analysis showed that this was a highly favorable agreement for de la Gardie, who knew that there was little or no possibility that the crown would repay the principal. At the time copper was selling at about RD 50 per skd.[59] If one uses that figure, the annual interest was RD 1,250 on a principal of RD 4,000 or 31 percent per year. Even if de la Gardie did use some of it to defray the mercenaries' wages and pay local debts, he would probably have use of the copper revenue long after the issue of the Russian succession was settled. The chancellor answered with a long discussion of the Russian war and the lack of support among the *Kammar-Råd* for it. He ended, however, with a terse acceptance of de la Gardie's proposal.[60]

What does this incident tell us? First, it was yet another example of the crown's chronic lack of cash. Would it have made sense to accept such an expensive loan if the king had cash to repay de la Gardie? Also, de la Gardie realized that asking for repayment in cash would have been futile, so he requested payment in copper, which he knew was more readily available than cash; he also included a substantial bonus to himself for his extra efforts.

This same element of payment and reward was also present in the transaction mentioned earlier involving Lorenz Kruse in Lübeck. In a letter of November 3, 1614 the chancellor began by congratulating Kruse for the loan he had obtained from the States General, and informed him that the king was prepared to ship 300 skd of copper to Lübeck to pay for the 30 to 40 barrels of gunpowder that Kruse was shipping back to Stockholm.[61] In other words, the crown did not have sufficient cash to send a bill of exchange to cover the cost of the gunpowder, so it was sending a parcel of copper. Kruse would sell the copper locally and use the proceeds to pay for the 30 to 40 casks of gunpowder. The problem with this type of arrangement was that once again Kruse was left to determine the price for the copper and the amount that he would keep for his commission. Using copper as currency for this type of transaction left the crown open to deceit.

58   AOSB, II, 5, 53.
59   G. Wittrock, *Kopparcompaniet*, 21.
60   AOSB, I, 2, 151.
61   AOSB, I, 2, 219.

The above examples of the crown granting a field officer a generous pension in copper in return for a loan to hire mercenaries, and the payment of 300 skd in copper for gunpowder in Lübeck, are only two incidents of the crown using copper for payments. There are countless more examples in the correspondence to prove that copper was already a currency of the realm. In fact, the crown had no choice in the matter. It was perennially short of silver currency, and all available *riksdalers* went toward the ransom. There were, however, problems with this copper policy. First, it was not possible to distribute copper in small denominations. The crown could not, for example, pay a troop of soldiers with *skeppunds* of copper. It would have to sell the copper first and wait for payment by bill of exchange, which could take several months. This was a serious drawback to the crown. The other problem was that the system remained inefficient and costly as demonstrated in the expensive payments to de la Gardie.[62] The transactions the crown negotiated were in either Swedish *dalers* silver mint, or in *riksdalers*, not in copper. If the transactions had been originally negotiated in copper, the crown could pay with a precise amount of copper. Since, however, the transactions were negotiated in silver currency, the crown was consistently overpaying in copper to protect the recipient from fluctuations in the relative prices of copper and silver. The crown needed an easier and more efficient method of negotiating with its copper.

Further examples can be found in Axel Oxenstierna's government budget proposals for the middle period of Gustav Adolf's reign. This included the final years of the Älvsborg ransom payments. The documents help us to understand the strong connection between copper and credit, and the struggle of the crown to finance the ransom while still paying state and military expenses. Since the Swedish economy had not yet developed credit facilities one must ask how the crown deployed copper as a substitute. An advance from a prominent merchant, Erik Larsson, is a good example of sources of domestic credit. In a letter written in December 1617 the chancellor mentioned to the king that he was negotiating with Larsson and two other merchants for a substantial advance.[63] The outcome was not clear until the following year, when the chancellor (on behalf of the *Kammar-Råd*) wrote to Peder Eriksson at the Stora Kopparberg. He instructed Eriksson to release 460 skd of copper to Erik Larsson. The chancellor also mentioned that while Larsson would be present at the mine to receive the goods, his

---

62   AOSB, I, 2, 219.
63   AOSB, I, 2, 324.

two partners, Lars Bengtssons and Peter Kruse (the brother of Lorenz), would not be present.[64]

It should not be a surprise, therefore, that in early January 1618, when the chancellor put together the budget for making the payment due on the third ransom installment, the advances made by the three partners in the copper purchase were included. Lars Bengtsson was the largest single contributor to the ransom payment. He lent the crown RD 56,316; Peter Kruse's advance was the second at RD 24,942; and Erik Larsson contributed a modest RD 1,575. Nonetheless, the three offered a total of RD 82,833. Since they received only 460 skd of copper on July 26 as collateral, we must conclude that there were other copper deliveries as well.[65]

It's curious how much this transaction resembled a futures contract, much like the advances made by merchants to miners at the Stora Kopparberg. Erik Larsson and his associates, in effect, paid for copper before delivery. They must have made the financial advances in January 1618, because the chancellor recorded it as part of the budget for the third installment. They did not receive the first copper delivery, however, until July 1618. They were buying, therefore, a six-month futures contract. The virtue of such a purchase was that beginning in January 1618, they could quote to their customers a fixed price for delivery in July 1618. There were, however, two major risks. If they could not sell the copper forward, they might be facing a lower price when they took delivery in July and be forced to sell at a loss. The other danger was that the king would not deliver on time. If they had sold ahead, they would have to deliver on time, even if that meant buying elsewhere to cover the sale. All three were sophisticated traders and they would have understood the risks. Having exhausted local sources of credit based on copper, the chancellor once again had to look abroad to raise funds.

Naturally he turned to The Hague for a loan, as he had for previous installments of the ransom. There were some compelling reasons the United Provinces would be interested in providing financial support to the Swedes. First, there was the constant threat to the republic from the Spanish armies stationed on their borders to the west and south. Second, Gustav Adolf was a Protestant king with a warlike reputation and therefore an attractive ally if they could divert his attention from Poland and the eastern Baltic. The other possibility open to the United Provinces was an alliance with Kristian IV of Denmark. Kristian IV did not possess, however, impeccable Protestant credentials. He was, as mentioned, guilty of secret negotiations

64 AOSB, I, 2, 324.
65 AOSB, I, 1, 446.

with the Spaniards.[66] Finally, Denmark controlled the Sound, and Kristian IV imposed tolls on all commercial traffic passing between the Baltic and the Atlantic. Since Dutch ships accounted for 90 percent of this traffic, they were perennially concerned that the Danish king would raise the tolls or ban Dutch shipping.[67]

To cultivate favor in the United Provinces, the crown maintained an ambassador, Dr. Jacob van Dijck, at The Hague. When a young humanist and lawyer, Jan Rutgers, finished his studies in France and came to The Hague to begin a legal practice, van Dijck recruited him to serve the Swedish crown. Rutgers traveled to Sweden early in 1616, where he met with the king, the chancellor, and the Queen Mother. He was back in Holland by mid-year to assist van Dijck.[68]

Rutgers had his first meeting with the influential Dutch statesman Johan van Oldenbarnevelt in July 1616. Rutger's uncle, Hugo Muys van Holy, an important politician, and a member of the States General, facilitated the meeting. Apparently, Rutgers explained the Swedish crown's plight and delivered a letter from Gustav Adolf to the States General requesting financial assistance. Rutgers was well received by both the elder statesman and the States General, but his timing was poor. King James I of England, in a fit of pique over British-Dutch commercial rivalries, demanded that the States General immediately repay an ancient loan of 28 barrels of gold.[69] The cities of Flushing and Brill were security for the loan so the States General had to focus on raising money to repay King James I, and could not entertain requests from far off Sweden.[70]

Later in the year, however, Rutgers reported some progress. He and van Dijck had met with every member of the Estates General and had the strong support of Johan van Oldenbarnevelt, who was determined to support a Protestant alliance with Sweden. Despite considerable internal opposition, the States approved a loan of RD 150,000. The Swedish crown was obligated repay the loan with shipments of copper during 1617. This, together with the loan from the Queen Mother mentioned earlier, would be sufficient to make the second payment toward the Älvsborg ransom. In January Rutgers wrote to the chancellor that he was enroute to Sweden, carrying a bill of exchange for RD 120,000 with him.[71]

---

66 AOSB, II, 13, 229–30.
67 De Vries, *The First Modern Economy*, 373.
68 AOSB, II, 13, 17.
69 Unfortunately, there was no indication of the weight of each barrel.
70 AOSB, II, 13, 231.
71 AOSB, II, 13, 253.

Rutger's next report on the States General came several months later. He was returning to Amsterdam after delivering the bill of exchange to the crown. It was already September 1617 and the king and the chancellor were worried about the third installment of the ransom. The king asked Rutgers to request another loan from the States to cover part of the new installment. Unfortunately, the Swedish crown had neglected to make any copper shipments to Amsterdam for principal and interest payments. Rutgers was not optimistic about another loan, however, unless the king made a substantial payment on the last loan. To this end, he urged the chancellor to expedite a shipment of 1,000 skd of copper to Amsterdam promised by the king.[72] Five days later Rutgers had another meeting with Johan van Oldenbarnevelt, who was unhappy that the Swedish crown had failed to make any payments. Rutgers took a risk and promised the imminent arrival of a large copper shipment. Oldenbarnevelt was still in the Swedish crown's camp, but he cautioned that any new loans would require approval from the representatives of the States.[73] Not surprisingly, Rutgers had been rash in promising a large payment. The copper shipment was delayed, and when it finally arrived in late November 1617, it was only 208 skd, which was less than the interest owed on the previous loan. By December another 200 skd had arrived, but again it was too little. In any case, the king would later order Rutgers to liquidate the 408 skd of copper now in Amsterdam and send the proceeds back to Stockholm via bills of exchange.[74] The crown, therefore, made no payments against outstanding interest and principal obligations during 1617. Rutgers was now frantic. Both he and his uncle, Hugo Muys van Holy, had been lobbying for the Swedish crown and their reputations were damaged.[75]

Frustrated by lack of progress with a new loan, the crown called on Johan Skytte, the crown's most skilled diplomat. As noted earlier, he was already in Lübeck overseeing the sale of copper there. In late autumn he departed for the Netherlands. His goal was to lobby for another loan and to collect intelligence. He was a keen observer and his long letters to the king are a fascinating combination of gossip and historical detail. Skytte had been the king's tutor, and his letters also have a pedagogical tone. He was blunt to the king on financial matters; more so than any other correspondent whose letters survive. His main task, however, was to raise money for the

72 AOSB, II, 13, 253.
73 AOSB, II, 13, 257.
74 ASOB, II, 10, 265.
75 AOSB, II, 13, 270.

third installment and in this endeavor, he was only partially successful. As explained, the king did not enjoy a favorable reputation in financial matters.

Skytte's letters were full of the details of his daily activities; in the first letter sent to the king on October 4, 1617, he remarked that he had just heard from Rutgers about a meeting with van Oldenbarnevelt, and that another loan of RD 100,000 from the States General was a real possibility. Skytte pleaded that copper be sent as soon as possible to Amsterdam. He, therefore, joined Rutgers in suggesting to the king and the chancellor that the new loan from the States General would depend on the timely arrival of a copper shipment.[76]

To understand the importance of Johan Skytte's visit to the Netherlands, it is necessary to recognize the Dutch antipathy toward the king of Denmark. During the last three decades of the previous century, the Dutch-speaking peoples were in open rebellion against their Spanish Habsburg masters. The warfare was brutal on both sides. After thirty years of conflict the parties were exhausted and agreed to a twelve-year armistice in 1609. The southern provinces, including Flanders and the Brabant, remained under Spanish rule. The northern provinces, which had been operating as if they were independent for several decades, were free to continue doing so. The two parties agreed to an armistice—not peace. Therefore, the northern provinces had to anticipate the resumption of hostilities when the armistice expired in 1621.[77] During the early years of the conflict, Dutch merchants had continued to trade with Spain. Ironically this trade greatly contributed to the growth and success of the young Dutch Republic. In 1598, however, Philip II of Spain banned all trade between the United Provinces and the Iberian Peninsula. This not only damaged Dutch trading volumes, but it also encouraged the Dutch merchants to look to the Baltic for future business. Between 1611 and 1620, an annual average of 1,708 Dutch vessels entered the Danish Sound enroute to Baltic ports. Given these figures, it is not surprising that the Dutch were exceedingly sensitive to threats from the king of Denmark.[78]

For his part, Kristian IV did his best to keep the Dutch off balance. During the War of Kalmar Kristian doubled the tolls he charged United Provinces' ships for passage through the Sound. Kristian was also vocal in his objections to the large Dutch population in the Swedish city of Göteborg (protected by the ransomed fortress of Älvsborg). As noted earlier, Göteborg was the

76   ASOB, II, 10, 192–93.
77   Parker, *Europe*, 98–99.
78   De Vries, *The First Modern Economy*, 372.

only Swedish port on the North Sea, and hence the only Swedish port the Dutch could reach without sailing through the Sound. Finally, Kristian openly flirted with the enemy; he sent and received delegations back and forth to Spain. Also, Spain attempting to persuade Kristian to ban Dutch shipping through the Sound altogether. The result was a Dutch-Swedish alliance signed in 1614. Its goal was to keep Kristian in check.[79]

It's not surprising, therefore, that Johan Skytte was well received when he reached the Netherlands. He arrived in October of 1617, still optimistic (after meeting with Jan Rutgers and Johan van Oldenbarnevelt) that the States General would contribute to the third installment of the ransom. In his report to the crown Skytte again raised the issue of the king's failure to send enough copper to pay the interest, and at least some of the principal on the loan of RD 150,000 that Rutgers and Muys de Holy had negotiated the previous year.[80] Although he was deferential and used the normal formal title E.K. M:T (Your Royal Majesty), he said repeatedly that there was little possibility of getting the States General to make another advance until the first advance was at least partly paid. There was an element of teacher to student in the tone. For example, when writing about the arrival of a small shipment of copper, he explained to the king that the Swedish crown's credit in Amsterdam was delicate and that he should be careful to fulfill his promised shipments. He indicated the same to the chancellor in the following letter: "When the copper didn't come to Amsterdam, we had to give many solemn assurances; after some copper came His Majesty's credit position improved, but he was still 'behind the horse.'"[81]

Skytte's assignment, however, was not yet finished. He continued to seek out new markets for Swedish copper. From the Netherlands he sailed to London, where he met James Spens, who was serving as the Swedish crown's ambassador. Spens was a colorful character; he was born and educated in Scotland and became Sweden's recruiter for Scottish mercenaries. Probably because of this Swedish connection, James I sent Spens to Sweden in 1611 as the British crown's representative at the Peace of Knäred. After the peace, Spens remained in Sweden and served in the Swedish army as General of the British Forces in Sweden. In return for his service, Gustav Adolf sent him back to London as his ambassador there.[82] Spens was well known in the court of James I, which made him a valuable connection. In fact, shortly after

79   Roberts, *Gustavus Adolphus*, 1, 150-52.
80   AOSB, II, 10, 203.
81   AOSB, II, 10, 221.
82   ASOB, II, 13, 12.

Skytte's arrival, Spens arranged an audience with King James I. Meetings with other influential members of the court followed, including one with the Prince of Wales, the future Charles I.[83]

Spens also had contacts with the world of commerce. During Skytte's visit, Spens facilitated a meeting with Thomas Smitt of the East India Company, John Merrick of the Constantinople Company, and W. Russell of the Moscow Company, all of whom were interested in purchasing copper in Sweden and importing it into Great Britain. Like all good merchants, they asked Skytte the terms and conditions under which the Swedish Crown would sell.[84] Skytte indicated that they required buyers to make an advance to the crown in either gold or *riksdalers* and give the crown full authority over it. This was to be delivered to Helsingör in Denmark (presumably for direct payment to the king of Denmark) or to Hamburg by midsummer. The King of Sweden would, in turn, deliver an unspecified quantity of copper over three years, beginning with the Feast Day of St. John (June 24). He promised to deliver good quality copper to the wharf at Stockholm for RD 46 per skd.[85]

Predictably, the English merchants wanted to consult with their colleagues before agreeing to these extended payment terms. They undoubtedly would have known about the crown's chronic late payments to The Hague and late copper shipments to Amsterdam. Their response was quite intriguing. Only Merrick and Russell returned the next day. They confessed that they were not experienced in copper trading. They asked how Stockholm weights compared to London weights, suggesting they could not do a proper accounting without understanding the difference. In truth, these weight differences bedeviled many merchants at the time. They also said that it was not possible for them to finance a three-year contract with payment up front, without charging interest. Finally, they argued that they would pay for copper only after delivery so they could, one suspects, check its quality before they made payment. What they did not address, or Skytte did not record, was the issue of market risk. As merchants, they were aware that copper was a volatile commodity. They would certainly be reluctant to enter a contract at a fixed price when the final delivery would arrive in three years. By then the market could have fallen substantially and they could take losses on the metal when they sold it. There was some considerable discussion,

83   AOSB, II, 10, 230.
84   Merchants try to avoid mentioning a price first because one does not know the price his opposite number has in mind. If you offer to buy at US$ 50.00 per pound and the seller would have sold at US$ 45.00 per pound you have paid too much.
85   AOSB, II, 10, 240. The price seemed reasonable on the wharf in Stockholm because Skytte had recently sold 200 skd in Amsterdam at RD 50 per skd.

and finally Russell made a counteroffer of RD 42 per skd with payment after delivery in Stockholm. Russell would arrange payment through his representative there. Skytte wrote to the king suggesting that he accept this first transaction. He noted that England was a new market for copper and that other new business in the metal could follow.[86] Skytte concluded that the merchants considered a large trade with a "potentate or a great person" to be dangerous because they had little recourse if the king failed to deliver. He added that they viewed His Royal Majesty with "very little trust."[87]

This incident was significant because it demonstrated once again that the king of Sweden's commercial reputation, even in England, was dismal. For the king to demand payment three years in advance was unrealistic and one is surprised that Skytte would even suggest such a transaction. It was also a signal to the English merchants that the Swedish crown was desperate. The one merchant who was seriously interested, W. Russell, offered payment at the time of delivery because he suspected that there was little chance that the king would deliver on time if he were paid in advance.[88]

The Hague was full of powerful merchants who lived by a code of conduct. If one paid his obligations on time, then he was credit worthy. If one did not pay on time he was not. The king of Sweden had not merely paid late, he had not paid at all. Apparently, the king did not yet realize, or had chosen to ignore, the fact that the entire trading and financial system was based on credit, which was, in turn, based on reputation. This failing doomed Skytte's mission from the beginning. The same was true for his trip to London. He met the king, the crown prince, and three important merchants. As they were familiar with the king's record, they would only do business with him on a "net cash basis." If he delivered the copper, they would deliver the cash. The mission was a major missed opportunity for the crown. The States General was now reluctant to lend a large amount of money to the king. They were willing to guarantee loans from private investors, and grant the occasional subsidy, but they balked at lending revenue from their own coffers. The Swedish crown had burned its bridges.

Let us return to the crown's desperate efforts to collect the funds for the third ransom payment. It was due on January 20, 1618, and the crown was short by RD 170,000. Jan Rutgers and Johan Skytte had warned the king repeatedly that no money would be forthcoming from the States General unless he began servicing the existing loans. It was only in December 1617,

86   AOSB, II, 10, 240.
87   AOSB, II, 10, 242.
88   AOSB, II, 10, 240.

a month before the third installment came due, that the king realized he might not be able to make payment on time.[89]

Now the king was distraught: "... the entirety of the States General has refused to help us with the third installment ... I do not see any solution until the money comes from the 2,000 skd of copper we sent to Amsterdam."[90] This statement, at least, tells us how the king finally paid the balance of the third installment; he used the proceeds from the 2,000 skd in Amsterdam that he ordered Johan Skytte to liquidate in January 1618. The actual payment, however, must have been months late. In the meantime, the king wondered how to handle the king of Denmark. Gustav Adolf now knew that he would not have the full amount of the ransom by January 20. As mentioned earlier, there was also the problem of the Danish king's duplicity regarding alliances. On one hand, he sent envoys to The Hague to advocate for a Protestant alliance that would include Sweden; on the other, he was simultaneously talking to the Spanish and to the Imperial court in Vienna. Kristian IV also had an "understanding" with the Catholic king of Poland that worried Sweden. If the Swedish crown made only a partial payment against the third installment now due, what would be the King of Denmark's reaction? Would he threaten Göteborg? This question was made more complicated by the "understanding" with Poland, whose king would certainly suggest that Denmark do anything possible to injure the Swedish crown. In the end, the king's fears were unjustified; there were no consequences for the late payment.[91]

This takes us to the fourth installment of the ransom, due in January 1619. Paying the third ransom installment to the Danish king had left the Swedish crown destitute; now it had to worry about the fourth and final payment. Because the crown no longer had access to loans made directly from the States General, the king and the chancellor developed another creative approach. They suggested to Johan van Dijck, the crown's ambassador to the United Provinces, that he contact Louis de Geer—an arms dealer based in Amsterdam with whom the crown had dealings—to form a syndicate of merchants. Hopefully, the syndicate would be willing to lend money to the crown, with copper as security, for the final ransom payment. De Geer agreed to the idea and set about forming a consortium of wealthy merchants. He "cleared the way and made possible the new project because of previous service he did for His Majesty [Gustav Adolf]."[92] The purpose

89 AOSB, II, 1, 105-08
90 AOSB, II, 1, 105-08
91 AOSB, II, 1, 107–10.
92 Louis de Geers *Brev och affärshandlingar* (LDGBOA), 26.

of a consortium was to spread the risk among several merchants. The risks included non-payment of the loan, as well as a steep drop in the price of copper. The consortium agreed to deliver the money in October 1618. In return, the Swedish crown pledged to deliver copper equal in value to DG 159,750 (the principal plus interest) one year later. This was only a preliminary offer. The real negotiations began in July.

The July contract was negotiated between Ambassador van Dijck for the crown and Louis de Geer as head of the consortium; it specified that the advance be used toward the last installment of the ransom. The members of the group appeared to be men of importance in the United Provinces. They were listed as Aelbert de Veer, Knight, and Lord of Callants Oge, Pauwels van Asperen, member of both the Council and the High Council (the court and the supreme court), Adriaen Tedingh, member of the Provincial Council in Holland, Zealand, and Friesland, Nicasius Kien, Commissioner General (quartermaster general), and Louis de Geer, merchant of Amsterdam.[93]

The syndicate confirmed that they agreed to advance RD 150,000 to the crown of Sweden at the interest rate of 6.5 percent. The Receiver General of the States would oversee the collection of money and exchange it into *riksdalers*. In return, the crown promised to repay the advance in copper. Specifically, the consortium would deliver the money to the Receiver General in October 1618, and the crown would deliver the copper in October 1619.[94] In exchange, van Dijck agreed to a price of RD 39 per skd copper. Finally, and most critically, the States General offered to reimburse the lenders if the Swedish crown defaulted.

One should emphasize that the States General had commercial reasons to want the Älvsborg fortress to pass back to the Swedish crown. They wanted access to the Swedish markets (without paying the Danish toll) as much as the Swedes wanted toll-free access to Amsterdam. They also had a military motive. The Twelve-Year Truce with Spain would expire in 1621 and the United Provinces had every reason to assume that hostilities with Spain would resume. They were, therefore, eager to keep Gustav Adolf in their camp as a future ally. With renewed hostilities with Spain almost a certainty, moreover, they needed money for their own defenses. They, therefore, agreed to insure the loan but not to make it.

Several questions arise from this agreement with the consortium; the first was the price. As recently as November 1617, Johan Skytte reported selling 200 skd of copper in Amsterdam at RD 50 per skd.[95] This alone

93   LDGBOA, 26.
94   LDGBOA, 26.
95   AOSB, II, 10, 203.

would not be significant except that de Geer agreed to purchase 272 skd in September 1619 at the same price, and there was no discussion in the correspondence about a price decrease. So, it is a fair assumption that the copper prices had remained steady for the year 1618. This would make the price of RD 39 to the consortium appear exceedingly generous. While it was a business contract, it was probably, therefore, also a diplomatic move. One can assume that the favorable price negotiated by van Dijck was a gesture of good will toward the powerful members of de Geer's consortium, and an effort to court favor for the future. Of course, an alternative explanation was that the consortium insisted on the discounted price to ensure a better profit when they sold the copper. Even with the guarantee from the States General, the consortium was taking a risk.

It was also now clear that Louis de Geer was making progress in establishing a solid and fruitful relationship with the Swedish crown; he floated a major loan through the States General. He and the crown were beginning to understand the advantages of doing business with one another. He was even doing little favors for the chancellor. In July he wrote to Oxenstierna asking if he was interested in obtaining some decent wine. He then sent samples of wine from the Rhine area, the Rhone Valley, and the Loire Valley,[96] and offered to supply which ever variety the chancellor preferred.[97]

In summary, I am reminded that prominent historians from the last century considered Gustav Adolf commercially inept because he continued to expand production at the Stora Kopparberg in the face of a stagnant copper market. I think this is the wrong basis for judgment; his goal was not to maximize the profit per *skeppund*. Rather, his goal was to manage the resource to further his immediate political and military ambitions. Paying his armies and the Älvsborg ransom was his overarching goal and he was successful in this endeavor because he was able to capture the bounty of the mine and turn it into *riksdalers*. He did so through loans from the States General, the Queen Mother and the merchants of Amsterdam. But the process also exposed the crown's vulnerabilities. While attempting to pay the ransom, Gustav Adolf was also drawn into expensive wars caused by his fear that the King of Poland would exercise influence in Russia and other parts of the Eastern Baltic. The king was especially worried about a Polish invasion of Swedish Estonia, which shared its southern border with Poland. This obsession with the danger from Poland occasionally diverted his attention from the central task of the decade, to pay the Älvsborg ransom.

96 LDGBOA, 27.
97 LDGBOA, 27–28.

The wars against Poland also contributed to the king's poor reputation and bad credit rating. He diverted copper shipments that he owed to the States General and used them to cover immediate military expenses. Forfeiting the fortress at Älvsborg and abandoning Göteborg to the Danes would have been a dear price to pay for the king's Polish policy.

There were, however, many positive aspects of this period. To begin, the king began to address the issue of the over-mighty Swedish subjects. Duke Johan died without heirs and his duchy passed to the crown. The Queen Mother remained a political problem, but the king was able to curb her forays into the copper market. Forcing her to give up the 3,000 skd of copper futures she held in 1617 was a major accomplishment. The king also forced her to limit copper purchases for the next several years. Once he neutralized the Queen Mother, the king was able to impose a strict monopoly on purchases at the Stora Kopparberg. By the end of 1619 the king had locked up all "officially" produced copper, thus fulfilling one of the fundamental goals of his reign. Smuggling certainly continued, but with few records it is impossible to measure the extent of this problem.

In 1611, when Gustav Adolf assumed the throne, the mine produced 5,665 skd of copper per year. By 1618 production surpassed 10,860 skd, an increase of over 90 percent in seven years. The existing sales channels were no longer able to accommodate the increased volumes. Before Gustav Adolf's reign, the transport of copper from the mine to foreign markets was leisurely and inefficient. It passed through a series of merchants or was purchased by local traders. Because Gustav Adolf opened the credit and arms markets in Amsterdam, the crown was shipping large quantities of copper there as payment. In Amsterdam it was put on smaller vessels and shipped up the Rhine to copper works and bronze cannon foundries along the way until reaching Aachen, the center for finished copper production. Or it went via ocean vessel on the Atlantic to cannon works and foundries in France. Overland freight from the northern German cities could not compete and the Swedish crown was now selling all over Europe.

The king had not yet, however, solved his central dilemma—how to convert *skeppund* of copper into currency. He had taken the innovative step of sending delegates to Amsterdam to float loans with the States General with copper as collateral. After damaging the relationship by failing to repay the loans, the king organized a group of prominent merchants to lend him money against future copper shipments. He was the first Swedish monarch to tap into the vast wealth of Amsterdam, but the results were not wholly satisfactory. Because the transactions were negotiated in Dutch Guilder, or Imperial *riksdalers*, both silver-based currencies, the king was forced to discount the copper against the silver currency to protect his creditors from fluctuations in the relative value of copper and silver. The king realized that this was not an ideal solution. We shall explore his response to the problem in the third chapter.

Bibliography

Archival Sources

Riksarkivet, SE/RA 1112.1/B120 (1613) Contract meds kopparbergz. Datum kopparberg. November 10, 1613.
Riksarkivet. SE/RA/1112.1/B/125 (1615) # 134, Fullmakt för Peder Pederson och Peder Jonsson. February 1615.
Riksarkivet, SE/RA/1112.1/B/125 (1615) Letter from Gustav Adolf to Mats Jöransson. March 3, 1615.

Printed Primary Sources

Dahlgren, Erik Wilhelm. ed. *Louis de Geers brev och affärshandlingar 1614–1652*. Stockholm: P.A. Norstedt & Söner, 1934.
Oxenstierna, Axel. *Rikskansleren Axel Oxenstierna skriften och brefvexling*, Series I, 16 vols. Stockholm: P.A. Norstedt & Söner, 1888–Present.
Oxenstierna, Axel. *Rikskansleren Axel Oxenstierna skriften och brefvexling*, Series II, 14 vols. Stockholm: P.A. Norstedt & Söner, 1888–Present.

Secondary Sources

Dahlgren, Erik Wilhelm. *Louis de Geer, 1587–1652, hans lif och verk*, 2 vols. Uppsala: Almqvist & Wiksells, 1923.
De Vries, Jan, and Ad van der Woude, eds. *The First Modern Economy, Success, Failure, and, Perseverance of the Dutch Economy, 1500–1815*. Cambridge: Cambridge University Press, 1997.
Frost, Robert I. *The Northern Wars: War, State, and Society in Northeastern Europe 1558–1721*. London: Routledge, 2014.
Heckscher, Eli Filip. *Sveriges economiska historia från Gustav Vasa*, 2 vols. Stockholm: Albert Bonniers. 1936
Lindroth, Sven. *Gruvbrytning och kopparhantering vid Stora Kopparberg intill 1800 talets början*, 2 vols. Uppsala: Almqvist & Wiksells, 1955.
Parker, Geoffrey, *Europe in Crisis, 1598–1648*. Oxford: Blackwell, 1979.

Roberts, Michael, *Gustavus Adolphus, a History of Sweden 1611–1632*, 2 vols. London: Longmans, Green and Co., 1957.

Wingquist, S. "Om det gamla koppar--compagneit och kopparmyntningen under Gustav II Adolfs tid." In *Skandia*, IV, 5–68. Lund: 1834.

Wittrock, Georg. *Svenska handelscompaniet och kopparhandeln under Gustav II Adolf.* Uppsala: Almqvist & Wikesell, 1919.

3. The Copper Company in the Early Years

Abstract

The birth of the Copper Company is the main feature of chapter three. The company charter, which we shall later examine in detail, contained a feature that was probably among the most important economic decision of Gustav Adolf's reign. The king granted the new company a full monopoly on purchases from the mine at a fixed price of SD 50 (RD 30.7 mine weight). Persuading the *bergsmän* to accept a fixed sales price and the purchasing monopoly was an important victory for the king. The price was adequate to keep the *bergsmän* satisfied, while, at the same time, allowing the crown to sell at a profit on the world market.

Keywords: Louis de Geer, *Råkoppar/Gårkoppar,* Peter Kruse, Livonian War, Säter

> *"Mit einem kleinen Verlust, kann mann jeden Geschäft machen."*
> (With a small loss you can do any business.) Old German/Yiddish trader saying

The focus of this chapter is the Swedish Trading Company or, as it was commonly called, the Copper Company, during its gestation period. In the introduction I mentioned that the company has been a lightning rod, drawing criticism from Swedish and foreign scholars alike, who examined the issue during the last century. If I were to judge the company as a financial analyst, I would not recommend investing in shares. If we consider the company, however, as an experiment that Gustav Adolf used to consolidate power at home, and to mobilize Sweden's metallic resources, it no longer appears misguided. It was rather a vehicle allowing the crown to develop a commercial enterprise, that might have brought the kind of wealth and prosperity that the Dutch East India Company brought to the United Provinces. We have

Stryker, L., *The Swedish Monarchy and the Copper Trade: The Copper Company, the Deposit System, and the Amsterdam Market, 1600–1640.* Amsterdam: Amsterdam University Press, 2024
DOI 10.5117/9789048560813_CH03

a singular advantage over earlier historians in the effort to determine the company's potential; we can explore the company's balance sheets for two separate years and tease out the numbers. Past commentators inexplicably ignored these sources.

Before we confront the company, however, we will explore the crown's financial standing after paying off the Älvsborg ransom. As he approached the end of his first decade in power, the king collected taxes all over the country and owned a considerable number of estates. We must consider the reason he did not use the revenue from his land base tax to fund his military ambitions. It would have been preferable to begin this discussion with a summary of royal revenue and expenses at the beginning of the 1620s. Unfortunately, this would be an exceedingly complicated business because the bulk of the king's tax revenue was paid in kind. Royal accounts for the year 1573 show that only 6 percent of the crown's revenue was paid in cash; by 1620 this had changed only marginally.[1] The balance was collected as grain, bread, iron, farm animals, wood, and other commodities. The local authorities would sell perishable commodities for cash or trade them for something more enduring.[2] When possible, the crown used the agricultural commodities collected to feed the army.

High government officials were not given a salary but were granted the revenues from various estates; they were responsible for managing the estate and exploiting whatever the estate produced. Even the army sometimes had to accept non-cash payments. Writing from Viborg during the Russian campaign in 1614, the king told the chancellor that he just received a shipment of cloth from Sweden that he would use to pay the troops.[3]

Although antiquated, the system seemed to function within Sweden. Problems arose, however, when international payments were necessary. The reason the Älvsborg ransom was a cruel shock to the crown's fiscal policy was the requirement that payment be made in *riksdalers*, which were rare in Sweden. If the king could have paid in pigs or charcoal, it would have been much less disruptive.

To understand the Swedish crown's revenue in the seventeenth century, one would have to aggregate the returns of every local and regional official with tax collecting and redistribution. The chancellor was not concerned about the collection and redistribution of commodities. He was attempting to budget for receipt and payment of cash items; therefore, it would be realistic

1   Roberts, *Gustavus Adolphus*, 2, 44.
2   Roberts, *Gustavus Adolphus*, 2, 44.
3   Axel Oxenstiernas, *Skrifter och brevväxling* (AOSB), II, 1, 54.

to view the budget solely as a cash-flow projection. In the budget for 1620, for example, the chancellor listed a combination of taxes and tolls with a total value of SD 486,600.[4] Of this total, the chancellor calculated that SD 110,000 would be available in the form of *avrad* copper, paid by the *bergsmän* on an estimated 5,000 skd (skd is the abbreviation for *skeppund*) of copper production. In addition, he calculated that the crown's own works at the mine would produce 2,600 skd of copper in 1620 and he expected to sell it for a total of SD 189,800. He was calculating with a copper value of SD 73 or RD 45 per skd Stockholm weight. This meant that for a cash revenue budget of SD 486,600 (RD 299,800), 56 percent would come from the sale of copper.[5]

Of course, it is also critical to know how the crown was spending the cash. Conveniently, for us, the chancellor budgeted anticipated payments for the year 1620, and they are rather revealing. The largest line item was SD 106,640 (RD 65,625), to the States General. This was a partial payment of interest and some principal toward the ransom loans. Not surprisingly, the second-largest line item was SD 50,000 for war materials. There were also large payments owed to family members.[6] The king's brother-in-law, Count Palatine John Casimir, was to receive SD 40,625 for what was described as "*brudskatt*" (dowry). In addition, he received yearly SD 30,000 for "*paraphernalier*" (miscellany). The Queen Mother and Duke Johan were entitled to SD 30,000 each, yearly, also under the category of "*brudskatt*," so the meaning must have evolved to a more general connotation. All together the king's close relatives were budgeted to receive slightly over SD 100,000, more than 20 percent of the budgeted revenue. In summary, 46 percent of the crown's projected revenue went towards servicing its debt and supporting family members.[7] Both applications were unproductive and did nothing to support the crown's political and military ambitions outside Sweden. These internal expenses were simply too high and threatened Gustav Adolf's military ambitions. The crown needed to find new sources of income if it planned to continue playing a role in northern Europe.

In the period immediately before the final payment of the Älvsborg ransom came due, the king appeared uncertain about future copper policy. He now had a true monopoly at the mine, but he did not have a post-ransom marketing plan. At about the same time, Louis de Geer began to maneuver

---

4   As a reminder, currencies are abbreviated as follows: SD for Swedish *dalers*, RD for *riksdaler*, and DG for Dutch Guilders. The exchange rate was RD 1=DG 2.5 and RD 1= SD 1.624.

5   AOSB, I, 1, 449–50.

6   AOSB, I, 1, 449–50.

7   AOSB, I, 1, 449–50.

for a position as the king's copper factor in Amsterdam. In November 1619, the crown negotiated a copper sales contract with de Geer and a new syndicate of investors for 4,500 skd.[8] The actual negotiation took place in Stockholm between the king and de Geer's assistant, Stefan Gerard. Before the first shipment was due, however, the king had decided to establish the Copper Company and direct all shipments of copper through it. The king ignored his obligations to de Geer and his syndicate. Naturally this developed into a bitter dispute, and it illustrates the risks taken by merchants when dealing with princes. It also demonstrates how such disputes could be solved amicably.[9]

In the midst of the controversy over the crown's failure to make the first shipment to the syndicate, the king discovered that de Geer had failed to make a payment to the States General, on behalf of the crown, in the amount of DG 17,494 (RD 6,997).[10] This was part of a much larger bill of exchange that the crown had previously executed through de Geer, and it appeared that de Geer simply never made the payment and hoped that no one would notice. This was rather clumsy on de Geer's part, because the king used this oversight, intentional or otherwise, as a pretext to ignore the copper contract for 4,500 skd. The dispute that followed lasted for months and cost de Geer prestige at home and with the crown.

The contract began "We Gustav Adolf etc." indicating that the contract was in the king's name. It went on to specify the sale of 4,500 skd of copper to be shipped in lots of 1,500 skd per year beginning in October 1620, and the final weights were to be determined on Stockholm scales. Accepting Stockholm scales was a substantial concession for Gerard to make, but he probably did so because the contract was in Stockholm *skeppund*, which were quite different from Amsterdam *skeppund*.[11] The price was RD 40 per skd and de Geer calculated the freight and expenses from Stockholm to Amsterdam at RD 5 per skd, so the price totaled RD 45 per skd (Stockholm)

8   Louis de Geers, *Brev och affärshandlingar* (LDGBOA), 39.
9   LDGBOA, 39.
10   The king, or his advisers, had obviously spent some time deriving the correct number because the original figure was DG 170,949, or almost ten times the final figure. His secretary struck out DG 170,949 and wrote DG 17,949 over it. Of course, it's impossible to know when the king noticed the mistake. It's intriguing to suggest that he wrote the letter and conveyed his annoyance when he thought that de Geer was holding a significant sum of money only to discover later, that the amount was a fraction of the amount that inspired his comments. See Riksarkivet. SE/RA/1112.1/B/135 (1620), 113–15, Letter from Gustav Adolf to Peter Falk concerning the contract with Louis de Geer. Stockholm, September 6, 1620.
11   As a reminder, an Amsterdam skeppund containted 317.24 Amsterdam pounds, a Stockholm *skeppund* 274.3 Amsterdam pounds and a Kopparberg *skeppund* 302.53 Amsterdam pounds.

delivered to Amsterdam.[12] This price was lower than sales made by Rutgers and van Dijck at about this time, and the other physical terms were a little vague. The king was, however, very specific on payment terms. He wanted payment in hard currency delivered to Amsterdam, or to any other location of his choosing. Each yearly payment would be RD 60,000. From the first payment, he requested that RD 22,840 be paid toward loans in Amsterdam, and the balance be given to him in cash. An essential part of the three-year contract stipulated that de Geer's syndicate would extend to the crown an unsecured loan of RD 60,000. No interest rate was mentioned. The syndicate would provide the funds at the rate of RD 20,000 per year and the loans would coincide with the deliveries of copper.[13] We should note that this contract contained two elements essential to the crown. It gave the crown a regular outlet for its copper production, and it provided a credit facility.[14]

There were some serious risks for de Geer and his associates in this contract. Making an unsecured loan to the crown must have caused some anxiety, but one could assume that the loan was the price of doing business. It was also possible that Gerard was able to secure the business because others were not willing to make such loans. The king would probably repay the loans, but it could take years. Another risk was market fluctuation. We must explore some arcane details of hedging to understand why buying copper four years out at a fixed price was fraught with danger. If the market price dropped below the purchase price, de Geer's syndicate would take a loss on every *skeppund* when they took delivery and resold. The only way to hedge this market risk would be for de Geer to sell immediately and deliver later. He had contracted to buy 1,500 skd per year over three years. Therefore, in theory, he could sell 4,500 skd of copper forward, and deliver 1,500 skd in October 1620, October 1621, and October 1622. The dilemma for de Geer was that he could not depend on the crown to deliver on time. If he sold 1,500 skd for delivery in October 1620, he, as a merchant, would be forced to honor the commitment. If he failed to do so, his reputation would be ruined, and he could no longer function as a merchant. News of such lapses traveled rapidly through commercial circles. Of course, he could reach a negotiated settlement with his customer, but it was also probable that whoever bought from de Geer for an October 1620 delivery would hedge by selling some or all the 1,500 skd to a consumer or merchant at a fixed price for the same delivery. This customer could then sell to someone else. Thus,

12   LDGBOA, 161.
13   LDGBOA, 39–40.
14   LDGBOA, 39–40.

depending on the market, there could be gains or losses at each trade. Today, this network of trades is called "the daisy chain," and it demonstrates why honoring commitments is so important for functioning markets.

Given the risks, why did de Geer and his syndicate "go long" by buying the 4,500 skd?[15] One obvious reason was that de Geer expected prices to continue to climb. The purchase price was fair, and de Geer thought it would be a profitable contract. Yet, there was probably an even more important reason. This contract cemented de Geer's relationship with the crown for direct business, unencumbered by agents and go-betweens in Amsterdam. In fact, the same day that Gerard negotiated the copper purchase, he also bought the crown's entire yearly production of sulfur at SD 30 per skd.[16] Sulfur was, of course, a key ingredient for gunpowder. This was a four-year contract and it fit nicely with de Geer's arms and ammunition business. De Geer was able to leverage this and similar contracts into a life-long and successful relationship with the Swedish crown. Explaining the risk de Geer and his colleagues were willing to take on this contract emphasizes their eagerness to develop a direct working relationship with the crown.

Considering this large purchase, one is reminded of a common saying in some trading circles, "Signing the contract is only the first stage of negotiations." Despite the rather specific shipping dates, and the fact that the syndicate had already paid the yearly loan of RD 20,000 to the king, no copper came from Sweden in October 1620. The Swedish crown did make a large shipment of copper. It went instead to Lübeck, under the auspices of the new Copper Company, not to de Geer's syndicate.[17] As part of the contract, de Geer and his consortium had advanced the king DG 56,826 or RD 22,730. (This was the RD 20,000 and some fees.) De Geer was understandably upset, and he wrote a letter to the States General because he knew that the king of Sweden also owed copper to them for past loan payments.

In 1621, Mars, the god of war, came to the aid of de Geer. In August of that year, King Gustav Adolf led an invasion force across the Baltic into Polish Livonia. This was no mere adventure, but a full-fledged war involving some 14,000 Swedish troopers. Gustav Adolf's intention was to create a buffer zone between Sigismund III, and Swedish Estonia. After a difficult siege, the king captured Riga and, later, Pernau. Fortunately for de Geer, the crown realized that it needed his expertise in supplying weapons,

---

15   The term "long" means that a merchant has purchased more than he has sold. If he bought 1,000 skd and only sold 500 skd he is long 500 skd.

16   LDGBOA, 38.

17   LDGBOA, 44.

and the dispute over the late payment of DG 17,949 to the Estates General was set aside. In July 1622, Jan Rutgers, on behalf of the king, completed negotiations with de Geer for a major arms purchase. The total purchase price of DG 84,420 was equivalent to RD 33,768. As a point of interest, the contract specified delivery to either Stockholm or to Riga, which the king was then occupying, and delivery was due in October 1622, which didn't give de Geer very much time to assemble such a large quantity of equipment.[18] The weapons were to be shipped in appropriate packing and "acceptance was conditional on the afore named de Geer giving a guarantee of quality to His Majesty." The agreement warned that the weapons were needed quickly. The critical clause, however, regarded payment. The crown would pay de Geer by finally delivering enough copper to repay the outstanding loan made by the syndicate and the new arms purchase.[19]

Obviously, the Livonian War was key to settling the ongoing dispute between de Geer and Gustav Adolf. De Geer realized that he could not force the king to honor the original contract for 4,500 skd. He learned, however, a valuable lesson. He was not valuable to the crown as a buyer of copper; copper was a commodity the crown could sell through any number of merchants. Rather, de Geer was essential to the crown as a supplier of weapons. It was his ability to subcontract and assemble large quantities of arms and ammunition that distinguished de Geer from every other copper buyer in Lübeck or Amsterdam. Of course, the fact that the crown could pay de Geer in copper made the transaction more convenient for the crown and more profitable for de Geer. He could make a profit on the arms he shipped and on the copper that he took as payment. The crown, moreover, saved time because it did not have to send copper to Amsterdam and wait for bills of exchange. It simply shipped copper to Amsterdam and received arms in return. Paying for arms and ammunition with copper was an efficient two-sided trade for the crown.[20]

In August 1622, de Geer informed the chancellor that he had assembled the weapons and ammunition and that Jan Rutgers had fully inspected it for quality. The value of the order came to over RD 43,000. De Geer would make the arms shipment as soon as he could charter the necessary cargo space. He estimated that he would need two ships. We do know that by the end of 1622, Stefan Gerard was back in Stockholm to negotiate pending issues. The new Copper Company was now fully operational and the king, therefore,

18   LDGBOA, 65.
19   LDGBOA, 65.
20   LDGBOA, 67.

had no further interest in shipping against the old contract. Yet, there was no reason for the king to abuse this position and lose "good faith and credit" in Amsterdam. The king, therefore, agreed to pay a penalty of RD 4 per skd for the 4,500 skd of copper owed to de Geer's syndicate.[21] This amounted to RD 12,000, which was not an insignificant amount. The money would go to de Geer and the members of his syndicate to cover their unrealized profits from the trade. In return, de Geer and the syndicate agreed to renounce all further claims on the unshipped copper: "... this contract is now terminated and dead ... my consortium and I are completely satisfied."[22] This compromise ended the dispute between de Geer and the king.

In summary, the blame for the fiasco did not rest only with the crown. Either by mistake or by deceit, de Geer failed to deliver DG 17,949 of the crown's money to the States General for repayment of a loan, thereby giving the king a plausible reason to ignore a contract. The real reason for the dispute was much simpler. The crown wanted to send the copper to Lübeck (under the auspices of the Copper Company) where it probably sold for a higher price than the price negotiated with the syndicate. Once the king realized, however, that he needed arms and ammunition to pursue the Livonian War, de Geer was back in favor, and a settlement was quickly reached. As an arms supplier, he was important enough for the crown to settle the dispute and purchase more weapons. Finally, de Geer accepted copper in payment, which made the transactions much easier for the king.[23]

The above dispute belongs in this discussion because it helps illustrate a fundamental issue under consideration. Earlier we observed the need for merchants to subscribe to the sanctity of formal contracts. The entire trading system relies on full performance of contracts because one interruption in the chain causes chaos. To take a modern example, a boatload of copper sailing from Santiago, Chile, to Shanghai, China, might change hands twenty to thirty times during the course of the voyage. If A sells to B and B sells to C and C sells to D etc., all the way to Y selling to Z then they are all interdependent. If F fails to deliver to G, then G would have to go into the market and purchase substitute copper in order to deliver to H. If the market had risen in the meantime, G could take a loss on the trade. This is the reason that merchants, in any age, normally only do business with companies or individuals with solid reputations for reliability and solvency.

21   LDGBOA, 68-69.
22   LDGBOA, 68-69.
23   LDGBOA, 67,75-76.

Because of market volatility, contracts are especially critical to commodity merchants. At the beginning of the copper chain is a mine or a smelter, and at the end a consumer. 95 percent of the problems with lack of delivery or arbitrary cancellations are with the companies at the beginning or at the end of the chain; this is simply because they are often not bound by the same mentality regarding the sanctity of contracts. The companies at the end of the supply chain are, in most cases, large industrial, smelting, or manufacturing companies that consume copper and other metals to produce finished products. The trading companies, in between, are financial companies with limited assets apart from people, a reputation, and credit lines. The companies at the beginning and the end of the chain occasionally break contracts because they have the power and prestige to weather a temporary embarrassment, and they enjoy a position very much like the king of Sweden. They often even avoid legal consequences because they are simply more important in the supply chain than the middlemen. For example, there are a limited number of companies producing alloys for aircraft engines. If one is a seller of tantalum, which is an essential ingredient in jet engine alloys, one has a limited number of potential customers. Let us say that ABC is an important industrial company producing alloys, and we sold them a large parcel of tantalum for delivery in six months. As the time for delivery comes close, company ABC announces that it no longer needs the shipment and tells us the contract is canceled. Naturally, we have the right to go to court and ask that the contract be enforced. Probably we would prevail if the case were as simple as presented. If we win the case, however, we will most likely never again sell to company ABC.

Yet, why was the king of Sweden able to resume commercial activities so soon after he breached a contract with Louis de Geer's syndicate? Did he enjoy a privileged position in the Netherlands? The answer is yes. The States General needed the Protestant king as an ally against the Habsburgs, and de Geer needed the king as a buyer of weapons and a supplier of copper. This was why the king could walk away from a contract and still do business.

Gustav Adolf was, however, not the first early modern monarch to abandon a contract. The crown of Spain declared bankruptcy in 1557, 1560, 1575, and 1596. Each time the bankruptcy was caused by military expenditure in the Mediterranean area or in the Netherlands. After each bankruptcy, the Spanish crown renegotiated the terms of its loans with its bankers, turning short-term obligations into long-term obligations at a lower interest rate. The crown's bankers agreed to make new loans, because the loans that were repaid were profitable. Only after declaring bankruptcy in 1575, did King Philip II (reigned 1556 to 1598) have difficulty with his

Genoese bankers. They suspended all loans, which resulted in Philip's failure to pay his army in the Netherlands. The foreseeable consequence was the sack of Antwerp in 1576 by Phillip's unpaid troops, which led to the death of 8,000 citizens.[24]

As we have learned, Louis de Geer's copper purchases were closely linked to his sale of arms to the crown. The arms business was complicated and required thorough knowledge of dozens of different suppliers. It also required making capital advances to most of them. It helped de Geer to establish, however, a long-term relationship with both the king and the chancellor. As explained earlier in this chapter, the same day that Gerard, back in Sweden, negotiated the cancellation of the ill-fated copper contract between de Geer's syndicate and the crown, he also negotiated a new weapons contract that looked extremely profitable for de Geer.[25] The new contract was based on "best efforts." The king specified that he wanted to spend RD 80,000 on weapons, and he granted Stefan Gerard full authority in Holland to purchase a list of items at a favorable price. The problem for the king was that the prices were doubtless more favorable to de Geer than to the crown. This sort of open contract, with few safeguards, was ideal for de Geer. Since this new weapons contract was negotiated on the same day that the old copper contract was officially cancelled, we can assume that the two were connected. De Geer accepted the relatively small penalty of RD 4 per skd copper because he obtained the new and probably lucrative arms contract. Yet, these open terms may also reflect a change in the arms market. The Thirty Years War was now well underway and there was doubtless strong demand for arms and ammunition. It was now a seller's market, and the crown could not easily limit de Geer's commission.[26]

De Geer had some difficulty performing on this contract and his problems speak to the local business conditions of his time. Over a year after signing the contract, the king wrote to de Geer asking for delivery information. De Geer replied that he had collected some of the arms that the king ordered, but that it was exceedingly difficult.[27] He had been dealing with a series of small arms manufacturers located in Liège, Cologne, Namur, Aachen, and Solingen, and "other family-owned factories." However, in order to pick up the arms he ordered from the Spanish Netherlands (Liège and Namur), he

24 Safley, Bankruptcy, 1, 20, and Parker, *The Army of Flanders*, 155.
25 LDGBOA, 69-70.
26 LDGBOA, 69-70.
27 LDGBOA, 77.

needed a pass granted by the Spanish *Infante*, resident in Brussels.[28] His agent in Brussels was working on the pass without success.

In addition, he reported that it was late in the season for raising troops and much of the iron used to make armor was now consumed. A shortage of iron plate had developed. The Spanish authorities were now issuing licenses to arms manufacturers to be sure that the armor and weapons being produced were for their use only. De Geer claimed to have made a substantial advance to a manufacturer in Namur as part of an arms contract. The Spanish procurer general learned of the advance, confiscated it, and arrested the manufacturer. Despite the difficulty, de Geer stated that he had made advances totaling RD 40,000 to various arms producers. He already had collected 650 skd of gun powder, 700 cavalry carbines, 350 pairs of pistols, 1,200 muskets, 800 sets of armor for cavalry, 2,000 for infantry, and 4,000 rapiers. These supplies were originally ordered by the king of France, but de Geer had somehow managed to divert them.[29]

This correspondence provides a vivid picture of de Geer's arms business. He first obtained an order from the king. Of course, the king's order was too large for one small workshop, but de Geer had established a network of craftsmen all over northern Europe. If he accepted an order for 4,000 rapiers or 1,000 muskets, for example, he could place orders with perhaps a dozen different sword makers and gunsmiths. In most cases, he gave the workshops an advance, so they could purchase the raw material they required. There were probably a very limited number of merchants capable of organizing such large shipments of arms. The letter also delineated the problems to be overcome. There were still bitter political and religious issues between the Spanish Netherlands and the United Provinces.[30] Such problems naturally spilled over into business. De Geer also had competition. The so-called "Palatine War," the first act of the Thirty Years War, was already in progress and France, under Cardinal Richelieu's direction, was about to embark on its own military adventure in the Italian Alps. The great nations of Europe were arming and there was growing competition for weapons and war supplies.

Now we come to a pivotal area of the king's copper policy, and his efforts to gain complete control over the purchasing and selling of copper. The purchasing monopoly was now in place at the mine; the king only needed a sales

28 He is referring to the *Infante* Archduchess Isabella Clara Eugenia, co-ruler of the Spanish Netherlands together with her consort, Albert of Austria. It is not at all clear, however, why the very Catholic regime in Brussels should grant a pass to a Protestant arms dealer.
29 LDGBOA, 77.
30 LDGBOA, 77.

monopoly to close the circle around the copper business. Earlier I mentioned the king's fascination with the idea of a new Swedish trading company, called the Copper Company, modeled on the Dutch East India Company. He hoped the new company would furnish the sales monopoly he needed.

Is there any reason to doubt the king's good intentions? Roberts follows Heckscher's lead in considering the formation of the company a calculated attempt to gain control over a lucrative asset, with the result, whether intentional or not, of stifling capitalism and free enterprise.[31] Heckscher's first objection to the company was that it grew out of the king's taxing system. As the crown had always received the *avrad* as tax, he believed the company was an extension of the power to tax and hindered the "normal" development of the copper industry.[32] His second objection was related to the first. While Heckscher recognized the contribution that the company made in moving from exporting *råkoppar* to exporting more finished grades, and to the development of the domestic refining industry, he calls the company a "disguise" for the crown's own copper-trading activities. In other words, the company was never independent; it remained under the control of the crown. In addition, the crown was guilty of exaggerating or even falsifying financial results to further its own ends.[33] Finally, in Heckscher's view, the main beneficiaries were foreigners. Louis de Geer owned twice as many shares as the Swedish native with the largest investment (the chancellor). Anthony Monier, a Walloon, and Peter Kruse, a native of Lübeck, were also both large investors. In fairness, this is more of an aside than an objection; without the foreign money, the improvements in the infrastructure at the mine would have taken much longer.[34] Heckscher's most serious objection, however, was the company's monopoly power over the export of copper: "The main question is whether the Swedish position could stimulate a higher copper price, or whether the monopoly, to the contrary, contributed to a price decline ..."[35] Heckscher leaves little doubt how he would answer this rhetorical question.

Clearly these objections should be considered, but perhaps the king's goal was not to create a free market for copper trading. He was more interested in turning the copper into revenue to further his political and military goals. I hope to show that the company had every possibility of success

31   Roberts, *Gustavus Adolphus*, 2, 94.
32   Heckscher, *historia*, 1:2, 283–84.
33   Heckscher, *historia*, 1:2, 451.
34   Heckscher, *historia*, 1:2, 373.
35   Heckscher, *historia*, 1:2, 451.

because its cost of goods remained considerably lower than the sales prices, even after the market began to decline in 1626. This point is demonstrated by the Copper Company's balance sheets that survive in the Riksarkiv in Stockholm.[36]

In 1619, when the king issued the first company charter, he would have been aware of the Dutch East India Company (founded in 1602 and known as the VOC). The VOC was sponsored by Johan van Oldenbarnevelt, whom we met earlier. In the later years of the sixteenth century Dutch merchants began actively trading in the East Indies. As the number of companies grew, Oldenbarnevelt and others, realized that the intense competition was preventing the companies from making a profit. He engineered a merger of the many companies into a single firm. It was not an independent enterprise, but rather it combined private interests with state interests. The VOC sold shares to the public and these shares were traded in the marketplace like copper or timber. In addition, the States General issued a charter to the company guaranteeing monopoly rights to trade in the East Indies. But the charter also granted the VOC the privilege of raising and funding an army and navy to protect Dutch interests in the Far East. After some early problems with corruption, the VOC proved to be highly profitable in the years that followed.[37]

Gustav Adolf's vision of the Copper Company's future was rather modest compared to the large and prosperous VOC. Gustav Adolf concentrated on marketing copper ingot and related commodities mainly in continental Europe. The Copper Company did, however, share one important characteristic with the VOC: it was neither exclusively a public joint stock company, nor a state-owned enterprise, but a combination of both. As such it promoted the state's interests as well as those of the individual investors.

The king's domestic goal for the Copper Company was to raise money through the sale of shares to improve the infrastructure of the Swedish copper industry. He wanted to develop refining capacity in Sweden. Hitherto, Sweden exported mainly raw copper or *råkoppar*, which required substantial refining before it was suitable for producing finished goods. Sweden's capacity to produce refined copper (*gårkoppar*) was limited.

Naturally, the ability to finance the government and the military was behind every economic decision the crown made. As mentioned in the last chapter, in 1611, the year Gustav Adolf ascended the throne, Sweden produced 5,665 skd, mine weight of copper. By 1618 it had produced 10,860

---

36   Riksarkivet. Leufsta arkiv, file 81, Cooper Platen Debit Anno 1626, Amsterdam. # 22.

37   Soll, *Free Market,* pp. 96–97.

skd, mine weight, a more than 90 percent increase.[38] In both 1623 and 1624 Sweden produced and exported over 10,000 skd of copper into continental Europe. The king, the chancellor, and all the members of the political and financial elite in Sweden realized that funding the crown's military and political ambitions would depend on high volumes of copper exports to the continent. The Copper Company was to be the vehicle for sales in northern Europe and for expanding refining capacity in Sweden.

What effect, however, did the increase in copper shipments have on the economy of continental Europe? There was a period of serious inflation in the Holy Roman Empire between 1619 and 1623 called the *"Kipper und Wipperzeit."*[39] The Thirty Years War had begun, and the various states and city-states of the empire were preparing for wartime expenditures. One of their steps was to devalue their local currency to gain a short-term advantage at the expense of their neighboring states and city-states. The debasement was accomplished by adding copper to silver coins without changing the face value. The strategy was then to export devalued currency at face value and import fully valued currency. Predictably, the neighboring states and city states retaliated by also devaluing their own currency either by changing the metal content or "clipping" the coins. The problem soon escalated into a race to the bottom and commerce slowed because sellers would not take coins whose value they could not trust. The result was inflation followed by economic stagnation. It is impossible to draw a direct connection between the increase in copper exports from Sweden to the continent and inflation in the empire. Some authors on the subject, however, have suggested that the increase in Swedish copper exports during the era of the Älvsborg ransom, and the period immediately after, contributed to the problem of inflation by adding to the supply of money that circulated.[40] I am skeptical because there does not appear to be evidence that pure copper coins were a factor in Germany between 1619 and 1623. If copper currency was already present in quantity, the Swedish introduction of copper coins to northern Germany later in the decade would not have met with such consternation.

Returning to the Copper Company, the king's introduction to the charter of 1619, survives in the Riksarkiv Stockholm. The document was called "An open letter on the Trading Company, July 24, 1619."[41] The king began by

38 Lindroth, Gruvbrytning, 2, ,389.
39 The meaning of the term is uncertain. Perhaps Kipper is related to "clipping" as in clipping of coins to remove metal. See Kindleberger, *The Economic Crisis* 150.
40 Paas, *The Kipper und Wipper*, 4.
41 Stiernman, *Samling*, 4, 708–10.

explaining that the balance of trade in Sweden was working against the interests of both the common people and the merchant classes. The country was importing more foreign goods every year, and the cost of those goods was increasing. The result was: "that all subjects, regardless of their class, have great difficulty obtaining the normal basics of life."[42] To increase the value of the copper produced at the mine the company would build facilities, on land donated by the crown, to expand refining capacity for copper, and to make finished wares from the copper, mainly for export. In fact, the king said the company would export only *gårkoppar* (refined copper). This was overly optimistic because at the time Sweden had refining capacity for only a tiny fraction of its output of copper. For the purpose of expanding this capacity, the crown had pledged that it would make a major contribution of capital to the company. At the same time, the crown asked that all subjects, regardless of class, buy shares; every subject whether nobleman, priest, merchant, or peasant had the right and freedom to contribute to the company's capital by purchasing shares.[43] Shares of the company were to be sold until the end of January 1620, and the minimum investment was SD 100. Once pledged, however, the capital was committed for three years. The king promised that the company would pay an annual dividend of 8 percent to all shareholders.

An early Swedish antiquarian, Anton von Stiernman, published the charter and many related documents in 1747. The company was to be headed by a governor, chosen from the nobility, and seven directors to be chosen from the burgher class. The king expected the shareholders to nominate candidates for the jobs of governor and directors, but he retained the right to screen candidates and to make the actual appointments. This and other provisions proved that the king was not willing to grant the company commercial autonomy.[44]

In the approximately five months between writing the "open letter" about the company and issuing the charter, the king realized that the company would not be exporting *gårkoppar* (refined copper) exclusively because of the small production rate. During this time, a Dutch metallurgist named Govert Silenz came to Sweden, at the king's behest, and developed a method for refining copper that was suitable for conditions in Sweden. The processing took place at the Queen Mother's mint in the town of Säter.[45] The procedure was expensive and could take as long as six months, but the

42 Stiernman, *Samling*, 4, 708–10.
43 Riksarkivet, Handel och Sjöfart arkiv, file 46 # 25.
44 Stiernman, *Samling*, 4, 718–20.
45 Riksarkivet. Kontractsböcker, special series (1613) 1620–22 (1624) # 18. See also Roberts, *Gustavus Adolphus*, 2, 91.

king understood the advantage of adding value to a commodity like copper, and he encouraged refining capacity expansion. Govert Silenz become an employee of the company; for compensation the king had agreed to sell him 100 skd of copper at SD 38 per skd, well below the value at that time. His specific job was to increase the production of refined copper.[46]

One thing is clear from the above, Gustav Adolf and Oxenstierna were willing to expand the infrastructure to increase the production of *gårkoppar* and Hungarian plate. Certainly, this was in recognition of the financial advantages, and the efficacy of creating as much value added on Swedish soil as possible. It also signaled concern to build the domestic economy and improve technology at the mine. Although we do not have employment figures, an industrial facility like Säter must have employed a hierarchy of skilled laborers from charcoal burners to master minters.

In that regard, it is difficult to judge the relative value of *råkoppar* to *gårkoppar* in 1619 because we have no price comparisons. De Geer wrote a letter in 1624, however, responding to an inquiry from the king regarding the sales price differential between the two. De Geer estimated that there was a RD 10 to RD 12 difference between the price of *råkoppar* and *gårkoppar* in Lübeck, Hamburg, and Amsterdam. He projected that if the company were to expand its facility in Sweden to do the extra refining, the cost would be recovered in two to three years. According to de Geer, the 1624 market for *råkoppar* in Amsterdam was RD 60 per skd, and the price for *gårkoppar* was between RD 70 and RD 72 per skd.[47]

The king proposed that the company immediately embark on a building program to produce refined copper for the European market. Moving Sweden from a producer and exporter of raw copper to a major producer of refined copper was one of the enduring successes of Gustav Adolf's reign. Unfortunately, no one was collecting statistics on what percentage of the copper produced at Falun was being refined. Minting copper currency, however, requires refined plate. By 1628, the company's final year, the mine produced 11,696 skd of *råkoppar*. That same year the crown turned 7,486 skd of copper into coins; meaning that this amount, at least, was refined. Thus, in nine years the kingdom had progressed from refining virtually no copper to refining at least 65 percent of the copper produced.[48]

Returning to the charter, the king's original plan was to establish a contemporary joint-stock company based on the Dutch and English models, but

---

46 Roberts, *Gustavus Adolphus*, 2, 91.
47 LDGBOA, 76.
48 See Lindroth, *Gruvbrytning*, 2, 389 and Wolontis, *Kopparmyntningen*, 252.

some traditional dynastic issues got in the way. The king was emphatic that the charter should grant the company the exclusive right to purchase copper from the Stora Kopparberg, and to market the copper both in Sweden and abroad. It should not come as a surprise, however, that the Queen Mother and Karl Felip were both given exemptions from the monopoly, demonstrating the Queen Mother's continued influence. In fact, both were allowed to continue buying limited copper quantities directly from the *bergsmän*.[49]

Perhaps the most important part of the charter was the section concerning the relationship between the company and the *bergsmän*. The company was to pay the *bergsmän* SD 50 per skd mine weight at the mine site. The payments were to be made in "ready cash"; for this purpose, the company was directed to keep a cash box on hand. Roberts maintained that the *bergsmän* complained bitterly about this price because the market was rising gradually, and they did not want to be tied to a fixed price. In support, he cites Dahlgren's biography of de Geer, but the citation concerned the king's purchase of copper for the Älvsborg ransom in 1615, not the company's activities. There is one immutable rule of mining; absent coercion, if miners cannot make a profit, they stop mining. If the *bergsmän* could not make a profit on the copper they sold to the company, they would stop selling. They would either resort to smuggling via unauthorized channels, or they would simply stop producing. Considering that production almost doubled at the Stora Kopparberg during the life of the company (1619 to 1628), it would be safe to assume that the *bergsmän* were able to make an adequate profit based on the SD 50 per skd (RD 27.7 per skd Stockholm weight) the company was paying them.[50]

The company's agent at the mine was to pay the *bergsmän* immediately, in cash, after the copper was weighed at the scales. Since the tax collector was also present, he recorded the transaction in the "weight book each day of the month for accurate accounting"; this insured that the king's *avrad* would be recorded for future payment.[51]

The charter also included a noteworthy section indicating the king's awareness of the vital role played by the local merchants in financing the mining operations at the Kopparberg. The king wrote that the company's agent should have cash available to make advances to the *bergsmän* for raw materials and other necessities. The company could also advance "goods," presumably meaning wood or other raw materials, needed to smelt the

49 Stiernman, *Samling*, 4, 923.
50 Production in 1619 was 6,294 skd and 11,696 skd in 1628. Lindroth, *Gruvbrytning*, 2, 389.
51 Stiernman, *Samling*, 4, 727.

copper ore. This would allow the company to take the place of the local merchants by helping the *bergsmän* finance those items needed for production. Unfortunately, the company's agents seldom had cash available, so payment was erratic at best, and the king's promise of cash, goods, or advances was nothing but a royal pipe dream. After paying the *bergsmän* SD 50 per skd (RD 27.7 per skd Stockholm weight), the company also had to pay the king a toll of SD 22 per skd (RD 13 per skd Stockholm weight), which came due on the Feast Day of St. John the Baptist (June 24) and the Feast Day of St. Martin (November 11).[52]

The final procedural issue was the quality control system the king dictated for the company. The king wanted to guarantee that the company's customers received high quality copper consistently. We saw in chapter one that each *bergsmän* was required to stamp his mark on each ingot of copper he presented to be weighed. This requirement was part of the privileges issued by Karl IX, the king's father, early in the century. The king repeated this requirement and instructed the company not to accept any copper that did not bear an individual mark. He also added a full sampling and analysis procedure. The company was to provide a sampling master (*Probere Mestare*) at the Falun scales who was to take samples "on both sides" of each ingot and do a chemical analysis of the samples to determine the quality of the copper. He would then declare "whether the copper was good or bad." The company was forbidden to purchase any copper not fully tested. After testing, the company's clerks were free to ship the copper "by the cheapest means" directly to the Stockholm scales where the toll collectors would make the appropriate entries into the Stockholm weight book.[53]

In addition, the company was forbidden to trade with peasants or small merchants in northern towns or in Norway. This was probably to prevent smuggling. In fact, the king remained worried about smuggling, probably with justification, because of the relatively low price the company was paying to the *bergsmän*. He would have been aware that the *bergsmän* could sell at a more favorable price to merchants from the nearby ports of Gävle and Hudiksvall, who were notorious for buying and exporting illegal copper. In a letter to Filip Scheiding, the new company governor (also the new governor of Dalarna after Carl Bonde), the king admonished him to be vigilant in preventing the *bergsmän* from selling copper to local merchants and thus escaping the king's SD 22 per skd tax.[54]

52   Stiernman, *Samling*, 4, 727–28.
53   Stiernman, *Samling*, 4, 728.
54   Riksarkivet, SE/RA/1112.1/B/144 (1623), # 10–13.

Finally, the king instructed the company directors to prepare a yearly "Extract of Balances" (balance sheets for the governor and the shareholders). These financial statements should be "correct and accurate," and be ready each December. We will examine two of these balance sheets to understand the internal costs the company faced. When the "Extracts" were available, there would be a meeting in Stockholm of sixteen people chosen by the stockholders and the governor of Uppland province (a historic province just north of Stockholm), the mayor of Stockholm, the city council, and the king. All the attendees would have full authority to examine the financial results.[55]

This was the framework for the Copper Company. The king's goals show through clearly. He wanted control over both the purchasing and the sale of copper. Establishing a fixed price with the *bergsmän* was an important strategy because it gave the company the ability to control its cost of goods and almost guaranteed a profit. The charter benefitted the *bergsmän* by removing the market risk. They were guaranteed a fixed price regardless of the current sales price. Of course, this advantage would be appreciated more by the *bergsmän* when the market was falling rather than climbing. The *bergsmän* would also have been more content if the company had paid them, as stipulated, in cash when the copper was weighed, instead of months later. Perhaps the most notable elements of the charter were those sections aimed at upgrading the quality of the product. The crown was obviously determined to bring refining capacity to Sweden and to export fully refined copper. It would take some time, but by the end of the decade most of the copper exported was refined copper.[56]

Because of the novelty of the enterprise, the Copper Company attracted considerable attention. As mentioned above, Filip Scheiding, a member of the *Riks-Råd*, was the first governor and the new directors included the chancellor, the treasurer, Jesper Kruse, and Johan Skytte. The king also appointed well-known businessmen, such as Peter Kruse, Anthony Monier, the quartermaster general, and Mårtin Wewitzer, a wealthy merchant and the leading tax-farmer, to the board. Before the end of 1620, the company had attracted SD 70,000 (RD 43,000) in capital; by the end of 1624, the company had SD 184,000 (RD 113,000) in capital and 56 shareholders. The company's capital peaked in 1626 with a total of SD 312,000 (RD192,000) and 84 shareholders.[57]

To raise capital, the king first appealed to friends and relatives. As mentioned, he committed the company to paying 8 percent yearly dividends to

55 Stiernman, *Samling*, 4, 730.
56 Lindroth, *Gruvbrytning*, 2, 389
57 Wittrock, *Handelskompaniet*, 25.

all shareholders. Of course, all the directors invested in the company. For example, Johan Skytte invested SD 10,084, Mårtin Wewitzer put in SD 22,700, and Anthony Monier committed SD 38,696;[58] the chancellor invested SD 14,022 (later much more). The king never invested more than SD 13,000, but other members of the royal family were also contributors. These included the Queen Mother, and her sister, Lady Agnes of Holstein. Most investors contributed SD 4,000 or less, and the list included institutions, such as the Hospital for the Poor in Danviken, which invested SD 3,969.[59] In addition, Louis de Geer and Erik Larsson, successful merchants, were also major investors. The fact that the company attracted investments from the most successful merchants and businessmen of the day, from Sweden and from abroad, indicates that the venture was taken seriously.[60] Such people would not have invested if, as Roberts suggested: "From the beginning, indeed, it was clear that the company had been called into existence, and continued to exist, for the benefit not of the shareholders but of the crown."[61]

By all accounts, the Swedish Trading Company did reasonably well during the first few years. This was partly the result of the upward price trend that had persisted during most of the century. Heckscher attributed this to the increasing consumption of copper by the Spanish mint. In fact, Heckscher stated that, "by Gustav Adolf's time, Spain was the most important end-market for Swedish copper." This trend continued into 1626.[62]

As indicated, the rising market helped profits. The company was buying copper at a fixed price of SD 50 per skd (RD 27.7 per skd Stockholm weight) and reselling it. If the company held the copper in inventory for a month, or a year, before finding a customer, it would make an additional profit on the copper because the prices were increasing faster than the cost of financing. In addition, the Copper Company had a built-in hedge because of the relatively low fixed purchase price. It would be helpful, however, to have some hard evidence of the company's early success. The fact that the astute Queen Mother and other investors were willing to increase their holdings meant that the news must have been generally good. In addition, we have some numbers for 1621. A balance sheet or "Extract" has not survived from the early years. What has survived, however, was a record of shipments from the Stora Kopparberg to Stockholm during 1621. That year the Copper

---

58   Van Dillen, "Amsterdamsche Notarieele," 29–30.
59   Van Dillen, "Amsterdamsche Notarieele," 29–30.
60   Wittrock, *Handelskompaniet*, 25.
61   Roberts, *Gustavus Adolphus*, II, 93–94.
62   Heckscher, *historia*, 1.2, 450–52 and LDGBOA, 76.

Company bought 2,827 skd, which it shipped to Stockholm at a cost of SD 5,002, equal to SD 1.75 per skd. Yet, why did the company purchase and ship only 2,827skd mine weight in 1621 when the Stora Kopparberg produced over 8,000 skd that year? The answer was simple; the company was too thinly financed that year to purchase and ship more than 2,827 skd.[63] As mentioned earlier, the company had raised only SD 70,000 by the end of 1620. The cost of 2,827 skd at SD 50 per skd mine weight was SD 141,350. That meant the company bought and sold copper with a cost equal to its equity twice that year.

We do not have solid figures for the early years of the company, but by most accounts, it was profitable through 1625.[64] Everybody was happy with the prospects of the company except the *bergsmän*. Despite the clause in the company's charter specifying that the *bergsmän* should be paid at the scales with "ready money," they soon realized that the company had adopted the same irresponsible payment habits from the crown. In 1621, a year in which the company was solvent, the *bergsmän* of the Stora Kopparberg wrote the chancellor to complain that they were not receiving payment for the copper they delivered: "Your loyal servants, noble and well born Lord Chancellor, are in great need and distress for lack of payment at the mine."[65] This was an unfortunate example of the company taking advantage of the most vulnerable segment of the supply chain. The wealthy merchants and the larger shareholders in the company had access to the king and the chancellor. At least in these years, their dividends were paid regularly. The *bergsmän* were the least well connected so they were paid last. This was particularly short sighted because the company rested on the shoulders of the *bergsmän*, who if sufficiently antagonized, could turn to smuggling, or simply stop producing.[66]

There were other early problems as well. In 1621 a truce with Poland expired, and Gustav Adolf renewed the dynastic war with his cousin, King Sigismund. Gustav Adolf cloaked his intentions under the banner of a Protestant alliance, although his Protestant allies thought his efforts would have been of more value elsewhere. The king began the campaign with the siege of Riga, which he captured in September 1621. From there he began the conquest of Livonia. This is yet another example of Gustav Adolf's acute discomfort over his Catholic cousin's intentions. The fact that

63   Riksarkivet, Handel och Sjöfart arkiv, file 46 # 25.
64   Riksarkivet, Handel och Sjöfart arkiv, file 46 # 25.
65   AOSB, II, 11, 363–65.
66   Kristiansson, *Falu*, 59.

the action was unprovoked makes one wonder if he was, perhaps, overly anxious about the Polish threat. The immediate result of this military action was an acute need for additional arms and munitions.[67]

It was about this time that the Sweden-based German trader, Peter Kruse, began a regular correspondence with the chancellor. He and Eric Larsson van der Linden, a Swedish merchant of Dutch descent, were in Germany, representing the company for sales of copper. They were both on good terms with the king. In fact, to third parties the king referred to the pair as "Peter and Eric."[68] The king was now at war, and he tended to rely on the chancellor to keep up with his normal correspondence. The king did, however, write a memo to "Peter and Eric" in March 1622, which he relayed through the chancellor. The memorandum instructed "Peter and Eric" to purchase a long list of weapons and munitions in Amsterdam for the war in Livonia, and he wanted the Copper Company to foot the bill.[69]

The king opened the letter by informing the pair that the Swedish Copper Company had now raised sufficient funds and was prepared to offer the crown a loan of SD 100,000 for arms purchasing. Since the king appointed the governor and had a veto over the appointment of the directors of the company, there was no counterbalance to his influence. One can imagine the discomfort of both Kruse and Larsson at the news that the king had voted himself a loan of SD 100,000, since both had invested heavily in the company. The king told them that he expected to have the money the following month. In the meantime, he was sending 250 skd of copper to the continent. This, however, was not going to cover the full cost of the required munitions, so the king requested that Kruse and Larsson leverage the company name locally for additional credit and make personal advances to complete the purchases. He also suggested that Kruse and Larsson contact Louis de Geer to help them assemble the weapons.[70]

Kruse replied to the chancellor on April 5 from Lübeck saying he had been in contact with de Geer and had traveled to Hamburg and Nuremberg where all the munitions were lined up and ready to ship if the king would only send the required payments. Kruse had tried to get an advance on the company's credit, without success: "It's a sad thing, but the people here know that the king has already borrowed money from the company; now they put their heads together and refuse any credit to the company for our

---

67   Roberts, *Gustavus Adolphus*, 1, 203.
68   AOSB, II, 11, 198.
69   AOSB, II, 11, 198.
70   AOSB, II, 11, 197–02.

purchases."[71] Such a result was inevitable. Once the merchants in Germany and the United Provinces realized that the king was taking money out of the company it decreased the possibility that the company would have the reserves to repay any credit granted.

This was the beginning of the end for the company. It was fewer than three years old and would continue to earn a profit for a couple more years, but it could not withstand the drain of capital that began with the first loan of SD 100,000 in 1622. Naturally, the king never repaid the loan, but borrowed even more. The king also asked for and received a loan of SD 16,000 in September 1622 from the company to pay for mercenary troops in Livonia.[72] Again, in 1624, the king requested an advance of SD 30,000 to cover expenses in Hamburg. The company complied. This time the king did repay the loan. Instead of paying cash, however, he resorted to a repayment plan that was all but extinct in other European countries; he turned over a revenue stream of feudal dues from the town of Brunnbäck in Dalarna to the company for a year.[73] Unfortunately, he was repeating the pattern we witnessed in the last chapter. He had a creative idea, the Copper Company, with a real chance for success. He nurtured it, providing it with shareholders and a profitable monopoly, but then he got involved in a war with his traditional enemy, Sigismund III, and he proceeded to drain the assets of the company. By so doing, however, he began the slow process of destroying the very tool that could have enabled him to develop the copper trade into an enterprise that could have funded more ambitious campaigns in the future. I would argue that it was an innovative experiment with every chance of success; if only the king had allowed it to prosper and grow.[74]

We began this section by asking whether the king would avoid draining money from the company. Unfortunately for the company, the answer is obvious. The king could not refrain from expensive military campaigns against Poland. During the period of the Älvsborg ransom, he had borrowed from the States General to finance the ransom. He then devised a clever strategy of gradually monopolizing the purchasing of copper so he could direct shipments to Amsterdam to pay the interest on the loans. In the meantime, however, he was drawn into a series of wars that strained the

---

71   Riksarkivet. Kontraktsböcker, huvudserie 1622. Contract between Gustav Adolf and the Copper Company. 11 September 1622.

72   Riksarkivet. Kontraktsböcker, huvudserie 1622. Contract between Gustav Adolf and the Copper Company. 11 September 1622.

73   Wittrock, *Handelkompaniet*, 37.

74   Riksarkivet. Kontraktsböcker, huvudserie 1622. Contract between Gustav Adolf and the Copper Company. 11 September 1622.

royal treasury, and the copper was directed to pay for weapons and troops instead of repaying the loans from the States General.[75] In the case of the company, his goal was to bring industry to Sweden so that the kingdom could face an uncertain future in Europe with sufficient resources. Yet, just as the company was showing promise, he renewed his endless war with Poland and commenced to drain assets from the company to fund his armies.

The copper currency was even more controversial. I observed earlier that the Stora Kopparberg was to Gustav Adolf the equivalent of the Peruvian Potosi silver mines to the king of Spain. It was his most important source of revenue.[76] The problem for the king of Sweden, however, was that he could not spend copper ingots as easily as the king of Spain could spend silver coins.[77] We have already established that the king used copper as currency, but there were two major difficulties. First, most transactions were negotiated in silver-based currency, such as *riksdalers*. If the king paid a *riksdaler* debt with copper, he would have to send enough copper to compensate for the fluctuations in value between silver and copper. So, he would invariably overpay. The second major difficulty was that he could not make payments in small denominations. It would not be possible to pay a company of soldiers their monthly wages, for example, by sending copper ingots to the front. Of course, if the king could have sent copper to financial and trading centers, like Lübeck and Amsterdam, and received back silver currency quickly, then minting copper would probably not have been necessary. As we have seen, however, the process of exchanging copper into currency was awkward and time consuming.

The traditional explanation for the copper currency, originally expressed by Heckscher and Wolontis, and later echoed by Roberts, was that Gustav Adolf wanted to mint copper to "absorb" excess copper production. This theory holds that if the crown turned copper ingots into coins, there would be fewer ingots to sell and, therefore, the price of the ingot would increase.[78] This view, however, does not survive scrutiny. The king intended to use copper to pay troops in Livonia and Prussia. That was the main reason he minted small denomination coins from copper. In fact, the crown's policy was to continue increasing copper production at the mine and to turn that production into currency. Minting copper coins did not actually absorb

---

75   Riksarkivet, Handel och Sjöfart arkiv, file 46 # 25.
76   We also observed earlier that the analogy does not survive a comparison of the local labor force.
77   Stryker, *The King's Currency*, 53.
78   Wolontis, *Kopparmyntning*, 52, Heckscher *Economic History*, 89, and Roberts, *Gustavus Adolphus*, 2, 95.

excess copper; but it did turn copper into small denominational coins quickly and efficiently, allowing the king to pay his troops without resorting to time-consuming bills of exchange back and forth to Amsterdam.

The king issued a new company charter in 1625.[79] The new charter increased the toll that the company paid to the crown from SD 22 to SD 60 per skd (that is from RD 13.5 to RD 37 per skd), meaning that the king was now being paid significantly more than the *bergsmän* for each skd of copper sold. Of course, this simply directed revenue away from the shareholders to the crown. The clause that rendered this charter most awkward, moreover, was the minimum price. The king decided that no copper should be sold below SD 150 per skd Stockholm weight (RD 92.3 per skd), and he instructed the company not to sell any form of copper below that price. Any copper that the company failed to sell would be transferred to the mint at that price.[80] The floor price mentioned was not arbitrary. The king wanted to set the copper-to-silver ratio at one *skeppund* copper to SD 150 silver mint. Therefore, he wanted all copper that could not be sold at an equivalent price to be delivered to the mint. What effect would such a high price have on the Copper Company? The floor price of SD 150 per skd was equivalent to RD 92.3 per skd. If we add the cost of transport from Stockholm to Amsterdam, the price was RD 97.3 per skd. This was a totally unrealistic price. Posthumus reported that refined copper was sold in Amsterdam during July 1625 for RD 74 per skd Stockholm weight.[81] Whether the king was aware of this or not, he condemned the company to either sell below the floor price, or to dump the entire yearly production onto the mint at an artificial price. This would, in turn, distort the mint's financial picture.[82] At the same time, the king also set up elaborate rules for the sale of his *avrad* copper. If the *Räntekammar* (the treasury) decided to sell the *avrad* copper, it had to achieve SD 150 per skd or more. If the king gave permission for the *avrad* copper to be forged or made ready for the mint, thereby increasing its quality, then he had an option to sell it to the company for SD 126 per skd. Alternatively, if the works at Säter made the copper into "Hungarian plate," which was a form that could immediately be fabricated with no further work, he had the option to sell the Hungarian plate to the company for a premium of SD 50, or a total of SD 176 per skd.[83] Based on the above, it was obvious that the

79 Wolontis, *Kopparmyntning*, 50–53.
80 Stiernman, *Samling*, 4, 924.
81 Posthumus, *Prices*, 371.
82 Stiernman, *Samling*, 4, 925.
83 Stiernman, *Samling*, 4, 925.

king favored production of Hungarian plate, and he included the following statement: "The company has the duty to produce as much Hungarian plate as possible and not to produce pre-mint copper or regular crude plate and never to export the *råkoppar* with small value."[84] The king had a laudable goal in this exhortation. He wanted to expand production capacity at Säter to upgrade the copper products being exported from Sweden at considerably greater value than raw copper. During 1625, prices for Hungarian plate reached between RD 91 to 93 per skd in Lübeck and Hamburg; later in the spring the prices reached RD 96 per skd.[85] The average reported price from Amsterdam that year for regular *gårkoppar* was DG 67.27 per hundredweight or RD 74 per skd Stockholm weight. This meant that *råkoppar* would have sold for only about RD 62 to RD 65 per skd.[86] The king was obviously intent on raising the value of exports.

Unfortunately for the king's goal of minting on a large-scale, the Säter facility was the only mint in Sweden and in the spring of 1625 a major flood destroyed it. The Queen Mother, who owned the mint, helped the king finance a new mint in Nyköping, further to the south.[87] Of course this caused long delays in implementing the crown's ambitious minting policy. Peter Kruse, meanwhile, was sent as a representative of the Copper Company, to remain at Säter and oversee the reconstruction of the mint. A year later he could report some positive developments to the chancellor. First, as part of the Charter of 1626, the company took over the management of Säter. Gobert Silentz was given a bonus of 104 skd of *råkoppar* but made to step aside as the primary manager; he would remain in the capacity of mint master. Writing from Säter, Peter Kruse thought the new arrangement would be an improvement, not least because it gave him clear authority over Silenz. In addition, he reported substantial progress in rebuilding the facility. He was able to salvage much of the old equipment and they were rebuilding the areas that had been destroyed. He had complaints as well. The lack of money was holding back progress. The plant required large quantities of charcoal, and he expected to run out by the summer.[88]

Despite the company's lack of liquidity, the expansion of refining capacity continued to be one of the crown's greatest achievements. The following summer, Kruse reported from Säter to the chancellor with good news: "The

---

84   Stiernman, *Samling*, 4, 925.
85   Wittrock, *Handelkompaniet,*62.
86   Posthumus, *Prices*, 371.
87   The Queen Mother died in Nyköping Castle in early December 1625.
88   ASOB, II, 11, 210.

Kopparberg mine, God be thanked, is producing the prettiest ore that we have seen for a long time, and much better than the ore we received last year …"[89] In addition to receiving favorable ore, Kruse reported that they had installed four new furnaces for refining *råkoppar*. He now claimed to have refining capacity of between 60 and 80 *skeppund* per day, which was three to four times the capacity he was able to muster shortly after the flood. He also stated that capacity to produce Hungarian plate was now at 50 skd per day. These figures must be seasonal. If annualized, Säter would have refining capacity far in excess of the Kopparberg's yearly output. However, it is an indication of real progress in the drive toward greater refining capacity.[90]

Kruse also gave the chancellor a report on the state of the mint at Säter. Minting copper began there in 1624 on an experimental basis and got underway in 1625. The early results were rather primitive. The mint would simply take sheets of pure copper and cut off pieces of approximately equal size, called *klippingar*. There were no markings or denominations. In 1626 the crown hired a professional mint master from Germany, Markus Koch, who came to Säter with a crew of colleagues. Sweden could, thereafter, mint copper into proper coins. In fact, Kruse wrote that according to Koch, the Säter mint was already far ahead of the new crown mint in Nyköping. The plan was that Koch and his crew would oversee the production of *klippingar* first, and, at the same time, gradually start producing round coins. Kruse believed that the copper mint would gain more widespread acceptance in the coin form rather than as *klippingar*.[91]

It is important to remember that copper currency, whether *klippingar* or coin, could not be made from *råkoppar*; only *gårkoppar* or plate would do. In 1625 the crown minted 595 skd, and the company 1622, skd. In 1626 the crown and the company together minted a total of 7,255 skd or almost 64 percent of the Stora Kopparberg output. This means that by 1626, despite the destruction of the Säter work in the previous year, at least 64 percent of the copper produced by the mine was being fully refined in Sweden. This was a major accomplishment when one considers that only five years earlier almost no copper was being fully refined in Sweden.[92]

Some of the king's contemporaries had reservations about the currency, especially over the issue of value. In 1626 Jakob de la Gardie wrote three times during May and June from the Russian front on the subject. The

89   AOSB, II, 11, 213.
90   AOSB, II, 11, 213
91   AOSB, II, 11, 213–14.
92   Wolontis, *Kopparmyntning*, 249.

first time he said his foreign mercenary troops were most unhappy when he attempted to pay them with copper coins. They understood that the coins were not accepted abroad; and even in the towns of Latvia they were charged double if they paid in copper. A few days later, de la Gardie again wrote to the chancellor telling him that he had "humbly" sent the king a letter asking that he send money, which was overdue, to pay the soldiers, who were a little restless. Most importantly, he asked the king not to send copper currency because "foreign troops will take the copper, but then leave the king's service." Finally, in June, de la Gardie wrote that the German infantry and cavalry had flatly refused copper currency and were demanding customary payment in silver.[93]

While the new currency was not well accepted in the beginning, it did survive for the next 150 years as an essential part of Swedish monetary policy. One must conclude, therefore, that it did, eventually, achieve grudging acceptance, at least in Sweden proper. The issue the critics missed, however, was the connection between the copper currency and the growth of the metallurgical industry in Sweden. The fact that currency cannot be made from *råkoppar* meant Gustav Adolf had to expand the refining capacity in Sweden. As explained, he began by attracting experts from Northern Europe and investing heavily in the refining works at Säter and Nyköping. Once Sweden could produce *gårkoppar* in quantity, it could also produce bronze. Within a few years, Sweden was regularly exporting copper products such as bronze cannon, copper wire, and copper kettles.[94]

Returning now to Amsterdam, copper prices (see figure 1 in the introduction), which had climbed steadily during the first two decades of the century, peaked in 1625. Then, when the Spanish mint left the copper market during 1625, prices began a downward trend that was to persist until 1632. Between 1632 and 1634, prices climbed once again but never regained the heights of 1625. After 1634 copper prices in Amsterdam returned to 1630 levels and remained in a narrow trading range until mid-century. We would expect the sharp price drop after 1625 to be reflected in lower production figures. Normally, such a price decrease signals a decline in demand, which should be reflected in lower production rates at the mine.[95] Why continue to increase production in the face of declining demand?

Markets are peculiar entities. The gradual realization in Amsterdam and Stockholm that the Spanish had left the market would have made

---

93   AOSB, II, 5, 399–405.
94   Boëthius and Heckscher, *Svensk Handelsstatistik*, 632–36..
95   Wolontis, *Kopparmyntning*, 22–23.

traders and consumers turn cautious, and this would change the character of the market. Markets almost never move in a straight line. We know that during the first twenty-five years of the seventeenth century, the copper market was trending upward because of growing copper consumption by the Spanish mint and the increase in production of bronze cannon. There would have been plateaus when the price did not move because of a dearth of transactions, and there would have been small declines in price when local inventories were temporarily greater than local demand. In a bull market, traders in Hamburg, Lübeck, and Amsterdam would take advantage of the dips in price to buy. The overwhelming mentality would be that any copper purchased today would be cheaper than copper purchased next month. This same mentality would apply to consumers of copper. If a copper fabricator in Aachen was competing for a large order of copper vessels for the brewing industry, he would use the current price of copper as a guide and quote accordingly. If he got the order, he would immediately buy the copper he needed from a local merchant. Likewise, the brewer, realizing that he would need new brewing vessels next year, would buy now to avoid higher prices next year.

The second major implication of the bullish mentality is inventory building, which takes place all along the supply chain. An exporter in Stockholm, for example, would buy more than he needed from the mine to fulfill current orders, so he was certain to have sufficient supplies for the future. He could take advantage of the rising prices by buying now and selling later at a higher price. Traders in European ports would do the same. They would have bought more copper from their suppliers in Stockholm than they needed for orders, thus maintaining inventory. The fabricators in Aachen would also have inventory. If they had orders for copper vessels requiring one *skeppund* of copper they would buy one and one-half *skeppund* from their suppliers in Amsterdam. In a long-term bull market, the only limitation was interest rates. The cost of financing must be less than the anticipated increase in price for holding inventories to be viewed as profitable.

When the market goes down, the process is reversed. Traders and consumers with inventory stop buying until their stocks are exhausted. If the exporter in Stockholm expected prices to fall, he would take an order in January to deliver in June, but he would not cover the sale until the last moment. For example, if he sold in January for delivery in Stockholm at RD 50 per skd, he would wait until May to buy copper, hopefully at RD 45 per skd, which he would deliver to his customer in June. The same was true for the consumer. In January he was asked to bid on copper brewing vessels for delivery in July. He would check with local copper merchants and quote a price based on RD 50 per skd copper. Rather than covering immediately, however, he would wait to cover the sale, hoping to buy at a price lower than the price he used to calculate his sale price. There are two factors that exaggerate the lack of demand in a falling market. First, inventories hang over the market, and second, buyers postpone purchases as long as possible to take advantage of declining prices.

For this reason, the picture for copper prices at the end of 1625 and the beginning of 1626 was grim. The Spanish stopped buying.[96] There were undoubtedly inventories in warehouses and factories all over Europe. Even if they did have orders, consumers would delay purchases as long as possible. The Copper Company could not sell in Europe. Production figures at the mine, however, did not decline. Instead, output continued to rise. Was the Stora Kopparberg defying the fundamental laws of supply and demand?

Simply put, I believe production was increasing, despite lack of demand, because of the company's monopoly on purchasing.[97] It was obligated to buy copper from the mine at SD 50 per skd, whether it was selling to customers or not. As long as the company was buying, the *bergsmän* would continue to produce at ever-increasing levels. The company may have been late with payments, but the *bergsmän* received weight certificates when they presented copper to the crown scales. When the company sent money to the mine, the *bergsmän* would present the certificates for payment. In the meantime, the *bergsmän* borrowed from local merchants using the weight certificates as collateral. Thus, the company monopoly shielded the *bergsmän* from market forces that previously would have adversely affected them. Because the company paid them a fixed price, the *bergsmän* increased production during the price decline. Even at SD 50 per skd, the more they produced, the more they earned.

There is one more vital piece to this artificial market. Because the *bergsmän* continued producing and the company continued to buy despite lack of consumption, prices remained low. Even when consumers had depleted their inventories and began to buy again, prices remained low

---

96 Heckscher, *historia*, 450–52.
97 Production figures for the Stora Kopparberg:

1625	9,211 skd
1626	11,061 skd
1627	11,354 skd
1628	11,696 skd
1629	10,674 skd
1630	12,986 skd

See Lindroth, *Gruvbrytning*, 2, 389.

because the company had inventory that weighed down the market. The company, by creating artificial demand when prices fell, had the effect of keeping prices low even when demand from consumers gradually returned.

It is no surprise, therefore, that starting in mid 1625, the company had difficulty selling copper. The directors blamed the king's floor price of SD 150 per skd or RD 92.3 because it was far above the real market.[98] When the king became aware of the problem, he wisely approached Mårtin Wewitzer, a company director and a prominent merchant, with a proposal. If Wewitzer would make a personal loan to the king totaling SD 157,000,[99] the king would allow Wewitzer to sell 2,057 skd of *råkoppar* in Germany at the discounted price of SD 118 per skd Stockholm weight, or RD 72 per skd. Wittrock, citing no sources, claimed that such an offer was unworkable because the market was only about RD 50 to RD 55 per skd at that time, implying that the king's offer to Wewitzer was foolish and out of touch. Based on two different sources, however, I have firm evidence that the market was still above the RD 50 to RD 55 per skd range in 1625 and early 1626. A contract liquidation in the *Leufsta arkiv* shows that de Geer sold Elias Trip 175 skd of *råkoppar* early in 1626 at RD 70 per skd.[100] That was still far above Wittrock's market estimate of RD 50 to 55 per skd. More to the point, we have the Copper Company's balance sheet for 1625, and it lists three separate sales made by Mårtin Wewitzer and his colleague, Peter Grönenberg, in Europe. These sales were based on the king's offer made in June of 1625 at SD 118 per skd or RD 72.[101]

The king was probably aware that indicators were pointing to a market turn. The Spanish were not buying, inventories were piling up across Europe, and the company was having difficulty selling through its normal channels. The king, realizing that his floor price of SD 150 was hopelessly unrealistic, lowered the bar and allowed Mårtin Wewitzer and his colleague to sell in Germany at SD 118 per skd. Despite these indications, the company continued to purchase copper from the *bergsmän* who remained unaffected by the change in the market.

I noted earlier that one of the king's goals in forming the company was to exercise control over the sale of copper to mirror the monopoly he had over the purchase of copper. Once established, the company became sole distributor of copper, thus giving the king the control he desired. He did

98 AOSB, II, 10, 283.
99 Wittrock, *Handelskompaniet*, 59.
100 Riksarkivet. Leufsta arkiv, file 81, Copper trade liquidation for Råkoppar. 1626.
101 Riksarkiviet. Handel och Sjöfart arkiv, file 46 # 43 to 48, Förslag opå Compagneidtz Stat pro Anno 1625.

not mandate a floor price until 1625, and as we have seen, it was not successful. In the introduction, I observed that Gustav Adolf was innovative
and not afraid to experiment. The floor price was an experiment which
he abandoned to prevent inventories from accumulating in Stockholm.
Instead, he sanctioned a new contract between the company and Louis de
Geer, and gave up, temporarily at least, his control over the distribution of
copper. Not only does this agreement between the company and de Geer
survive, but de Geer's balance sheet for the contract can be found in the
Leufsta arkiv, allowing us to conduct an analysis of the transaction.[102] This
will tell us about freight rates, insurance, and other transaction costs related
to shipping. Most importantly, it will allow us to calculate the company's
profit on the trade, thus providing insight into the nature of its business.

The details of this new agreement were negotiated between de Geer, in
Amsterdam, and Anthony Monier, in Stockholm, through an Amsterdam
attorney. De Geer agreed to finance 2,000 skd of the Copper Company's
excess inventory at RD 50 per skd; a total of RD 100,000. The company
would ship this parcel to Amsterdam, where de Geer would attempt to
sell it. Letters to all parties confirmed the contract on August 12, 1625.[103]
The company promised to ship the 2,000 skd copper during the balance of
1625. The parcel would consist of *råkoppar*, *gårkoppar*, and copper plate; the
contract did not specify the ratios of each type. The parcel would be shipped
to de Geer in Amsterdam "on consignment." This is a term still current
today, meaning that the metal remained the property of the seller until the
buyer released it into his own inventory. Immediately after the contract
was signed, de Geer sent a loan of RD 20,000 to the company, which was
desperately needed to cover payments to the *bergsmän*. Upon the arrival of
the copper in Amsterdam, de Geer would pay the company RD 50 per skd
in cash, regardless of the quality, after deducting the RD 20,000 advance.
The company promised to pay de Geer interest at the rate of 8 percent per
annum on the full advance of RD 100,000. Further, de Geer would arrange
for insurance to cover the shipment and storage in Amsterdam.[104]

One could draw a couple of conclusions from the last clause. The framers
of the contract placed some emphasis on the issue that de Geer should insure
the copper. Perhaps this meant that insurance facilities were not available in
Sweden at the time, at least not for such large shipments. One of the reasons

---

102 Riksarkivet. Leufsta arkiv, Cooper Platen Debit Anno 1625 Amsterdam # 22, Garcooper
Debit Anno 1626 Amsterdam # 25, Rouwcoper Debit Anno 1626 # 27.
103 LDGDOA, 84.
104 LDGDOA, 84–85.

the king worked with de Geer in Amsterdam was that there were no adequate credit facilities in Sweden to provide liquidity for the company, and it is not surprising, therefore, that sophisticated insurance instruments did not yet exist. The second important issue was the price. One must remember that at this stage, de Geer was not buying the copper from the company, as the company retained ownership; de Geer was lending money to the company at a fixed interest rate, and the copper was the security for the loan.[105] The contract specified that the copper would be insured at the rate of RD 80 per skd for *gårkoppar* and RD 70 per skd for *råkoppar*. This conformed well to Posthumus's price survey, which shows an average price in 1625 of RD 79.14 for *gårkoppar* in Amsterdam.[106] In this negotiation, de Geer was faced with difficult choices. He certainly wanted to be as helpful to the company as possible in order to cement his relationship with it and with the crown. Yet, he also must have realized that there was a chance that the company would fail to pay the interest or even cease to exist, in which case he would then own the copper at the price he advanced. The price they agreed upon, RD 50 per skd Stockholm weight, seemed reasonably safe, although de Geer would have known that they were already in a falling market. If he had been forced to dispose of the copper in 1627, the next year for which Posthumus located copper price currents, de Geer would have made a profit on the *gårkoppar*, but the *råkoppar* would have been breakeven.

One of the more striking features of this contract was the freedom and discretion that it granted de Geer; he was not merely the financier for the company, but he was also its sales agent in Amsterdam. As such, he was granted "absolute authority and full power and discretion to sell the copper for the benefit of the company, but not to sell below the price of RD 50 per skd Stockholm weight."[107] Obviously, this type of delegation of authority was necessary because of slow and uncertain communications. If de Geer had to get permission from Sweden before making a sale, the opportunity would be gone before a reply could arrive.

By good fortune, as mentioned, the records for the liquidation of this contract have survived in the *Leufsta archiv*.[108] (Please see Appendix A) The most immediately useful information in the document, the key to all the analysis that follows, was the difference between Stockholm weight

105 LDGDOA, 84–85.
106 Posthumus, *Prices*, 1, 372.
107 LDGDOA, 85.
108 Riksarkivet. Leufsta arkiv, Cooper Platen Debit Anno 1625 Amsterdam # 22, Garcooper Debit Anno 1626 Amsterdam # 25, Rouwcoper Debit Anno 1626 # 27.

for copper and Amsterdam weight. In his liquidation of copper plate, de Geer reported that he had received 317.2 skd Stockholm weight totaling 87,020 Amsterdam pounds. With this information, we can calculate that a Stockholm *skeppund* contained 274.3 Amsterdam pounds. Understanding this ratio is critical for calculating and comparing prices in Amsterdam and Stockholm.

De Geer sold the *gårkoppar* and the *råkoppar* to Elias Trip. De Geer and the Trips cooperated on many business transactions. In fact, de Geer and the Trip family were possibly the only trading group in Europe, at the time, capable of handling such a large transaction in copper. In addition to providing an insight into transaction costs, the balance sheets in Appendix A provide the cost of shipment from Stockholm to Amsterdam. Without this information, price calculations are meaningless. Here, de Geer presented a neat package with even the financing cost included. Based on the figures in Appendix A, the full transport costs per *skeppund* were as follows:

Plate Copper: DG 17.4 per skd (RD 7 per skd)
Gårkoppar: DG 18.2 per skd
Råkoppar: DG 17.1 per skd

That is an average cost of DG 17.56 per skd (RD 7 per skd).[109] Once the transaction and transportation costs have been extracted from the balance sheet, we can proceed to the main purpose of this exercise: to reconstruct the profit/loss calculation (see figure 3, Total Profit column 4). For the sake of simplicity, I have converted the figures to *riksdaler* per *skeppund*.

It is not possible to test the conventional wisdom that the Copper Company was a poor business decision that hurt rather than helped the crown's efforts to develop copper production, without understanding the numbers for a typical company trade. The cost "in warehouse Stockholm" includes the expenses at the mine, the cost of refining, and the inland freight. The cost "in warehouse Amsterdam" includes the ocean freight, the expense to import, and de Geer's sales commission. The next line is the sales prices in Amsterdam derived from Appendix A, followed by the profit per *skeppund*. The profit margins from the plate, *gårkoppar*, and *råkoppar* were 44 percent, 43 percent, and 42 percent of the sales price respectively.

---

109 In 1628 de Geer calculated these same costs for *råkoppar* and *gårkoppar* at RD 5 per skd, minus financing. LDGBOA, 161.

Figure 3. The Copper Company's 1625-1626 Trade with de Geer, the Profit Calculation110 GRAAG LIJNEN OP DECIMALEN

	Plate RD per skd	Gaarkoppar RD per skd	Raakopper RD per skd	Total Profit
Cost at Mine (SD 50 per skd) Mine Weight	27.7	27.7	27.7	
Premium to upgrade into plate or Gaarkoppar	9.0	6.0	0.0	
Freight to Stockholm	1.0	1.0	1.0	
Cost in warehouse Stockholm	37.7	34.7	28.7	
Freight etc. to Amsterdam	7.0	7.0	7.0	
Cost in warehouse Amsterdam	44.7	41.7	35.7	
Sales price in Amsterdam	79.9	73.7	61.6	
Profit per skd	35.2	32.0	25.9	
Total Weight sold in skd	316.4 skd	190.0 skd	702.5 skd	
Total Profit	RD11,137.3	RD6,080.0	RD18,194.8	RD35,412.0

This is a generous profit margin, made possible by the monopoly purchase price at the mine, and the elimination of the layers of merchants between the mine and Amsterdam. The Copper Company was a sound and forward-looking concept with a solid cost structure. If the king had allowed it to concentrate on the business of buying and selling copper, it could have contributed to the development of Swedish industry and made its shareholders wealthy.

Bibliography

Archival Sources

Riksarkivet. Handel och Sjöfart arkiv, file 46 # 25.
Riksarkiviet. Handel och Sjöfart arkiv, file 46, # 43 to 48 Förslag opå Compagneidtz Stat pro Anno 1625.
Riksarkivet. Kontractsböcker, special series (1613) 1620–1622 (1624) # 18.
Riksarkivet. Kontraktsböcker, huvudserie 1622. Contract between Gustav Adolf and the Copper Company. September 11, 1622.

110 The premiums for upgrading are located in the Company Balance Sheets for 1625. See Riksarkiviet. Handel och Sjöfart arkiv, file 46, # 43 to 48 Förslag opå Compagneidtz Stat pro Anno 1625.

Riksarkivet. Leufsta arkiv, Cooper Platen Debit Anno 1625 Amsterdam # 22, Garcooper

Riksarkivet. Leufsta arkiv, file 81, Cooper Platen Debit Anno 1626, Amsterdam. # 22.

Riksarkivet. Leufsta arkiv, Cooper Platen Debit Anno 1625 Amsterdam # 22, Garcooper Debit Anno 1626 Amsterdam # 25, Rouwcoper Debit Anno 1626 # 27.

Riksarkivet. SE/RA/1112.1/B/135 (1620), 113–15, Letter from Gustav Adolf to Peter Falk concerning the contract with Louis de Geer. Stockholm, September 6, 1620.

Riksarkivet, SE/RA/1112.1/B/144 (1623), # 10–13.

Printed Primary Sources

Dahlgren, Erik Wilhelm, ed. *Louis de Geers brev och affärshandlingar* 1614–1652. Stockholm: P.A. Norstedt & Söner, 1934.

Oxenstierna, Axel. *Rikskansleren Axel Oxenstierna skriften och brefvexling*, Series I, 16 vols. Stockholm: P.A. Norstedt & Söner, 1888–Present.

Oxenstierna, Axel, *Rikskansleren Axel Oxenstierna skriften och brefvexling*, Series II, 14 vols. Stockholm: P.A. Norstedt & Söner, 1888–Present.

Stiernman, Anton von, ed. *Samling utaf kongl. brev, stadgar och förordordningar i angående Sweriges Rikes*, 4 vols. Stockholm: Kongl. Tryckeriet, 1747.

Van Dillen, Johannes Gerard, ed. "Amsterdamsche Notarieele Acten Betreffende den Koperhandel en de Uitoefening van Mijnbouw en Metaalindustrie in Zweden." In *Bijdragen en mededeelingen van het Historisch Genootschap*, 58. Utrecht: 1937.

Secondary Sources

Dahlgren, Erik Wilhelm. *Louis de Geer, 1587–1652, hans lif och verk*, 2 vols. Uppsala: Almqvist & Wiksells, 1923.

Heckscher, Eli Filip, *Sveriges economiska historia från Gustav Vasa*, 2 vols. Stockholm: Albert Bonniers, 1936.

Kindleberger, Charles P. "The Economic Crisis of 1619 to 1623" *The Journal of Economic History* 51, no. 1 (March 1991): 149–175.

Kristiansson. *Sture, Falu kopparvåg 1546–1873, historiska inblickar i en institution och livet kring denna*. Filipstad: Bronells Tryckeri AB, 1993.

Lindroth, Sven. *Gruvbrytning och kopparhantering vid Stora Kopparberg intill 1800 talets början*, 2 vols. Uppsala: Almqvist & Wiksells, 1955.

Paas, Martha, Schoolfield, George C., and Paas, Roger. *The Kipper und Wipper Inflation, 1619–1623: An Economic History with Contemporary German Broadsheets*. New Haven: Yale University Press, 2012.

Parker, Geoffrey. *The Army of Flanders and the Spanish Road 1567–1659*. Cambridge: Cambridge University Press, 1974.

Posthumus, Nicolaas Wilhelmus. *Inquiry into the History of Prices in Holland*, 2 vols. Leiden: E.J. Brill, 1946.

Roberts, Michael. *Gustavus Adolphus, a History of Sweden 1611–1632*, 2 vols. London: Longmans, Green and Co., 1957.

Safley, Thomas Max. "Bankruptcy." In *Europe 1450 to 1789, Encyclopedia of the Early Modern World*, 6 vols, edited by Jonathan Dewald, 1, 219–22. New York: 2004.

Soll, Jacob. *Free Market, the History of an Idea*. New York: Basic Books, 2022.

Van Dillen, Johannas Gerard. *Van Rijkdom en Regenten. Handboek tot de Economische en Sociale Geschiednis van Nederland tijdens de Republiek*. The Hague: Martinus Nijhoff, 1970.

Wittrock, Georg. *Svenska handelscompaniet och kopparhandeln under Gustav II Adolf.* Uppsala: Almqvist & Wikesell, 1919.

Wolontis, Josef. *Kopparmyntning i Sverige 1624–1714*. Helsingfors: 1936.

4. The Copper Company: The Years of Decline

Abstract

The euphoria over the company's early success did not last. In Chapter four we examine the decline of the company's fortunes. Beginning in 1625 the king demanded a series of loans from the company. At first the king's requests were moderate. During the latter part of the year, however, as the king was preparing to campaign in Prussia, his demand for loans from the company increased. In this chapter we ask the important question, "did Gustav Adolf mis-manage the Copper Company." If he had allowed the company to function without financial interference, could it have developed into a reliable source of revenue in its own right?

Keywords: VOC (Dutch East Indian Company), Avrad Copper, Elias Trip, Elbing, Charter of 1625

> "A *mitsiye* (bargain) today, a loss tomorrow."
>
> Old Yiddish trader saying

In April of 1625, the chancellor received a disturbing letter from Copper Company director Peter Kruse. He wrote from the newly expanded mint at Säter to explain that he had been to the Stora Kopparberg, Nyköping (the other location for refining and minting capacity), and Stockholm. In the course of his travels, Kruse wrote, he had met with a number of the other company directors, and they were all concerned about the company's cash flow. As was his prerogative from the charter of 1625, the king had transferred all the *avrad* copper to Säter, and asked Kruse for payment at the agreed price of SD 126 per skd or RD 77.5 per skd.[1] This was an inflated price for

---

1   As a reminder, currencies are abbreviated as follows: SD for Swedish *dalers*, RD for *riksdaler*, and DG for Dutch Guilders. The exchange rate was RD 1=DG 2.5 and RD 1= SD 1.624. *Skeppund* is shortened to skd.

Stryker, L., *The Swedish Monarchy and the Copper Trade: The Copper Company, the Deposit System, and the Amsterdam Market, 1600–1640.* Amsterdam: Amsterdam University Press, 2024
DOI 10.5117/9789048560813_CH04

råkoppar and Kruse did not have sufficient company reserves to make the payments. He asked the chancellor to intervene with the *Kammar-Råd* to pay for the *avrad* copper.[2]

The king was obviously in need of funds. At the beginning of 1625, he had borrowed SD 150,000 from the company. Then, in November 1625, he wrote to the directors of the Copper Company informing them that he would require another loan for the amount of SD 30,000 (RD 18,472),[3] most likely to help fund his war in Livonia. The king also wrote a separate letter to his old tutor, Johan Skytte, an investor, and a member of the company's board. Perhaps because he had certain reservations about the request and felt it necessary to justify his actions, the king's letter to Skytte contained a much longer and fuller explanation.[4]

Skytte, who was not shy about objecting, must have written a testy reply because two days later the chancellor wrote to Skytte on behalf of the king. He was conciliatory. Skytte's letter has not survived, but judging from Oxenstierna's response, he must have complained that lending the king SD 30,000 now, would encourage him to seek another loan in the new year. The chancellor assured Skytte that the king only wanted the SD 30,000 and he would not be requesting any additional loans until there were "more favorable conditions." This indicated that both the chancellor and the king realized that conditions in the copper market had changed and that the company could no longer be considered an unlimited source of loans to the crown.[5]

Despite the chancellor's assurances, Johan Skytte was not appeased. He wrote again to the chancellor in early December about his fears for the company's future; this time he was blunt in his criticism of crown policy. Skytte had just received the year-end balance sheet from the compiler of the numbers, Johan Sparre, a company director and the chancellor's brother-in-law.[6] Skytte was upset. The numbers not only showed no profit for the year, but also showed a sharp decline in working capital.[7] He was direct in assigning blame. He wrote that he and his fellow directors did everything

---

2   Axel Oxenstiernas, *Skrifter och brevväxling* (AOSB) II, 11, 206.

3   Riksarkivet SE/RA/1112.1/B/150 (1623), # 123 Letter from Gustav Adolf to the Directors of the Koppar Companie. November 6, 1625.

4   Riksarkivet/SE/RA/1112.1/B/150 (1624), Letter from Gustav Adolf to Johan Skytte. 6 November 1625.

5   AOSB, I, 3, 217.

6   AOSB, II, 10, 282–83.

7   Riksarkiviet. Handel och Sjöfart arkiv, file 46 # 43 to 48, Förslag opå Compagneidtz Stat pro Anno 1625.

"humanly possible" to make the company profitable, but the king imposed impossible conditions on the directors (such as the unrealistic floor price of SD 150 per skd or RD 92.4).

Skytte was apparently ready to wage a campaign against the floor prices. He reminded the chancellor that Mårtin Wewitzer was able to sell in northern Germany only with the help of a large discount below the floor prices. Skytte saw no reason to maintain an artificial minimum price that ignored the actual market. He, like many of his contemporaries, still believed that the Spanish would resume buying copper if the company offered them prices more in line with the market. He was writing, of course, before it was understood that the Spanish would not return as buyers.[8]

He provided more evidence by quoting a letter from Dietrich von Falkenberg, the Queen Mother's court chamberlain, who doubled as her copper salesperson. Falkenberg wrote that it was no longer possible to sell copper in northern Germany at RD 55 per skd, and that the prospect for any price increase soon was doubtful. He was selling at whatever price he could get. Skytte, therefore, made the point that while the Queen Mother was selling at the market price and still making a profit, the king was preventing the company from doing any business. "The house of Her Majesty the Queen Mother is full of profit while His Majesty the King demands that the copper must remain unsold. May God stand by us because human help is not coming."[9] We cannot judge the accuracy of Falkenberg's report without knowing whether he was referring to *gårkoppar* or *råkoppar*. We do know, however, that de Geer sold *gårkoppar* in Amsterdam at RD 73.7 per skd at about this same time, and *råkoppar* at RD 61.6.[10] Despite the aggressive tone of Skytte's letter, the chancellor did not mention it in his next letter to the king. He merely wrote that he had received a letter from Johan Skytte regarding the Copper Company. He added, "I'm not well versed on the subject, but the letter is no doubt full of sound advice."[11]

Johan Skytte's letter underlined a central flaw in the Swedish Trading Company, the interconnection between the crown and the company. This linkage led to benefits and to problems as well, particularly on the issue of corporate governance. In comparison, the Dutch East India Company had

8   Riksarkiviet. Handel och Sjöfart arkiv, file 46 # 43 to 48, Förslag opå Compagneidtz Stat pro Anno 1625.

9   AOSB, II, 10, 283–84. (Skytte wrote this letter two days before the Queen Mother's death on December 8, 1625).

10   Riksarkivet. Leufsta arkiv, Cooper Platen Debit Anno 1625 Amsterdam # 22, Garcooper Debit Anno 1626 Amsterdam # 25, Rouwcoper Debit Anno 1626 # 27.

11   AOSB, I, 3, 253.

quite a different standard of governance. To begin, the Swedish Trading Company was Gustav Adolf's creation, and there was very little in the Swedish trading experience to provide precedents for the company; we should not be surprised, therefore, that the company suffered from the heavy hand of its creator. In contrast, the Dutch East India Company evolved within a mature, commercial community with all the facilities necessary to carry out international trade. The different Dutch provinces had originally acted independently, sending separate trading expeditions to Asia. In 1598, for example, there were five separate and competing Dutch companies with twenty-two vessels committed to Asian trade. At the turn of the century, Johan van Oldenbarnevelt, the Dutch politician, proposed uniting the separate companies and granting an official monopoly through the States General.[12]

Gustav Adolf retained the right to approve the governor and the directors of the Swedish Copper Company and company officials were chosen from among the shareholders, many of whom felt obligated to buy shares in order to sustain royal favor. At its peak, the Swedish Trading Company had only eighty-two shareholders. In contrast, the Dutch East India Company (VOC) had over eighteen hundred shareholders. The Dutch board was selected from the seventy-six largest investors with eight coming from Amsterdam and eight from the other provinces. The governorship revolved among the smaller provinces. This body came to be known as the Heren XVII. The Swedish Copper Company was quite different; the king dictated policy to its directors, and consequently, Johan Skytte was powerless to prevent the king from leading the company into disaster. The opposite was the case with the VOC. The Heren XVII acted in tandem with the States General: "Privately financed, it was the international arm of the Dutch government, and for almost a hundred years, it made little Holland the center of world trade."[13] In Asia, for example, the VOC erected fortresses, waged war, and set policy.[14]

Finally, there was the issue of the shares. The amount the investors in the VOC risked was limited to the value of their initial investment. In other words, the VOC was a limited liability company.[15] This allowed the investors to buy and sell their shares along with other commodities and securities on the Amsterdam Exchange. Shareholders in the Swedish Trading Company had no such flexibility. Yet, in accordance with the paternalistic nature of the company, when the king finally dissolved it in 1628, he repaid the investors

12   De Vries, *Economy*, 385.
13   Soll, *The Reckoning*, 78.
14   Van der Muijssenbergh, *Corporate Governance*, 63.
15   Van der Muijssenbergh, *Corporate Governance*, 63.

the amount of their original investments plus interest at 20 percent. The king made the decisions and, therefore, accepted responsibly when things went wrong.[16] Most shareholders were repaid by the middle of 1629; however, Roberts contends that three charitable investors, the Danvik poor house and the dioceses of Växjö and Kalmar, were still waiting for payment in 1643.[17]

In summary, the problems with the company were not commercial. From the beginning the company was founded on the sound principle of buying from the *bergsmän* at the low price of SD 50 per skd mine weight or RD 27.7 per skd Stockholm weight, refining as much copper as possible, and selling into the European market. The numbers show that it could have been viable. The king, however, was less interested in creating a thriving commercial entity than in using this resource to finance his wars.

In consequence, he hamstrung the company with a charter that allowed him to make unrealistic demands. In 1625 he put the company at risk by resuming a war in Livonia and discussing an invasion of Prussia. If we conclude that the long-term purpose of the company was to furnish the crown with resources to further its military goals, then, there is strong evidence that the king's company could have been successful. Considering the advantages that Sweden had as a producer and distributor of copper to Europe, the king would have been better served by allowing the company to operate independently until it reached a level of unquestioned prosperity. Then the Copper Company could have contributed to the king's military campaigns while continuing to grow.

The balance sheet for 1625 shows that the Copper Company had a strong base; unfortunately, it also shows that the shareholders' equity was being drawn down to finance the king's wars and investments in infrastructure. The former had no long-term benefit for the company, except for creating demand for bronze cannon. Investing in infrastructure, on the other hand, was a perfectly legitimate capital expenditure that a modern board of directors would probably sanction without fear of questions at an annual shareholders' meeting.

Since 1625 was a watershed moment, it is fortunate that the balance sheets for that year have survived in the company papers now located in the *Handel och Sjöfart* archive housed in the Riksarkiv in Stockholm (see Appendix B). First, a word of caution, one cannot judge a balance sheet written in 1625 by modern accounting standards.[18] For example, this balance

16   Wittrock, *Handelskompaniet*, 59.
17   Roberts, *Gustavus Adolphus*, 2, 98.
18   Riksarkiviet. Handel och Sjöfart arkiv, file 46 # 43 to 48, Förslag opå Compagneidtz Stat pro Anno 1625.

sheet is divided into two parts, January 1, 1625, to September 26, 1625 and September 26, 1625 to January 1, 1626. The second part of the balance sheet also contains a summary of the first part and, of course, there are numerous inconsistencies. In addition, the balance sheet itemizes individual transactions, so it is more like a combination of a profit-and-loss statement and a balance sheet. These documents are, nevertheless, an important window into the workings of the Copper Company. The king's critics maintained that the company was ill conceived and inappropriate for Sweden.[19] We will see if the profit-and -loss-statement we have teased from the balance sheet will support this contention. There is nothing complicated about reading a seventeenth-century balance sheet. The debit side is money out, and the credit side is money in (see Appendix B).

What is the purpose of using a balance sheet as a source? First it fills in gaps in the written correspondence. The king's offer to Wewitzer, discussed in the previous chapter, is a good example. Wittrock reported that the price was not workable, but the balance sheet shows that Wewitzer did, indeed, make sales at SD 118 (or RD 73) per skd. The nature and quantity of the company's loans to the king is another. There is no mention, for example, of the many arms purchases made by the company for the king in the letters we discussed. Probably, however, the most valuable contribution of the balance sheets is supplying information that will permit us to develop a profit-and-loss statement. The only way to judge the potential of the Copper Company is to understand its ability to make a profit.[20]

The trouble with seventeenth-century balance sheets is that they do not give us a clear picture of the profit and losses for the period covered. We will, therefore, look at the company as an investor would, and consider the fundamentals of the business. This requires stripping out the one-time expenditures, such as the repayment of past debts to Peter Gröneberg and Mårtin Wewitzer, and the purchases of arms that clearly provided no benefit for the company. The company, however, was paying a tolling charge to refine *råkoppar* into plate and *gårkoppar*. This was negotiated independently between the vice-governor of the company, Lars Skytte, and Gobert Silentz, so it is fair for inclusion. On the other hand, there is no justification for large subsidies to the Säter plant, especially since the Queen Mother owned it. It would be realistic, however, for the company to help pay for the rebuilding. In the modern world, it is common for a company seeking conversion capacity

19   Heckscher, *historia*, 1, 451–56.
20   Riksarkiviet. Handel och Sjöfart arkiv, file 46 # 43 to 48, Förslag opå Compagneidtz Stat pro Anno 1625.

Figure 4.   Purchases and Sales for 1625 in SKD

	Quantity in skd	Price in SD	Extension	Cost in SD	Extension	Gross Profit
Purchases						
Company	4,911.5	50.0	245,575.0			
Avrad	140.0	126.0	17,640.0			
Avrad	448.6	116.0	52,037.6			
Avrad	794.2	116.0	92,127.2			
Company	3,088.0	50.0	154,400.0			
Company	1,500.0	50.0	75,000.0			
Total	10,882.3		636,779.8			
Sales						
Wewitzer	1,623.3	118.0	191,549.4	50.0	81,165.0	110,384.4
Groenenberg	103.0	148.0	15,244.0	50.0	5,150.0	10,094.0
Groenenberg	257.7	118.0	30,408.6	50.0	12,885.0	17,523.6
Avrad[1]	400.0	150.0	60,000.0	50.0	20,000.0	40,000.0
De Geer[2]	1,167.3	115.0	134,239.5	50.0	58,365.0	75,874.5
Company	527.4	118.0	62,233.2	50.0	26,370.0	35,863.2
Company	491.2	118.0	57,961.6	50.0	24,560.0	33,401.6
Avrad	879.4	126.0	110,804.4	116.0	102,010.4	8,794.0
Avrad	169.0	126.0	21,294.0	116.0	19,604.0	1,690.0
Avrad	430.0	126.0	54,180.0	116.0	49,880.0	4,300.0
Company	1,396.0	118.0	164,728.0	50.0	69,800.0	94,928.0
Company	2,000.0	150.0	300,000.0	50.0	100,000.0	200,000.0
Total	9,444.3		1,202,642.7		569,789.4	632,853.3

1   Avrad copper was the toll paid in copper to the crown by the *bergsmän* in return for mining rights. The sales of 400 skd and 2,000 skd at SD 150, the king's floor price, were sales the company made to the mint.
2   These figures are based on de Geer's trade for the company in 1625.

to contribute capital to smaller independent companies. In short, we will consider only those items on the debit side that relate to the operation of the business. Given these guidelines, we can construct a simple income statement for the company. The first step is to calculate the sales revenue. We know the cost of goods from the debit side. We know from Wittrock that the company paid the crown SD 116 per skd (RD 71.4) for *avrad* copper.[21] Otherwise, the calculations are straightforward.

21   Wittrock, *Handelskompaniet*, 56.

The "book" for the year (see figure 4) includes all purchases and sales recorded in the separate balance sheets (see Appendix B). Note that at the end of the year, column one, the company had purchased slightly more copper (1,438 skd) than it had sold. It would probably be impossible to maintain a totally "square book" or have sales match purchases exactly in an era of slow communication and transport. Of course, in an unstable market,[22] it would have been ill advised to have a large "long position" or a large "short position;" as both put the owner at risk. Another issue that can be clearly seen from the table of sales and purchases was the variation in prices. Obviously, the king's insistence in the Charter of 1625 that nothing be sold under SD 150 per skd was unrealistic and was abandoned.

The only customer willing to pay the king's price was the mint, which also operated at the king's command. The critical numbers are the gross sales of SD 1,202,643 (end of column 4) and gross profit of SD 632,853 (end of last column). With capital of only SD 312,000, (stated in in the previous chapter), the company managed top line sales of SD 1,202,643, or almost four times capital. That was most impressive but possible only because of late payments to the *bergsmän*.

To establish the company's expenses, one also must calculate yearly conversion costs at Säter. (See figure 5 for the refining work done for the company that year.) It is important to keep in mind that we are only including refined copper processed and sold in 1625. The total is SD 31,830 for refining costs.

Finally, we have all the elements necessary to assemble an income statement (see figure 6). As mentioned, only expenses that are not relevant to the operation of the company, such as loans to the king and arms purchases, are excluded. Note also that the king's tolls on company purchases are included. In the Charter of 1625, the toll was set at SD 60 per skd. The amount mentioned in the year-end balance sheet was SD 111,080. But that would be the toll on only 1,851 skd of copper, a small fraction of the company's sales for the year. One possible explanation was that the king, realizing that he had to move copper to pay his troops, allowed the toll to lapse, or, more probably, charged a lower rate. In the end, the toll went the way of the SD 150 floor price. With these provisos in mind, the company showed a gross profit of SD 632,853 on sales of SD 1,202,642.7 or 52 percent of sales. The operating profit after expenses was SD 374,052 or 31 percent of sales.

Why did the Copper Company look so good on paper, even as copper prices were beginning to falter? The advantage the company had was its

22   AOSB, II, 10, 283.

control over costs at the mine. It was buying copper from the *bergsmän* at a predetermined cost, thereby eliminating the most difficult hurdle in this kind of transaction, the ability to buy at a price that would allow a profit. It would be misleading to think that the crown could dictate any price to the *bergsmän*. We should recall the negotiations between the crown and the *bergsmän* discussed in the first chapter. If the *bergsmän* were unhappy or felt exploited, they would simply stop producing or turn to smuggling. The crown understood that the *bergsmän* had to make a profit. They were independent operators, not serfs; they decided whether to produce or not to produce. The king had succeeded in establishing the company as the middleman between the *bergsmän* and the world market. He, therefore, took the normal profit away from the merchants and channeled it to the company coffers. The key, which the king discovered, was to control costs at the mine.

Figure 5.   Calculation of Processing Cost at Säter January through December 1625

Company Conversions	SKD	Cost in SD	Total in SD
Raakoppar to Hun. plate	103	16.5	1,699.5
Raakoppar to Pre-mint	2,400	10.0	24,000.0
De Geer Trade			
Raakoppar to Hun. plate	261.5	16.5	4,314.8
Raakoppar to *Gaarkoppar*	181.6	10.0	1,816.0
Total			31,830.3

Figure 6.   Income Statement for 1625 January to December in SDK

1 Sales Revenue	1,202,642.7
2 Cost of Goods Sold	569,789.4
3 Gross Margin	632,853.3
Operating Expenses	
4 Director and Employee Salaries	49,731.0
5 Contribution to Rebuild Saeter	36,000.0
6 Write-Off of Copper in Flood	30,160.0
7 Cost to Refine at Saeter	31,830.0
8 Toll Paid to His Majesty	111,080.0
9 Total Operating Expenses	258,801.0
10 Operating Profit	374,052.3

This exercise proves a couple of things. First, it shows the value of analyzing the Copper Company's balance sheets. There is no alternative for determining the financial viability of the company. The correspondence can provide price information, the state of the market, the names of customers and traders, but it cannot tell us whether the company was capable of making a profit for the crown and for the shareholders. Second, it shows the criticism that Heckscher and Roberts directed at the concept of the Copper Company was, at least partially, unjustified. The numbers show that properly managed, the company should have made a substantial profit, and probably would have done so year after year. One of the great misfortunes of Gustav Adolf's reign was his failure to nurture the company to maturity; he had other priorities. By withdrawing money at an early stage, he doomed the company to a premature demise. If he had given it time to develop, the company might have brought prosperity to Sweden in the same manner as the Dutch East India Company did for the United Provinces. Once mature, the company could have contributed further toward the king's political and military ambitions and Sweden's march towards statehood.

Despite the loss of shareholder equity during 1625, the king was eager to keep the company alive. In January 1626, he issued a new charter of privileges.[23] Surprisingly, he repeated some of the mistakes from the previous year. For example, he continued to demand a toll of SD 60 per skd for each *skeppund* the company purchased from the *bergsmän*, despite collecting the toll on only a fraction of the copper purchased by the company the previous year. In addition, he continued to insist on an unrealistic floor price. This was probably his way of preventing his underlings in the company from selling at a price he considered inappropriate. Presumably, the floor price forced them to check with him before selling below it.

Meanwhile, events on the political and military front intensified the crown's hunger for revenue. The most important political issue in 1626 was the preparation for war across the Baltic Sea. A coalition engineered by The Hague, consisting of Sweden, Denmark, and Transylvania, had come undone because of Kristian IV of Denmark's lack of success on the battlefield against the Catholic Imperial army. This left Gustav Adolf,[24] and Bethlen Gabor, king of distant Transylvania,[25] to protect Protestant northern Europe

---

23 A copy of the Charter of Privileges for 1626 is found in Riksarkivet, Handel och Sjöfart arkiv, file 46 # 3–12.
24 Of course, he might also have been influenced by the wealth of Prussia, a rich farming area with prosperous trading cities. There were also generous tolls to be collected at river mouths.
25 Of whom Roberts writes: "He was a not unfamiliar type of ambitious barbarian, unscrupulous, ruthless, able after his own fashion, with a veneer of civilization and a strong superficial piety." Roberts *Gustavus Adolphus*, 2, 309.

against the Catholic armies of Tilly and Wallenstein. Gustav Adolf and his councils began plans to invade Prussia. The first action took place in July 1626; the king landed with his army at Pillau, on the Prussian coast, and took it without a fight. He then proceeded along the Baltic coast all the way to Königsberg, the ancient seat of the Teutonic Order in East Prussia, and now part of the duchy held by the king's father-in-law, the Margrave of Brandenburg. While he now controlled most of the Baltic coast from Danzig to Königsberg, the king was careful not to interfere with trade, and he allowed Danzig to maintain its status as a free city.

While the king was preparing for war, the chancellor had been engaged in purchasing supplies and equipment for the expedition, which explains, in part, his sporadic involvement in company affairs during 1625. After the invasion, the king appointed the chancellor governor-general of Prussia, and Oxenstierna moved his base of operations to Elbing. In December 1625, he wrote to the king about assembling supplies of grain for the army, and he began ordering other provisions as well.[26] He was still ordering weapons through de Geer by mid-year, after the invasion fleet had already sailed.[27]

Since he was now located in a seaport, the chancellor was also able to gather intelligence and he fed the king a steady diet of critical information. For example, the number of the troops available to the king of Poland in the event he attacked Gustav Adolf: "Regarding the troops under the king of Poland there are many. My source has observed a total of 20,000 men." As always, the chancellor was also concerned about funding this new war and he wrote encouraging the king to impose an excise tax on the Prussian cities "that are not yet plundered, like Frauenberg and Christburg." He also told the king that he must send a bill of exchange to their agent in Hamburg, in the amount of RD 80,000, to pay for arms and ammunition. He brought up the possibility of sending the bill of exchange through the company but concluded that its credit was not good enough for the bill to be accepted in Hamburg. This was yet another negative sign for the company.[28]

By the second half of 1626, there was no question that the price of copper was turning south. The king sent Conrad von Falkenberg, a Livonian nobleman and a member of the king's inner circle, as the crown's financial agent in northern Germany and the Netherlands. In September 1626, Falkenberg was in Lübeck waiting for a copper shipment from Stockholm that he was directed to sell. He reported that the news was not good. There was a large

26 AOSB, I, 3, 250–53.
27 AOSB, I, 3, 344–46.
28 AOSB, I, 3, 392.

copper shipment bound for Spain that had been sitting on the pier for several months. The market remained quiet with the best Hungarian and German plate copper selling at around RD 65 per skd.[29]

Two months later, Falkenberg was in Hamburg completing the exchange of Swedish *dalers* into *riksdalers* in order to pay a mercenary regiment that was on the way to Prussia to join the king of Sweden's army. He reported to the chancellor that additional copper had arrived in Hamburg from Sweden, and there was now a total of 3,000 skd in inventory; he asked the chancellor for full authority on behalf of the Copper Company, to sell the copper in Hamburg.[30] We will shortly refer to the company's balance sheet (see Appendix C) covering 1626, and the first quarter of 1627; there is no evidence of the 3,000 skd that Falkenberg discussed. Falkenberg thought it was company copper, but I think it was not. An examination of the company's balance sheet for this period shows that it traded only 2,451.27 skd of copper that year and the transactions were all included on the credit side of the equation.[31] The mine produced 11,061 skd in 1626,[32] and 2,518 skd were minted into currency. Subtracting the copper used for the mint and the copper traded by the company, there remained 6,092 skd to be sold. If the crown shipped 3,000 skd of copper to Hamburg, it was almost certainly a trade the crown intended to make outside the company. This was significant because it signaled that the crown was looking for new outlets for copper. It was the first sign that the king was growing impatient with the Copper Company as an instrument of crown copper policy. Perhaps the king's main disappointment with the company was his realization that the company was not able to supply him with constant loans. The shareholder equity was shrinking, and Johan Skytte, and perhaps other directors as well, criticized him for draining company assets. He needed another source of funds.

In fact, the balance sheets for January 1626 through April 1627 (see figure 7 and Appendix C below) show a company in trouble. Purchases and sales were vastly diminished compared to previous years. In the meantime, however, the company was still investing in infrastructure and paying generous salaries to its directors. Clearly it could no longer support these overhead costs with shrinking sales and profits.

29   AOSB, II, 11, 546–52.

30   AOSB, II, 11, 546–52.

31   Riksarkivet. Handel och Sjofart arkiv, file 2 # 100–104. Copper Company Balance Sheets for April 1927.

32   Lindroth, *Gruvbrytning*, 2, 389 and Wolontis, *Kopparmyntningen*, 250.

Figure 7. Summary of Balance Sheet for April 1627

Purchases	skd	Cost per skd	SD
Copper	2,451.27	111.97	274,474.4
Sales			24,486.9
Other Expenses			
Capital Spending		77,884.5	
Operating Costs		30,016.8	

The largest expenditure was SD 77,698 for buildings, which once again underlines the emphasis that the crown placed on capital improvements and production facilities. The operating expenses, which included the salaries, payments for charcoal, and purchase of miscellaneous goods, come to a total of SD 30,016.8, meaning that they exceeded gross sales by over SD 5,000 that year. Finally, the company was still supplying the crown with ammunition. Even at this late stage, the king continued to regard the company as a source of revenue.

As mentioned above, the company purchased only 2,451.3 skd of copper from various sources in 1626 and the first quarter of 1627; where was the rest of the copper produced that year? A balance sheet from Erik Larsson, who was operating in Amsterdam,[33] shows he traded more than 1,000 skd of Swedish copper in 1626 and about 1,600 skd in 1627, all at a profit. This was more evidence that the king had already decided to find alternative channels for the sale of "his" copper. In January 1627, Louis de Geer was in Hamburg, on the way to visit the king of Sweden; he wrote to inform his partner, Pieter Trip, that there were now between 4,000 and 5,000 skd of Swedish copper rumored to be available in Hamburg from the crown's agent, Leonard von Sorgen, at RD 40 per skd. This was certainly the copper that Conrad von Falkenberg had imported into Hamburg and was attempting to sell for the crown, proof that the king was selling copper outside of company channels.[34]

There is one more glaring problem. The company had practically no recorded sales from January 1626 to April 1627. To develop a gross sales figure, we will assume general statements like "diverse creditors" means that the creditors were copper customers. Thus, the gross sales figure for the period was SD 24,486.9, or less than 10 percent of the amount spent to buy copper. If this was the case, it means the company ended the fiscal

---

33   Riksarkivet. Handel och Sjöfart arkiv, file 2 # 105, Erik Larsson's Balance sheet for 1628.
34   Louis de Geers, *Brev och affärshandlingar* (LDGBOA), 105.

year with a long position (inventory) of SD 249,987.5, or slightly less than the shareholders' equity. This was untenable.

What do these documents tell us? The company was doomed. For the year 1626, its combined capital spending and operating cost equaled SD 107,901.3. By contrast, we estimate its gross sales to be a mere SD 24,486.9. Even if gross profits on these sales were comparable to the previous year, it would amount only to SD 7,345.8, or less than 7 percent of capital spending and operating costs. After deducting the sales for the year, copper inventory remained at SD 249,987.5. From a cash-flow perspective, the company was finished. Only a massive sale of inventory could have prolonged it. Clearly the king had lost interest and was preparing to move on to another venture. The Copper Company would linger for another year, but its power and influence was over. In fact, during 1626, the king had decided to end the company's monopoly on the sale of copper. He concluded that it would be more efficient to sell through individual representatives and he began to export copper to northern Germany and Amsterdam for that purpose. This greatly diminished the company's sales and profit potential. Without profits the company could not continue to invest in infrastructure and pay salaries.

The Copper Company's fall from royal favor made room for other sales channels, and Louis de Geer was on the ground and ready to fill the void. There were a couple of testy exchanges between the crown and de Geer during the period of the Älvsborg ransom when the crown decided not to ship copper under contract. That was, however, solved amicably and de Geer became an important investor in the company during its period of influence.[35] This was also the period in which de Geer began to make substantial investments in Sweden's immature metallurgical industry. From this point de Geer and his company gradually took over the role that had been assigned to the Copper Company and greatly assisted the crown's overall plan for using copper to further its political and military objective.[36]

In April 1626, de Geer, Elias Trip, and Trip's second cousin, Pieter Trip formed a company with an initial capital of DG 27,000. The business of the company was to be "saltpeter, gun powder, grenades, and all other manner of weapons and armor."[37] De Geer would purchase arms in France, Bremen, and Hamburg, and saltpeter from Danzig. Pieter Trip was to be the administrator in Amsterdam. Their target market for sales was Sweden. In fact, Anthony Monier, the quartermaster-general in Sweden, had already supplied the new

35   LDGBOA, 44–49.
36   See, for example, LDGBOA, 81–87.
37   Van Dillen, *Notarieele*, 230–32.

company with a list of needed arms. The mechanism was now in place for de Geer and his partners to play a larger role in Sweden's future.

In January of 1627, de Geer was traveling to Stockholm to meet the king. It turned out to be a critical trip, and it marked a turning point in his relationship with Gustav Adolf. De Geer had just concluded a major arms sale to Sweden, on behalf of his company, and he wanted to be present for the unloading of the arms and to arrange payment from the crown. His partner, Pieter Trip, remained in Amsterdam to oversee the shipment of weapons. As he traveled, de Geer bombarded Trip, via letters, with ideas and commentary, and it is instructive to record the development of his thoughts, as he got closer to Stockholm. While still in Hamburg, de Geer wrote that he encountered a group of German mercenaries enroute to join the Swedish army in Prussia; the group included 2,000 foot soldiers and 1,000 cavalrymen. Smelling profits, de Geer instructed Pieter Trip to find and ship an additional 1,000 carbines and an unlimited quantity of helmets and body armor. He now knew there would be greater demand than he originally expected.[38]

Once de Geer arrived in Sweden, he began discussions with the king on many subjects, but copper was high on the list; in a letter to both Pieter and Elias Trip, de Geer reported that he would accompany the king on a visit to the Stora Kopparberg.[39] During this trip—and whenever the king was back in Stockholm—de Geer and the king continued to discuss copper. Once the king understood the extent of de Geer's financial resources and his ability to market copper in Amsterdam, the fate of the Copper Company was probably sealed.

In April 1627, de Geer wrote to Trip explaining that he had learned from Johan Skytte and Erik Larsson that the king would seek a new channel for copper sales in Holland, and that an agreement between the crown and de Geer was possible.[40] This was, however, information that the crown wished to keep secret. De Geer related to Trip that, in fact, he and the king were discussing a shipment of 1,000 skd copper, over the year, in lots of 150 to 200 skd per shipment. As the negotiations progressed, de Geer reported that the king would prefer that he (de Geer) not act as a principal, but as a commissioned agent and banker, and that the quantities involved could be much larger than originally mentioned.[41]

38 LDGBOA, 105.
39 LDGBOA, 110
40 LDGBOA, 120.
41 LDGBOA, 120.

After negotiations, the king and de Geer agreed on a broad concept. Every year, as soon as the harbors were free from ice, the crown would begin shipping copper to the ports of Lübeck and Amsterdam at the rate of between 5,000 and 6,000 skd per year. Upon receipt of the copper, de Geer's company would make an advance for the full value of the copper at a price to be agreed upon. The crown would pay interest on the advance at 8 percent per year.[42] This was a major step for de Geer. There was, nonetheless, substantial risk. If the crown shipped the copper, and did not pay the interest, de Geer would take it as collateral. If the two parties agreed on a delivery price of RD 50 per skd, and the market fell to RD 30 per skd, de Geer would be at risk for the difference if the crown defaulted. It would be similar to having an outstanding mortgage of US$ 250,000 on a house with a market value of US$ 150,000. De Geer minimized this risk by specifying that the copper price should be established only on the date of shipment. On the other hand, there were benefits for de Geer and his associates. First, except for the possibility of a default, the entire market risk remained with the crown. De Geer received a commission when he sold, but if the market went down, the crown suffered the loss. Second, it would make de Geer and his company the most important copper merchants in Europe almost overnight. No entity would have control of such a large percentage of European copper consumption. This would give them considerable influence over the market. Finally, they gained a stronger position as business agents and financial partners with the crown. This alone would justify the endeavor because it would inevitably lead to other, perhaps more profitable, business.

As an example of the added benefits for de Geer and his associates, in the letter to Pieter Trip, de Geer mentioned that the first shipment of copper would go to Lübeck. De Geer would make the advance payment on it, but instead of sending it to the crown, he would use the advance to purchase gunpowder and ship it to Stockholm. De Geer expected to make a handsome profit on the sale, and he asked Trip to contact his friends in Lübeck to start assembling parcels of gunpowder. Presumably, most future advances would also be used to purchase weapons; thus, de Geer and his associates anticipated a steady stream of profits on the sale of copper in Lübeck and Amsterdam, and on the weapons delivered to the crown.[43]

One of the original purposes of de Geer's visit to Sweden was to collect payment for the vast amount of weaponry and ammunition that he and Pieter Trip were shipping to Stockholm. We do not have an exact amount,

42   LDGBOA, 110-12.
43   LDGBOA, 123–24.

but based on the correspondence, it must have been substantial. In April, moreover, de Geer asked Pieter Trip to find and ship 100,000 pounds of gunpowder and DG 100,000 worth of cheese and herring to Elbing where the Swedish army in Prussia was headquartered.[44] This meant that de Geer was now a major creditor to the king, a position he had managed to avoid in the past. Previously, he had always waited for some form of payment before he shipped to Sweden. Now he complained that the crown, through Erik Larsson, had offered to make some payment to him in copper currency; de Geer was reluctant to accept it: "Here the copper coins are considered bad and, in the end, it prevents men from buying and selling."[45] He was, however, a realist and he feared that he would have to accept it in the end. He informed his correspondent in Hamburg, Leonard von Sorgen: "Everybody here seeks silver coins [in preference to copper] ..."[46]

Otherwise, the king had every reason to keep de Geer content because he would continue to need large quantities of weapons, despite the nascent production capacity in Sweden. Later in 1627 he arranged for 1,000 skd of *gårkoppar* to be shipped to de Geer through Erik Larsson. That would cover much of the outstanding balance. Taking copper ingots was an advantage for de Geer over copper coins. If he accepted coins, he would have to negotiate the exchange rate between silver coins and copper coins. The exchange rate between *riksdaler* and Swedish *daler* silver mint was fixed at RD 1 to SD 1.624 because they both contained a specified content of silver. The original contracts were all in *riksdaler* or Swedish *daler* silver mint. If the crown paid de Geer in copper currency, they would have to negotiate a new rate of exchange. The crown, desiring to defend the integrity of the copper currency, would propose a ratio favoring copper, and de Geer, wanting to protect his profits, would propose a more realistic ratio, and the whole issue would be highly political. By paying de Geer in copper ingots, therefore, the crown and de Geer avoided much unpleasantness.[47] Unfortunately, de Geer did not mention a specific price at which he would accept the copper ingot in payment. He did, however, mention that the outstanding bill for weapons alone was RD 40,000, and that the king was shipping 1,000 skd from Riga, where it had originally been shipped for use as barter for food supplies.[48] Hence, the price was RD 40 per skd Stockholm weight.

44 LDGBOA, 117.
45 LDGBOA, 112.
46 LDGBOA, 115.
47 LDGBOA, 115.
48 LDGBOA, 142.

This price was supported by another document. In November of 1627 the king negotiated a loan of RD 80,000 from de Geer and Erik Larsson. It is not clear if Larsson was a principal in the loan, or if he was acting as a factor for the crown. The loan was in the form of a bill of exchange to be sent to Holland for redemption.[49] In return the king was to supply 2,000 skd of copper in different grades, *råkoppar, gårkoppar*, and Hungarian plate copper, and he would ship "at the first free water," or as soon as the Baltic was navigable. In effect, therefore, de Geer was buying copper futures for spring delivery. We also know the outcome. A balance sheet in the *Leufsta arkiv* for 1628 lists the purchase on the debit side as 2,000 skd at RD 40 per skd. The credit side lists a series of sales for that year and none of the sales was below RD 50 per skd. Elsewhere, de Geer calculated his full costs from "in warehouse Stockholm" to "in warehouse Amsterdam" at DG 12.3 or RD 5.00 per skd.[50] This meant that de Geer made a profit on the sales in Amsterdam of at least RD 5.00 per skd on *råkoppar*, and much more on the *gårkoppar* and the Hungarian sheet.[51]

The pattern of the trade that began in 1627 becomes clear. With the help of his relatives by marriage, Elias and Pieter Trip, de Geer would ship weapons from Amsterdam to Stockholm (and later, directly to Elbing in Prussia, the headquarters of the Swedish army in Germany). He would ship on credit, trusting that the crown would eventually pay. He was able to make this leap of faith because he was now living and working in Sweden, at least most of the time, and he had invested in Swedish industry. In addition, he had access to the king and had become indispensable to the crown. He was in a position now to lobby for payments directly, rather than relying on ambassadors in The Hague to pass on his requests. The crown would invariably pay him in various forms of copper, which he would ship to Amsterdam and sell himself or through the Trip family. He made a profit on the weapons he sold to the crown, and a profit once again on the copper he took in return.[52]

From the crown's side, the king came to realize that dealing through de Geer was more expedient than selling through the Copper Company. First, there was an issue of expense; the company was costly to maintain. As noted, a significant part of the budget went to pay directors and employees, plus the company had to pay annual dividends to its shareholders. In

---

49 LDGBOA, 154.
50 LDGBOA, 161.
51 Riksarkiver. Leufsta arkiv, file 81 # 111, Calculation for purchased copper in 1628.
52 LDGBOA, 114.

addition, de Geer provided his connections in Amsterdam and beyond. The company's representatives in Europe, Mårtin Wewitzer and Peter Gröneberg, could not sell enough copper in small lots to keep up with production, and the crown invariably ended up selling to de Geer. It would have taken the company time to develop the kind of European contacts necessary to sell the large quantities that de Geer could place. Why keep the company in the middle? When the crown first established the company, marketing copper was simple. The company would ship to Lübeck and a German merchant would take it from there to Spain. That all changed in 1626 when Spain withdrew from the marketplace. After that year, the crown needed more sophisticated marketing, and rather than attempt to develop domestic expertise within the company, the crown sought an alliance with de Geer and the Trip clan. They could bring large lots of copper to Amsterdam and distribute them among smaller customers. The fact that de Geer also acted as a banker to the king meant that he had, by 1627, usurped the role of the Copper Company completely.[53] If we look, however, at the larger picture, these short-term advantages were not necessarily the best path for Sweden's industrial development. Had the king devoted resources to the company, it certainly could have developed the expertise to sell as well as de Geer and his associates in Amsterdam. Then the company and the country would have reaped the full benefits of the largest copper mine in Europe, with metal available at a steady and relatively low price.[54]

Gustav Adolf delivered the final blow to the company on April 28, 1628, with a distinct lack of fanfare. Indeed, it was almost a non-event compared to the publicity, including open letters from the king to the burghers of Lübeck and elsewhere, that preceded the company's first charter in 1619. This time the king merely issued a letter to the "participants," or shareholders, announcing the revocation of the charter of 1626. All the company's assets would revert to the crown. The king pledged to repay each shareholder's investment, plus 20 percent interest, until fully paid. He also gave extensive directions for the transition period to the new regime.[55] The next day, the king issued a detailed letter to Erik Larsson and Louis de Geer, formalizing the new copper deposit plan agreed upon and implemented almost a year before.[56]

53 Riksarkivet, SE/RA/1112.1/B/159 # 305–7 Försakning för Participanterne I handels Compagniet. April 28, 1628.
54 LDGBOA, 114–24.
55 Riksarkivet, SE/RA/1112.1/B/159 # 305–307, Försakning för Participanterne i handels Compagniet. April 28, 1628.
56 LDGBOA, 165–68.

In the final analysis, what was the legacy of the Copper Company on the Swedish domestic copper industry? The balance sheets demonstrate that the company invested heavily in the refining capacity at Säter and later at Arboga. This resulted in an important shift in the grades of copper that the company exported by the end of its term. In addition, the company was involved in expanding minting capacity at Säter, Arboga, and Nyköping. It was impossible to produce copper currency from *råkoppar*; refined copper sheet was necessary. Therefore, the king's drive to circulate a copper currency had the added benefit of encouraging more refining capacity. It is important to note that almost all the improvements in copper refining and processing took place after the king granted the first charter to the company. Before 1619, *råkoppar* was smelted at the crown's works in Born and at other locations near the Stora Kopparberg. The older Swedish works made little *gårkoppar* and no plate. Therefore, what the king was able to accomplish with the company is worth repeating. There was scarcely any additional refining capacity added until the king brought Govert Silentz from Holland, and the company financed the rebuilding of the works at Säter. The company also contributed to developing copper refining capacity at Norrköping. In 1628, the company's last year, the Stora Kopparberg produced 11,696 skd of *råkoppar*. That year the company minted 7,486 skd, meaning that at least 64 percent of all copper produced was made into *gårkoppar* or sheet for minting.[57] We know that the actual percent was greater, because some was shipped to the continent as well. Sweden's transition from a producer of *råkoppar* to a producer of thousands of *skeppund* of *gårkoppar* and copper plate a year was the legacy of Gustav Adolf's Copper Company.

There was, however, a dark side to the years of the company's dominance; it tended to exploit the *bergsmän*. The company was chronically late in paying these essential participants in the supply chain. Every charter issued by the king with privileges for the company specified that the *bergsmän* were to be paid in ready cash, and that a "*cassa*" was to be kept at scales in Falun for this purpose. This never occurred. Almost before the ink was dry on the 1621 company charter, complaints from the *bergsmän* about payment began to arrive on the chancellor's desk. We repeat a quotation from October of 1621: "Your loyal servants, Noble and well born Lord Chancellor, are in great need and distress for lack of payment at the mine."[58] As we have seen, the company was listing the payments to the *bergsmän* on the balance

---

57   Wolontis, *Kopparmyntningen*, 221 and 303.
58   AOSB, II, 11, 363.

sheets, but not making payments according to the charter. As the manager at Säter, Peter Kruse was also responsible for the company's purchasing activities at the mine. In a report to the company directors written in 1626, he complained: "At the Kopparberg I only hear about [lack of] payment. Many people plague me, who are in real need."[59]

Because of the undependable stream of payments, a curious alternative developed at the Kopparberg. When a *bergsmän* brought his copper to the city scales, the company official would issue a weight certificate called a *sedlar*, or *kopparsedlar*. When money did arrive at the mine, the *bergsmän* would present the *sedlar* for payment. In the meantime, however, the *sedlar* became a kind of currency. The local merchants would lend money to the *bergsmän* and take the *sedlar* as security. They also accepted *sedlar* as payment for wood and charcoal. The *bergsmän*, however, were not happy with this system. The merchants would only accept *sedlar* as security for loans or as payment for goods at a discount against the face value; and this discount fluctuated based on the prospects for payment to arrive.[60] Assuming an interest rate of 8 percent per year, each month one held a *sedlar* the value would decrease by 0.67 percent. In addition, one would have to hope that payment showed up at all. Although, when payment did arrive, it was not always distributed in an orderly fashion.[61]

In his history of the city of Falun, K.G. Hilderbrand relates an incident in 1625. There was a rumor in Falun that a wagon with payment would arrive. The *bergsmän* holding *sedlar* formed one group at the town gate, and the merchants also holding *sedlar* formed another. When the wagon arrived, a riot ensued with the *bergsmän* battling the merchants for possession of the coins. In the confusion, the money simply disappeared, and the company wrote a stern letter to the mayor of Falun seeking to recover it.[62]

Regardless of the implications for a free market economy, from Gustav Adolf's point of view, enforcing a purchasing monopoly on the *bergsmän* was one of the key achievements of his reign. It allowed him to exploit the copper resource by selling at home and abroad at the current market price, while keeping his cost of goods low and consistent. This leads us to pose again a central question of the chapter. Was the Copper Company a plausible idea with a reasonable chance for success? Given the crown's ability to control

59 ASOB, II, 11, 210–11.
60 Hilderbrandt, *Falun*, 42.
61 Hilderbrandt, *Falun*, 42.
62 Hilderbrandt, *Falun*, 42.

the cost of copper to the company, the basic concept appeared to be sound. In fact, the company had potential beyond what it achieved.

Investments in bronze cannon foundries, for example, or copper wire drawing facilities, would have allowed the company to export finished goods with a considerably higher profit margin than copper ingot. The crown had access to the largest copper mine in Europe, and the king's purchasing monopoly guaranteed that the mine would increase production, regardless of prices in Amsterdam. The competing mines in Saxony and the Tyrol were producing less every year, while the Stora Kopparberg produced more.[63] The company could have given the king the means to distribute not only copper into Europe, but also bronze cannon, copper coinage, copper wire, and copper sheet—in short, all the products made on the continent at that time. There was no particular reason that the king should simply sell copper ingots in Lübeck and Amsterdam and allow traders like de Geer and the Trips to make margins on Swedish exports. Given time, the company men, such as Mårtin Wewitzer and Peter Gröneberg, would have made their way to Aachen and to other centers of copper consumption and sell directly to the consumers there. If there were margins to be made, they would eventually find the end-users of copper and copper products. The employees of the Dutch East India Company did not build an empire by sitting behind desks in Amsterdam. The employees and representatives of the Copper Company should have been encouraged to make contacts with European consumers beyond Lübeck and Amsterdam, and to sell more than just copper ingot.

Unfortunately for the long-term funding of his expensive military projects, the king did not really give the company a chance to develop. Only a few years from its inception, Gustav Adolf was requesting large loans from the company. Then, in 1626, the king was trying to sell in Lübeck without the company's assistance. By the following year, he was dealing with de Geer and Trip, and profit margins that could have contributed to Swedish industrial development went to Amsterdam instead. One could defend the king against those critical of his monopoly on purchases of copper because his focus was on harnessing the copper resources to further his military and political goals. The same logic forces one to question his wisdom in abandoning the company after draining its financial resources. If the king had nurtured the company, and developed the export market, the company could have been the vehicle that financed his military ambitions in Poland and Germany. It was a missed opportunity for Gustav Adolf to solve his chronic financial difficulties.

---

63 Westermann, *Zur Silber und Kupferproduction*. (No pages noted).

Bibliography

Archival Sources

Riksarkiviet. Handel och Sjöfart arkiv, file 46 # 43 to 48, Förslag opå Compagneidtz Stat pro Anno 1625.

Riksarkivet. Handel och Sjöfart arkiv, file 46 # 3–12.

Riksarkivet. Handel och Sjöfart arkiv, file 2 # 100–104. Copper Company Balance Sheets for April 1927.

Riksarkivet. Handel och Sjöfart arkiv, file 2 # 105, Erik Larsson's Balance sheet for 1628.

Riksarkivet. Leufsta arkiv, Cooper Platen Debit Anno 1625 Amsterdam # 22, Garcooper Debit Anno 1626 Amsterdam # 25, Rouwcoper Debit Anno 1626 # 27.

Riksarkivet. Leufsta arkiv, file 81 # 111, Calculation purchased copper in 1628.

Riksarkivet. SE/RA/1112.1/B/150 (1623), # 123 Letter from Gustav Adolf to the Directors of the Koppar Companie. November 6, 1625.

Riksarkivet. SE/RA/1112.1/B/150 (1624), Letter from Gustav Adolf to Johan Skytte. November 6, 1625.

Riksarkivet. SE/RA/1112.1/B/159 # 305--07 Försakning för Participanterne I handels Compagniet. April 28, 1628.

Printed Primary Sources

Dahlgren, Erik Wilhelm, ed. *Louis de Geers brev och affärshandlingar* 1614–1652. Stockholm: P.A. Norstedt & Söner, 1934.

Oxenstierna, Axel. *Rikskansleren Axel Oxenstierna skriften och brefvexling*, Series I, 16 vols. Stockholm: P.A. Norstedt & Söner, 1888–Present.

Oxenstierna, Axel. *Rikskansleren Axel Oxenstierna skriften och brefvexling*, Series II, 14 vols. Stockholm: P.A. Norstedt & Söner, 1888--Present.

Stiernman, Anton von, ed. *Samling utaf kongl. brev, stadgar och förordordningar i angående Sweriges Rikes*, 4 vols. Stockholm: Kongl. Tryckeriet, 1747.

Van Dillen, Johannes Gerard, ed. "Amsterdamsche Notarieele Acten Betreffende den Koperhandel en de Uitoefening van Mijnbouw en Metaalindustrie in Zweden." *Bijdragen en mededeelingen van het Historisch Genootschap* 58. Utrecht: 1937.

Secondary Sources

Dahlgren, Erik Wilhelm. *Louis de Geer, 1587–1652, hans lif och verk*, 2 vols. Uppsala: Almqvist & Wiksells, 1923.

Heckscher, Eli Filip. *Sveriges economiska historia från Gustav Vasa*, 2 vols. Stockholm: Albert Bonniers, 1936.

Hilderbrand, Karl-Gustav. *Falu stads historia 1641–1687*. Falun: Falu nya boktryckeri, 1946.

Lindroth, Sven. *Gruvbrytning och kopparhantering vid Stora Kopparberg intill 1800 talets början*, 2 vols. Uppsala: Almqvist & Wiksells, 1955.

Roberts, Michael. *Gustavus Adolphus, a History of Sweden 1611–1632*, 2 vols. London: Longmans, Green and Co., 1957.

Soll, Jacob. *The Reckoning, Financial Accountability and the Rise and Fall of Nations*. New York: Basic Books, 2014.

Van der Muijssenberch, Winifried. "Corporate Governance, The Dutch Experience." *Transactional Law* 63 (2002–2003).

Wittrock, Georg, *Svenska handelscompaniet och kopparhandeln under Gustav II Adolf*. Uppsala: Almqvist & Wikesell, 1919.

Wolontis, Josef. *Kopparmyntning i Sverige 1624–1714*. Helsingfors: 1936.

5.   The Deposit System

Abstract

Chapter five examines the representatives the crown employed in Amsterdam. The king's ambassadors and commissioners in Amsterdam were competent men with experience in law and administration. They were not, however, capable of overseeing or even fully understanding, the complex world of buying and selling commodities in Amsterdam. The trading and financial experts, like Elias Trip and Louis de Geer simply ran circles around the king's administrators. This resulted in repeated financial setbacks for the crown. Chapter five also recounts the attempt of Louis de Geer, one of the king's closest financial advisors, to mislead the king and the chancellor. De Geer made a series of false claims, asserting that he could manipulate the copper market in Amsterdam.

Keywords: Louis de Geer visits Sweden, Erik Larsson, Conrad von Falkenberg, the deposit system, Prussian invasion, copper currency

> "When the sums are large, the merchants cannot be trusted."
> Gustav II Adolf

As we saw in the previous chapter, when King Gustav Adolf grew impatient with the Copper Company, he sought other means to market copper. The ideal solution would provide him with periodic loans which were necessary to expand his military intervention in northern Germany. During the winter of 1627, Louis de Geer and the king met in Sweden to discuss these issues. The result was the "deposit system," which gradually replaced the Copper Company as the king's preferred method for turning copper into silver-based currency. The principle was quite simple. The crown would send copper to Lübeck or Amsterdam and leave it there "on deposit." The crown would then mortgage the copper to a lender and receive a cash advance for its value. Naturally, the crown would also owe interest on the loan.

Stryker, L., *The Swedish Monarchy and the Copper Trade: The Copper Company, the Deposit System, and the Amsterdam Market, 1600–1640*. Amsterdam: Amsterdam University Press, 2024
DOI 10.5117/9789048560813_CH05

After much discussion and negotiation, the king appointed Louis de Geer and Erik Larsson to oversee and manage the "deposit system," so he could concentrate on military activities. Gustav Adolf relied on de Geer and Larsson to act on his behalf. Since Conrad von Falkenberg was stationed in Amsterdam during this period, he was also involved in the administration of the deposits there. The king summarized the new program in a detailed memorandum dated April 29, 1628.[1]

The deposit system allowed the king to turn copper into revenue, without putting the copper directly on the market for sale. His objective was to slow the supply of copper to the market, hoping to prevent the price from falling. At the same time, however, he still needed income from the mine, so he initiated this creative strategy of mortgaging the copper in Lübeck and Amsterdam, because they were commercial centers with access to capital. There were, however, serious drawbacks to this solution, which we will discuss in this chapter.

Regarding the deposit system, the historians from the last century are strangely silent. In fact, with the exception of Josef Wolontis, they were much more concerned with condemning the expansion of copper currency which also occurred during this period. This is puzzling because the deposit system was still in effect when the king was killed in battle in November 1632. Citing Dahlgren as his source, Roberts calls the deposit system "rather more successful" than some of the king's other ventures.

On April 29, 1628, after announcing the demise of the Swedish Trading Company, the king issued a memorandum confirming the agreement he had reached with de Geer and Larsson.[2] First, the agreement gave de Geer and Larsson full authority over all copper that the king controlled through a purchasing monopoly at the mine. This included *avrad* copper, purchased copper, and any copper still in company warehouses. In addition, the king instructed Peter Kruse and Gobert Silentz at Säter to give de Geer and Larsson a full accounting of company copper in storage, and all work in progress. While the king granted de Geer and Larsson sweeping powers over the disposal of copper, he did not relinquish his authority over them. They were required to submit monthly accounting reports to the *Rekninge-Kammar* (a Treasury Council office).

As mentioned in the last chapter, this deposit system was in effect from the middle of 1627 and, therefore, overlapped the company for a year. There were already small company owned copper inventories in Lübeck and Amsterdam, and the king wanted a full accounting of them, including all

1   Louis de Geers, *Brev och affärshandlingar* (LDGBOA), 166–68.
2   LDGBOA, 166–68.

expenses involved. He accepted that de Geer and Larsson should receive yearly interest payments on any copper they financed.[3] Although he neglected to mention it in the memorandum of April 29, 1628, the interest rate was set at 8 percent. As usual, the king imposed a floor price of RD 66 per skd for *gårkoppar* and RD 50 per skd for *råkoppar* on the current inventories.[4] De Geer and Larsson could sell from the deposit if they found customers above the floor prices. The original agreement specified that the copper be placed on deposit in Amsterdam in return for loans from de Geer and Larsson at the rate of RD 40 per skd.[5] As we shall see when we examine the balance sheets for deposits made in 1627 and 1628, the king's floor prices prevented any sales from this deposit.

The king also noted the schedule of intended new shipments; the first shipment of 2,000 skd *råkoppar* would leave promptly from Stockholm for Amsterdam. He instructed the factors (de Geer and Larsson), to make payments via bills of exchange, in the amount of RD 12,000 directly to Jakob de la Gardie in Riga, to support the army there. The balance went to the chancellor in Elbing, where he remained governor of the occupied territories in Prussia. The king also announced that 1,500 skd of *gårkoppar* would be ready for shipment in early August and that de Geer and Larsson should be ready with the payment of RD 90,000.[6] The proceeds from this shipment were again divided; RD 40,000 was to go to the defenders of Riga; RD 20,000 to de la Gardie personally, and RD 20,000 directly to one Heinrich Wulff, a merchant in Riga, for grain and other foodstuffs needed by the army there.[7] The king did not give directions for the balance but the pattern was clear. The crown shipped copper to Amsterdam or Lübeck, mortgaged the shipment, and directed de Geer and Larsson to send the revenue to pay and supply the armies abroad.

In addition, the king granted power and authority to de Geer and Larsson over the company's facilities: "The factors [de Geer and Larsson] shall have authority over the Kopparberg, Säter, and all the other mint works. The factors shall report directly to us [the king] and in my absence to the *Riks- and Kammar-Råd*."[8] Of course, there was a good reason for the king to

---

3   LDGBOA, 166–68.

4   As a reminder, currencies are abbreviated as follows: SD for Swedish *dalers*, RD for *riksdaler*, and DG for Dutch Guilders. The exchange rate was RD 1=DG 2.5 and RD 1= SD 1.624. *Skeppund* is abbreviated to "skd."

5   LDGBOA, 166-68.

6   Riksarkivet. Leufsa arkiv, file 81#119, Koppar Recknings meds Erik Larsson 1627–1628.

7   Axel Oxenstiernas, *Skrifter och brevväxling* (AOSB), II, 5, 423.

8   LDGBOA, 166-68.

grant de Geer and Larsson power and authority in Amsterdam. In addition to their financing and managing the copper deposits, he was depending on them to furnish SD 40,000 copper mint per month in currency to pay his military expenses. The king decreed that the factors should oversee the delivery of not fewer than 7,000 skd of copper each year to the mints, and that 7,000 skd should yield SD 480,000 copper mint per year, or SD 40,000 copper mint per month. This was so critical to the king he further specified that the factors were to make personal guarantees of performance. If the mint did not supply the SD 40,000 per month, de Geer and Larsson would supply it from personal funds.[9]

While the king granted de Geer and Larsson vast powers and responsibilities over copper trading and copper processing, they took on serious personal risk in return. A problem, such as the flood that interrupted minting at Säter two years earlier, could ruin both de Geer and Larsson if the king chose to enforce this clause. Gustav Adolf included an incentive clause as well. He stated that if he was satisfied with the performance of de Geer and Larsson on the projects outlined in the memorandum, he was prepared to grant them further privileges to expand production facilities in Sweden. So that the factors "might benefit themselves and others in the realm," the king would grant privileges for the development of bronze foundries, brass mills, and copper sheet mills. Of course, the agents would be investing their own capital on such projects. In return for the privilege of making the capital investment in Swedish industry, the agents would be obligated to pay the king a toll of SD 50 per skd of copper sold as finished product.[10]

Not surprisingly, there was often some difference between the king's intentions and the actual execution. As mentioned in the last chapter, in May of 1627 the Swedish army landed at Pilau in Prussia and proceeded to occupy the Baltic coast from Königsberg in the east to Elbing in the west. From this position, the king continued his intermittent war against his cousin, King Sigismund of Poland, who was now allied to the Imperial Hapsburg army under Count Wallenstein. We noted earlier that Gustav Adolf had appointed the chancellor governor of Prussia. When the campaign season ended, the king returned to Stockholm, but Oxenstierna remained at the military headquarters in Elbing. During these periods of separation, the king and the chancellor exchanged information frequently. In November 1627, the king wrote to the chancellor that he had shipped all the copper available to Amsterdam, and that he expected to receive RD 157,500 from that shipment

9   LDGBOA, 166–68.
10   LDGBOA, 166–68.

through Erik Larsson and Louis de Geer.[11] We also learn from the king's letter that de Geer's brother-in-law, Elias Trip, was financing the deposits. De Geer and Larsson were acting as factors for the king, Pieter Trip was their partner in Amsterdam, and Elias Trip was the banker.

The king also wrote that he had yet another shipment of copper en route from the Stora Kopparberg to Stockholm, worth RD 78,750, and he was anxious to get it aboard a vessel and sail it to Amsterdam before the Stockholm harbor froze. If he could not get it to Amsterdam, he wrote, the Trip family would not agree to accept collateral still in Stockholm. They would, therefore, not make the loan.[12]

The procedure for the deposit system was complex. The crown would notify Trip's agent in Stockholm, Arnold Huberts, that a shipment was ready. Then, Erik Larsson would draw up a contract, stating that the Trip family was lending the king RD 78,750, with copper as security. When the bill of lading was presented to the Trip family, they would accept it and send a bill of exchange to the crown.[13] The crown would present that to Trip's local agent for payment. In this case, the king asked Oxenstierna to inform Larsson, who was traveling in Germany on business, that the Treasury Council at Elbing would compose the conveyance documents for the copper and present them to the Trip family. He also requested that the Trip family direct the bill of exchange to the head of the Treasury Council, Gerdt Dirichsson. The king stated that he would ask Dirichsson to certify to the Trips that Arnold Huberts had been notified of the shipment.[14]

Within a couple of days, the king informed Oxenstierna that another RD 200,000 was available in Amsterdam.[15] These sums were the proceeds from the sale of grain the crown had collected as taxes. The king wanted this also to be transferred to Elbing by bill of exchange. This meant that king had anticipated the transfer of a total of RD 436,250 to maintain the army in Prussia.

But the money did not arrive. In February the king wrote to the chancellor complaining that he had finally heard from Peter Trip, who claimed that Erik Larsson had left instructions that no funds should be transferred until he was sure that the final copper shipment had sailed before the Stockholm harbor froze.[16] Meanwhile, Larsson was traveling in Germany and unreachable.

11   AOSB II, 1, 359–61.
12   AOSB II, 1, 359–61.
13   A bill of lading is a title document for shipped goods issued by the carrier, and it accompanies the shipment.
14   AOSB, II, 1, 359–61.
15   AOSB, II, 1, 359–61.
16   AOSB, II, 1, 381.

The head of the Elbing Treasury Council, Gerdt Dirichsson, drew up the shipping documents and the title documents conveying the copper to Trip. When Trip received the conveyance documents, he rejected them out of hand as incorrect. This put Dirichsson in a bad light and he immediately protested to Trip by letter but received no reply. Because of this debacle, the Trip family also refused to forward the RD 200,000 to Elbing by bill of exchange until the matter was resolved. This prompted the king to observe: "When the sums are large, merchants cannot be trusted."[17]

The chancellor also reacted with anger, as the head of the Treasury Council, Gerdt Dirichsson, reported to him. It was also clear from his reply that Oxenstierna knew about the problem before receiving the king's letter. He explained to the king that Dirichsson executed the conveyance documents under his supervision and that Dirichsson would not have sent the documents without his approval. Further, Oxenstierna wrote that Trip had no legal right to reject the conveyance, because all the documents were correct. Oxenstierna warned the king that it would be most difficult to begin the spring campaign with unpaid and mutinous troops. The chancellor further complained that Larsson was fully aware of the delicate situation in Prussia, which made his action unpardonable.[18]

One must wonder about Peter Trip and Erik Larsson's motive. Oxenstierna offered the king one possible explanation. When the crown was preparing to make the November shipment the previous year, there were already doubts about the ships getting through the ice. Larsson was in Germany, and he could not check whether the copper sailed. The last thing Larsson, de Geer, and the Trip family wanted was to mortgage copper that would sit all winter in a warehouse in Stockholm. So, Larsson had told Pieter Trip not to pay until he could verify the shipment. In doing so, Trip had to label the Dirichsson documents flawed in order to have a valid reason to reject them. This was, of course, simple to refute. The copper, once shipped, would arrive in Amsterdam at the same time, or shortly after, the bill of lading. Then Pieter Trip could verify the shipment by strolling down to the port and inspecting the cargo as it was unloaded from the vessel. The real reason must have been that the three partners were stalling for time. They had to find RD 236,250 to mortgage the copper and perhaps they did not have it either in cash or credit. In fact, on the same day that the chancellor wrote to the king, he received a bill of exchange from Larsson for RD 80,000.[19]

17   AOSB, II, 1, 382.
18   AOSB, I, 4, 73.
19   AOSB, I, 4, 73.

This partial payment seems to be convincing evidence that the partners did not have the funds to make the full mortgage payment.

Another explanation is equally probable, especially for the RD 200,000 that the partners held in cash from Wewitzer's sale of grain in Amsterdam, mentioned earlier. The Trip family had been holding this large sum, interest free, in Amsterdam at least since November. It was now almost March.[20] They seemed to be playing a traditional merchant game—delay payment for as long as possible and use money to make money. If they lent it in November for five months at 8 percent per annum, they would have earned RD 6,666 in interest. Or, perhaps they needed the money to finance a short-term trade that could yield 25 or 30 percent return. That is a strong motive to gain time. Apparently, the king was correct. One cannot trust merchants with large sums of money. There are too many reasons to delay payment.

This was just the beginning of the unfortunate treatment the crown experienced under the deposit system. The idea of mortgaging copper in Amsterdam was valid so long as one was dealing with honest and reliable partners. None of the merchants involved in this transaction lived up to this requirement. Once again, we are struck with the difficulties the crown faced trying to do business in Amsterdam without proper safeguards. The king was never able to prevent the Amsterdam merchants, on whom he depended, from exploiting their positions for their own benefit.

When the chancellor finally confronted Larsson, he did not disguise his annoyance with the agent. In a letter to the king, the chancellor wrote that Larsson had acted in his own narrow self-interest and disregarded the welfare of the Swedish Army in Prussia.[21] In his letter to Larsson the next day, he voiced his own personal disdain over the incident. "We deny that the shipment was not authorized, and we answer that you have caused untold harm and injury with your letter to Trip [causing a delay in payment]."[22] He also mentioned that the king was personally upset, and that Larsson had jeopardized the health and success of the army in Prussia. Larsson did not reply to this letter for several months.

When Larsson finally did answer the chancellor's critical letter of March 12, 1628, it was not a very satisfactory reply. He began with an excuse for not answering sooner: "I have not presumed to answer during the summer because I know that I am in disgrace from Your Honor's letter … I am innocent and I

20   AOSB, II, 1, 381-385.
21   AOSB, I, 4, 70–71.
22   AOSB, I, 4, 77–79.

take God as my witness."[23] Then Larsson once again blamed the head of the Treasury Council, Gert Diricksson, for creating the problem. He claimed that Diricksson sent the bill of lading without an "*uttinnan ordher*" or literally an "out in order." This must have been a letter stating that the copper was not to be consumed in the United Provinces but was there "in transit." The point being that if the copper cargo was to be shipped out of the United Provinces to Germany, for example, it was probably exempt from Dutch import duties. It would have been standard practice to issue an "in transit" letter for any shipment whose ultimate destination was unknown at the time of shipment. If the partnership did, in the end, sell the copper to a Dutch consumer, the import duty would be due. Today this is called shipping "in bond" and probably 99 percent of shipments to Rotterdam today are in bond. If Trip had accepted the bill of lading without the letter he probably would have been forced to pay the import duty. Therefore, according to Larsson, Trip rejected the bill with protest.[24] Larsson's explanation, however, does not survive scrutiny. He was, after all, in Germany in 1627 when he wrote the letter to Pieter Trip instructing him not to accept the conveyance of copper from Gerdt Diricksson. He would have no way of knowing that Diricksson had not sent a letter of transit with the conveyance. He was obviously making excuses for sitting on the money for five months. In any case, the missing letter of transit should not have delayed the RD 200,000 from grain sales that Wewitzer had turned over to Pieter Trip so that he could send a bill of exchange to Elbing.

Given recent experience Oxenstierna remained skeptical of the Trip connection and he sent a trusted financial type from Elbing, Isaac Spierinck, to Amsterdam to do a complete audit of the existing deposits there. Spierinck was met with a withering lack of cooperation from Trip and his associates: "They have appealed to Trip for assistance, but in his typical merchant style, he ignores them."[25] Spierinck wrote to the chancellor recommending that no more shipment be made until the accounting was in order. But necessity intervened. Despite unresolved discrepancies, Oxenstierna recalled Spierinck and resumed shipping copper to Amsterdam in order to ensure the continuous flow of credit.[26] Apparently, Trip also realized that he was indispensable and behaved accordingly. On the other hand, the crown never fully trusted Trip after this incident and it would have repercussions on his future business with Sweden.

23   AOSB, II, 11, 424–25.
24   AOSB, II, 11, 424–25.
25   AOSB, I, 4, 257.
26   AOSB, I, 4, 257.

Surprisingly, a little more than a month later, the king sent a formal written contract confirming the new deposit agreement (discussed at the beginning of this chapter) to de Geer and Larsson, which leads us to ask why the crown would continue to do business with the group after the payment fiasco?[27] The answer was probably that it had little choice. The king still needed credit; a monarchy in the seventeenth century with military ambitions ran on credit. As discussed earlier, it was not possible for the crown to obtain the credit necessary in Sweden, so the king had to rely on the most prominent money center in northern Europe, Amsterdam. His experience with the States General was mixed at best; he was still paying off debts to the States. The king and the chancellor realized that they needed access to the Trip family for credit and, at this point, de Geer and Larsson were the only connection. The chancellor acknowledged as much to the king in a letter toward the end of the year.[28]

One should also remember that de Geer was now a critical investor in Swedish industry and in that role, he was important to the crown in his own right. In 1628 alone, de Geer contracted to enlarge the shipyards in Norrköping, leased the saltpeter works at Linköping, leased two iron works from a defunct company making armor in Nora and Lindes, and he expanded once again the iron works at Norrköping to accommodate the growing exports of iron goods and cannon. In this last venture, one of his partners was Louis Trip, the cousin of Pieter Trip, and a nephew of Elias Trip.[29]

Nonetheless, it seems the crown was beginning to realize that closing the Copper Company, and trusting its future to the merchants of Amsterdam had some disadvantages. As a result of the payment debacle, the crown sent Conrad von Falkenberg to Amsterdam. He was to be the crown's watchdog over bills of exchange and other administrative details of the deposit system. Unfortunately for his performance, Falkenberg was not a merchant, and had only limited success in managing events for the crown's benefit. He also tended to feud with other crown representatives in Amsterdam.

Even without agent and banker problems in Amsterdam payments by bills of exchange took months to reach Stockholm or Elbing. This problem encouraged the crown to continue the copper currency experiment because of the time saved by turning copper ingot into low denomination coins. As noted earlier, the crown started minting copper in 1625 on a rather limited basis. By the end of the decade, however, minting copper

---

27 LDGBOA, 166–68.
28 AOSB, I, 4, 256–57.
29 LDGBOA, 180.

was fully developed. As the governor of occupied Prussia, Oxenstierna was responsible for promoting copper coins as valid currency, because the crown was anxious that the new currency be accepted by the troops and enjoy equal status with the silver coins of the Holy Roman Empire. If the population in general did not agree to transactions in the copper standard, then soldiers would be reluctant to accept payment in copper coins. If successful, however, the crown could turn copper directly into money without the slow and troublesome task of sending it to Amsterdam, selling it for cash, and then waiting for the merchants to remit the bills of exchange. Minting copper coins meant a serious improvement in the crown's cash flow.[30]

There was, unfortunately, a downside to the standard. The large quantities of copper specie that the crown used to pay its armies, and the *bergsmän*, resulted in the devaluation of the copper coins. This, in turn, discouraged local acceptance. In an attempt to address the devaluation, the chancellor fell into the trap of trying to peg one currency to another, rather than letting them float against one another. In August the chancellor issued a mandate stating that henceforth, one silver *riksdaler* would be at parity with three Polish copper *florins*. He further stated that copper currency was to trade freely with silver currency at the above exchange rate. To put teeth into the mandate Oxenstierna stated: "Our Royal Majesty, our merciful lord, orders all governors, officers and soldiers of the army, all members of the established classes, travelers and people involved in trafficking to observe these conditions to avoid severe punishment."[31]

He sounded serious about the punishments, although it is not clear if they were really enforced. For the first offense of refusing to accept currency at the above ratio, the unfortunate trader forfeited the goods involved in the transaction, plus any money involved, and paid a 10 *florin* fine. The fine increased to 20 *florins* for the second offense and 100 *florins* for the third, plus forfeiture of goods and money. A repeat offender could suffer a sentence of hard labor, confinement, and confiscation of goods. It was the duty of all governors, *burgermeisters*, members of the local governing councils, and any other officials to enforce this statute.[32]

The chancellor was both a scholar and a practical man of the world. Given his wide breathe of knowledge and experience one wonders if he really expected such a decree to make a difference. Clearly it did not. Within

---

30 AOSB, I, 4, 263–64.
31 ASOB, I, 4, 263–64.
32 ASOB, I, 4, 262–64.

months the ratio of *florins* to *riksdaler* had deteriorated further. Four months after his decree, instead of trading, as ordered, at one *riksdaler* per three copper *florins*, the ratio was between five copper *florins* and six copper *florins* per *riksdaler*. Oxenstierna attributed this to the weak copper market in Amsterdam. He was aware of prices in Amsterdam at RD 58 to RD 60 per skd, which are in line with prices reported by Posthumus for 1629.[33] In addition, the chancellor reminded the king of his recent sale of 1,000 skd of copper in Hamburg at RD 41 per skd. News of this sale had reached the port cities and the copper currency reacted.

In addition, the large quantities of copper currency mentioned were simply overwhelming the local economies. The chancellor wrote: "I know it was not from bad intentions, but particularly that part of Prussia occupied by Your Majesty is too full of copper currency ...." It would appear that, in general, inflation was not the problem, because the chancellor went on to write "... since the truce[34] the price of grain from Königsberg had fallen from 180 *florins* (silver mint) to between 150 and 160 *florins* (silver mint), and from Mewa one can buy grain at 130 *florins* (silver mint). But it's hardly possible to buy grain in any quarter for 600 *florins* (copper mint)."[35] It was the same, he reported, for all food and basic supplies.

The devaluation of the copper currency was particularly hard on the soldiers. The commissariat had difficulty purchasing grain and other supplies and the soldiers could not purchase supplies on their own. To this point, Oxenstierna observed, most of the officers and common soldiers had been patient; however, he feared trouble in the future. He suggested that the crown switch from minting copper to selling copper in Amsterdam to raise money for the troops;[36] and he was clearly upset: "I ask Your Majesty to judge for himself in this matter, if Your Majesty could help me. For a long time I have not been able to resolve this problem."[37]

Although he seldom mentioned the issue, we know that the king was well aware of the problem. First, the chancellor reminded him often from his headquarters in Elbing, as we have seen above. Second, he made an occasional rueful remark. For example, in a letter to the chancellor from Stockholm written in late April 1628, the king remarked, "I will not bring any more copper coins [into Stockholm] because they are overflowing here

---

33   ASOB, I, 4, 263–64 and Posthumus, *Prices*, 371.
34   Here the chancellor is referring to the cessation of hostilities between Denmark and the Imperial Armies under Count Wallenstein.
35   AOSB, I, 4, 436.
36   AOSB, I, 4, 436.
37   ASOB, I, 4, 435–37.

and I do not want to do more damage [to the value]."[38] So the king was not ignoring the problem; he just had no immediate solution.

The chancellor tried to gain acceptance for the copper currency, but he was swimming against the tide. The price of copper was falling on the Amsterdam markets, and, at the same time, the crown was pouring copper currency into coastal Prussia. Nothing would have prevented a decline against silver currency. It is worthwhile to emphasize, however, that the copper currency was not causing a generalized inflation. As cited earlier, the chancellor wrote that the price of grain had fallen in silver currency but was higher in copper currency. Thus, the issue was not inflation, but lower copper prices.

To answer the questions posed at the beginning of this section, I must repeat a point made many times before. To judge the success of the copper currency, we must once again consider the king's military and political goals. He was now in Prussia, poised to defend northern Germany against the Imperial armies; more than ever, the king required currency to feed and pay his armies. The copper currency was not perfect, but it was a solution. We saw in the beginning of this chapter the delays and difficulties the crown experienced when exporting copper to Amsterdam and receiving payment by bills of exchange. This was not only because of the inherent awkwardness in the process, but also because the merchants with whom the king did business in Amsterdam were self-serving and greedy.[39] I conclude, therefore, that despite the dislocations caused by the copper currency, it sufficed as a relatively quick means of turning copper ingot into low denominational currency.

Now we turn from the vast plains of eastern Prussia and Livonia to Amsterdam to consider the effect that copper coins had there. Residents of the city reported regularly to the crown that quantities of copper coins were arriving in the city and that their presence resulted in lower prices for copper ingot.[40] Is this logical? Would it matter whether the copper showed up in the form of ingot or coins? We know already that the crown was going to ship copper regardless of the price. What did it matter that it appeared as coin? How did these coins make their way from Sweden, Prussia, and Livonia and why were they not accepted locally. The term used in trading circles for this phenomenon is "arbitrage." It means simply that if the prices for a commodity are different in two separate and distinct locations, the commodity will be drawn to the location with the higher price, until the prices in both locations even out.

38   AOSB, II, 1, 405.
39   Stryker, *Sharp Practice*, 131–62.
40   AOSB, II, 11, 568 and AOSB, II, 11, 578.

One can see the effects of arbitrage as local secondary markets developed for the copper coins. The regional merchants would buy the copper coins at an ever-increasing discount from the soldiers stationed in Prussia and pay them in silver coins that were acceptable to providers of food and lodging. What did the merchants then do with the copper? Conrad von Falkenberg, the crown's commissioner in Amsterdam, provided the answer. Writing to the chancellor in September 1629, he described the endless supply of copper coins that were arriving in Amsterdam: "One cannot sell one pound of copper here ... copper coins arrive daily and are going for as low as DG 48 to DG 50 per hundredweight [RD 55 per skd]."[41]

Again, writing to the chancellor in January of the following year Falkenberg says: "Copper trading, Merciful Lord, goes very badly here because there are too many copper coins coming from Sweden, Prussia, and Livonia."[42] Erik Larsson also joined the chorus in his report to the chancellor after returning from Amsterdam in April 1631: "The copper coins are replacing all other kinds of copper in Amsterdam ... Some casting works are now melting coins instead of ingot for their castings. What is the point of spending the money to make copper into coins if it will be melted?"[43] It was only one year earlier, when the chancellor arrived in Elbing, that he decreed henceforth the copper currency would be valued at one *riksdaler* to three *florins* copper mint.

There was plenty of evidence that the copper currency, being minted by the king and used to pay his soldiers, local suppliers, and *bergsmän*, was pouring into Amsterdam between the years 1628 and 1631. The following are the quantities of copper sent to the mint during this period. We will soon understand, however, that because of capacity restraints, not all of it was turned into coins in the year it arrived.

Figure 8.   Minted Copper[44]

1625	595 skd
1626	7,255 skd
1627	2,518 skd
1628	7,486 skd
1629	6,435 skd
1630	3,483 skd
1631	1,082 skd
1632	4,118 skd

41   AOSB, II, 11, 570.
42   AOSB, II, 11, 578.
43   ASOB, II, 11, 439.
44   Wolontis, *Kopparmyntning*, 249–52.

Nevertheless, a significant amount of copper currency was sent every year from Sweden to Prussia and Livonia. The puzzling issue was the mechanism for drawing the copper coins out of the far reaches of the Swedish Empire onto the market in Amsterdam. When Falkenberg and Larsson wrote that the copper market was quiet, they must have meant that the market for ingots was quiet. For copper coins to travel from Livonia or inland Sweden to Amsterdam meant that the silver mint currency price for them in Amsterdam had to be higher than elsewhere. Otherwise, there would be no reason for the coins to make the journey to Amsterdam. This is arbitrage; the higher prices in Amsterdam drew the copper coins from the local markets in Prussia, Livonia, and Sweden. For example, Falkenberg wrote repeatedly that copper currency was being sold in Amsterdam at around DG 50 per hundredweight, or RD 55 per skd Stockholm weight.[45] We know the freight and expenses from Stockholm to Amsterdam totaled about RD 5 per skd. The equivalent price in Stockholm, and probably elsewhere, therefore, would have been RD 50 per skd, remembering that the *riksdaler* was a silver coin. If the local merchants in Stockholm, Riga, Elbing, and Königsberg could exchange the copper currency at an equivalent of RD 45 per skd then they could ship it to Amsterdam, sell at the Amsterdam exchange at RD 55 per skd, and make a profit of RD 5 per skd before financing. In practice, there would have been other middlemen involved, but the principle is clear. Every part of the Baltic area occupied by Swedish troops, or supplying Swedish troops, was involved in a copper arbitrage trade with Amsterdam.

Another obvious question, then, is why merchants in Amsterdam were able to pay a significantly higher price for copper coins than the merchants in Riga or Elbing. The answer applies not just to copper coins, but to copper in general. The merchants of Amsterdam had business connections with copper consumers in northern and southern Netherlands and, most importantly, in the Aachen region, the center for the early modern copper and bronze industry in Europe. Copper arriving in Amsterdam would be loaded aboard riverboats and shipped up the Rhine and the Maas Rivers to customers in Aachen. Because Amsterdam merchants knew their customers in Aachen, they also knew the latest sales prices and, therefore, could buy at a price that would allow them a profit. In addition, they also knew which customers were buying and how much they were buying. In many cases, they would probably be covering short contracts they had already made for delivery in the future. In summary, they enjoyed an information edge over the merchants in Riga or Elbing, just as those merchants would have

---

45   AOSB, II, 11, 570.

an advantage over an Amsterdam merchant wanting to sell into their markets.[46]

We discussed in the last chapter the king's desire that the copper currency should trade, or be exchanged, with silver currency at the rate of one *skeppund* copper currency to SD 150, which was the reason he imposed a floor price on the Copper Company's sales.[47] The copper coins were being sold in Amsterdam at the equivalent of RD 55 per skd Stockholm weight, which was equal to SD 89.37 per skd Stockholm weight. This was a long way from the king's original goal. We must, therefore, ask was the policy beneficial? As we mentioned in the introduction, Heckscher objected to the policy on the grounds that it kept the price of copper low. On the issue of putting pressure on the price, one can only agree. When copper is put on the market, in whatever form, it increases supply and works against higher prices. It was not, however, as if the crown had any choice. In 1630 the chancellor wrote in the candid "Considerations": "While there was general agreement that copper was undervalued, and would soon recover, the crown was financially weak; the crown's situation was poor so that it could not afford to let copper lie, as it would have preferred."[48] This is the clearest possible statement of our persistent theme. It appears to me that Prof. Heckscher and his followers objected to the king's monopoly purchasing policy, and to his copper mint, without considering the king's priorities. As the chancellor stated, the crown was financially weak, it would have preferred to leave the copper in the ground at current prices, but it had no choice. In June of 1630 Gustav Adolf landed his army at Peenemunde, near Stettin in northern Germany. He was now fully engaged in the war against the Imperial armies, and he needed every resource available. To criticize the king's allocation of copper is to miss an important point; he had no choice unless he changed his broader political and military goals.

It is also clear that the amount of copper that made its way to Amsterdam was essentially the same whether or not the crown chose to mint it. The path would have been different, but whether as ingot or coins, the same amount of copper would have eventually reached Amsterdam due to the elaborate collection system that developed in areas where the crown was spending the copper currency. The advantage for the crown was time. By minting copper, the crown did not increase the amount of copper to reach the

---

46   For a discussion on the importance of information see Lesger, *The Rise*, chapter 6.
47   Stiernman, *Samling*, 4, 924.
48   AOSB, I, 1, 345.

markets, it simply turned copper into currency more quickly, thus improving the crown's cash flow. The time saved was worth the cost of minting.

We saw above that starting in 1629 the king's agents in Amsterdam were reporting to the crown that the abundance of copper coins was depressing the copper market; so, the crown was aware that the copper coins were damaging the price. If, as suggested by the commentators of the last century, the purpose of the copper currency was to withhold copper from the market, the crown then knew the strategy was not working. Nevertheless, the crown continued an aggressive policy of minting copper coins until after the king's death in 1632.[49] This is probably the most convincing argument that the purpose of the copper mint was not primarily to cause an artificial shortage. If that had been the primary purpose, the king would have ended the project just the way he abolished the Copper Company when that proved ineffective. The reason the crown continued to mint copper coins was to provide large quantities of low denominational currency to pay the soldiers abroad and the *bergmän* at home.

The question of the parallel standard is subtler and brings us to the issue of bimetallism. This term usually applies to countries that have parallel gold and silver standards. Milton Friedman defines bimetallism as "a government commitment to buy either gold or silver at fixed prices in money designated as legal tender." And he refers to the period between 1837 and the American Civil War during which the US Government set the ratio at one ounce of gold to 16 ounces of silver. The second aspect of bimetallism is open access to minting. Every individual has the opportunity to mint silver and gold into currency. Thus, while the price of the two metals is fixed, the supply of coins is not stable and could change constantly. Economists do not all agree on the benefits of the dual currencies. Friedman believes that bimetallism can contribute to stability. When the supply of gold in not sufficient to support an expanding supply of money, silver can be minted in its place. He refers to France's dual standard that functioned successfully from the end of the Napoleonic era to the Franco-Prussian War in 1871.[50]

A different group of economists, represented by Angela Redish, consider a bimetallic regime to be unstable because of changes in the inherent values. If the market value for gold advanced rapidly, silver would become undervalued against the official ratios. The result would inevitably be an increase in the quantity of silver circulating and a decrease in the quantity of gold circulating as individuals spent their undervalued silver, and hoarded

---

49 Wolonits, *Kopparmyntningen*, 303.
50 Friedman, Bimetallism Reivisted, 85–86, 95.

their overvalued gold. If the market prices continued to diverge gold would disappear entirely, and the regime would revert to a single currency.[51] This is precisely what happened in Stockholm, Riga, Livonia, and Prussia. The local economies were overwhelmed with copper currency, with the result that silver coins disappeared from circulation.

As is often the case with innovation, time appears to fix the problem, at least partially. By April 1630, the copper currency was gaining limited acceptance in some locations. The chancellor wrote that he had been able to hire German foot soldiers and cavalry with the promise of payment in copper. He was also pleased to report that the exchange rate to *riksdalers* had remained steady at between five *florins* (copper mint) and 5.5 *florins* (copper mint) and that he was able to supply the army in Prussia over the winter relying mostly on the copper currency. He pointed out, however, that he could not pay all debts in copper, as some creditors still demanded silver-based coins.[52] By the summer of 1631, the copper currency had gained general acceptance in occupied Prussia—perhaps aided by the lack of silver currency—and the ratio had climbed to one *riksdaler* for four *florins* (copper mint). Oxenstierna was using this rate to collect the important port tolls in Pilau and Königsberg.[53]

These tolls were a critical part of the crown's war chest. When the king first occupied Prussia, in 1626 through 1627, he levied import and export tolls on all Prussian ports. He began with Danzig and then appropriated the tolls in Pillau from his father-in-law, the Margrave Elector of Brandenburg. The tolls ranged from just over 7 percent in Pilau to 14.5 percent in Danzig on the value of the goods.[54] By the end of 1628, the crown levied tolls at every port in occupied Prussia, and some internal tolls as well. As governor, Oxenstierna oversaw the entire enterprise, but the actual administration was carried out with withering efficiency by Pieter Spierinck, the brother of Isaac Spierinck, whom we met earlier on the chancellor's business in Amsterdam. The tolls were the largest overseas source of revenue. In 1629, for example, the crown collected RD 584,000 from the tolls.[55] That same year, the chancellor estimated that revenue from copper would amount to RD 805,000.[56] Thus, when the chancellor asked the king for directions on Prussian toll issues, it was in earnest. Hitherto, the tolls were levied in

---

51   Redish, *Bimetallism*, 184–85.
52   AOSB, I, 5, 257–58.
53   AOSB, I, 5, 253–58.
54   Roberts, *Gustavus Adolphus*, 2, 82.
55   Roberts, *Gustavus Adolphus*, 2, 84.
56   AOSB, I, 1, 455.

copper currency to assure circulation of the coin. The chancellor now asked the king, in light of the shortage of *riksdalers*, if he should begin collecting the tolls in *riksdalers* to force them back into circulation. The chancellor was concerned that the copper currency was driving silver coins out of circulation in northern Germany. He knew that had already happened in Sweden because of his correspondence with Count-Palatine Johan Casimir, the king's brother-in-law, and a member of the *Kammar-Råd*.[57] This observation demonstrated the chancellor's grasp of the currency issue, which he shared with the king.

Not surprisingly, the king replied that he had been discussing the issue with a mint master, Balthasar Zwirner. Since the king was still in Saxony, we can assume that he was referring to a German mint master. He wrote that he and Zwirner had decided that the crown had put too much copper currency into circulation in northern Germany, which threatened the copper standard.[58]

The king and the mint master thought the solution was to continue to mint copper, and, at the same time, begin, once again, to mint silver *riksdalers*. This plan had been approved by both the *Riks-Råd* and the *Kammer-Råd*. The king hoped that circulating both currencies would help commerce and avoid the problem of one currency overwhelming another. Once again, this demonstrated that the king was aware of the problem. Unfortunately for the local economy, this suggestion did not result in a quick solution to the devaluation of the copper currency. Apparently, the authorities could not organize a return to minting silver until after the king's death in 1632. Once the silver currency was readily available, moreover, the relationship between the two currencies stabilized both in Sweden and in the occupied areas of Germany and Poland.[59] This contradicts the position taken by Heckscher,[60] and repeated by Roberts with his usual eloquence: "Gustav Adolf was at the mercy of economic forces he could not control and only dimly appreciated."[61]

We opened this chapter with a discussion of the contract between the king and the business partnership of Louis de Geer, Erik Larsson, and the Trip family. One should not forget, however, that the deposit system really began shortly after de Geer's visit to the Stora Kopparberg in April 1627 with the agreement outlined by de Geer to Pieter Trip in letters written in April

57   AOSB, II, 10, 563.
58   AOSB, II, 1, 743.
59   Wolontis, *Kopparmyntiningen*, 92-93.
60   Heckscher, *historia*, 1, 455-61.
61   Roberts, *Gustavus Adolphus*, 2, 98.

and May of 1627. By the time the king issued the formal contract, therefore, the deposit system was already functioning.[62]

The period after the Copper Company, during which de Geer's consortium handled copper trading and minting is covered by a balance sheet for the years 1627 and 1628 (see Appendix D). The most striking feature of these years was the large quantity of copper on deposit in Amsterdam. At the end of 1628 there were 9,547.1 skd of copper on deposit, guaranteeing a loan from the de Geer consortium of RD 430,220.8. These amounts would be staggering even for the de Geers and the Trips. Certainly, the partners enriched themselves by remortgaging the copper at a higher price and borrowing at a lower interest rate, because de Geer mentioned it later in another context—as if it were common practice.[63] The king was paying them 8 percent interest on a loan priced at RD 45 per skd. We must remember that because the crown did not enjoy a favorable credit rating in Amsterdam, the price was lower than market value. The market value, at the time, for *gårkoppar* was RD 62 per skd. The copper was located in a warehouse in Amsterdam under the control of the partners. They could mortgage the same 9547.1 skd to others at a price of at least RD 55 per skd. This would allow them to take RD 95,471 from the transaction. They were, in effect, borrowing the money interest free. In addition, since the partners enjoyed a favorable credit rating among their peers, they probably borrowed money at 5 percent or below, using the king's copper as collateral. Since they were lending to the king at 8 percent, they had an additional profit of 3 percent or more per year. Most important, the partners got back their capital so they could employ it for other, more profitable purposes. We assume this was standard procedure during the entire period of the deposit system, and it explains the large differential between the copper values that the merchants lent against versus the market value of copper. In fact, in a letter from Louis de Geer to his assistant, he proudly boasts of lending the crown money against a deposit of crown copper in Amsterdam at 8 percent and borrowing against the same copper for 4 percent.[64] If the assumption is correct, this was yet another example of the merchants in Amsterdam taking advantage of the crown's distance to exploit the situation.

The copper deposit contract between the crown, Louis de Geer, and Erik Larsson expired at the end of 1628; the king and the chancellor pondered how best to proceed. While the chancellor was established in Elbing, the

---

62 LDGBOA, 115–25.
63 LDGBOA, 236.
64 LDGBOA, 252–53.

king was mostly in Prussia, but frequently back in Stockholm. Nonetheless, it was typical of the king to remain fully informed on both the copper market and the latest copper mint and *riksdaler* exchange rate. The king and the chancellor, however, faced a dilemma: de Geer, their preferred deposit partner, was now living in Sweden. In the past, he was an ideal buffer between the crown and the Trips. With de Geer gone from Amsterdam, the crown would be forced to have Falkenberg deal directly with the Trips. In a letter at the end of 1628, the chancellor complained to the king about a residual problem from the last deposit contract with de Geer. Elias Trip had "remonstrated" against Erik Larsson's last accounting for interest because a parcel of copper had remained in Hamburg for some time, and Trip refused to make an advance until it arrived in Amsterdam: "He made remonstration as only Trip, so full of his merchant bravado, could do."[65] The chancellor was clearly exasperated with Trip. It was with some trepidation, no doubt, that the crown instructed Falkenberg, a courtier, not a merchant, to negotiate a new deposit contract with the Trip family.

Despite second thoughts in Stockholm, Falkenburg successfully negotiated a new agreement on May 16, 1629,[66] and it furnishes us with an example of the accuracy of correspondence versus balance sheets. The contract is published in full in J.G. van Dillen's collection of documents on the copper trade. As background, Conrad Falkenberg's brother, Dietrich, was in Amsterdam to purchase arms and to hire mercenaries. There was pressure from the crown to conclude a new deposit agreement to cover these expenses. The new contract was for a total of 21,000 skd of copper to be delivered at the rate of 7,000 skd per year for three years. Trip was to mortgage the copper at DG 40 per hundredweight or RD 44 per skd Stockholm weight for *råkoppar* and DG 50 per hundredweight or RD 55 per skd Stockholm weight for *gårkoppar*. The crown agreed to pay Trip interest at the rate of 7 percent per year. The interest was payable in copper or in currency, and if the crown failed to pay the interest on time, Trip had the right to seize enough copper to cover the interest payment and sell it. In addition, Trip had the ability to sell the copper to others if he could obtain the minimum price of DG 50 per hundredweight or RD 55 per skd Stockholm weight for the *råkoppar* or DG 60 per hundredweight or RD 66 per skd Stockholm weight. As in previous contracts, Trip was responsible for arranging the logistics, such as freight and insurance.

As mentioned, the terms of the contract are published and easily accessible. The well-known expert on the Trip family, P.W. Klein, even calculated

65   AOSB, I, 4, 257–60.
66   Van Dillen, *Notarieele*, 234.

that this transaction would consume up to RD 386,000 in Trip family credit if the full 21,000 skd were actually shipped.[67]A balance sheet that survives in the Riksarkivet, however, makes clear that of the 21,000 skd mentioned in the contract, only 441 skd were shipped.[68] Shortly after the contract was signed the copper prices began to fall, and Elias Trip used a legal escape clause to refuse future shipments.

In the beginning of this chapter, I observed that the deposit system was hampered by disloyal and self-serving actions of the merchants on whom the king depended. In January 1631 the king appointed Erik Larsson the factor in Amsterdam and gave him full authority to dispose of all the copper to be exported for the next three years. The king explained these powers in a memorandum that he sent to Larsson early in the year.[69] The end result of Larsson's discussions with Elias Trip was a highly unfavorable deposit contract that left the crown in considerable debt to Trip. Unfortunately, there is no possibility of proving or disproving that Larsson profited personally from the trade, or that he merely negotiated without conviction on the king's behalf. Falkenberg was convinced that Larsson had betrayed the king, but he was also interested in assuming the full authority that the king had granted to Larsson, so his motives are suspect. Both the king and the chancellor also expressed doubts about Larsson's loyalty when they learned about the unfavorable contract conditions.

The terms of this suspect agreement were negotiated in February 1632, when Larsson met with Elias Trip in Amsterdam. To put these discussions in context, we will review the market events at the time. In June 1631, Larsson had informed the chancellor that prices in Amsterdam were softening and *gårkoppar* was selling at to RD 44 per skd Stockholm weight for lots of 100 skd.[70] According to Larsson, this meant that he would probably not be able to negotiate a mortgage contract for more than RD 40 per skd. Also at this time, Larsson was engaged in a negotiation with the representative of the king of France for a shipment of 4,000 skd of *gårkoppar* for the royal cannon foundry. He had offered the copper at DG 46 per hundredweight (RD 50 per skd) but was told by the customer that copper was available at DG 41 per hundredweight (RD 45 per skd). Larsson was also trying to sell the king's *gårkoppar* in Aachen. He had offered 1,000 skd to a merchant there at DG

67 Klein, *De Trippen*, 360.
68 Riksarkivet Stockholm, Handel och Sjöfart vol. 46 "Gustavus Adolphus Conick van Sweden" 1633.
69 Riksarkivet. SE/RA/1112.1/B/172 (1631) #23–27, Memorial för Erik Larsson, January 16, 1631.
70 This price is confirmed by Wolontis who also reported a sale in June 1631 at RD 44 per skd.

44 per hundredweight and was again told that the prices there were DG 41 per hundredweight (RD 50 per skd).[71]

Ten days before he began discussions with Elias Trip regarding a new contract, Larsson wrote to the chancellor complaining that copper coins were coming from Danzig (most likely currency from the army) and that mortgages on copper might not be possible above RD 40 per skd Stockholm weight.[72]

The above was Larsson's assessment of the market, communicated to the crown, in early February 1632, as he prepared to begin discussions with Elias Trip. The negotiations with Trip lasted four days. In the end, Trip agreed to mortgage 18,000 skd of copper at RD 40 per skd for *gårkoppar*, and RD 30.75 for *råkoppar*. The interest rate was set at 7 percent. Trip had the right to sell the copper if the interest was not paid, and the king had the right to redeem the copper, either partially or in full, upon payment of the mortgage and the unpaid interest. Unlike the deposit agreement of 1629, which was hardly implemented, the crown shipped a total of 4,535 skd against this new agreement during the year. At the end of 1632, the total value of the mortgaged copper and unpaid interest owed to Trip alone, was DG 885,783[73] (RD 354,313), an amount that the crown could never have paid given its military expenditures.

Conrad von Falkenberg wasted no time informing the king about the new terms of the contract. First he explained the details outlined above, then he launched into a polemic: "Because of this unfavorable contract ... I think that I could have achieved more favorable deposit terms if Your Majesty would grant me full authority."[74] Falkenberg could have added that the price currents for February 1632 reported an average price of DG 44 per hundredweight, or RD 48.4 per skd Stockholm weight.[75] This was a much higher price than Larsson had been reporting to the crown.

The Falkenberg letter is noteworthy because it is so self-serving. First, he described the meeting between Larsson and Trip as if it were a conspiracy rather than a business negotiation. Then he distanced himself from the contract and claimed that he could have achieved a better result. Unfortunately for the crown, there were probably very few merchants, even in Amsterdam, with the resources to mortgage 18,000 skd of copper with a redemption bill

71   AOSB, II, 11, 454–55.

72   AOSB, II, 11, 477.

73   Riksarkivet. Handel och Sjöfart arkiv, file 46. # 206–208, 210 Gustavus Adolphus Coninck van Zweden (1629).

74   AOSB, II, 11, 596.

75   Posthumus, *Prices*, 371.

of approximately RD 300,000, so whoever did the negotiation would almost certainly have to deal with Elias Trip.

In the final paragraph of his report, Falkenberg turned informer. He referred to a letter sent by the king on January 30, 1632, to both him and Erik Larsson in which the king ordered secrecy regarding copper sales.[76] Falkenberg claimed that Larsson passed on sales information to Trip.[77] While keeping sales prices secret might make sense from the king's military headquarters in Bavaria, it was not realistic in a city full of merchants like Amsterdam. All sales would quickly become public knowledge. Even if the merchants themselves were discrete, their clerks and the people executing the transfer of ownership documents would use such information to trade for favors or other information. Falkenberg would have known this and informing on Larsson for trading information with Trip was just another method to discrediting him.

Despite Falkenberg's prejudices his suspicions were probably justified, especially in light of the misleading price information that Larsson fed to the crown. In addition, in January 1632 de Geer made a sale of *gårkoppar* in Amsterdam at RD 51.[78] This is convincing evidence that the market was moving upward in early 1632. This trend continued through out the year. One must conclude that Larsson had supplied the crown with misinformation in order to justify the low mortgage price. Then, without informing the crown the terms of the new agreement, Larsson went on an extended business trip to Germany. He finally wrote to the chancellor from Schwabach, near Nuremberg, on March 21, and he made no mention of the new contract at all. Instead, he allowed his rival, Falkenberg, to make the announcement to the king with a self-promoting slant.[79] When he learned of these new terms, the king was furious with Erik Larsson and Elias Trip. He accused Larsson of having a secret agreement with Trip in order to benefit personally from the unfavorable agreement.

The other important issue is that prices began to recover in early 1632. It is impossible, or course, to analyze the cause without better production and consumption statistics, but the crown's policy of mortgaging copper in Amsterdam, rather than selling it, may have contributed to the price increase. In addition, the Thirty Years War was then fourteen years old, and

76   Riksarkivet. SE/RA/1112.1/B/176 (1632) # 24, Till alle Gubernatorerne och [illegible] om mijntesz.

77   AOSB, II, 11, 596.

78   Riksarkivet Stockholm. Leufsta arkiv, v. 109 #016.

79   Riksarkivet. Handel och Sjöfart arkiv, file 46. # 210, Gustavus Adolphus Coninck van Zweden (1632).

the Swedes had been campaigning in Germany for two years. There was, no doubt, a strong demand for the implements of war, including bronze cannon.

What was Larsson and Trip's motive for setting the price low for the copper to be mortgaged and setting the interest rate high. The answer is key to understanding the deposit system and is supplied by Louis de Geer who obviously wanted to be back in the trade. He wrote to the chancellor after the negotiation. The letter is dated only 1632, but it probably arrived mid-year.[80] De Geer explained to the chancellor that the copper shipped against the new contract was all being remortgaged. Trip was paying RD 40 per skd, but he was remortgaging it at not less than RD 55 per skd and perhaps up to RD 60 per skd. The difference between the RD 40 and the RD 55 to RD 60 now became part of Trip's working capital. As mentioned earlier, the crown shipped 4,535 skd by the end of 1632. If Trip remortgaged this quantity at RD 55 per skd (using de Geer's lower end estimate) he would increase his working capital by RD 68,025. Of course, he would have shared this windfall with Larsson. By the end of the year the crown had about 23,000 skd on deposit in Amsterdam and northern Germany. Probably every *skeppund* was similarly remortgaged.[81]

In summary, the deposit system was a creative idea, but an inappropriate solution to the crown's dilemma. The crown's objective was to turn copper into silver-based currency, without actually putting it on the market when prices were low. But the system was expensive. It cost the crown 7 to 8 percent per year in interest alone. If left unpaid, the interest would compound. The majority of the copper was stored in Amsterdam where the crown had difficulty with accounting and administration. It also opened the king to exploitation and abuse by merchants located too far away to control. It is not probable that merchants in Stockholm could have remortgaged the copper at better rates without the crown discovering the ploy. Finally, storing the copper in Amsterdam worked against the crown's stated goals. The crown was afraid that selling copper would force the prices down. Yet keeping large stockpiles of copper in Amsterdam, the center of the European copper market, also had a negative effect on prices. Every merchant in town would have known about the inventory, and its existence would discourage merchants from holding onto copper. They also would have known that the king could, at any moment, decide to liquidate his position and prices would plunge. The crown would have been better served by simply selling copper

80   LDGBOA, 236.
81   Stryker, *The King's Currency*, 66, and AOSB, II, 11, 596.

into the market. Let us not forget that the king still was buying from the *bergsmän* at a price that guaranteed him profit even at lower copper prices.

With Larsson and Trip both out of favor with the crown because of the February contract, Louis de Geer saw an opportunity to once again dominate the copper market in Amsterdam. If successful, he could combine exporting both grades of copper to Europe with the export of end products from his factories in Sweden. This would have been a powerful tool and a step towards a true monopoly position. De Geer's strategy was to fabricate a market manipulation and report it to the king and the chancellor. He hoped to appear as the master trader in the eyes of the crown. There was a brief price recovery in the summer of 1632. This followed rumors among traders in Amsterdam that the king would stop all copper shipments to Amsterdam throughout the year.[82] Through a series of letters de Geer described fictitious trades to the crown and succeeded not only in convincing the king and the chancellor, but also convincing two generations of historians that he had manipulated the copper market in Amsterdam.

This is a classic case of correspondence versus balance sheets. The correspondence from de Geer to the crown is convincing. It is only by analyzing the balance sheets that I was able to contradict de Geer's account. The story began in 1629 when the king asked de Geer to put 720 skd of copper on deposit in Amsterdam.[83] De Geer agreed. It was these 720 skd that de Geer claimed he used to manipulate the market. The balance sheets, however, tell a different story.

Before we analyze the numbers, however, we must understand de Geer's exaggerated account and the reaction to this account by historians of the last century. In August of 1632 de Geer wrote the following to the king:

> Sire,
> Since I left the company of Your Majesty, I have continued to work to bolster the copper price, because it remained low. To this end I have developed a strategy; the siege of Maastricht has cut off transportation to the city of Aachen, and nothing can now be shipped there. We have "cast the ball" [or, cast the die] with a parcel of 720 [ship pounds] here [in Amsterdam] that is the property of Your Majesty ... it has now been sold and resold five, six, or seven times daily, and passed from hand to hand and sold and sold again, for not one additional ship pound can reach Aachen.

82   AOSB, II, 11, 596.
83   LDGBOA, 196.

This caused pressure ... the price is now DG 55 per hundredweight,[84] or RD 60 per skd, and that is up from DG 45 per hundredweight. My plan was to make several sales and then to buy back at a higher price. We now sell at DG 55. Twice as much copper as is located in town [Amsterdam] and its environs ... has been sold by other merchants as well, who sell among themselves.[85]

De Geer then explained his technique to the king. He sold a small quantity of copper at DG 45.62 then bought the same parcel back at DG 46 per skd. Then he bought another small parcel at DG 49. He then sold 125 skd at DG 49 and, a short time later, he bought back a mere 20 skd at DG 50 per hundredweight. He sold 500 skd at DG 50.50 and bought some of it back at DG 51, DG 52.50 and DG 53. Each time he sold, he bought back at a slightly higher price, knowing that he was paying above the market. He claimed that through this series of purchases and sales he had turned a stagnant market into an active bidding war. Later in the month he wrote to the chancellor taking full responsibility for moving the copper price in Amsterdam from DG 46 per hundredweight (RD 50.50 per skd) to almost DG 60 per hundredweight (RD 65.8 per skd).[86]

Some further explanation of de Geer's letter is necessary. Maastricht was a heavily fortified bastion on the river Maas garrisoned with Spanish troops. This fortress overlooked the normal route, via the river Maas, for shipments of bulk commodities between Amsterdam and Aachen, the center for early modern copper and bronze production. As part of the interminable War of Dutch Independence, in June 1632, the Dutch general Frederick Henry, Prince of Orange, laid siege to the fortress, thus blocking shipments of copper to Aachen. The city surrendered on August 28, 1632.

Continuing with the theme that the crown was not well served by its servants in Amsterdam, let us examine the extravagant claims that Louis de Geer made to the king and the chancellor. He claimed full credit for the 1632 recovery in the copper market.[87] De Geer clearly realized that since both Trip and Larsson were out of royal favor, the time was right to regain control over the marketing of Swedish copper in Amsterdam. His strategy was to invent a brilliant piece of market manipulation aimed at demonstrating his prowess as a trader. In August 1632, de Geer first wrote to the king and to

84 Just to remind the reader, Dutch gilders or DG traded at RD 1 = DG 2.5 for the entire period under discussion.

85 LDGBOA, 237.

86 LDGBOA, 239.

87 LDGBOA, 236.

the chancellor. In case they failed to see the significance of his news, a few days later he wrote again, claiming to have moved the market up to RD 60 per skd. On August 28, he wrote that, through buying and selling, he moved the market above RD 65 per skd in Amsterdam.[88]

Historians of the last century accepted de Geer's fanciful story, perhaps because of the intriguing image of a single trader manipulating a market. It is noteworthy that Wittrock, writing in 1919, never mentions the incident. He may have found it too implausible to repeat. In his 1923 biography of de Geer, E.W. Dahlgren accepted the merchant's manipulation claims uncritically and he quoted the entire letter that de Geer wrote to the king in August 1632 cited above. In fact, Dahlgren believed that the king's effort, through the deposit system, to starve the copper market in the west was finally having an effect. De Geer anticipated this and through his "brilliant manipulation"[89] turned an upward price trend into a feeding frenzy.

In his multi-volume economic history of Sweden, published in 1936, E.F. Heckscher did not spend pages on the incident. Yet he did mention the manipulation and praised de Geer for the results. Heckscher described de Geer's technique of selling small parcels and then buying them back as creating a "trading mentality" of climbing prices. The result was a 60 percent price increase. Most importantly, however, Heckscher recognized de Geer's motive. By manipulating the price de Geer distinguished himself from other potential rivals in Amsterdam, such as Trip, Larsson, and Falkenberg, who also sought a lucrative copper monopoly.[90]

George Wolontis, in his work on the copper currency, repeated Dahlgren's account of the manipulation. In fact, he quoted the letter shown earlier and did not question its validity. Nevertheless, he states, "[i]t is true that Louis de Geer 'cast the ball,' as he called it, and he certainly had a hand in moving the market." Wolontis accepted de Geer's role as a successful market manipulator, but he was convinced that the king's policy of withholding copper from the market through the deposit system made the manipulation possible. As long as the crown maintained the discipline of not selling off large lots, the market remained relatively high.[91]

This summary of the literature on the manipulation shows how pervasive it was in Swedish economic history. It also made its way into English and Dutch historical literature. In his 1958 biography of Gustav Adolf, Michael

---

88 LDGBOA, 236–39.
89 Dahlgren, *Louis de Geer*, 1, 204.
90 Heckscher, *historia*, 1, 453–54.
91 Wolontis, *Kopparmyntingen*, 38–39.

Roberts described the events much like Hecksher and Wolontis. The king's copper policy was beginning to bear fruit, but it was de Geer's prowess as a market maker that made the change "more pronounced," and directly caused the market to move upward.[92]

In his later account the historian of the Trip family, P.W. Klein, accepts de Geer's description of the "house maneuver" without question or objection. He describes the maneuver as a series of anonymous trades through which de Geer would offer copper to the market and then buy it back at a higher price. Again, it is noteworthy that Klein accepts de Geer's own description of the events without question.[93] The same is true of the final and most recent description of the events. Writing in 1995, the eminent Dutch historian, Thomas Lindblad, described de Geer's maneuver as "actions that presuppose control over a substantial proportion of the total supply," or approaching a monopoly position. Like his predecessors Lindblad accepted Heckscher's version of events.[94]

This was a rather curious story, and one wonders that accomplished historians publishing between 1923 and 1995 fell for this unlikely tale without some verification beyond de Geer's self-serving correspondence. The first notification that de Geer gave of his market manipulation was in a May 19, 1632 letter to Pieter Spierinck. The letter concerned bills of exchange that de Geer was helping Spierinck to float in Frankfurt for the chancellor. In it de Geer claims that he caused the market to increase from RD 44 per skd to RD 57 per skd.[95] He asked Spierinck discretely to tell the chancellor what he had accomplished and asked that the chancellor relate the news to the king. Either the chancellor never learned of de Geer's accomplishments, or he was otherwise occupied because he did not relay the tale to the king. The king was similarly occupied with the war in Germany. He defeated the Catholic army under Count Tilly in March of 1632 at the Battle of Rain and, after a sojourn plundering Bavaria during the summer, the king was preparing to face a new Catholic army under Count Albrecht von Wallenstein.

Altogether de Geer wrote once to Peter Spierlinck, three times to the chancellor and five times to the king.[96] In each letter he claimed to have manipulated the copper market in Amsterdam, and he mentioned specific trades that accomplished this goal. Each letter was designed to promote his

---

92   Roberts, *Gustavus Adolphus*, 2, 103.

93   Klein, *De Trippen*, 375.

94   Lindbad, *Louis de Geer*, 81.

95   LDGBOA, 226.

96   LDGBOA, 226, 236–39, 242–43.

cause. To investigate the veracity of these claims we will begin by asking whether the trades de Geer described actually occurred.

The letters that de Geer wrote to the crown are available in a collection of the merchant's correspondence edited by E.W. Dahlgren during the time he spent in the de Geer family archives (the *Leufsta arkiv*). This collection is now located in the Riksarkiv in Stockholm. Dahlgren's edition contains, however, only a fraction of the archive and includes no balance sheets and limited financial information. Dahlgren included the correspondence between de Geer and the crown, but he did not include the balance sheet for the 720 skd of copper[97] that de Geer had on deposit and claimed to have used for the manipulation. Nor did it include de Geer's financial records for the year 1632, which are necessary to prove or disprove the series of trades that de Geer pretended to make after he sold off the 720 skd. One must visit the Riksarkiv to encounter these documents.

The 720 skd remained the property of the king on deposit in Amsterdam until de Geer began to sell off the parcel in April of 1632. The balance sheet for the sale of the 720 skd is a separate document in the unpublished part of the *Leufsta arkiv* because de Geer was acting as agent for the king when he sold from this inventory. De Geer was the seller, but the king owned the copper, and the records were kept by Trip, acting as banker. Once de Geer sold the lots listed, however, they were no longer part of the king's inventory. If de Geer bought and sold copper for his own account, as he claimed, these transactions would be listed in his personal ledgers for the year 1632. The ledgers show, however, only one copper sale; he sold 40 skd to Adam Floris at DG 46 per hundredweight in January 1632.[98] He made no purchases of copper in Amsterdam that year. The elaborate detail in which de Geer's assistant, Johan le Thoor, recorded the business that de Geer did transact in Amsterdam in 1632 is a further argument against the manipulation. If transactions such as the sale of bronze cannon, personnel salaries, even the purchase of wine were included in the business ledgers, then a series of sales and purchases of copper, meant to move the market, would surely be included as well.[99] There is no record showing his participation in the manipulation he claimed. I also checked the Handel och Sjöfart arkiv (Trade and Shipping Archive) with similar results.[100]

97 Riksarkivet. Leufsta arkiv, file 81 # 137–39, Con. Mat. Coperreecken
98 Riksarkivet. Leufsta arkiv, file 109 # 16, Jan le Thoor, Credit, Laus Deo Anno 1632 Amst.
99 Riksarkivet. Leufsta arkiv, file 109 # 2–16, 30–41. Jan le Thoor, Credit, Laus Deo Anno 1632 Amst.
100 This archive contains much of the Copper Company sources.

De Geer was able to sell the king's copper at higher prices in June 1632 than when he began the campaign in April. This is clear from the sales listed in Appendix E.[101] De Geer, however, was certainly guilty of exaggeration and perhaps worse in the series of letters he composed for the crown. For, while the price did go up, it appears that de Geer did nothing to affect the price except to sell into a rising market; which is, in itself, commendable. His tales of buying and selling for his own account, however, were pure fantasy.

The dates were also puzzling. De Geer made the sales registered on the balance sheet (see Appendix E) between April and the end of June. He mentioned to Pieter Spierinck, on May 19, that he had raised the price from RD 44 to RD 57 per skd, and asked Spierinck to pass the information on to the crown, but then he dropped the subject.[102] De Geer's last sale was in late June of 1632. He only informed the king of his manipulation in mid-August, or more than six weeks after his last sale; further, he presented the information as if the sales were contemporary with the letter. The best explanation was that he wanted to be sure that copper was in a sustained rally before he took credit for the manipulation. If he had started his "copper campaign" in June, and watched the market collapse in July, he would have gained nothing. By August 21, when he first wrote to the king on the subject, he was convinced that the king's policy of mortgaging copper had kept enough copper off the market to move prices up for a sustained rally. He decided in August, therefore, to begin the campaign to receive full authority, and hopefully to take over the mortgage on the parcel of 23,000 skd on deposit with Elias Trip as well.

The kind of manipulation that de Geer described to the crown is possible for short periods of time only if there was a fundamental change in the supply/demand curve.

If the king's policy of keeping copper off the market had finally begun to bear fruit, then a series of trades at higher prices could change the participant's perception and turn the stagnant market into a bull market. It's important to note, however, that the manipulation does not cause the change, it merely uncovers a change in the fundamentals. A manipulation without a secular movement is doomed, because the higher the price goes, the more copper that is attracted to Amsterdam. The manipulator is then faced with a distasteful choice. If he fails to continue buying, the price will fall. If, however, he continues to buy he increases his risk position at high prices. Eventually the manipulator runs out of money or credit and

101 Riksarkivet. Leufsta arkiv, file 81 # 137–39, Con. Mat. Coperreecken.
102 LDGBOA, 226.

the price returns to levels dictated by the supply/demand curve. A recent example is the Hunt Brothers' attempt to manipulate the silver market in the late 1970s and early 1980s. By buying large quantities of silver the Hunt Brothers were able of push the market from US$ 11.00 per troy ounce in September 1979 to nearly US$ 50.00 per troy ounce in January 1980. At this level, however, the brothers could no longer borrow against inventory, and their credit was exhausted. The predictable result was a sharp decline in the price of silver. By March 1980 the price of silver was back to US$ 11.00 per troy ounce. De Geer was much too astute to fall into such a trap. He sold the king's inventory into a rising market, and then invented a self-serving story to curry the crown's favor.

Despite de Geer's carefully crafted plan to draw attention to his skill as a trader neither the king nor the chancellor acknowledged his supposed efforts. In his final letter to the king dated October 20/30, 1632 de Geer announced that the price of copper was now above RD 75 per skd, and that the frenetic buying and selling (caused, of course by de Geer's clever scheme) was continuing.[103] This final letters somehow gained the king's attention and he replied warmly to de Geer: "Our mercy and appreciation goes to you, honored and special friend. We read with interest your letter about the business affairs ... We have considered your communication and we would like to propose that we confer on the subject in person ..."[104]

Finally, all the maneuvering and correspondence had succeeded. The king was at last ready to meet with him to discuss the future. De Geer doubtless had hopes of controlling the export of copper from Sweden along with the export of copper bearing products such as bronze cannon from his Swedish production facilities. In short, he was in striking distance of his goal. Suddenly, however, his plans came undone. While engaging Albrecht von Wallenstein and the Imperial armies at the critical battlefield of Lützen, King Gustav Adolf was killed, and his armies left leaderless.

We stated at the beginning of this chapter that the king was not well served by his business associates in Amsterdam. De Geer's deception was perhaps the cruelest of all. He waited until his serious rivals for control of the copper trade in Amsterdam, Elias Trip and Erik Larsson, were in disgrace. Now he was the only remaining merchant in the city who enjoyed the crown's full confidence. He then used this confidence to invent a story of heroic intervention in the copper market, which resulted in a 50 percent increase in prices in Amsterdam.

103 LDGBOA, 243.
104 Dahlgren, *Louis de Geer*, 1, 206.

De Geer's goal in inventing this story must have been to regain the lucrative deposit business from the crown. Because he spent most of his time between 1628 and 1632 in Sweden consolidating his industrial investments there, he missed the three-year deposit starting in 1629. Since he had originally persuaded the king to try the system during their travels together in 1627, he must have felt a certain ownership over the policy. It turned out to be lucrative for the lender, and expensive for the crown. It is not surprising that de Geer wanted his place of dominance back, and the myth he invented for the crown was the ideal vehicle for him to recover lost ground. By all appearances, it was working. The king wanted to meet with him to discuss his plans. Had the meeting taken place, de Geer might well have achieved his goal. In addition, because of the torrent of letters de Geer wrote, later published by Dahlgren, the story appeared in books written by some of the most distinguished historians of northern Europe.

Although the Trip mortgage would stay intact for some time, the deposit system ended with the death of the king. It certainly had not worked as the king planned. The ideal strategy would have been for the crown simply to withhold copper from the market. Unfortunately, as the chancellor repeatedly observed, this was not a realistic option. By the end of the 1620s Sweden had invaded northern Germany. In 1631 Sweden was campaigning aggressively and confronting the power of the Imperial Hapsburg armies. The crown needed to turn copper into specie in order to fund its ambitious political and military agenda.

The deposit system developed by the king and de Geer had one advantage: copper did not reach the market unless the crown chose to release it. De Geer and his associates proposed the system in the first place because it greatly benefited the merchants. Even after the interest rates fell to 7 percent on copper mortgaged at RD 50 per skd, it added a cost of RD 3.5 per skd the first year, and it compounded thereafter. If the crown had chosen to redeem the copper from the May 1629 mortgage contract in May of 1631, the cost would have been RD 57.25. The difference is RD 7.25, representing two years of interest compounded yearly. If the crown had sold the copper into the market, and the market dropped more than RD 7.25 during the period, the king would have benefitted. However, this sort of calculation is impossible to predict and probably the crown should have sold at the best price possible all along. The cost from the *bergsmän* (RD 27.7 per skd Stockholm weight) was so low that the crown would probably always have made a profit.

On the other hand, the deposit system was a source of revenue for de Geer, Larsson, and most of all for Elias Trip. They received the interest and used much of the mortgage money to purchase arms for the crown, on which they also made a profit. In addition, I am convinced that they were guilty of various "sharp practices" mentioned in this chapter.[105] The most obvious was remortgaging the copper in Amsterdam at a higher price and a lower interest rate than the mortgage with the crown. They could, therefore, take a profit and still make 3 to 4 percent on the interest. We have de Geer's accusation that Larsson and Trip were remortgaging copper from the highly suspicious contract negotiated in early 1632. More to the point, de Geer boasted to Johan Le Thoor of doing the same with the 720 skd; lending to the king at 8 percent with the king's copper as collateral and borrowing at 4 percent interest again using the king's copper.

The merchants it trusted served the crown poorly. The kind of abuse mentioned above would never have been possible under the Copper Company regime. I am quite sure that remortgaging was a common feature of all involved in the deposit system, and it was a highly profitable practice as well. Even de Geer, the crown's favored merchant, was guilty of egregious conduct. Since he had designed the deposit system in 1627, he realized the potential for profit. When he noticed the weakened condition of his rivals, he created an elaborate hoax to court royal favor and regain the mortgage.

Bibliography

Archival Sources

Riksarkivet. Handel och Sjöfart arkiv, file 46. # 206–208, 210 Gustavus Adolphus Coninck van Zweden (1629).

Riksarkivet Stockholm, Handel och Sjöfart arkiv file 46 "Gustavus Adolphus Conick van Sweden" 1633.

Riksarkivet. Leufsta arkiv, file 109 # 2–16, 30–41. Jan le Thoor, Credit, Laus Deo Anno 1632 Amst.

Riksarkivet. Leufsa arkiv, file 81#119, Koppar Recknings meds Erik Larsson 1627–1628.

Riksarkivet Leufsta arkiv, file 109 #016.

Riksarkivet. Leufsta arkiv, file 81 # 137–39, Con. Mat. Coperreecken.

Riksarkivet. Leufsta arkiv, file 109 # 16, Jan le Thoor, Credit, Laus Deo Anno 1632 Amst.

Riksarkivet. SE/RA/1112.1/B/172 (1631) #23–27, Memorial för Erik Larsson, January 16, 1631.

Riksarkivet. SE/RA/1112.1/B/176 (1632) # 24, Till alle Gubernatorerne och [illegible] om mijntesz.

---

105 See Stryker, *Sharp Practices*, 131–62.

Printed Primary Sources

Dahlgren, Erik Wilhelm, ed. *Louis de Geers brev och affärshandlingar* 1614–1652. Stockholm: P.A. Norstedt & Söner, 1934.

Oxenstierna, Axel. *Rikskansleren Axel Oxenstierna skriften och brefvexling*, Series I, 16 vols. Stockholm: P.A. Norstedt & Söner, 1888–Present.

Oxenstierna, Axel. *Rikskansleren Axel Oxenstierna skriften och brefvexling*, Series II, 14 vols. Stockholm: P.A. Norstedt & Söner, 1888–Present.

Stiernman, Anton von, ed. *Samling utaf kongl. brev, stadgar och förordordningar i angående Sweriges Rikes*, 4 vols. Stockholm: Kongl, Tryckeriet, 1747.

Van Dillen, Johannes Gerard, ed. "Amsterdamsche Notarieele Acten Betreffende den Koperhandel en de Uitoefening van Mijnbouw en Metaalindustrie in Zweden." *Bijdragen en mededeelingen van het Historisch Genootschap* 58. Utrecht: 1937.

Secondary Sources

Dahlgren, Erik Wilhelm. *Louis de Geer, 1587–1652, hans lif och verk*, 2 vols. Uppsala: Almqvist & Wiksells, 1923.

Friedman, Milton. "Bimetallism Revisited." *The Journal of Economic Perspectives* 4, no. 4 (1990): 85–104.

Heckscher, Eli Filip. *Sveriges economiska historia från Gustav Vasa*, 2 vols. Stockholm: Albert Bonniers, 1936.

Klein, Peter Wolfgang. *De Trippen in de 17e Eeuw, een Studie over het Ondernemersgedrag op de Hollandse Stapelmarkt*. Rotterdam: Assen, 1965.

Lesger, Clé. *The Rise of the Amsterdam Market and Information Exchange: Merchants, Commercial Expansion, and Change in the Spatial Economy of the Low Countries, 1550–1630*. Translated by J.C. Grayson. Aldershot: Ashgate. 2006.

Lindbad, Thomas. "Louis de Geer (1587–1652) Dutch Entrepreneur and the Father of Swedish Industry." In Lesger, Clé and Noordegraaf, Leo. eds. *Entrepreneurs and Entrepreneurship in Early Modern Times, Merchants and Industrialists within the Orbit of the Dutch Stable Market*, edited by Clé Lesger and Leo Noordegraaf, . The Hague: Hollandse Historische Reeks XXIV, 1995.

Posthumus, Nicolaas Wilhelmus. *Inquiry into the History of Prices in Holland*, 2 vols. Leiden: E.J. Brill. 1946.

Redish, Angela. *Bimetallism, an Economic and Historic Analysis*. Cambridge: Cambridge University Press, 2000.

Roberts, Michael. *Gustavus Adolphus, a History of Sweden 1611–1632*, 2 vols. London: Longmans, Green and Co. 1957.

Soll, Jacob. *The Reckoning, Financial Accountability and the Rise and Fall of Nations*. New York: Basic Books, 2014.

Stryker, Lawrence. "'Sharp Practice' Among Merchants in Seventeenth-Century Amsterdam 1620–1632." *The Journal of European Economic History* XLIII, no. 3 (2014): 131–62.

Wittrock, Georg. *Svenska handelscompaniet och kopparhandeln under Gustav II Adolf.* Uppsala: Almqvist & Wikesell, 1919.

Wolontis, Josef. *Kopparmyntning i Sverige 1624–1714.* Helsingfors: 1936.

6. After the King

Abstract

In chapter six we witness the outcome of a dispute between the Trip family and the Swedish crown. In abbreviated terms, in 1632 the crown owed the Trip family RD 836,000 plus an annual interest bill of RD 58,500. The sum was crippling and there was no chance of a conventional settlement. The Chancellor made several attempts to pass oversight responsibility to the Swedish *Riks-Råd* (the privy council) without success. Over the next couple of years the crown carried out a desultory negotiation with the Tripp Family but it ended in harsh recrimination on both sides. Finally, the crown lost patience and defaulted on its loans from the Trip family. The resulting legal suits were finally settled in 1873.

Keywords: Queen Kristina, Elias Trip, Walloons, John Casimir, the Count Palatine, Axel Oxenstierna

> *"Wer lobt, kauft nicht.* (Whoever praises will not buy.)"
> Old German/Yiddish trader saying

Predictably, immediately after the king's death uncertainty reigned in Sweden, Amsterdam, and Germany regarding copper policy. There was the usual scramble for power and influence, especially over the question of who would dominate copper distribution on the continent. The candidates soon prepared for battle. De Geer clearly had not abandoned his ambition to regain control of the sale of Swedish copper in Amsterdam and the north German cities of Hamburg and Lübeck. To that end, he began a letter writing campaign to the *Riks-Råd* and the *Kammar-Råd* to demonstrate his expertise. The *Riks-Råd* was the traditional medieval council populated by the hereditary nobility. The *Kammar-Råd* was an administrative body that controlled the contemporary functions of government, such as tax collection. Johan Skytte, born a commoner, was a prominent member of the *Kammar-Råd*.

Stryker, L., *The Swedish Monarchy and the Copper Trade: The Copper Company, the Deposit System, and the Amsterdam Market, 1600–1640*. Amsterdam: Amsterdam University Press, 2024
DOI 10.5117/9789048560813_CH06

As part of his own campaign to gain control over copper sales in Amsterdam, Conrad von Falkenberg initiated a lawsuit against de Geer and attempted to discredit him both in Sweden and in Amsterdam.[1] Meanwhile, Chancellor Oxenstierna, now head of the armies in Germany and leader of the regency counsel, wanted to turn copper policy over to the *Riks-Råd*. He began a dialogue with the *Riks-Råd* and the *Kammar-Råd* on the subject, but there was no rapid resolution.

Gustav Adolf was killed at the battle of Lützen on November 6, 1632. The copper market's immediate response to the king's death was a sharp fall in prices, because traders expected the liquidation of the copper deposit inventories in Amsterdam. No one was certain how to proceed. In early December, de Geer wrote to Pieter Spierinck. De Geer was worried about continued supplies of copper to his industrial plants in Sweden after the king's death, and he asked Spierinck to seek assurance from the chancellor. He commented on the effect the king's death had on prices: "Regarding copper prices, I helped to drive them up to DG 70 [per hundredweight or RD 77 per skd]. Now after the sad events they have fallen to DG 64 [per hundredweight or RD 70.5 per skd]."[2]

Meanwhile, back in Stockholm, Gustav Adolf's six-year-old daughter, Queen Kristina, succeeded to the throne. To no one's surprise, Axel Oxenstierna became the head of the regency council as well as the new supreme commander of the Swedish armies in Germany. Initially the chancellor attempted to maintain the late king's copper policy. He wrote to the *Riks-Råd* on November 14, 1632, from his current headquarters at Frankfurt, only days after the king's death. Apparently, Falkenberg had written to the king recommending that the crown liquidate some of its large copper deposit inventory in Amsterdam. The chancellor replied that Gustav Adolf had been determined to sell only enough copper to cover interest costs and his policy was still in effect.[3]

Prior to this the chancellor sent the *Riks-Råd* a long formal announcement of the king's death, and information on the decisions that were pending. Regarding copper, he simply reiterated that for the moment the king's policies should remain. The king had authorized Erik Larsson, for example, to sell inventories in Hamburg and Amsterdam to pay the Trip family some

---

1   Axel Oxenstiernas, *Skrifter och brevväxling* (AOSB), II, 11, 621.
2   Louis de Geers, *Brev och affärshandlingar* (LDGBOA), 248.
     As a reminder, currencies are abbreviated as follows: SD for Swedish *dalers*, RD for *riksdaler*, and DG for Dutch Guilders. The exchange rate was RD 1=DG 2.5 and RD 1= SD 1.624. *Skeppund* is abbreviated to "skd."
3   AOSB, I, 7, 649–50 see also AOSB, I, 7, 663.

of the interest owed on the large deposit still in their hands.[4] In early December Oxenstierna wrote again to the *Riks-Råd*; he directed the letter to the council's secretary, Lars Grubbe. First, he made clear that he supported a program of ceasing all further shipments of copper to the continent. The chancellor stated, however, that the *Riks-Råd* should make the difficult decisions on how best to proceed. He would make suggestions, but the council had the final say.[5]

After the king's death, the *Riks-Råd* quite naturally rose in importance. John Casimir, the Count Palatine, and husband of the late king's sister, dominated this body. Gustav Adolf had preferred to rely on the *Kammar-Råd*; some prominent noblemen, such as the chancellor, were members of both bodies. In January 1633, the chancellor wrote to Claus Fleming, also a member of both councils, with a copy to Johan Casimir, indicating his desire that the *Riks-Råd* take over the administration of copper policy. He wanted Fleming and the Count Palatine to oversee the effort. In his letter, the chancellor included a brief history of copper prices. He explained the price rise that had occurred over the previous year, noting the tightening of supplies, and attributing it to the king's policy of selling as little as possible. He also mentioned the destruction of the mines at Mansfeld in Saxony because of military action, and the fact that the Imperial Army in Germany blocked Transylvanian copper from reaching western markets. The main consuming areas in Germany: Aachen, Frankfurt, Nuremberg, and Meissen were, therefore, forced to pay a premium for copper.[6]

He explained, in addition, the copper monopoly, the supply lines and the deposit system. He estimated that the total amount owed to the *bergsmän* for their copper and to the merchants in Amsterdam, Lübeck, and Hamburg for interest on copper in deposit would exceed RD 300,000. Despite the cost, the chancellor recommended that the *Riks-Råd* continue the deposit at least for the immediate future: "Despite other hindrances the best advice is to leave the copper where it is now in Lübeck, Hamburg, and Amsterdam and pay the interest."[7]

The chancellor also commented that the merchants involved in the deposit system all hoped that the crown would be forced to sell the inventory so they, the merchants, could buy the copper at distressed prices. He then provided a brief description of the important copper merchants with whom

4   AOSB, I, 7, 649.
5   AOSB, I, 7, 707-09.
6   ASOB, I, 8, 94-95.
7   AOSB, I, 8, 96.

the crown did business. This was the only instance the chancellor gave a frank opinion of the players in writing (apart from frequent complaints about Elias Trip). Regarding Erik Larsson, the chancellor wrote: "He has the right intentions, but he is not good at defending his actions … he bears watching, but I do not think him guilty of disloyalty or embezzlement."[8]

On de Geer and Trip the chancellor commented: "De Geer and Trip, and others like them, care about nothing except their own profit. One day they serve the crown and the next day they insult it." Mårtin Wewitzer fared rather better; Oxenstierna wrote he was "fully good." Conrad von Falkenberg, however, "means well, but he fights with Erik Larsson and the other merchants in Amsterdam."[9]

I do not agree with the chancellor that the merchants involved in the deposit system hoped that the crown would be forced to sell the copper rather than mortgage it. The deposit system was a great boon for the merchants, and a continuing cash drain for the crown. When the idea first arose in discussions between de Geer and the king, in 1627, the system was an innovative method for absorbing copper immediately after Spain left the market and caused a surplus. By 1632, however, the policy had outlived its advantage. By the end of that year Elias Trip had 23,885 skd[10] (6.8 million modern pounds) of copper in inventory at an average value of RD 35 per skd for a total value of RD 836,000 and an annual interest bill of about RD 58,500.[11] This was too high a price to pay in the long run, and the system was doomed because the crown could not pay the ever-increasing interest. The merchants also profited by remortgaging the copper at a lower interest rate and often at a higher price. They were, therefore, able to turn the deposit into a profitable business with little risk.

In 1630 the king requested the chancellor's views on the future of copper policy. In response, the chancellor wrote "*Betänkande om kopparhandeln och kopparmyntningen*" (Considerations on Copper Trading and Copper Minting).

The chancellor's "Considerations" are a useful measuring stick. He stated his position on many subjects regarding copper and copper minting, and in such detail that one can compare the chancellor's performance, after the king's death, to his stated goals in the "Considerations." Was he able to implement the reforms that he suggested to the king, or did the pressures of feeding and supplying armies in the field force him to adopt expediencies

---

8   AOSB, I, 8, 98.
9   AOSB, I, 8, 98.
10   Stryker, *The King's Currency*, 66.
11   Stryker, *The King's Currency*, 66.

that ran counter to his stated views? We have noted the connection between Sweden's exports of copper and her insatiable need for cash to fund the wars in Germany. Did the chancellor fall victim to these same historic problems?

Oxenstierna introduced the "Considerations" with the following description quoted earlier: "Copper is the noblest commodity that the Swedish Crown produces and can boast of, wherein also a great part of the crown's welfare stands."[12] He then further wrote "the crown's situation was poor so that it could not afford to let copper lie, as it would have preferred."[13] As we have seen, the crown was not willing to sell at the low prices recorded after 1626, so it decided to ship copper to Amsterdam and borrow against it. In retrospect, Oxenstierna considered this a thoroughly bad idea. He believed that the merchants (such as Elias Trip) who received the copper had the use of the resource given to the crown "by the grace of God." The chancellor went on to call the deposit system an insult. He observed that the merchants realized over time that the crown was not going to be able to redeem the copper by paying the principal and the interest. The growing stocks, therefore, caused prices to fall further. The chancellor believed that the merchants were waiting for the crown to liquidate these positions at low prices. They waited "with open mouths like a wolf after a lamb."[14]

The chancellor also had serious reservations about the idea of minting copper. In deference to the king, however, he was circumspect. He wrote that if copper remained at an even price, and the amount minted was limited, it could work. The crown's goal, he thought, should be to keep the proportion of copper to silver reasonable. Otherwise, a fall in the copper price relative to silver would cause deep discounts in the relation of copper currency to silver currency. Simply selling the copper in Amsterdam in return for silver would increase the supply of silver to the crown. While it was true that copper would fluctuate against silver, selling consistently would guarantee that the crown would benefit from price increases as well as suffer from price declines. He also believed the crown could still participate in the occasional speculation by holding copper back from the market.

Somewhat surprisingly, given the obvious benefits of a monopoly, the chancellor expressed a preference for a free market in copper at all levels, which endeared him to Heckscher and his followers. Regarding the monopoly held by the now defunct Copper Company, the chancellor wrote that although he had "small understanding of these commercial issues," he

12   ASOB, I, 1, 344 (Translation by Michael Roberts).
13   AOSB, I, 1, 345.
14   AOSB, I, 1, 345.

thought that the Copper Company's monopoly on copper sales caused more trouble than benefit: "Therefore, I respectfully submit that there should be free trade in copper at the Kopparberg, and the freer the better."[15] He reasoned that the Copper Company could buy copper from the *bergsmän*, but that the prices should not be ordered from above. They should be set in the public forum where buying and selling was done openly, and where prices were set by the perception of the buyers and sellers of the future. Then, once a transaction was agreed upon, the actors must execute it or face judgment by the community. Of course, the fact that an agreement was concluded, and the trade executed was not a guarantee that it was a wise decision. In fact, the chancellor seemed to have a rather low opinion of the participants in the marketplace: "In general one lacks the sense, the other lacks the will and the third lacks prudence."[16] All these shortcomings were just part of the market.

The problems created by the old Copper Company's monopoly did not stop at the mine. According to the chancellor, the monopoly also hurt the burghers and their cities because both benefited from the widespread trade in copper. The chancellor's solution was simple. A new Copper Company could contribute to the Swedish economy not by monopolizing internal trade, but rather by concentrating on trade overseas. When it operated in Sweden with a monopoly, it reduced commerce between cities and the countryside because it deprived merchants of access to copper ingot. He wrote that a new company should direct its efforts to developing business with Spain, the Duchy of Moscow, Persia, India, and the Mediterranean. If it operated overseas, a company could help to expand the Swedish economy. As the chancellor stated in the beginning of his memorandum, this advice was meant for ideal times. The chancellor knew as well as the king that given the current state of war, the crown had to maintain its monopoly to finance the war.[17]

The chancellor's next complaint about the company monopoly was that it stifled manufacturing. He wrote that the monopoly prevented the development of finished product manufacturing. The company exported raw copper overseas and then imported finished goods that the inhabitants needed for daily life. The result was to discourage domestic manufacturing. The company-held privileges (which the chancellor helped to write) presented barriers to those interested in establishing manufacturing and forging

15   AOSB, I, 1, 347.
16   AOSB, I, 1, 347.
17   AOSB, I, 1, 347.

works. This meant that much of the expensive work of making copper kettles or bronze cannon, for example, was being done overseas and the realm derived no benefit from it.

Finally, and most critically, the chancellor believed the crown should have the right to charge a fair toll on the sale of copper. It should, however, first reform the "old menagerie of rights" that existed then. A fixed toll on more transactions would, he wrote, increase crown revenue. The chancellor ended the section with the comment that these suggestions may seem remarkable but failing a better set of ideas the changes could be accomplished in "our time."[18]

Here is a summary of the chancellor's main points:
1) Eliminate the deposit system.
2) Eliminate the crown monopoly on purchases of copper at the mine.
3) Allow the *bergsmän* to sell freely to whomever they wished at negotiated prices.
4) Charge a toll on each *skeppund* sold by the *bergsmän* but have no other connection to the mine.
5) Allow completely free trade in copper within Sweden.
6) Restrict minting of copper to a balanced level with the minting of silver.
7) Revive the Copper Company and direct it to focus on developing foreign markets for copper and copper products.
8) Encourage the development of domestic manufacturing by allowing the free exchange of goods.

We now have a template by which we can judge the chancellor's actions during the next decade on copper policy.

One can already detect some of the chancellor's plans in his correspondence with the *Riks-Råd* immediately after the king's death. In a letter to Lars Grubbe, the council secretary mentioned earlier, the chancellor included a section on the Stora Kopparberg. He suggested eliminating the purchasing monopoly: "We [the *Riks-Råd*] can either continue the present system of the crown having a monopoly ... or we can give the *bergsmän* freedom to sell but to pay a toll ... We suggest a toll of RD 20 per skd should be paid by the miners for freedom to trade."[19] The debate over the crown's purchasing monopoly would continue to rage for several years after the king's death.

As discussed, the chancellor was not the only one to weigh in on copper policy immediately following Gustav Adolf's untimely death. In a letter to

18   AOSB, I, 1, 348.
19   AOSB, I, 7, 708.

Pieter Spierinck, a month after the king's death, de Geer offered to send his views on the copper market to the *Riks-Råd* and the *Kammar-Råd* in Stockholm to help them make decisions about the future. Apparently, his offer was accepted because later, in December 1632, he wrote a letter expressing his views on how best to proceed. There were major differences between de Geer's letter to the *Riks-Råd* and *Kammar-Råd*, and the letter Oxenstierna wrote to the same recipients. The chancellor was concerned with the larger issues; he was speculating on how to improve and reform the relationship with the *bergsmän*, how to encourage more investment in local industry; he was looking for a path to the future. For him the main question was whether they should restore freedom of trade to the Stora Kopparberg or keep the purchasing monopoly intact.[20]

De Geer, to the contrary, focused on the immediate issue of preventing the price of copper from falling. At the king's death there was a moment of panic as the merchants who followed this market assumed that Sweden would now stop paying interest on the mortgaged copper in Amsterdam, and would, therefore, be forced to liquidate stocks. De Geer confirmed this to the *Riks-Råd* and the *Kammar-Råd*, telling them that the price of copper in Amsterdam had fallen since the king's death from RD 77 per skd to RD 72 and would probably return to RD 55 per skd.[21]

In his "Considerations" on copper trading, the chancellor called the deposit system an affront, because the copper had been given to the crown "by the grace of God" and now the grasping merchants in Amsterdam had the use of it. De Geer's first suggestion was that the *Riks-Råd* and the *Kammar-Råd* should use "any means" to pay the interest owed to Elias Trip, preventing him from taking possession of copper and selling it to fund the missing interest. Second, since everyone in Amsterdam expected Sweden to ship copper to Amsterdam for sale as soon as the Baltic ports were opened in the spring, de Geer suggested an alternative strategy. The *Riks-Råd* and *Kammar-Råd* should make a shipment in the spring, but they should place it in deposit with Trip or some other merchant in Amsterdam. In addition, they should announce that future shipments would also be mortgaged and not sold into the market. This would force the consumers in Aachen and elsewhere to "come and pray to be allowed to purchase" the *Riks-Råd* and *Kammar-Råd* could then sell quietly for delivery in three to six months.[22]

20   LDGBOA, 250-51.
21   LDGBOA, 250-51.
22   LDGBOA, 250–51.

The chancellor wanted to open sales in Sweden so that copper could move freely within the country. He would use a company only to develop overseas markets. De Geer, to the contrary, suggested that the crown restrict sales of copper in Sweden to prevent competition from Swedish merchants shipping abroad. The crown's past practice was to have copper available for sale in Hamburg, Lübeck, and in Amsterdam. De Geer wrote that all copper intended for export should be sent to Amsterdam only. This would prevent a factor in Hamburg from selling at different conditions than a factor in Amsterdam. In other words, de Geer was confirming P.W. Klein's view discussed in the introduction, that early modern capitalists, like Schumpeter's entrepreneurs, sought monopoly control over trade to reduce risks. Further, de Geer wrote that for the immediate future, Sweden should export for sale only what was necessary to pay the *bergsmän*.[23]

De Geer was concerned that the *bergsmän* be treated fairly, although he did not share the chancellor's view that the *bergsmän* should have freedom to sell in a free market. That would have worked against de Geer's vision of a closely controlled supply line. Of course, as always, he was most concerned with his own business. He wrote to the *Riks-Råd* and the *Kammar-Råd* that since the *bergsmän* had certainly been living on credit from the local merchants in Falun during the winter, they had to be paid by June or July so they could repay their debts. To provide money to pay the *bergsmän*, he would accept a large shipment of copper in Amsterdam and mortgage it. He would then either transfer money by bill of exchange or send cash at the first "open water." This offer confirms my contention that the mortgaged deposits were much more profitable for the mortgagee than beneficial to the crown.[24]

Regarding the market, de Geer made some observations hinting at the devastation that was occurring in Germany during this stage of the Thirty Years War. One reason de Geer remained hopeful that copper prices could recover was, "[b]ecause of trouble and war, the copper mines in Germany are now full of water and it will be difficult to bring them back to production."[25] The main German copper mine was located at Mansfeld, in Saxony. Today it is referred to as "Luther City" because Martin Luther grew up in the town and his father owned a smelting furnace there. Because of its location, Mansfeld was a major supplier of copper to central German towns, such as Nuremberg in Franconia.[26] During part of 1631 Gustav Adolf and his army were quartered

---

23 LDGBOA, 250–51.
24 LDGBOA, 250–51.
25 LDGBOA, 250–51.
26 Timm, Die Bedeutung, 185.

in Halle, about thirty-five kilometers from Mansfeld. On September 4, 1631 Gustav Adolf defeated Count Tilly and the Imperial army at Breitenfeld, north of Leipszig. The presence of two marauding armies and a major battle not far away would certainly explain the temporary abandonment of the mine; and neglected hard-rock mines soon fill with water.

De Geer also noted that the long war had destroyed "the common people's goods," so demand for replacement copper kettles and other domestic goods must have been strong. For some reason he does not mention demand for bronze cannon, the chief consumer of copper. The amount of copper used for cannon production must have been considerable. Between January and July of 1632, for example, de Geer's foundries in Sweden sold 1.03 million Amsterdam pounds of cannon or 3,745 skd Stockholm weight.[27] These were not all bronze cannon, and perhaps the majority was iron, but many were bronze. If de Geer was selling such quantities, other cannon foundries in France, Germany, Italy, and Spain were also casting and selling bronze cannon. De Geer wrote to the *Riks-Råd* that if they took his advice, prices should once again exceed RD 70 per skd in Amsterdam.[28]

Obviously, de Geer was still eager to be appointed factor for copper sales in Amsterdam. Erik Larsson retained the position coveted by de Geer despite his abysmal performance in the copper deposit negotiations with Elias Trip in February 1632. De Geer was particularly solicitous, therefore, to both the *Riks-Råd* and *Kammar-Råd*, and to the chancellor, immediately after the king's death. He wrote to the chancellor in January 1633 with another fanciful claim that he had once again singlehandedly moved the market by purchasing about 200 skd of copper: "I purchased about 200 skd of copper. When I began the market was between DG 56 and DG 54 per hundredweight, or about RD 60 per skd Stockholm weight. Before I finished buying, I had raised the copper prices to RD 65 to RD 70 per skd."[29]

One should be skeptical of these claims for all the reasons mentioned in the last chapter. This time, however, de Geer's ledger for the period is not available, so it is not possible to refute him. The fact that in the next paragraph de Geer asks the chancellor to intercede on his behalf and prevent Falkenberg from proceeding with legal action against him in Amsterdam makes one more skeptical. As we shall see further on, the legal action was probably at least partially justified.[30]

27 Riksarkivet. Leufsta arkiv, file 109 # 2–10, 30–41. Jan le Thoor, Credit, Laus Deo Anno 1632 Amst.
28 LDGBOA, 250-51.
29 LDGBOA, 270.
30 LDGBOA, 271-72,

The king's death could have been a turning point in crown copper policy, and de Geer obviously wanted to benefit from any change. His main interest was to be the primary sales conduit for all copper exported to the continent. He was also hoping to benefit from the continued policy of mortgaging copper in Amsterdam. De Geer, however, must have realized that mortgaging copper presented a complex problem for the crown. It could not afford to redeem the inventory, nor could it permit Trip to sell it onto the market. For this reason, I doubt that de Geer had only the crown's interests in mind when he advised the *Riks-Råd* and the *Kammar-Råd* to continue the policy of depositing copper in Amsterdam to keep it off the market. It is more likely that he hoped the mortgaging would continue and that he would participate in the practice. De Geer might have been a friend of the crown, but he was also a businessman in search of profits.

Dahlgren summarized de Geer's ambitions as follows: "De Geer considered himself the most likely candidate for the position of the crown's factor in Amsterdam … He wanted to combine this position with privileges from the crown."[31] De Geer had met with the king in Kissingen[32] earlier in 1632; we do not have the exact date, but de Geer refers to the meeting both in letters to the king and in letters to Johan Casimir.[33] He apparently discussed these ideas with the king at that meeting. After his reported manipulation, the king suggested another meeting, presumably to discuss de Geer's ambitious plans to combine expanded copper manufacturing and foundry capacity in Sweden, and a monopoly on the sale of copper ingots and finished copper products in continental Europe. He certainly hoped the chancellor would be sympathetic to his cause. He was not prepared, however, for the intense infighting that followed immediately upon the king's death.

We recall from the last chapter that Conrad von Falkenberg was highly critical of Erik Larsson's three-year deposit contract negotiated with Elias Trip. At that time, Falkenberg suggested that he could do a much better job for the crown if he had full authority to negotiate.[34] With Larsson and Trip both in disgrace, Falkenberg probably realized that de Geer was his main rival in Amsterdam for full authority and the lucrative position of factor. After the king's death, he wasted no time in attempting to discredit de Geer both in Amsterdam and in Sweden.

---

31 Dahlgren, *Louis de Geer*, 1, 209.
32 Kissingen (today Bad Kissingen) is in Lower Franconia (present day Bavaria).
33 LDGBOA, 259, 273.
34 AOSB, II, 11, 596.

In December 1632, soon after the king's death, Falkenberg lodged a formal protest and lawsuit against de Geer through his notary, Jacob Jacobsson. In the protest Falkenberg accused de Geer of misusing a subsidy in the amount of RD 20,000 that the States General made to the Swedish crown in 1631 to aid the Swedish war effort in Germany. The States General paid the subsidy directly to de Geer to cover the cost of a shipment of arms owed by de Geer to the crown. It was now several months later, and de Geer had not made the shipment. Falkenberg was suing de Geer to recover the RD 20,000 plus interest. Falkenberg also alleged that de Geer had failed to pass on a payment to the States General that the king had directed him to make a year earlier. Falkenberg wrote that de Geer never made this payment.[35] With the advantage of hindsight, we know that de Geer did make this payment to Mayor Knipquyler in the amount of RD 16,344. Falkenberg was either ignorant of this fact or chose to ignore it.[36]

This was a rather complicated affair, potentially damaging to de Geer's reputation with the crown and with his business associates in Amsterdam, so he answered Falkenberg's accusation promptly. De Geer's explanation, in a letter to the *Kammar-Råd*, was complex.[37] He wrote that in March 1631, when he was still in Stockholm, he made a contract with the crown to supply weapons to several regiments of foot soldiers and 8,000 cavalry troopers for the wars in Germany. The total cost was well over RD 100,000. In the meantime, to support Gustav Adolf's wars in Germany against the Catholic Habsburg armies, the Dutch States General granted a subsidy to the crown of RD 60,000, payable at the rate of RD 20,000 per month in August to October 1631.[38] Falkenberg, however, failed to mention that part of this subsidy was to be used to purchase arms for the Swedish crown in Amsterdam.

We saw in the last chapter that Falkenberg was not shy about using his position as watchdog for the crown, and to discredit others to advance his own position. Falkenberg began complaining to the chancellor in March 1632, that interest was due to the States General for a loan from December 1629. He stated that de Geer was supposed to have used the proceeds from the 720 skd shipped to him in 1630 to make an interest payment to the Estates General. Falkenberg again raised the issue to the chancellor in April, this time he wrote that the crown was now three years in arrears on interest

---

35 Riksarkivet. Leufsta arkiv, file 80 # 26, Protest van Valkenburch.
36 Riksarkivet. Leufsta arkiv, file 81 # 137–39, Con. Mat. Coperreecken.
37 LDGBOA, 254–56. For a copy of the request see LDGBOA, 257.
38 Riksarkivet. Leufsta arkiv, file 80 # 26, Protest van Valkenburch.

payments.[39] He had never mentioned to the chancellor, however, the RD 20,000 subsidy that de Geer allegedly confiscated.

In fact, according to de Geer's response to the protest, the States General had turned the August 1631 subsidy over to him directly as the first payment toward the March 1631 arms contract that he had negotiated with the Swedish crown. It was not until December 1632 that de Geer was ready to make the first shipment to Germany on the contract.[40] To explain the delay, de Geer wrote to the chancellor about the long lead-time for weapons; he had to make advances to the manufacturers so they, in turn, could purchase the necessary raw materials.[41]

He also had a plausible explanation for the 720 kgs. He had received this in 1630 and the crown had instructed him to mortgage the parcel and use the revenue to pay interest due on a loan from the States General. He wrote to the chancellor that he discussed this very issue at the meeting with the king in early 1632 at Kissingen. The king asked about the delay in making the interest payment and de Geer told the king that the situation was complicated. The States General of the United Provinces made the loan, but it was the estate from the province of Holland to whom the interest was owed. De Geer told the king that he had long ago made the payment, thus confirming that the payment made to Mayor Knipquyler for RD 16,344, recorded in 1632, was indeed the overdue interest payment.[42]

De Geer then launched a counterattack against Falkenberg claiming that he had caused enormous trouble for the crown in Amsterdam and in The Hague by his actions. Now the matter was public and officials in The Hague were inquiring about the problem. Further, subsidies from the States General that the crown had planned to use to finance another arms shipment due from De Geer were now blocked.[43] It appeared that Falkenberg's latest example of self-serving political maneuvering had done real damage to the crown's position in The Hague. By late summer, the chancellor was desperate for the arms shipment but the subsidy from the States General, necessary to pay de Geer for the arms, was still blocked.

Short of cash, and apparently not happy with the *Riks-Råd*'s performance of managing copper policy, the chancellor was forced to take action. In September, without consulting anyone in Stockholm, the chancellor met with

39   AOSB, II, 11, 603
40   LDGBOA, 264.
41   LDGBOA, 254-57.
42   Riksarkivet. Leufsta arkiv, file 81 # 137–39, Con. Mat. Coperreecken.
43   LDGBOA, 258–60.

de Geer in Frankfurt. During the meeting, it was agreed that de Geer should form a new copper company, and the crown would sell the approximately 24,000 skd currently held by Elias Trip to de Geer's new company. In addition, the chancellor promised the new company the right of first refusal on any additional copper to be exported during the next twelve months. Not surprising, part of the copper to be transferred to de Geer was in payment for weapons.[44] We can assume, therefore, that this new copper contract was necessary to pay de Geer for the weapons to be delivered to the armies in Germany. This new contract was the final stage in a string of consequences begun by Falkenberg's protest against Louis de Geer.

The entire incident has the odor of a Greek drama. Motivated by the desire to discredit de Geer, Falkenberg made a series of accusations against him. These accusations prompted the States General to suspend a subsidy to Sweden to pay for a large arms shipment that de Geer was preparing for delivery to Hamburg. This, in turn, forced the crown to seek an alternative method for funding the arms shipment. The chancellor's solution was to propose a vast copper contract to de Geer. Thus, Falkenberg's plan to discredit de Geer and become the copper factor in Amsterdam backfired; Falkenberg had failed to grasp that de Geer remained critical to the crown as an arms supplier. In that role, he was much more important than a mere copper factor in Amsterdam.

As has been made clear, it was not part of the chancellor's master plan to establish a new copper company with a monopoly on purchases after the king's death. Probably the idea was suggested by de Geer to solve the problem of payment for the arms. It also gave de Geer, moreover, the very thing he had been seeking since he returned to Amsterdam. If implemented, it would have restored his position as the preeminent copper trader in the city and given him a monopoly on the sale of Swedish copper in continental Europe. Based on these maneuvers, I believe that his plan for the company was to control the flow of copper from the Stora Kopparberg to the markets in Europe. This would allow him to take advantage of the crown's monopoly of purchases at the mine to limit costs. He could also be certain that enough copper stayed in Sweden to feed his growing industrial enterprises there. De Geer planned to control the flow of copper into continental Europe and direct the distribution to his own advantage. Finally, he would combine the sale of copper ingot with the sale of finished products from Sweden. For example, he could supply the French king's cannon foundries with copper at the same time he was supplying the French quartermaster with finished

44 LDGBOA, 291-294.

bronze cannon from Sweden. This would have given him considerable power over prices.

This prospective new company was a triumph for de Geer, and a defeat for all the other contenders for the monopoly to distribute Swedish copper. The first document, issued by the chancellor in the second half of September, was innocently called "Conditions Agreed to Between His Excellency, the Lord Imperial Chancellor, and Sr. Louis de Geer." As part of this agreement, the chancellor would supply 1,000 skd of copper to one of de Geer's works in Sweden. De Geer would pay RD 65 per skd for a total of RD 65,000. From this payment, de Geer would immediately credit the crown RD 46,449, which was the invoiced amount for the weapons already delivered by de Geer to Hamburg.[45]

The chancellor issued the second contract on the same day as the first, and it was probably the largest copper sales contract issued in the history of Europe to date: "Whereas Sr. Louis de Geer has agreed to purchase 24,000 skd copper now stored in Amsterdam, Hamburg, Lübeck and Sweden."[46] They agreed to a price of RD 55 per skd for *gårkoppar* and finished products such as kettels and sheet, and RD 50 per skd for *råkoppar*.[47] It is important to note that this was a "provisional" contract, meaning that it was not binding at this point, but subject to reconfirmation on both sides. The prices were in line with the market at that time, but considerably lower than prices at the peak of the price spike the previous year. The average price for *gårkoppar* sold in Amsterdam in 1633 was RD 66.25.[48]

The contract was also specific about the time and place for delivery: "Since it is already late in autumn, it will be too late to ship copper from Sweden." The contract stipulated, therefore, that the immediate shipments would come from the copper on deposit in continental Europe. The chancellor mentioned that the deposits in Hamburg and Lübeck were insignificant, so the great majority would come from the deposit still with Elias Trip in Amsterdam. The copper coming from Sweden would begin with a shipment in May 1634 and continue with subsequent shipments every two months. One major issue was taking possession of the copper in Amsterdam. The chancellor clearly expected trouble with Trip. He commissioned de Geer to be the crown's representative to negotiate with Trip. De Geer would pay Trip directly the money owed to Trip by the crown and deduct that amount

45 LDGBOA, 291.
46 LDGBOA, 291–94.
47 LDGBOA, 291–92.
48 Posthumus, *Prices*, 371.

when he paid the crown for the copper. As we shall see, the chancellor's premonition that there would be difficulties with Elias Trip proved to be more than correct.[49]

If implemented, this contract would have given de Geer control over all the copper then deposited in continental Europe plus the next year's production from Sweden. He would be the leading copper trader in Amsterdam. Equally important, it recognized his intention to develop copper manufacturing facilities in Sweden, and the agreement guaranteed supplies of copper for this purpose. Finally, the contract gave de Geer the right of first refusal on all additional copper sold by the crown for the next eighteen months, beginning in January 1634.[50] The contract also put de Geer on track to establishing a copper manufacturing empire in Sweden in partnership with the Swedish crown.

We cannot cover the beginning of de Geer's manufacturing career in Sweden without mentioned his dependence on political and religious refugees from the low countries. De Geer himself was born in Liege but moved to Amsterdam to escape religious persecution in the Catholic Southern Netherlands. De Geer's initial investments in the nascent Swedish industry were in partnership with another Walloon, William de Besche, who had already established a Swedish iron works in the early 1620s. De Geer acted as a recruiter, and hired skilled laborers such as carpenters, bookkeepers, iron casters, musket makers, and so on to work for de Besche in Sweden.[51]

To take an example, in 1623 a certain Jean Cred agreed to travel with his assistant, Gillet Pavet to Sweden where he would work as a supervisor in a metallurgical plant owed jointly by de Besche and de Geer. His contract was for six years, and his salary was RD 104 per year; also, the cost of his passage to and from Sweden was covered.[52] Although the sources are quiet on the subject one can assume that many young Walloons elected to stay in Sweden after their contracts expired.

While most of the contracts, as those above, were for individuals or small groups, in one, dated April 29, 1624, de Geer agreed to hire thirty-two Walloon charcoal burners and wood cutters. They were to work for six years

---

49 LDGBOA, 291–94.

50 LDGBOA, 293. The right of first refusal in commodity trading is an extremely valuable right. It meant that if the crown wanted to sell additional copper it would negotiate with a third-party buyer. Once a price was reached, the crown would be obligated to offer the copper to de Geer at the price established. It gave de Geer the power to prevent any competitor from buying copper from the crown for eighteen months.

51 LDGBOA, 7.

52 LDGBOA, 73.

and were paid 3½ Dutch Guilders per *last* of charcoal they delivered. De Geer also agreed to pay transport costs for the wives and children of the workers.[53] Once arrived in Sweden the migrants were well treated, enjoying tax exemptions and freedom from military duty. De Geer sponsored 275 Walloons between 1620 and 1630 and they brought with them current technical knowledge. It is not an exaggeration to describe the Walloon emigres as the backbone of Sweden's metallurgical industry.[54]

Many Walloons, like de Geer, rose to important positions. Anthony Monier was the head quartermaster for the Swedish army, and he also served a term as head of the Copper Company. The number of Walloons working in the metallurgical sector became so large that de Geer also hired a Calvinist minister to preach on Sundays and teach the catechism. For this service he was to be paid RD 120 per year.[55]

Now that we have recognized Sweden's debt to the Walloon immigrants we can return to de Geer's Swedish investments. What were the advantages for the crown? The chancellor was devoted to expanding Swedish industry, especially the copper industry, and this agreement would have encouraged Louis de Geer with a guaranteed supply of copper. In addition, the agreement would have ended the deposit system, and, therefore, ended the crown's obligation to pay interest on the large mortgage to Elias Trip. As planned, it would mean the crown could transfer much of the administration of the mine and the shipment of copper to the new company. Sitting in Frankfurt-am-Main, the chancellor could not oversee the business. Having the new company shoulder the responsibility would be a definite advantage. Finally, the agreed price was fair. The crown would get the weapons it needed, and de Geer finally would have the leverage over copper distribution that he so eagerly sought. It appeared to offer advantages to both sides.

In October, the chancellor wrote to the new queen, Kristina, with a full explanation. The queen was only seven years old at the time. She was widely regarded as precocious, but to believe that she understood such a letter at the age of seven does strain credulity. One must assume, therefore, that the correspondence was intended for her advisers and members of the regency council. When he left for Germany, in 1630, Gustav Adolf entrusted the care and education of his daughter to his sister, Catherine, the wife of John Casimir, the Count Palatine. This was probably because Kristina's mother, Queen Maria Eleonora was emotionally unstable. The count was on the

---

53 LDGBOA, 78.

54 Roberts, *Gustavus Adolphus*, I, 119.

55 LDGBOA, 157.

regency council and a member of the *Riks-Råd*. As noted, in the months
after the king's death the chancellor had hoped that the *Riks-Råd* would
take control over copper trading. It is logical to assume that the chancellor's
letters were really intended for John Casimir since the young Queen was
part of his household.[56]

Returning to the chancellor's letter of October 1633, he explained the
copper deposits in Amsterdam, Hamburg, and Lübeck as if the new queen
was already familiar with the situation. He wrote that the existence of large
inventories in Amsterdam were "prejudicial" to an improving market. In
addition, "manufacturing and commerce of the world is suffering [from the
wars]" and the chancellor did not want "Your Majesty to be forced to sell [at
a lower price] later." The most important reason for selling, however, was to
end the expensive and troublesome interest payments that were bleeding
the kingdom and greatly enriching the Trip family, with little or no benefit
to Sweden. He explained the price structure and added that he had contact
with businessmen who expected prices to go down further, so he wanted
to lock in a sales price before that happened. He urged the queen (and her
advisers) to take an interest in the shipments coming from Sweden so they
were not late because "when the crown is late [in shipping] the foreign
merchants rejoice in penalties and remedies they will charge."[57]

As mentioned earlier, the chancellor's "Considerations" on copper policy
can be used to measure his behavior after the death of the king. He was
attempting to reestablish a copper company, but one without a monopoly
on sales in Sweden. As he suggested to the king in the "Considerations," the
new company should concentrate on developing exports abroad as well as
increasing manufacturing and casting capacity in Sweden. On this count
the chancellor was consistent with the recommendations in his testament.
The question of freedom to sell for the *bergsmän* was, however, quite a
different matter. On this issue the contract was silent, but he commented
in his letter to Queen Kristina that the copper buying at the mine should
continue through the winter months to avoid late shipments in the spring.
Clearly, the monopoly was still firmly in effect. As chancellor, he had the
privilege of advocating a free market for the miners; as the head of the army
in Germany, he wanted shipments on time and at a fixed price.[58]

Unfortunately for de Geer and Oxenstierna, the agreement began to fall
apart almost immediately. It was not evident in the initial agreement that de

56   Nordstrom, *Christina*, 486.
57   AOSB, I, 10, 161-63.
58   AOSB, I, 10, 162.-63

Geer had not yet formed his company. That is, he did not have commitments from other investors to form a consortium. This explains why the contract was "provisional." According to Klein, de Geer did not have the resources to finance the purchase of 24,000 skd of copper on his own, so he had to reactivate his partners in Amsterdam from previous syndicates.[59] While Klein does not cite a source for this contention, a letter written by de Geer on November 1, 1633, confirms it.[60]

The letter did not specify a recipient, so we do not know for certain to whom it was sent. De Geer wrote the letter, or had the letter written in German, which was unusual for him. Therefore, we can be certain it was not going to Peter Spierinck, a Dutchman. It mentioned the chancellor by name, so he was not a likely recipient either. Probably, it was meant for the *Riks-Råd*, or an individual member of the *Riks-Råd*. It was brief but disturbing. He wrote that the copper he had purchased in Amsterdam and elsewhere was encumbered in debt from unpaid interest and, therefore, he could not take possession of it. His negotiations with Trip, moreover, had come to a complete standstill, and nothing further could be done until the outstanding interest was paid. Furthermore, because of the position of the army (he did not clarify which army), Aachen was once again cut off from Amsterdam. We learn from a later letter that two wagon trains of copper en route from Amsterdam to Aachen were confiscated near Nijmegen, and a merchant was "much inconvenienced." The Maas River was also again closed for the same reason.[61]

Because Aachen was no longer accessible, the price of copper in Amsterdam had dropped precipitously. De Geer claimed that it was down below RD 66 per skd and sinking fast; "There are twenty sellers for every buyer," he lamented.[62] Under the circumstances it was not possible for de Geer to recruit a syndicate to invest in the 24,000 skd of copper. Since he now realized that he would not be able to raise the funds necessary for the large purchase from his normal backers, he was seeking to retreat without losing credibility.

By mid-November 1633, therefore, the chancellor realized that his agreement with de Geer was over, and he was obligated to inform the young Queen Kristina (and her advisers) about the new difficulties. He wrote that the crown's creditors in Holland (Elias Trip) were blocking his plans to sell the

59   Klein, *De Trippen*, 377.
60   LDGBOA, 295-96.
61   LDGBOA, 296–97.
62   LDGBOA, 295–96.

crown copper by exaggerating the interest owed on the deposits. He pledged to the queen that he would devote full attention to the issue. It does show, once again, the disadvantage of mortgaging copper in distant Amsterdam, far from the crown's ability to monitor and control the proceedings. The chancellor was obviously frustrated, and he blamed the Dutch merchants for the problem: "Our copper remains in Holland for all to see, and the Dutch, who, when it comes to trade, are both wise and cunning, will take notice. No doubt they are plotting to force us to sell our copper at low prices."[63]

The chancellor informed the queen that the crown must now make a large shipment of copper to the continent to pay creditors. Apparently, the crown also needed to find money quickly to pay the army in Mecklenburg and Pomerania.[64] The chancellor wrote to the *Riks-Råd* and the *Kammar-Råd*, as well, urging them to make a large shipment of copper to the continent. He expected to sell the copper at RD 66 per skd, and he would inform the creditors that payment would follow the shipment of copper.[65] The chancellor was concerned because the Swedish army, under General Banér, was facing the Imperial Army, under Duke Wallenstein in Mecklenburg and Pomerania, and they could not neglect paying the troops at such a critical juncture. They must have acted quickly, because at the end of the month de Geer wrote to Pieter Spierinck telling him that 500 skd of copper had arrived in Amsterdam and another 2,000 skd was in Hamburg en route to Amsterdam. He told Spierinck that he would prefer to keep the new shipment in Hamburg because prices were falling quickly in Amsterdam. The first 500 skd, brought in by Erik Larsson, was not selling, despite Larsson's offering it at RD 63.8 per skd, well below the RD 66 price that the chancellor was expecting. De Geer also mentioned that another 350 skd of copper currency had arrived from Hamburg, which only added to the oversupply.[66]

One also learns from de Geer the nature of the calculation he was making. He told Spierinck that he would not be able to convince his normal copper investors to participate in the purchase of the 20,000 to 24,000 skd because of recent market conditions. De Geer estimated that it would take at least three years for the investors to liquidate such a large quantity of copper (24,000 skd equals 7.2 million present-day pounds or 3,264 metric tons). He reasoned that even if de Geer and his associates bought from the crown at RD 55 per skd, the crown would have to grant two years "interest free"

63   AOSB, I, 10, 274–75.
64   Dahlgren, *Louis de Geer*, 1, 214.
65   AOSB, I, 10, 284-85.
66   LDGBOA, 298.

to help them finance it. Even if they were able to sell at RD 65 per skd, it would still only yield a 20 percent profit over three years. It would be more profitable for the merchants to lend out their capital at current interest rates, plus they would avoid the risk of owning copper in a falling market.[67]

We now clearly see the fundamental problem with the deposit system. The crown had made the mistake of putting too much copper into the system. In the beginning when the quantities were small, the idea had some benefit for the crown. It allowed the crown to turn copper into cash, without putting metal onto the market when prices were low. As the quantity in the stockpile increased, however, the existence of copper in Amsterdam acted as a deterrent to price increases. As Oxenstierna observed, "our copper remains in Amsterdam for all to see," meaning that as long as the inventory overhung the market, and the merchants believed that the crown would eventually liquidate stocks, the price would not go up.[68] Meanwhile, the interest costs continued. The crown had made payments in copper, but by 1633 the crown had fallen seriously behind in payments and the inventory was, therefore, now encumbered with debt. The crown now understood that it would have to pay large amounts in back interest, in addition to the principal, to redeem the copper and stop the interest accumulation.

On the other hand, the system was a great boon for the merchants. They made a secured loan to the crown at 8 percent based on a copper price of, perhaps, RD 60 per skd. They then remortgaged the same copper, perhaps at RD 70 per skd. This allowed them to take RD 10 per skd out of the transaction. They would eventually have to repay the loan, but meanwhile they had their capital back, including an extra RD 10 per skd interest free. That amounted to RD 20,000 on a shipment of 2,000 skd. They were probably borrowing, moreover, at only 4 percent per year so they were also making the difference in interest. As explained in the previous chapter, de Geer's correspondence with the chancellor, and with Johan Thoor, indicates that the crown was unaware of these financial maneuverings in Amsterdam.[69]

The obvious question is how the crown found itself in such a difficult position? Part of the problem was that Amsterdam was far away, and the crown did not have a reliable mechanism to monitor the activities of the merchants, or to keep track of the accumulating interest obligations. The second issue was the crown's representatives in Amsterdam. Some, like de Geer, were quite naturally more interested in their own personal fortunes.

---

67 LDGBOA, 298–99.
68 AOSB, I, 10, 284–85. see also ASOB, I, 10, 356.
69 LDGBOA, 236. See also, LDGBOA, 252.

Others, like Falkenberg, were too busy making political points to involve themselves directly in the execution of the copper transactions. Only Erik Larsson was doing the actual accounting, as we shall soon see, and he also was not above suspicion. Once the chancellor realized the extent of the problem with the deposits in Amsterdam, he understood that the crown had been ill served. Writing to the *Riks-Råd* he complained: "Good sirs, judge if there is any evil that merchants will not do. I find that great wrong and damage has been done to the crown." The chancellor went on to complain that when Erik Larsson negotiated with Elias Tripp in February 1632, Larsson accepted Trips accounting without inspecting the numbers. The same was true in 1629 when Falkenberg negotiated with Trip. How could the chancellor refute Trip's figures when his representatives had accepted them without a proper auditing? "The crown's servants have been made to look foolish."[70] The chancellor's frustration was understandable. The previous year he had a report from Falkenberg stating that he had an interest bill from Elias Trip for one of the copper deposits, which he thought was incorrect. He could not, however, find his copy of the original agreement so he could not confirm his suspicion.[71]

As the year ended, there was a complete impasse with Trip, and de Geer had made clear he was no longer interested in the grandiose plan of buying the 20,000 to 24,000 skd copper from the crown. Meanwhile, General Banér's army was still in Pomerania in need of pay.[72]

Until now, we have considered the deposit dispute only from the crown's point of view. Elias Trip, however, also faced certain problems. In December 1633, the market was still above RD 60 per skd for *gårkoppar* and RD 50 for *råkoppar*.[73] The deposit system was a mortgage, however, and when the mortgagor stopped paying the mortgagee, the mortgagee had no income from his capital outlay. The Swedish crown was now seriously behind on interest payments and Trip was getting no cash flow from the mortgage. One should not be surprised, therefore, that he attempted, in mid-January, to confiscate a shipment of 2,300 skd of copper newly arrived from Sweden. The crown intended to sell this outright to pay the army in Pomerania. As the copper was being moved from the pier to the warehouse in small transport vessels, Trip showed up with a municipal court official and two small transports of his own and attempted to sequester the shipment. He claimed that it was in

70   AOSB, I, 10, 355–59.
71   AOSB, II, 11, 639.
72   LDGBOA, 300–01.
73   LDGBOA, 300–01.

payment for past interest and a weapons delivery. To execute a sequestration, Trip had to swear to the court that his claim was valid and that the amount he was attempting to confiscate was appropriate. De Geer somehow learned of the maneuver and showed up at the warehouse with his own notary to contest the actions as a commissioner of the Swedish crown.[74] De Geer argued that the value of the copper in question was greater than the amount of the debts mentioned in Trip's pledge. De Geer also argued that the copper was the private property of the crown and, therefore, not subject to the claim. Unfortunately for the crown, de Geer's arguments did not convince the court, and Trip's claims were declared valid. To prevent further erosion of the crown's reputation in Amsterdam, de Geer persuaded Trip to delay the action. The copper went into the warehouse, but it was still vulnerable if Trip decided to renew the action for sequestration.[75]

De Geer then executed a separate document with Trip, promising to pay personally for the outstanding interest on the copper deposits, and for some of the principal due. He offered to pay Trip DG 300,000 in advance and the balance over a six-month period. It was, of course, subject to the crown's agreement. De Geer then suggested that all this would only be possible if the crown allowed him to put the recently arrived 2,300 skd of copper into a mortgage at 7 percent per year, and to sell the copper if he could find a buyer. If he sold the copper, he would receive a 2 percent sales commission. He would use the principal to repay Trip. The crown would have to agree, in addition, to ship 3,500 skd to him in Amsterdam. In other words, de Geer was now proposing to resurrect his agreement with the chancellor from their September 1633 meeting.[76] At that meeting, however, they had agreed to a sales price of RD 66 per skd for *gårkoppar*. Now, de Geer would certainly insist, based on a letter of December 24, 1633, to Pieter Spierinck,[77] that the mortgage price be set at RD 50 per skd. This was significantly lower than the price he agreed in September with the chancellor. De Geer wanted to take over Trip's mortgage position, at a low price, with the added advantage of being able to sell from the position when it suited him.

In the end, the crown did nothing and Trip was successful in enforcing the sequestration for the 2,300 skd. The reactions were mixed. Erik Larsson was furious, and he wrote to the chancellor explaining the problems that this action would create. First, it ruined the crown's already damaged reputation

---

74 LDGBOA, 305.
75 LDGBOA, 305–06.
76 LDGBOA, 305–06.
77 LDGBOA, 300.

in Amsterdam. Now no one would buy copper from the crown for fear that it could, at any moment, be confiscated. The action also caused prices to plunge. Once again, there were no buyers for Swedish copper, only sellers. This meant that the value of Trip's deposit inventory also went down: Larsson opined, "I think the Swedish crown now has the right to force Trip to keep all the copper in his deposit because by executing the sequestration he has lowered the value of copper everywhere."[78]

At Larsson's request the *Rik-Råd* wrote to the States General and to the Amsterdam city council requesting that the sequestration order be annulled, to no avail. The chancellor's reply was more measured, but he still disputed the legitimacy of this action. His initial reaction was disbelief that the Amsterdam courts would execute such an order. That did not mean, however, that the chancellor was not displeased. If they were under the threat of "merchant tyranny," they must find an alternative method of marketing. The chancellor told Larsson that he did not have time to examine the problem, but that Larsson should come up with some ideas and reach a compromise with Trip. The chancellor's preference was to form a new company that would distribute copper in Hamburg, Lübeck, and Amsterdam, but to limit the amount sold to 6,000 skd per year. Sweden would consume the balance herself in foundries or in other manufacturing operations. He even suggested selling off some of the excess in Russia. The key to this new strategy would be to limit the amount sold per year in the large continental trading cities.[79]

As we shall soon see, Trip's sequestration was not the end of the deposit system as a means for the crown to generate cash without selling copper. I have maintained that it was a plan that heavily favored the merchants over the crown for several reasons. First, the mortgaged price was always below the market price to protect the mortgagee against a falling price in the event of a default by the mortgagor. Second, the interest rates were either 7 or 8 percent. On a mortgage price of RD 50 per skd this meant the interest per year was RD 4 per skd. Since the crown failed to pay interest in a timely fashion, it compounded. In Appendix F we examine one deposit for which we have relatively complete records. This will help us to decide if it was truly as one-sided in favor of the merchants as I have suggested.

The conclusion is obvious. The crown could never hope to redeem the deposits. The cost in May 1634 to redeem the parcel of 5,714.3 skd that we analyze in Appendix F would have been RD 419,429. This was a sum the crown

78   AOSB, II, 11, 528–30.
79   AOSB, I, 11, 605–607.

could never hope to repay. As we saw earlier, when Elias Trip sequestered the 2,300 skd copper for interest payment, he had 24,000 skd on deposit. We know that he accumulated this large lot starting in 1629 and there were different mortgage prices. It is safe to assume that the average mortgage cost was about RD 47 per skd and the average interest cost was RD 12 per skd.[80] To put it in perspective, that meant the redemption cost for the entire parcel was roughly RD 1,416,000 or almost one-third more than the Älvsborg ransom. Annual simple interest at 7.5 percent would be RD 106,200 per year. It was simply not possible for the crown to consider redeeming copper at such a high cost. What, then, was to be done?

After the angry words that de Geer and Larsson aimed at Elias Trip during his attempt to sequester the crown's copper, all Amsterdam must have been surprised on April 8, 1634. On that day, Elias Trip announced the formation of a consortium of investors who would enter a three-year contract with Erik Larsson, the commissioner of the Swedish crown in Amsterdam. We, however, need not be surprised because we have access to the chancellor's more measured reply to Larsson, and his advice that Larsson find a solution to the problem and compromise with Elias Trip. By 1634, thanks to French subsidies and the Prussian river tolls, the crown was no longer in the desperate financial situation that characterized the early years of the decade,[81] but it still wanted to maintain good relations with the merchant community. When Larsson wrote to the chancellor to inform him of the new agreement with Trip, therefore, he acknowledged that he had been following the chancellor's instructions: "High born and merciful lord, Herr Chancellor, Your Excellency, in fulfillment of your advice and instructions and in conformance with my commission, I have enclosed a copy of the contract [negotiated with Elias Trip]."[82] He went on to tell the chancellor that Louis de Geer was a helpful participant in the discussions. In conformance with the chancellor's wishes, the contracting parties would take only 6,000 skd per year from Sweden. In addition, they would take over the Trip inventory, so the problem would be, at least, postponed.

The following were the more significant participants in the consortium and their contributions:

---

80   The parcel contained both *råkoppar* and *gårkoppar*. To calculate interest on an inventory that was accumulated at a regular rate over time; one assumes that one-half the inventory was financed during the entire span.

81   By 1634 Sweden was receiving an annual subsidy from France and the Prussian Tolls were in full operation. See Åström, *The Swedish Economy*, 95.

82   AOSB, II, 11, 531–32.

Elias Trip	DG 675,000 (RD 270,000)
Louis de Geer	DG 500,000 (RD 200,000)
Jacob Crivius	DG 300,000 (RD 120,000)
Erik Larsson	DG 150,000 (RD 60,000)

There were several other participants and together they raised DG 2,400,000 or RD 960,000, a vast sum.[83]

It was curious that de Geer and Larsson participated in this consortium. They were, of course, both commissioners for the crown and both were involved in the negotiations. This should have raised some serious concerns on the crown's side, but the chancellor did not mention it. On the other hand, it was a triumph for Trip because he adroitly turned two potential rivals into allies and partners. He also, no doubt, thought it would help eliminate problems on the crown's side. Dahlgren, at least, expressed surprise by the defection of de Geer and Larsson over to Trip's camp: "That Erik Larsson and also de Geer should now appear side by side with a person from whom they so recently distanced themselves, and openly accused, must have been one of the fruits of compromise, in which, however, the advocate for the crown drew the short straw."[84] It once again indicates that the crown was not well served by those with whom it chose to do business in Amsterdam.

The main points of the new agreement were as follows: The consortium would assume possession of the 24,000 skd in Trip's inventory as well as the new 2,300 skd that Trip had sequestered. This ended the legal action.[85] The consortium would mortgage the copper at RD 55 per skd for the *gårkoppar* and RD 44 for the *råkoppar*. In other words, the prices were the same as in the original deposit of 1629. In addition, as suggested by the chancellor, the consortium agreed to take 6,000 skd per year for three years. This would, again, be a deposit to be mortgaged.[86] But redemption of the copper was unlikely because of the quantity. Meanwhile, de Geer and other members of the consortium would seek to sell copper from both the original deposit and from the newly arriving batches. They would be free to sell at a floor price of RD 66 per skd for *gårkoppar* and RD 55 for *råkoppar*. Sales, however, would be unlikely because the average price in Amsterdam in 1634 for *gårkoppar* was RD 62.20.

83   LDGBOA, 317–20.
84   Dahlgren, *Louis de Geer*, 1, 221.
85   LDGBOA, 321.
86   LDGBOA, 317-320.

The agreement also called for the crown to give the consortium a sales monopoly on copper for six years from ratification. The crown could not sell to any other merchants for export. The crown could, of course, sell internally to Swedish foundries and manufacturing ventures.[87] This sales monopoly (like all monopolies) was designed to prevent competition, and it was a common feature of Elias Trip's contracts. He insisted on the same terms in the 1629 negotiations with Falkenberg.[88]

Erik Larsson kept the chancellor informed on the progress of the negotiations. Once negotiations were completed in April, Larsson was to take the document to Stockholm for ratification by the *Riks-Råd* and the *Kammar-Råd*. The chancellor, however, a member of both councils, disliked much about the agreement. As early as April 11, before the conclusion of the discussions, he had written to Queen Kristina and her advisers on the subject. He recognized that the crown had to address the issue of its debts to Elias Trip, but he was not willing to allow Trip to bully the crown on the issue of a monopoly. He wrote that granting Trip a monopoly on copper sales in continental Europe for six years would "put the crown's control over commerce and trade in the hands of Elias Trip to do with whatever he pleased."[89] In addition, the chancellor wanted the crown to retain power over sales prices. He feared that the consortium would sell below market to its members, who would then resell at a profit, thereby cheating the crown once again.

In May when the negotiations were complete and Larsson was on the way to Stockholm with the finished contract, the chancellor sent his opinion on the document to the *Riks-Råd* and the *Kammar-Råd*. He clearly disapproved of the finished document claiming that it "made the crown the slave of the Amsterdam merchants."[90] More specifically, he objected to the restrictions on exports and was unhappy that Trip was allowed to keep the 2,300 skd that he had sequestered, which appeared to add legitimacy to his position.[91]

According to Oxenstierna, moreover, there were several unresolved issues. For example, Elias Trip had submitted an accounting for the growing debt on the 24,000 skd currently on deposit. This accounting differed by RD 80,000 from the accounting done by the Swedish *Ränte-Kammar*. The chancellor wanted Trip to travel to Stockholm and explain the difference to the Swedish authorities. Also, the chancellor did not want the copper on deposit in

---

87 Dahlgren, *Louis de Geer*, 1, 222.
88 Van Dillen, *Notarieele*, 238.
89 AOSB, I, 11:2 590–91.
90 ASOB, I, 11:2, 737
91 ASOB, I, 11:2, 738.

Hamburg and Lübeck to be part of the contract. He wanted to redeem those lots and sell them into the market. This would, of course, conflict with Trip's requirement that the contract include a six-year monopoly on the sale of copper in continental Europe, to which the chancellor would never agree.[92]

In the end, the Trip consortium came to naught. The joint committee of the *Riks-* and *Kammar-Råd* rewrote the contract to remove the restrictions that Trip wanted to impose on the crown's sales abroad. They also increased the crown's oversight on sales in Amsterdam. The main problem, however, was that the chancellor simply did not trust Trip or his associates.[93] By summer the chancellor reported to Queen Kristina and her advisers that Trip had renounced the contract and that his consortium was dissolved. They would now have to seek other means to finance the debt in Amsterdam.[94] During these negotiations the crown had continued to sell copper, mostly through de Geer, in Amsterdam, Hamburg, and Lübeck. The chancellor informed the queen (and the regency council) that crown debts in Hamburg and Lübeck had now been paid with shipments of copper.

The problem for everybody concerned was the quantity of copper mortgaged. If the crown formally announced a default, the price of copper could fall sharply. This was a situation that Trip could not tolerate because he might be forced to sell at a price well below his mortgage price. If it formally defaulted, the crown might also face higher interest rates for future loans. That, at least, was the experience of the Spanish Hapsburgs.[95] So both sides continued to pretend. Trip pretended that there was a chance that the crown would redeem the copper, and the crown pretended that it would not finally have to default on the mortgaged copper.

Finally, however, the chancellor lost patience. He had received a letter from Trip demanding full payment. He told the queen (and the regency council) not to worry about Trip because there was enough copper in the Amsterdam deposit to pay everything owed to him.[96] The chancellor clarified his new position toward Elias Trip in a letter to his brother, Gabriel Gustavsson Oxenstierna: "He is now fully paid, no, overpaid, but he is clever and has invented additional expenses, which he demands. He will have to come to Stockholm and appear before the *Kammer*, like any other creditor."[97] This meant that the chancellor was finally calling Trip's bluff. He would

92   ASOB, I, 11:1, 738.
93   Dahlgren, *Louis de Geer*, 1, 224.
94   AOSB, I, 12, 282.
95   Safley, "Bankruptcy," 1, 218.
96   AOSB, I, 12, 626.
97   AOSB, I, 12, 648.

inform Trip (through Larsson) that the crown considered the matter settled. Trip should keep the copper now in his possession as full payment for the principal and interest. Of course, this was not the end of the controversy.

Meanwhile the crown still had bills to pay. In his letters to the young queen (she was now eight years old), and the regency council, the chancellor fretted about not being able to sell the 6,000 skd that he had planned to sell to the Trip consortium yearly. He told the queen that he was looking for other means. He does not say so, but he was probably now afraid to ship the copper to Amsterdam for fear that Elias Trip would attempt another sequestration. He reported that the crown had been selling copper all along through de Geer in Amsterdam. He would now probably move the location to Hamburg or Lübeck for future sales.[98] In the meantime, de Geer reported to his assistant in Stockholm, Johan Le Thoor, that he had just sold the last part of 1,000 skd that the crown had sent to him to sell as an agent. He asked Le Thoor to request more from the *Riks-Råd* and the *Kammar-Råd*. In addition, he wanted another 600 skd copper for his cannon foundry in Nyköping.[99] The crown was selling copper, but not at the desired rate.

Despite the chancellor's bluster about forcing Elias Trip to appear before the *Ränte-Kammar* in Stockholm before he would consider any settlement, he knew that the crown needed the ability to sell copper in Amsterdam without the threat of further sequestrations of copper shipments. It is, therefore, safe to assume that the chancellor knew that some accommodation with Trip would be necessary. That does not mean that he would tolerate being bullied by Trip, or that he was any less ruthless than Trip when the crown's solvency was at stake.

In April, however, Trip addressed a long and exhaustive petition to the States General and to the *Riks-Råd* in Stockholm; it detailed the copper deposits for the Swedish crown, beginning with negotiations with Conrad von Falkenberg in 1629. He reviewed every transaction and requested that the crown send a representative to settle the matter.[100] In June of 1635 the chancellor wrote to Erik Larsson in Amsterdam telling him to approach Trip to inform him that he should settle outstanding debts using crown copper in his possession. But, of course, the chancellor expected to see a full accounting and the return of all copper not used for payment.

On the same day, the chancellor wrote a formal letter to Trip announcing that Larsson was his official delegate and authorized to act on the crown's

---

98   AOSB, I, 12, 625-26.
99   LDGBOA, 323-24..
100 Van Dillen, *Notarieele*, 269.

behalf. To intimidate the obstreperous Trip, the chancellor began his letter with a highly uncharacteristic list of titles: "Her Royal Majesty's and the Swedish Empire's Chancellor, all powerful legate over Germany and the Army, Director of the Protestant League, Axel Oxenstierna, Lord of Kimitto, Lord of Fijholm and Tijdön, Knight, etc."[101] He then requested that the merchant accept Larsson's fair settlement offers.

Larsson was not able to settle the matter with Trip. In the end, both parties agreed to arbitration, which took place on October 20, 1635. Two local doctors of law, Hercules Roch and Pieter Cloeck, were chosen by the parties of the dispute to act as arbitrators. Legal counsel represented the crown and Trip. There was no dispute over the fate of the 24,000 skd of copper. Both parties agreed that the crown had decided to default on its loan from Trip and turn the copper deposit over to him. Neither party, however, used the term "default." The arbitrators recognized that the crown was granting Trip "his rightful share" by releasing ownership of the copper. The hurdle to settlement was Trip's attempt to collect not only past due simple interest, but "interest on interest," or compounded interest.[102] The crown had calculated simple interest only. The arbitrators agreed with Trip on the interest issue and awarded Trip an additional DG 160,742 (RD 98,979) on top of the copper he now owned outright. Furthermore, the crown still owed Trip for an old weapons contract in the amount of DG 127,214, which brought the total settlement to DG 287,956 or RD 115,182 on top of the copper deposits. Erik Larsson, on behalf of the crown, agreed to pay this amount over three years.[103]

This was an expensive lesson for the crown, but the disadvantages of the deposit system were now clear for all to see. The crown had forfeited 24,000 skd of copper still in deposit and was responsible for paying compounded interest on the loan it secured. But it had no alternative. It had to settle or face the possibility of sequestration of its copper whenever it shipped to Amsterdam, and it could not ignore the most important center for copper trading in Europe.

The crown also finally understood the problems with large deposits. Since the copper was far away, the crown lost control over the administration of the loans. It also failed to make yearly reconciliations with Elias Trip. Such a simple step would have informed the crown of the growing problem. As we have observed repeatedly, the crown was not well served by its servants in

101 AOSB, I, 13, 317–18.
102 Van Dillen, *Notarieele*, 273.
103 Van Dillen, *Notarieele*, 277.

Amsterdam. Between 1629 and 1633, Conrad von Falkenberg was stationed in Amsterdam; Erik Larsson had full authority over copper trading from 1630; de Geer was the crown's commissioner from 1632 onward. Any of them could have looked after the administration.

Oxenstierna reluctantly assumed a new role in copper trading, while modestly claiming that he was not an expert in financial matters. We recall, however, that he strongly condemned the deposit system in his "Considerations" to the king written in 1630.[104] As we shall shortly see, the fiasco with Trip ended the deposit system. The chancellor had plans for the future of copper trading, but these plans did not include a new deposit system. The chancellor, meanwhile, had learned that he could not rely on merchants in Amsterdam to look after the crown's interests.

In a July 1635 letter to Jacob de la Gardie, a fellow member of both the *Riks-Råd,* and *Kammar-Råd*, and the commander of the army in Livonia, the chancellor suggested, once again, that a new copper company might be a solution.[105] He also proposed the idea to the young queen and the regency council in August. He suggested a company with capital of only RD 100,000. It would handle all the copper exported from Sweden, but not copper that was to be consumed internally. By autumn the new copper company was taking shape. The chancellor wrote that Erik Larsson was organizing the company. There would be a Swedish company that handled the purchasing of copper from the mine and the inland shipments, and an Amsterdam company that would oversee the sale of copper in continental Europe.[106] But the chancellor was concerned about certain details of the new agreements. As he mentioned in his testament, Oxenstierna observed that the new company should not interfere with the development of copper manufacturing and foundry production in Sweden. Obviously distrustful of Elias Trip, he told the queen and the council that he had specified to Larsson that if Trip was involved in the company in Amsterdam, Larsson should oversee the Amsterdam company's accounting. Finally, the new company would have a life of three and one-half years, after which it would be dissolved.[107]

The crown's handling of the copper exports, in chaos since the death of the king, were finally back on track. The chancellor was too far away to oversee the day-to-day business and he no longer trusted the *Riks-* and *Kammar-Råd* to take an active role. Putting Erik Larsson in charge of a

104 AOSB, I, 1, 345.
105 AOSB, I, 13, 346.
106 AOSB, I, 13, 513–15.
107 AOSB, I, 13, 513–15.

new copper company appeared to be an ideal solution. In January 1636, Larsson wrote from Stockholm to give the chancellor a full report. Between members of the *Riks-Råd* and the Stockholm merchant class he had raised capital in the amount of RD 52,000. Their goal was to raise a total of RD 100,000,[108] but Larsson said he would visit Hamburg and Amsterdam soon and was confident of raising the balance.[109] He also reported that he was the largest contributor, at the time contributing RD 8,000. Oxenstierna's court-chancellor in Hamburg, Johan Salvius, was drawing up the privileges for the company, which is probably the reason that they have not survived with Oxenstierna's papers. Larsson reported that he was eager to get under way and informed the chancellor that the first 1,300 skd of copper were ready for shipment from Stockholm.[110] This was the last letter the chancellor ever received from his long-time acquaintance. Shortly after writing the letter, Erik Larsson died unexpectedly.

This left the copper plans in ruins. In his first letter to the queen and the regency council in the new year, the chancellor lamented the death of Larsson because "it will mean great difficulty raising the additional capital." The chancellor wanted to find a replacement for Larsson, an "upstanding and well-respected merchant," who could fill Larsson's role as a fundraiser and oversee the company operations.[111] He was convinced that the new company "could not help but make money"; in fact, he would have liked to run it himself, but he lacked the training. De Geer would have been an obvious choice, but according to his biographer, E.W. Dahlgren, de Geer was no longer interested. By now he was back in Sweden, and fully involved in the copper manufacturing and bronze cannon foundry business. In fact, statistics support the contention that beginning in the mid-1630s, notably less copper went for export because more was being consumed in Sweden for domestic industrial activities.[112] De Geer, no doubt, had spotted this trend and decided that the future was brighter in the copper-manufacturing sector rather than in copper trading.

This trend was also affected by the war. The chancellor wrote to his brother, Gabriel Gustavsson Oxenstierna, that there was now a Spanish garrison in Aachen and the town was cut off from Amsterdam once again. This caused a price decline, because without a market the copper was

108 AOSB, I, 13, 514.
109 AOSB, II, 11, 537–39.
110 AOSB, II, 11, 536–38.
111 AOSB, I, 15, 190.
112 Boëthius and Heckscher, *Svensk Handelsstatistik*, 632–36.

accumulating in Amsterdam.[113] The chancellor also mentioned, moreover, that many of the copper masters and copper workers had left Aachen for the Netherlands. He sent his financial trouble-shooter, Pieter Spierinck, to Amsterdam with a commission to find and hire as many copper workers as possible for migration to Sweden.[114]

De Geer's new interests were evident from his correspondence. He was now living at his copper works in Norrköping and corresponding with his son, Laurens, who was still in Amsterdam. Instead of offering *gårkoppar*, he wrote that he was offering 350 spools of copper wire and copper sheet. He also mentioned that he would make 12,000 copper kettles at his works in Finspån.[115] Naturally, he was now following prices for fabricated copper goods with the same keen interest he had shown for copper ingot prices during the previous decades. He wrote to his business partner in Hamburg, Jan van Sorgen, that he was monitoring copper wire prices in Amsterdam because the English were now buying at DG 57 per hundredweight (RD 62.7 per skd) there. He added that recently he could have sold brass rolls at DG 75 to DG 80 per hundredweight, but now they were selling at DG 70 (RD 77 per skd). He also wrote that he was exporting copper kettles to Bremen and selling them at DG 60 to "important buyers." In short, de Geer had transferred his interest from trading in copper ingots to manufacturing copper and bronze goods.

De Geer was also attempting to develop his arms manufacturing business. In June of 1637 he wrote to the chancellor asking for privileges to expand his cannon foundry in Norrköping. De Geer complained that he had the opportunity to sell both iron and bronze cannon in England, but his limited production capacity would not allow the additional business. His correspondence during this period was full of such requests.[116] To expand copper goods and bronze cannon production, he needed more trained people. Fortunately, the chancellor's efforts to recruit displaced copper workers from Aachen and Wallonnia was working. As mentioned earlier in this chapter the movement changed from a mere trickle to a flood as de Geer continued to sign contracts with many metal workers from French-speaking Calvinist areas of northern Europe during this period.

When de Geer did mention copper ingot, he complained about the lack of it. He wrote to his trading partners in Danzig, Mattaes and Abraham

---

113   AOSB, I, 15, 333-34.
114   AOSB, I, 15, 334.
115   LDGBOA, 367.
116   LDGBOA, 390-91.

Clemens, probably at their request, telling them that all copper leaving Sweden went to Amsterdam via the Amsterdam Copper Company, which was the sister company of the New Swedish Copper Company.[117] This demonstrates that the new company was functioning, but it must have done so quietly, because there is very little correspondence surviving to document its activities. What is clear, however, is that much more copper was being consumed in Sweden and exported as finished product.

In summary, the king's death, in November 1632 left a power vacuum for copper policy. This, in turn, led to a series of political maneuvers in Amsterdam. With Erik Larsson temporarily out of favor, Louis de Geer showered the chancellor and the *Riks-Råd* with advice on copper sales, hoping to be appointed, once again, the factor in Amsterdam. This prompted a lawsuit from Conrad von Falkenberg, who wanted the position for himself. At first, the chancellor tried to shift the responsibility for copper policy to the *Riks-Råd*. This administrative body, however, failed to develop a strategy. Meanwhile, various parties attempted to organize consortiums to handle the purchasing and marketing of copper. The vast deposits in Amsterdam, however, and the associated debts, presented an insurmountable barrier to an agreement. Finally, the chancellor lost patience and announced that interest payments would stop and Elias Trip, the financier in Amsterdam, now owned the entire lot outright.

In his "Considerations" on copper policy, which we reviewed earlier in this chapter, the chancellor made several recommendations to the king that differed radically from Gustav Adolf's copper policy. For example, the chancellor was opposed to the deposit system, and he explained his opposition in the "Considerations." He wrote that the merchants who mortgaged the copper had use of a resource given to the crown "by the grace of God." And he was outraged by the cost of interest on the deposit. He may have seen its value as a temporary expedient to keep copper off the market. By 1630, however, when he wrote the testament, the king was already abusing the system. By 1632 the deposit had become a burden that the crown could no longer support.[118]

De Geer's efforts to form a new copper company in 1633 also fell flat when Trip demanded interest payments on the deposits.[119] When none came, Trip went to the authorities and sequestered a large shipment belonging to the crown. This caused an uproar, but shortly thereafter, Trip himself attempted

---

117 LDGBOA, 390-91.
118 AOSB, I, 1, 345.
119 LDGBOA, 291.

to form a syndicate to purchase the inventory and import copper from Sweden. This attempt was, in turn, doomed because the chancellor would not entertain Trip's low mortgage price and his demand for a monopoly on the sale of copper in all of Europe. The common problem behind these failures was the size of the deposit of copper in Amsterdam and the mortgage on it. The principal and interest had become too large a debt for the crown to repay or refinance. In the end, the chancellor did the inevitable. He defaulted on the previous agreements. Although no one called it a default at the time, there is no other way to describe the facts.

In 1635 Trip took possession of all the copper in the deposit, which included the original 24,000 skd plus the 2,300 skd that he sequestered. The total was 26,300 skd of copper, equaling 7.5 million modern pounds of copper.[120] The deposit system was over. At the arbitration in Amsterdam later that year, Trip was awarded RD 115,182 in interest payments. The crown demonstrated its unhappiness with the outcome by not making the payments, despite numerous promises to do so. The issue was still pending when the last claimant died in 1873.[121] We can conclude, therefore, that the chancellor ended the deposit system, thus fulfilling his promise in his 'Considerations.'

The issue the chancellor mentioned most often in the "Considerations" was the necessity for Sweden to develop a domestic copper industry through investment in copper manufacturing, bronze cannon production, and the development of brass works.[122] Before his death on the battlefield, the king had also advocated building Sweden's domestic copper manufacturing and casting industry. The process began in the late 1620s when de Geer temporarily moved to Stockholm and invested in the iron and copper works being established by his fellow countryman, Willem de Besche. To this day, de Geer is known as the "father of Swedish industry" because of his role as the first major industrialist in Sweden.[123]

Oxenstierna voiced serious reservations, however, on the copper minting issue, which earned Heckscher's praise for the chancellor's wisdom. In the "Considerations," the chancellor clearly stated that he would prefer selling copper in return for silver, rather than minting copper itself. As we have observed, however, there was a substantial wait between shipping copper to a continental port and receiving payment in the form of a bill of exchange. As

---

120 A skeppund Stockholm weight equals 136 kgs or 300 US pounds. See Wolontis, *Kopparmynt-ningen*, n. 31.
121 Dahlgren, *Louis de Geer*, 1, 250.
122 AOSB, I, 1, 348.
123 Nováky, "Inledning," 16.

governor of the German possessions, and head of the Swedish armies on the
continent after the death of the king, Oxenstierna was suddenly responsible for
feeding, paying, and supplying many thousands of soldiers. He accomplished
this task by continuing to mint copper at rates like those before the king's
death.[124] Despite reservations, the chancellor did not follow his own advice.

Heckscher disliked the copper currency, yet he reserved his sharpest
criticism for the purchasing monopoly the king established at the Stora
Kopparberg. To Heckscher this was an unwarranted crown intrusion into a
smoothly functioning market system.[125] In his "Considerations" the chancellor argues eloquently for complete freedom of trade between the *bergsmän*,
the local merchants, and local manufacturers. He made his point with a
memorable phrase: "Therefore, I respectfully submit that there should be
free trade in copper at the Kopparberg, and the freer the better."[126] Heckscher
quoted the phrase to contrast the chancellor's enlightened position (in his
view) with the king's copper policy. The chancellor's logic was compelling. He feared that the crown's copper monopoly was working against the
king's efforts to develop a domestic copper manufacturing industry. The
crown bought all available copper from the *bergsmän*, then turned it into
copper currency, or sent it to Amsterdam to pay local creditors. This view
is supported, to some extent, by de Geer's efforts to purchase copper for his
Swedish manufacturing operations during the king's life.

Heckscher praised Oxenstierna's copper "Considerations" and quoted from
it frequently. It is a major irony, therefore, that despite Oxenstierna's position
in his testament, once he became the head of Queen Kristina's regency
council, the chancellor took no steps to amend the crown's purchasing
monopoly at the mine. In fact, in planning the new copper company the
chancellor specified that the monopoly would continue.[127] It was not until
1639, with copper exports through the new copper company in decline, that
the chancellor and the *Riks-Råd* granted the *bergsmän* limited freedom to
sell copper to local merchants. The reaction of the *bergsmän* was mixed.
The commonality of *bergsmän* wrote to the chancellor in February 1638
mentioning that Peter Kruse had explained that they were now free to
sell copper to local merchants. They thanked the chancellor for the new
freedom, but they complained that the local merchants showed no interest

---

124 Wolontis, *Kopparmyntningen*, 252. In 1628 the crown minted 7,486 skd. In 1629 the figure
was 6,435 skd. It never exceeded 5,000 skd per year thereafter.
125 Heckscher, *historia*, 1, 451, 456.
126 AOSB, I, 1, 347.
127 AOSB, I, 13, 513-14.

in their copper. Therefore, they appealed to the chancellor and the queen to buy copper from them. Otherwise, they would not be able to buy the wood and charcoal needed to continue mining and refining.[128] Early in the following year, the *bergsmän* wrote again to the chancellor asking that the traditional *avrad* tax of four *skeppund* per quarter *par* be eliminated until "copper can be sold at a better price."[129]

The above indicates that the chancellor did follow his own advice in the "Considerations" and restored to the *bergsmän* the freedom to sell at least some of their copper to local merchants. It was, moreover, apparently a mixed blessing. The *bergsmän* had become accustomed to selling everything they produced to the crown at a fixed price. They were not happy to be subject once again to the mercies of the copper market. Letters from the *bergsmän* to the chancellor, complaining about low prices and high tolls, continued throughout the decade.[130]

Bibliography

Archival Sources

Riksarkivet. Leufsta arkiv, file 109 # 2–10, 30–41. Jan le Thoor, Credit, Laus Deo Anno 1632 Amst.

Riksarkivet. Leufsta arkiv, file 80 # 26, Protest van Valkenburch.

Riksarkivet. Leufsta arkiv, file 81 # 137–39, Con. Mat. Coperreecken.

Printed Primary Sources

Dahlgren, Erik Wilhelm, ed. *Louis de Geers brev och affärshandlingar 1614–1652.* Stockholm: P.A. Norstedt & Söner, 1934.

Oxenstierna, Axel. *Rikskansleren Axel Oxenstierna skriften och brefvexling,* Series I, 16 vols. Stockholm: P.A. Norstedt & Söner, 1888–Present.

Oxenstierna, Axel. *Rikskansleren Axel Oxenstierna skriften och brefvexling,* Series II, 14 vols. Stockholm: P.A. Norstedt & Söner, 1888–Present.

Van Dillen, Johannes Gerard, ed. "Amsterdamsche Notarieele Acten Betreffende den Koperhandel en de Uitoefening van Mijnbouw en Metaalindustrie in Zweden." *Bijdragen en mededeelingen van het Historisch Genootschap* 58. Utrecht: 1937.

---

128 AOSB, II, 11, 364.
129 AOSB, II, 11, 369.
130 AOSB, II, 11, 360–73.

Secondary Sources

Boëthius, Bertil and Eli Flip Heckscher. *Svensk handelsstatistik 1637–1737*. Stockholm: Thule, 1925.

Dahlgren, Erik Wilhelm. *Louis de Geer, 1587–1652, hans lif och verk*, 2 vols. Uppsala: Almqvist & Wiksells, 1923.

Heckscher, Eli Filip. *Sveriges economiska historia från Gustav Vasa*, 2 vols. Stockholm: Albert Bonniers, 1936.

Klein, Peter Wolfgang. *De Trippen in de 17e Eeuw, een Studie over het Ondernemersgedrag op de Hollandse Stapelmarkt*. Rotterdam: Assen, 1965.

Nordstrom, Byron J. "Christina (1626-1689)." In *Europe 1450 to 1789, Encyclopedia of the Early Modern World*, 6 vols, edited by Jonathan Dewald, 1, 486–487. New York: 2004.

Posthumus, Nicolaas Wilhelmus. *Inquiry into the History of Prices in Holland*, 2 vols. Leiden: E.J. Brill, 1946.

Roberts, Michael. *Gustavus Adolphus, a History of Sweden 1611–1632*, 2 vols. London: Longmans, Green and Co., 1957.

Safley, Thomas Max. "Bankruptcy." In *Europe 1450 to 1789, Encyclopedia of the Early Modern World*, 6 vols, edited by Jonathan Dewald, 1, 219–22. New York: 2004.

Stryker, Lawrence. "The King's Currency: Gustav II Adolf and the Copper Standard 1619-1632." *Scandinavian Economic History Review* 65, no. 1: 52–69.

Timm, Albrecht. "Die Bedeutung des Mansfelder Kupfers zwischen 1500 und 1630." In *Schwerpunkte der Kupferproduktion und des Kupferhandels in Europa 1500–1650*, edited by H. Kellenbenz, 184–89. Cologne: 1977.

Wittrock, Georg. *Svenska handelscompaniet och kopparhandeln under Gustav II Adolf*. Uppsala: Almqvist & Wikesell, 1919.

Wolontis, Josef. *Kopparmyntning i Sverige 1624–1714*. Helsingfors: 1936.

Conclusion

Abstract

The conclusion brings together the many strands of this rich story. We examine the place that Gustav II Adolf occupied in the European hierarchy, particularly his role as the leader of the Protestant armies. During this period, he dominated the battlefields of the German territories. The king was also faced with the task of building a bureaucratic state to support and regulate his vast armies in the field. He was, at the same time, chronically short of resources to underwrite his ambition plans. This prompted him to reorganize and make more efficient his one major asset, the Stora Kopparberg copper mine. He tried, in particular, to expand the crowns control over the purchasing and sales of copper, and to improve the quality of metal exported.

Keywords: Baltic Naval Rivalry, Truce of Altmark, Stockholm, Mainz, Spain

"I would take even the *Kölner Dom* (the Cologne Cathedral) as a firm offer."
Old trader saying

In a footnote to the opening pages of this work, I recounted the story of the young Gustav Adolf's attempt to exterminate the local population of serpents. While probably a myth, it does reflect an aspect of his personality. The king was persistent and aggressive in pursuit of his dual goals of defending the realm at home while, at the same time, expanding his overseas empire. Gustav Adolf understood the importance of copper to achieve his goals and he built on the foundations put in place by his father, Karl IX, who brought German mining experts to Falun to construct improved pumping and hoisting technologies. Yearly production at the mine doubled between 1611, the year the new king assumed the throne, and 1632, the year of his death.

When writing about charismatic figures, like King Gustav Adolf, or competent statemen like Axel Oxenstierna, it is too easy to focus on the

Stryker, L., *The Swedish Monarchy and the Copper Trade: The Copper Company, the Deposit System, and the Amsterdam Market, 1600–1640*. Amsterdam: Amsterdam University Press, 2024
DOI 10.5117/9789048560813_CON

individuals at the expense of their surroundings. It's also important to measure their influence beyond the borders of their kingdoms, and in the case of Gustav Adolf, also beyond the borders of his conquests. We have, for example, referred to the growth of "state building," the "fiscal state" and the "military state." All three are concepts that inform us about the emergence of early modern society. We should remember, moreover, that the changes heralded by these concepts were not peculiar to Sweden. In fact, one might observe that Sweden was hardly the most revealing example of state building.

Sweden certainly came late to the game, and this will allow us to examine her place among other emerging military states. Already in the first half of the sixteenth century Spain had a well-organized military consisting of a professional officer corps, and an army with separate branches of infantry, artillery, and engineering; and Spain was not shy about using its miliary resources on the European continent. Along with the professional army came a professional bureaucracy to oversee and regulate it.[1] Perhaps of greater importance, given the threat of Muslim incursion, Spain had a fully functioning fleet capable of defending her interest in both the Atlantic and the Mediterranean oceans. In contrast, during the War of Kalmar, the armies of Karl IX and Gustav Adolf were small, ill equipped, and did not do all that well against their hereditary foes, Poland and Denmark.[2] The Swedish navy was too small to face a pitched battle, which allowed the Danes to dominate the Swedish coast. Sweden's combined military forces never exceeded 15,000 men.[3]

A comparison with the Dutch Republic also shows how far behind Sweden remained in naval warfare compared with her contemporaries. As late as the outbreak of the Thirty Years War in 1618 Sweden had limited naval resources, despite an economy based on the export of raw materials and later the export of weaponry.[4] One obvious reason for the naval superiority of the Dutch Republic was its almost total dependence on commercial activities. A fully developed navy was essential to protect this commerce. It was a great irony that raw materials and, later, goods manufactured and processed in Sweden were shipped to Amsterdam in Dutch vessels. In 1627, for example, Peter Trip shipped 6,751 skd of copper from Stockholm to Amsterdam using Dutch vessels. The cargo was to serve as collateral for a loan the Trip family

1   Glete, *War and the State*, 82.
2   Downing, *The Military*, 194
3   Downing, *The Militarly*, 195 and Roberts, *Gustavus Adolphus*, I, 61.
4   Glete, *War and the State*, 200–201.

made to the Swedish crown in the amount of DG 687,000.[5] Thus, the need for credit led to the shipment of copper. Amsterdam's stable of international bankers guaranted a constant flow of goods to the city as security for loans.

In another example, Louis de Geer shipped cannons, ammunition, weapons, armor, and horseshoes from his industrial plants in Sweden to be sold in Amsterdam by his own trading company.[6] Why did he use Dutch ships? Because they were secure. As part of the Dutch Republic's eighty-year war of independence they had developed an elaborate convoy system. In fact, it was the largest convoy network thus far attempted. One can imagine the importance for Dutch trading to have the resources to protect commerce in the face of Spanish belligerence. This was especially true after the Spanish truce with the Dutch Republic expired in 1621. When the war resumed, it was mostly at sea.[7]

There was yet another weakness in Sweden's naval efforts. Sweden did not have a substantial merchant marine to train naval officers. Beginning in 1602, the Dutch VOC (The Dutch East India Company) dominated trade with the East Indies. While founded as a trading company, the VOC also functioned as a training ground for officers, when needed, for the Dutch Navy. Sweden did not possess an ocean bound trading network and, therefore, lacked an inventory of seasoned naval personnel.[8]

Despite this limited naval presence in the Baltic, Gustav Adolf sought to enlarge his influence there. Finland had been part of the Swedish empire since the twelfth century. Estonia joined after the Protestant Reformation. The king added Ingria, and Karelia in 1617 after the Russian wars, and he successfully invaded the important Polish trading city of Riga in 1621. The rest of occupied Livonia followed in 1629 as part of the Truce of Altmark.[9] Territories in Germany such as Pomerania where only officially recognized as Swedish possessions after the Peace of Westphalia in 1648.[10]

To put the Swedish effort in perspective, her ambition for a limited Baltic empire suffers by comparison to the enormous oversea Spanish Empire that reached from the Philippines in the East to the American continent in the West. A Swedish Empire was necessary if the goal was to dominate the Baltic Region. But compared to the territories of the Spanish empire or even the early colonial empire of France, Sweden paled. This is important to

5   Lesger, *The Rise of Amsterdam*, 208–209.
6   Lesger, *The Rise of Amsterdam*, 208–209.
7   Downing, *The Military*, 220.
8   Glete, *War and the State*, 200,
9   Roberts, *Gustav Adolf,* 2, 398.
10 Lundkvist, *The Experience*, 21.

remember because Spain, itself, was interested in expanding its influence in the Baltic region and used her position to threaten Sweden's revenues from the Prussian port tolls along the Vistula. This was followed by "rumors" that Spain was contemplating sending subsides to Gustav Adolf's Catholic arch enemy, King Sigismund of Poland.[11]

Empire building and fighting foreign wars in Germany, in general, strained the Swedish economy, but also had some positive effects. First, there was the flow of war plunder from the Holy Roman Empire to the northern homeland, and as a counter-balance, the export of copper, iron, and weapons moving from Sweden to the warring parties in the empire.[12] Sections of Stockholm like the Skeppsbron, were established to accommodate the flood of foreign merchants drawn to the raw materials trade as the war economy blossomed.[13] Some, like Louis de Geer, moved to Sweden and invested in the wave of industrialization founded mainly on the manufacture of weapons to feed the wars in Germany. In 1634, the chancellor sponsored a round of government reforms that fueled the need for educated and talented bureaucrats serving in both Stockholm and Elbing. Between 1620 and 1668 the population of Stockholm quadrupled.[14] Yet, in 1632, after Gustav Adolf's death, the city elders did not invite other reigning monarchs to the funeral because they feared that such visits would expose the city's barrenness. "Stockholm was rather a scruffy little town at the time," and with a population of a mere 40,000 it was a village compared to other imperial capitals such as London, Paris or Vienna.[15]

A significant portion of the Swedish Empire's business was carried on in Germany, closer to the armies. As we have noted previously, the maintenance of armies requires administrative services. This apparatus included payroll, weapons acquisition, and most importantly the collection of taxes and mandatory contributions from the local population. These services work more efficiently if they are located closer to the theater of war. It also helps if the administrators speak the same language as their colleagues. After entering the Thirty Years War, Sweden established a permanent administrative center in Mainz. It was tasked with virtually every function of the army. So naturally, as the Swedish presence in Germany grew, the bureaucracy in Mainz expanded at the same pace. And when the army in Germany was

---

11   Roberts, *Gustav Adolf,* 2, 336
12   North, *The Baltic,* 117.
13   North, *The Baltic,* 117.
14   North, *The Baltic,* 117.
15   North, *The Baltic,* 117.

no longer needed the German speaking administrators were send home along with the German mercenaries. After the Peace of Westphalia in 1648, Sweden was unable to fund either the vast military or the bureaucracy that it spawned.[16]

We have, thus far, shown the disadvantages Gustav Adolf suffered compared with his allies and rivals, which makes his undeniable success even more commendable. One area, however, in which the king excelled was mining copper. Production levels are available for the sixteenth century, and for the early years of the seventeenth century for the three primary non-Swedish European mines. There was the Neusohler mine in Hungary, the Schwaz mine in the Tyrol, and the Eisleben mine in Mansfeld mentioned in the last chapter. All three showed a steady decline in mineral output beginning in the first years of the seventeenth century and lasting until the statistics end in 1622.[17] The cause of this shift is obvious; the Stora Kopparberg's production levels were growing at the expense of the competition. The reader will remember that until 1626 the copper prices in Amsterdam were increasing, so Gustav Adolf was motivated to produce and sell. Even when copper prices fell, however, the Stora Kopparberg continued to produce at capacity. In 1600 the Neusohler mine produced 12,004 skd, in 1622 that figure fell to 10,782 skd. The mine at Schwaz produced 9,396 skd in 1,600 and 5,548 in 1622. And the Mansfeld mine, 5,442 skd in 1,600 and 3,344 skd in 1622. During this same period the production of cooper at the Stora Kopparberg rose from 2,405 skd to 7,733 skd.[18]

Running the mine at full capacity in a falling price environment would not win praise from modern mineral economists, but it made perfect sense to the king in the early years of his reign. He was facing a RD 1 million bill for the Älvsborg ransom. These payments were critically important for Sweden's military and commercial future. The city of Göteborg, protected by the Älvsborg Fortress, was Sweden's only North Sea port and her only access to the West avoiding the heavily fortified Sound controlled by Denmark. Without Göteborg, Sweden could be isolated from her commercial markets and blockaded in time of war; to maintain Göteborg, the crown had to pay the Älvsborg ransom in full.

Yet, how was the war-torn and disorganized nation, that Gustav Adolf inherited in 1611, able to pay? Just as the king had to consolidate control over his subjects, he had to exercise control over the most important natural

---

16 Downing, *The Military*, 200.
17 Westermann, *Zur Silber und Kupfer*, (not numbered).
18 Lindroth, *Stora Kopparberg*, 2, 389.

resource that his kingdom offered—copper. He began this process, with the help of Carl Bonde, by negotiating favorable supply contracts with the *bergsmän*, keeping in mind that they always had the alternative of smuggling, or simply not producing copper. In other words, the king had to negotiate in a reasonable fashion with the *bergsmän* and take care not to trample on their time-honored rights and privileges.

During this same period, we noted the king's propensity for military action. He fought a number of wars against Russia and Poland, fueled mostly by fear that his cousin and rival, Sigismund III of Poland, would extend his power and influence in the eastern Baltic region. Not only was Sigismund a strong proponent of Counter-Reformation Catholicism, but he also had a legitimate claim to the Swedish throne. The fact that Poland shared borders with Swedish Estonia meant that Gustav Adolf was constantly in fear of invasion. Regardless of the justification, these wars were expensive. One could argue that such military adventures jeopardized the equally important task of paying off the ransom. In the end, however, the young king was successful; he fought his wars, and at the same time, paid the ransom. Göteborg remains to this day a major trading center for Sweden and is now the second largest city in the country.

By 1619 the young king was finally able to enforce a purchasing monopoly on the *bergsmän* of the Kopparberg. This was an important achievement because it gave the crown power over the purchase price. He set the purchase price high enough to satisfy the *bergsmän*, yet low enough to insure a profit in the continental markets. Having a monopoly on purchasing meant that the crown was taking the place of the local merchants. In the long run, this led to greater efficiencies in marketing and transportation; it also provided the crown with the profits previously made by the string of merchants who brought the copper to market. In addition, this monopoly allowed the king to proceed with two important goals in the second decade of his reign. He established the Copper Company to handle the purchase and export of copper and he began minting copper as currency.

A copper company loosely based on the model of the Dutch East Indies Company had potential. If properly nurtured, such an organization could have overseen the sale of Swedish copper all over Europe, without involving merchants in Amsterdam. It also could have provided marketing and technical expertise, that would have benefitted Sweden in the long run. Unfortunately for the company, the king was not patient. He expected profits from the company, and he borrowed from its equity.

This doomed the enterprise almost from the beginning. The leading Swedish economic historians of the last century had reservations about the Copper Company. Wittrock, the first to tackle the subject, wrote of the king, "[t]ime and again his financial plans and decisions were murky at best."[19] This was mild compared to Heckscher's criticism of the company monopoly, which was driven by his ideological commitment to free markets, unhampered by government interference. Since he wrote his most important works in the 1930s, the examples of Soviet and German state-control over industry certainly colored his opinions of Gustav Adolf's copper monopoly. He was critical of crown involvement at the mine and considered the effort counterproductive.[20]

The king's other significant initiative was the introduction of a copper currency. His logic was compelling. Spain had been minting copper for decades. The king made copper a more flexible currency by minting lower denomination coins to pay soldiers and local suppliers to the army. Heckscher's primary objection to the copper currency was the fact that much of it ended up for sale on the Amsterdam market in competition with copper ingot.[21] The case for the copper currency had an important dimension that I have never seen discussed but seems self-evident. It was a fast and efficient way to turn copper into currency and was a critical improvement for the royal cash flow. This was an important benefit because the crown needed a rapid turnaround time from copper ingot to copper coins in order to pay and feed the armies in the field. The alternative was to send copper to Amsterdam for sale and wait for payment by bills of exchange. We now know that this could take many months, especially if the merchants with whom the crown was dealing temporarily diverted the money for their own benefit. One must also acknowledge that by minting copper, the crown was not putting more copper onto the market than previously. If the *bergsmän* produced it, then the crown would sell it as ingot, mortgage it in Amsterdam, or mint it. It reached the market one-way or another. When one considers this fact, Heckscher's criticism appears less relevant.

Even the undisputed English language expert on the subject, Michael Roberts, was critical of the crown's economic policy. He wrote: "The history of Gustav Adolf's copper policy ... had, indeed, been uniformly unfortunate. And ... Gustav Adolf was at the mercy of economic forces, which he could not control, and only dimly appreciated."[22] As I have mentioned repeatedly, I think this criticism is misdirected. The crown's primary goal was not to

---

19 Wittrock, *Handelscompaniet*, 161.
20 Heckscher, *historia*, 1, 451, 593–94.
21 Heckscher, *historia*, 1, 458.
22 Roberts, *Gustavus Adolphus*, 2, 102.

create the ideal environment for free-market trading in commodities. The crown's objective was to mobilize copper in the service of the state in the same manner it mobilized the Swedish army. Copper was an essential chess piece in this economically backward country's attempt to pay the Älvsborg Ransom and, at the same time, field armies to protect Protestant interests in northern Europe. In short, the crown used copper to further its political and military goals; it did not have the luxury of husbanding the resource to achieve distant goals of economic growth.

Ironically, the king's critics ignored or downplayed the deposit system, which turned into a financial disaster for the crown. The practice of mortgaging copper ingots in Amsterdam was a way to avoid selling copper in a falling market. If the crown had used the practice sparingly, the consequences might have been positive. Unfortunately for future policy, the crown decided to mortgage the majority of the copper it produced after the demise of the Copper Company. At the time of the king's death, Elias Tripp had 26,300 skd copper in his inventory. The crown could never hope to redeem such a large quantity. Meanwhile, other merchants competed with Trip to be the contracting party because of the potential profits to be made from remortgaging the metal.

It was against this background that de Geer staged his manipulation hoax, claiming that he had singlehandedly moved the copper market in Amsterdam from RD 45 per skd to RD 80 per skd by selling small lots of copper and then buying them back at higher prices.[23] Based purely on de Geer's published letters, every historian to touch the subject has accepted his claim at face value. De Geer even convinced the king of his superhuman talents, and the king was ready to meet with him to discuss a more comprehensive copper policy.[24] Unfortunately for de Geer, the king died in battle before that meeting could take place.

Regarding the copper on deposit, in the end, the chancellor instructed Erik Larsson to tell Elias Trip that the crown would make no further payments and the copper now belonged to him. This was simply a default on the loans that Trip had made to the crown. Despite being largely ignored by history the default had severe consequences. Trip now had a copper inventory of approximately 26,300 skd, which he undoubtedly wanted to sell. Every merchant in every prominent trading city would have known about the inventory. A large inventory, hanging over the market, must have a negative influence on prices. A glance at figure 1 in the Introduction will show that prices came down in 1634 and 1635 and stayed at relatively low

---

23   Louis de Geers Brev och affärshandlingar (LDGBOA), 237.
24   Dahlgren, *Louis de Geer*, 1, 206.

levels for the next fifteen years. It is more than likely that the 26,300 skd in Trip's inventory had a major influence on this long-term price retreat.

Regardless of the praise, or criticism, the king received from historians in the last century, we should remember that when he came to the throne in 1611, the mine was producing fewer than 6,000 *skeppund* of copper per year. By the year after his death, the production rate had doubled to slightly under 12,000 skd per year. Clearly, the king's policy of increasing the number of active *bergsmän*, which we discussed in the first chapter, led to this important expansion. In addition, he moved Sweden from mining and processing *råkoppar*, a partially refined intermediary, to a producer and exporter of *gårkoppar* and plate. This meant that the expensive work of refining and forging was taking place in Sweden, and the extra revenue remaining in the country. It is likely that the Thirty Years War contributed to this trend. As production was interrupted in Germany and in the Southern Netherlands, more copper masters and copper workers, mainly religious refugees from Wallonia, were recruited to Sweden from the continent. The Copper Company made large investments in the royal works in Säter and elsewhere to improve the country's refining and manufacturing capacity. Part of this program was to encourage investment from overseas as well. The Walloon, Willem de Besche came to start iron foundries during the reign of Gustav Adolf's father, Karl IX. Gustav Adolf invited Louis de Geer to Sweden and encouraged him, with grants of privileges, to begin the process of developing the Swedish copper and armaments industry.

Gustav Adolf's role in increasing mining capacity and modernizing Swedish industry was connected to the royal monopoly on purchasing copper from the *bergsmän* and the minting of copper. Both were key elements in the king's plan. The purchasing monopoly guaranteed a supply of copper for the mint and for other applications. The fact that copper coins could only be made from *gårkoppar* was an important factor in the king's decision to improve refining capacity. The chancellor continued this effort after the king's death. In 1635 Louis de Geer returned to Sweden and increased his investments in copper manufacturing and casting. Because of the resulting growth in the domestic copper manufacturing industry, the crown became less reliant on sales of copper ingot to fund the military and political machinery. De Geer did not bother to join the new copper company formed by Erik Larsson at the end of 1635. Rather, he was now focused on Swedish industry and eventually became the leading industrialist in early modern Sweden. The expansion of Swedish industry, begun by Gustav Adolf, and continued by the chancellor until his retirement in 1654, was an enduring legacy for the king, and a direct result of his policy of harnessing copper production and sales to further his political and military ambitions in northern Europe.

Bibliography

Printed Primary Sources

Dahlgren, Erik Wilhelm, ed. *Louis de Geers brev och affärshandlingar 1614–1652*. Stockholm: P.A. Norstedt & Söner, 1934.

Oxenstierna, Axel. *Rikskansleren Axel Oxenstierna skriften och brefvexling*, Series I, 16 vols. Stockholm: P.A. Norstedt & Söner, 1888–Present.

Oxenstierna, Axel. *Rikskansleren Axel Oxenstierna skriften och brefvexling*, Series II, 14 vols. Stockholm: P.A. Norstedt & Söner, 1888–Present.

Stiernman, Anton von, ed. *Samling utaf kongl. brev, stadgar och förordordningar i angående Sweriges Rikes*, 4 vols. Stockholm: Kongl. Tryckeriet, 1747.

Van Dillen, Johannes Gerard, ed. "Amsterdamsche Notarieele Acten Betreffende den Koperhandel en de Uitoefening van Mijnbouw en Metaalindustrie in Zweden." In *Bijdragen en mededeelingen van het Historisch Genootschap* 58. Utrecht: 1937.

Secondary Sources

Dahlgren, Erik Wilhelm. *Louis de Geer, 1587–1652, hans lif och verk*, 2 vols. Uppsala: Almqvist & Wiksells, 1923.

Downing, Brian M. *The Military Revolution and Political Change, the Origins of Democracy and Autocracy in Early Modern Europe*. Princeton: Princeton University Press, 1992.

Glete, Jan. *War and the State in Early Modern Europe, Spain, the Dutch Republic, and Sweden as Fiscal-Military States, 1500–1660*. London: Routledge 2002.

Heckscher, Eli Filip. *Sveriges economiska historia från Gustav Vasa*, 2 vols. Stockholm: Albert Bonniers. 1936.

Lindroth, Sven. *Gruvbrytning och kopparhantering vid Stora Kopparberg intill 1800 talets början*, 2 vols. Uppsala: Almqvist & Wiksells, 1955.

Lesger, Clé. *The Rise of the Amsterdam Market and Information Exchange: Merchants, Commercial Expansion, and Change in the Spatial Economy of the Low Countries 1550–1630*. Translated by J.C. Grayson. Aldershot: Ashgate. 2006.

Lundkvist, Sven. "The Experience of Empire: Sweden as a Great Power." In *Sweden's Age of Greatness*, editct by Michael Roberts, 20–57. New York, 1973.

North, Michael. *The Baltic, a History*. Translated by Kenneth Kronenberg. Cambridge, Ma: Harvard University Press, 2017.

Roberts, Michael. *Gustavus Adolphus, a History of Sweden 1611–1632*, 2 vols. London: Longmans, Green and Co., 1957.

Westermann, E. "Zur Silber-und Kupferproduktion Mitteleuropas vom 15 bis zum Frueher 17. Jahrundert." *Der Anschnitt* 38 (1986): 187–211.

Wittrock, Georg. *Svenska handelscompaniet och kopparhandeln under Gustav II Adolf.* Uppsala: Almqvist & Wikesell, 1919.

Wolontis, Josef. *Kopparmyntning i Sverige 1624–1714.* Helsingfors: 1936.

Appendices

Appendix A[1]

Figure 9.   Louis de Geer's Copper Liquidation[2]

	Copper Plate Debit in the Year 1625 Amsterdam Weight in Pounds		
	Shipper	Stockholm	Skd
1	Shipper Cornelius	10.1	2,775
2	Peter Jacobsen	61.2	16,782
3	Jarich Jarichson	140.0	38,413
4	Theunis Simonson	58.8	16,127
5	Jacob Paules	47.1	12,920
6	Totals	317.2	87,017
7	Equivalent in Amsterdam *Skeppund*	274.3	
	Expenses in Dutch Guilder		**DG**
8	Freight on 10.1 skd		7.0
9	Freight for convoy with balance of plate		217.5
10	Harbor fees, wharfage and other minor and extra costs		79.2
11	Discharge from vessel, freight, and handling into the warehouse		65.2
12	Various nights when copper was guarded		10.0
13	Supervision of workers		43.5
14	Cost of security (*waechgeld*)		221.8
15	Customs broker		130.5
16	God's penny for the poor		10.5
17	Insurance on 317 skd Stockholm wt. at RD 80 per skd (4%)		2,534.4
18	Insurance broker		110.9
19	Three months warehouse rent		14.0
20	Three months interest on 317 skd at RD 50 per skd		790.0
21	De Geer sales commission (2%)		1,265.6
22	Total expenses		5,500.1
23	Payment due to the directors on the feast day of St. Martin		57,780.7
24	Total		63,280.8

1   Because of rounding, and use of decimal units instead of currency extension the reader will note some minor discrepancies in the "sum column."
2   Riksarkivet. Leufsta arkiv, file 81, Cooper Platen Debit Anno 1626, Amsterdam. # 22.

Stryker, L., *The Swedish Monarchy and the Copper Trade: The Copper Company, the Deposit System, and the Amsterdam Market, 1600–1640*. Amsterdam: Amsterdam University Press, 2024
DOI 10.5117/9789048560813_APP

Copper Company Credits

	February **Copper Plate**	100 wt.	**DG**
25	Jordan Slicher bought at DG 71 per 100 wt.	42.98	3,051.60
26	Mattys van Ceulen at DG 72	42.50	3,060.00
27	Jacob van Leyen at 72	43.35	3,121.20
28	Jeronimo Rodriges Mendez at 72	83.65	6,022.75
29	Piter van Leyden at 72	126.14	9,334.30
30	Volquin Momma at 72	23.3	1,667.00
31	Jeronimo Rodriges Mendez on March 17 at 72	111.75	8,046.00
32	Jan Stassart at 72.5	171.3	12,419.30
33	Philip Pelt at 73	172.3	12,577.90
34	Cornelis Rutchers at 75	44.8	3,360
35	Mattys van Ceulen	<u>8.13</u>	<u>609.75</u>
36	Totals	870.20	63,280.80

Summary of *Gårkoppar* Liquidation 1625[3]

	Debit		**DG**
37	Full value of *gårkoppar* sold by de Geer (5,224.2 pounds or 19.05 skd)		35,002.10
38	Less expenses and de Geer's sales commission		3,458.75
39	Total owed to Company directors in April Credit		31,543.35
40	5,224.2 pounds sold to Elias Trip at DG 67 per 100 wt.		35,002.10

Summary of *Råkoppar* Liquidation 1625[4]

	Debit		
41	Full value of *råkoppar* sold by de Geer (19,336.0 pounds or 70.5 skd)		108,281.60
42	Less expenses and de Geer's sales commission		12,048.80
43	Total owed to Company directors in April Credit		96,232.8
44	19336.0 pounds sold to Elias Trip at DG 56 per 100 wt.		108,281.60

Like most early modern financial documents, this liquidation was organized as a balance sheet with debit and credit sides for the transaction. I have included the complete credit side for copper plate only because the shipping details for *gårkoppar* and *råkoppar* are identical to the shipping details for copper plate. I simply summarized the debit side for *gårkoppar* and *råkoppar*. In this context one should think of the debit side as expenses, or money out, and the credit side as revenue, or money in.

Starting with the first plate entry, it is noteworthy that the freight arrived on five different vessels (see lines 1 to 5). This may have been a function of the size of the vessels, or the quantity of copper available when vessels were loaded. It may also have been a form of insurance. If a large portion of

3   Riksarkviet. Leufsta arkiv, file 81, # 25, Garcooper Debit Anno 1626, Amsterdam.
4   Riksarkivet. Leufsta arkiv, file 81, # 27, Rouwcoper Debit Anno 1625, Amsterdam.

the copper were shipped in one vessel, and it fell prey to storms or pirates, the entire cargo would be lost. Splitting the cargo increased the odds that most of the shipped copper would reach its destination. Based on modern standards, the ocean freight was inexpensive for a metal commodity at 1/3 of 1 percent of the cargo value. It is important to reiterate that Amsterdam built its trading empire on inexpensive freight.[5]

Another noteworthy issue was security. There was the cost to guard the copper after discharge from the vessel, which was a modest DG 10. But the watch money (*waechgelt*) was DG 221.3, which must have been the cost of security while the copper remained in the warehouse (see lines 12 and 14). The ocean insurance was notably expensive, especially by today's standards. At DG 2,534.3 it represented 4 percent of the overall transaction; that tells us that such shipments were fraught with danger (see line 17). This would also explain de Geer's reference to a convoy, which would have a significant advantage over a single vessel against piracy (see line 9). De Geer's sales commission at 2 percent was the standard of his day; but he was also collecting interest on the advance. This is only one of three transactions, and he made commissions on all three (see lines 21, 38, and 42).

The credit side of the copper plate balance sheet lists the customers to whom de Geer sold and the prices. The prices are listed, as Dutch guilder per hundredweight; for example, the average sales price for plate was DG 72.7 per hundredweight equal to RD 79.9 per skd (see lines 25 to 35). It is noteworthy that de Geer sold off the plate in relatively small parcels. Unfortunately, there is no way to tell whether the buyers were merchants or consumers. Most likely they were local merchants with connections in copper and bronze productions centers, such as Aachen and Nuremberg, who would resell the plate to consumers at a higher price.

Looking to the credit side for both *gårkoppar* and *råkoppar*, we note that de Geer sold both parcels to Elias Trip. De Geer sold the *gårkoppar* at DG 67 per hundredweight or RD 73.7 per skd Stockholm weight, and the *råkoppar* at DG 56 per hundredweight or RD 61.6 per skd (see lines 40 and 44). Since Mårtin Wewitzer sold *råkoppar* in Germany at SD 118, or RD 72.6 per skd Stockholm weight, de Geer's sale to Trip was rather low by comparison. It was, in fact, low enough to arouse suspicion in Stockholm. Surviving correspondence, however, contains no hint of controversy over the price.

5   De Vries, *Economy*, 352.

Bibliography

Archival Sources

Riksarkivet. Leufsta arkiv, file 81, # 22 Cooper Platen Debit Anno 1626, Amsterdam.
Riksarkviet. Leufsta arkiv, file 81, # 25, Garcooper Debit Anno 1626, Amsterdam.
Riksarkivet. Leufsta arkiv, file 81, # 27, Rouwcoper Debit Anno 1625, Amsterdam.

Secondary Sources

De Vries, Jan, and Ad van der Woude, eds. *The First Modern Economy, Success, Failure, and, Perseverance of the Dutch Economy, 1500–1815*. Cambridge: Cambridge University Press, 1997.

Appendix B[1]

Company Balance Sheets 1525

Figure 10

Part A1	Company Balance Sheet January to September 1625 Debits	In SD
1	To yearly lease of building from Gobert Silentz for refining *avrad* and other copper	23,839.5
2	To contracted copper ruined in the flood at Säter refinery 232 skd at SD 130 per skd	30,160.0
3	To the sum that the director calculate is necessary to spend on new buildings and improvements of the works	36,000.0
4	To the losses on crown raw copper sold in Lübeck	5,000.0
5	Inventory	753.3
6	To Gobert Silentz for refining charges at Säter	17,430.7
7	To the mint master's contribution to wages	3,637.3
8	To copper buyer at Falun skd 4,911.5 at SD 50 per skd	245,582.0
9	To the first loan to His Majesty	150,000.0
10	To the order that Peter Grönenberg be paid	41,460.0
11	To Grönenberg and Wewitzer for weapons ordered in Holland	28,669.0
12	To interest on the loan provided by Grönenberg and Wewitzer for SD 28,669	2,982.0
13	To the order that Wewitzer be paid	84,556.0
14	To the interest on 2,000 skd copper on deposit in Holland calculated at 3 percent per year	5,225.0
15	To provision for losses on 2,000 skd copper on deposit in Holland	8,000.0
16	To *avrad* copper promised as plate or pre-mint copper 140 skd at SD 126	17,640.0
17	To pay the king for *avrad* copper (116 per skd)	52,048.0
18	To pay for loan copper	8,820.0
19	Salaries for directors and other employees	20,220.0
20	Sum	782,022.8
21	Remaining Capital	290,728.0
22	Total	1,072,750.8
Part B1	**Company Balance Sheet January to September 1625 Credit**	**In SD**
1	From the sum of company capital	311,773.7
2	Interest on capital at 1 percent	3,387.9

1 Because of rounding, and use of decimal units instead of currency extension, the reader will note some minor discrepancies in the "sum column."

3	From 1,623.3 skd *råkoppar* sold by Mårtin Wewitzer at SD 118 per skd	191,556.0
4	From 103 skp copper plate sold by Peter Grönenberg at SD 148 per skd	15,258.8
5	From 257.7 skd *råkoppar* sold by Peter Grönenberg at SD 118 per skd	30,405.7
6	From 400 skd copper mint in forecast at SD 150 per skd	60,000.0
7	From 2000 skd copper on deposit with Louis de Geer at SD 104 per skd	208,000.0
8	From 527.4 skd copper sold at SD 118 per skd	62,239.0
9	From 491.2 skd copper sold at SD 118 per skd	57,956.0
10	From the sale of *avrad* copper collected from His Majesty 879.4 skd at SD 126 per skd	110,808.0
11	From the sale of copper collected from His Majesty against the loan 169 skd at 126 per skd	21,294.0
12	Total	1,072,679.1

Figure 11

Part A2[2]	Company Balance Sheet September to January 1626 Debit	In SD
1	To His Majesty for avrad copper at full calculation	92,128
2	To loan copper still unpaid	12,474
3	To miscellaneous expenses	13,553
4	To His Majesty for war expenses	50,000
5	To the purchase of 3088 skd at SD 50 per skd from the Kopparberg	154,400
6	Subtotal	322,555
7	Remaining Company capital	183,932
8	Total	506,487
Part B2	**Company Balance Sheet from January 1625 Debit**	**In SD**
1	To His Majesty's copper toll for 1625	111,080
2	To lease and for work done at Sater	58,984
3	To Säter for refining 2,000 skd copper into Hungarian plate at SD 16.5 per skp	33,000
4	To Säter for refining 2,000 skd raw copper into mint plate at SD 10 per skp	20,000
5	To Säter for refining 2,000 skd gar copper into mint plate at SD 4 per skd	8,000
6	To Governor, Directors and other employees and foremen	29,511

2   Riksarkiviet. Handel och Sjöfart arkiv, file 46 # 43 to 48, Förslag opå Compagneidtz Stat pro Anno 1625.

7	To the purchase of 1,500 skd raw copper from the Kopparberg at SD 50 per skd	75,000
8	To Säter for refining 1,500 skd raw copper into Hungarian plate at SD 16.5 per skd	24,750
9	Subtotal	360,325
10	Remaining Company capital	133,607
11	Total	493,932
Part C	**Company Balance Sheet September 1625 to January 1626 Credit**	**In SD**
1	From the sum of Company Capital now held	290,728
2	From the sale of avrad copper 430 skd at SD 126 per skd	50,936
3	From the sale of 1396 skd *råkoppar* at SD 118 per skd	164,823
4	Total	506,487
Part D	**Company Balance Sheet from January 1625 Credit**	**In SD**
1	From the sum of Company Capital now held	183,932
2	From the sale of 2000 skd copper in the form of pre mint plate at SD 150 per skd	300,000
3	Total	483,932

One of the great accomplishments of Gustav Adolf's reign was expanding the refining capacity for *råkoppar* by building the facilities to produce Hungarian plate and *gårkoppar*. As mentioned in the main text, a Dutch copper-processing expert, Gobert Silentz, originally managed the refinery at Säter although the facility was owned by the Queen Mother. The first item on the debit side (see Part A1), SD 23,839.5, lists a payment to the Queen Mother for the lease of the buildings at Säter. In May 1625 a major flood occurred at Säter and the works were severely damaged. After the flood, the king appointed Peter Kruse, a company director, to oversee the plant. He repaired the damage and expanded the facility. This was important because selling refined copper added value to exports and improved the profitability of the entire operation.

Item 2 (Part A1) is the Copper Company's inventory at Säter that was destroyed in the flood. The company wrote off the value of the inventory. The figure of SD 130 per skd is curious as the company bought from the *bergsmän* at SD 50 per skd and paid the king a toll of SD 60 per skd mine weight. That totals SD 110 per skd. The balance must be freight and financing, or perhaps some of the refining was already done. In addition to the information on the balance sheet, line item 3 (Part A1) on the debit side, while not specific, no doubt refers to repairs at Säter. The company's mandate, however, was to build additional refining capacity so that eventually the company would not export any *råkoppar*. The king insisted on this point in his Charter of 1619 and again in the Charter of 1625. Moving to line item 6 (Part A1), SG 17,430.7 is the amount spent on the refining process mentioned earlier. Fortunately, the contract negotiated between the vice-governor of the company, Lars Skytte, and Gobert Silentz has survived and provides evidence of the refining charges.[3] In the contract, the charge is listed as four *lipspund* per *skeppund*, meaning that payment was in copper. However, in the second balance sheet, the charge was defined as SD 16.5 per skd. (Part B2 line 3). Also, the contract does not list losses of copper, which would be normal in a refining operation. The losses must, therefore, be included in the refining charge.

An established part of the king's budget was to borrow from the company. This is reflected in Part A1 line item 9. Wittrock reports that the king originally wanted the full amount of the loan in May, but Peter Kruse convinced him to take the money over three months, to ease the burden on the company's cash flow.[4] The king also wanted to sell *avrad* copper to the company and here he succeeded. Line item 17 (Part A1) reflects at least part of the sale. Wittrock reports that the king demanded SD 116 per skd for the *avrad* copper and that Johan Skytte and Peter Kruse objected strongly. They were, however, overruled by the king.[5] Another entry for the purchase of *avrad* copper (item 16, Part A1) was for Hungarian plate or pre-mint plate at the price specified in the charter, SD 126 per skd.

Line items 10 and 13 (Part A1) are a little baffling, especially since there was a substantial amount of money involved. Both Grönenberg and Wewitzer were frequent travelers to northern Germany and the Netherlands to purchase weapons and to sell copper for the company. Therefore, we would speculate that the money owed was for weapons purchased. However, there is a separate entry, line item 11 (Part A1) that covers a loan made by Grönenberg and Wewitzer specifically for the purchase of weapons; and item 12 (Part A1) was for interest on the loan. There is a larger issue here. Unlike the Dutch East India Company, which did purchase weapons and hire soldiers for its own use, the Copper Company had no such authority. The arms, after all, were for the crown, not for the company. This was further evidence of the murky line between company business and crown business; such transactions hurt the shareholders.

The remaining items to be discussed are related to the copper trade engineered by Louis de Geer in Amsterdam. Item 15 (Part A1) is a provision

---

3   Riksarkivet. Handel och Sjöfart arkiv, file 46 # 43 and 44, Contract between Lars Skytte and Gobert Silentz. March 11, 1625.
4   Wittrock, *Handelskompaniet*, 55. See also AOSB, II, 11, 206.
5   Wittrock, *Handelskompaniet*, 56.

for loss, meaning the author of the balance sheet was anticipating a small loss on the deposit with de Geer. And item 18 (Part A1), "to pay for loaned copper," was almost certainly the anticipated interest owed to de Geer for the copper sent to Amsterdam on deposit. The amount, SD 8,820, would represent about seven months interest. We now know, of course, that the deposit was successful, and the interest owed was much less.

Note that on the credit side of the balance sheet for January to September 1625, the sum of capital, line 1 (Part B1), is SD 311,773. If we turn to the company balance sheet from January, the remaining capital is listed on line 10 (Part B2) at SD 133,607.0. We can now understand why Johan Skytte was alarmed when he read these balance sheets. The company capital, or the shareholder equity, dropped during the year by SD 178,166.7 (57 percent). Such a decrease was obviously unsustainable. However, we must remember one important issue; SD 200,000 went from the company into the royal coffers, at least three quarters of it as a loan. Such a fall in equity was not related to the success or failure of the company in the marketplace; rather it reflected the crown's demand for cash.

Returning to the credit side of the balance sheet for January to September 1625, we see that the king's offer to Mårtin Wewitzer to sell copper at SD 118 per skd (RD 72.7 per skd) bore fruit because he sold 1,623.3 skd (item 3, Part B1) and later Peter Grönenberg sold a smaller parcel at the same price (item 5, Part B1). There were two more sales at this price, but we do not know the details (items 8 and 9, Part B1). It is also noteworthy that Peter Grönenberg made a smaller sale of plate at SD 148 per skd (RD 91.1 per skd) (see line 4, Part B1). These were the sales that Wittrock stated were not possible because the market had already dropped to the RD 50 to 55 per skd range.[6] It is obvious that despite his exhaustive use of original source materials, Wittrock never consulted this balance sheet.

Item 7 (Part B1) was Louis de Geer's shipment to Amsterdam that we analyzed earlier. The author of the balance sheet, Johan Sparre, listed the price as SD 104 per skd, or RD 64 per skd. This was because the results of the trade were not known at the end of 1625. He listed the revenue at SD 208,000 (RD 128,000). We know from the liquidation discussed earlier that the actual revenue was RD 185,555.[7]

The final point to be made on the credit side was that there were no sales of *gårkoppar* at or near the king's floor price of SD 150 per skd (RD 92.4). The only sale approaching the king's floor price was the small sale

6   Wittrock, *Handelskopaniet*, 59.
7   Riksarkivet. Leufsta arkiv, file 81 # 22–27, Copper Trade Liquidation. 1626.

of plate mentioned above, and plate sold for a premium over *gårkoppar*. The king's floor price was clearly unworkable, and much higher than the market. If the king had been stubborn on the issue neither the company nor its servants, Wewitzer and Grönenberg, would have sold one *skeppund* of *gårkoppar* in 1625. Fortunately for the company and the crown, the king realized his mistake and allowed some exceptions. Only the unfortunate mint was obligated to take 400 skd at the inflated price (see item 6, Part B1).

In Part A2 and B2 we can examine the balance sheet for the remainder of the year, and a second balance sheet for the full year. Curiously, at several points the balance sheet for the full year of 1625 appeared to contradict the balance for the first three quarters in Part A1 and B1. One possibility would be that the later version superseded the earlier version. The earlier version, however, contained the de Geer trade, which we can corroborate from de Geer's letters, but the later version does not. A probable explanation is that the later version was meant as a supplement to the earlier version, rather than as a replacement for it. The fact that the sales figure for the combined balance sheets is 9,444.9 skd, which is only slightly less than the Stora Kopparberg's output that year,[8] supports this position. There is some even more compelling evidence for this explanation in the form of an error in accounting noticed by Oxenstierna. In February 1626, the chancellor wrote to the king on the subject: "Gracious Majesty, I have now received another copy of the combined company balance sheets [for 1625] and they do not balance! I will attach them when I can correct them."[9]

Obviously, only the uncorrected copy has survived. Please note that the Company Balance Sheet from the January 1 debit side shows a total of SD 493,932 (line 11, Part B2). The credit side shows a total of SD 483,932 (line 3, Part D). This is certainly the error that the chancellor caught. The author of the balance sheets, Johan Sparre, simply changed the debit side to match the credit side without looking for his mistake in addition. Of course, my Excel worksheet and Axel Oxenstierna both caught this untidy accounting practice.

---

8   Total output in 1626 was 11,061 skd. Lindroth, *Gruvbrytning*, 2, 389.
9   AOSB, I, 3, 308.

Bibliography

Archival Sources

Riksarkivet. Handel och Sjöfart arkiv, file 46 # 43 and 44, Contract between Lars
   Skytte and Gobert Silentz. March 11, 1625.
Riksarkiviet. Handel och Sjöfart arkiv, file 46 # 43 to 48, Förslag opå Compagneidtz
   Stat pro Anno 1625.
Riksarkivet. Leufsta arkiv, file 81 # 22–27, Copper Trade Liquidation. 1626.

Secondary Sources

Wittrock, Georg. *Svenska handelscompaniet och kopparhandeln under Gustav II
   Adolf.* Uppsala: Almqvist & Wikesell, 1919.

Appendix C[1]

Figure 12. Balance of Debits for April 1627 (The Copper Company)[2]

	Balance of Debits for April 1627 (The Copper Company)	In SD
1	To *Cassa* Stockholm	1,866.3
2	To *Cassa* at Säter and Nyköping	2,000.0
3	To *Cassa* Falun	515.0
4	To *råkoppar* from Falun: 115.5 skd at SD 110 per skd	12,752.0
5	To *råkoppar*: 114.3 at SD 110 per skd	12,600.3
6	To diverse types of plate and sheet 887 skd at SD 110 per skd	97,677.3
7	To mint plate from Säter 22.8 skd at SD 132.8 per skd	3,044.2
8	To William Coyint in payment for refining mint plate 88 skd at SD 132.7 per skd	11,648.0
9	To plate from Säter 132.3 skd at 132.7 per skd	17,591.7
10	To Gobert Silentz for refining gårkoppar 5 skd at SD 127 per skd	706.8
11	To ditto to Silentz for refining *råkoppar*	4,589.0
12	To *gårkoppar* in Stockholm 241.5 skd at SD 127.8 per skd	30,902.1
13	To *lakakoppar* from Säter 15.3 skd at SD 312.7 per skd	4,784.5
14	To merchants for refined plate 122.5 skd at SD 135.8 per skd	16,659.9
15	To purchase refined plate from Säter 1.47 skd at 147.8 per skd	217.1
16	To purchase of refined plate from Säter 2.4 skd at SD 167.8 per skd	403.5
17	To contribution to the bells and God's gift in Säter	386.0
18	To purchase of Hungarian plate at Säter 30.3 skd at 130.8 per skd	3,996.0
19	To purchase of Hungarian plate in Stockholm 45 skd at SD 130.8 per skd	5,894.5
20	To bell copper from Falun 1.85 skd at SD 60 per skd	111.0
21	To bell copper from Stockholm and råkoppar 2.23 skd at SD 100 per skd	223.0
22	To stick copper from Stockholm 6.1 skd at SD 100 per skd	610.0
23	To Bell copper from Stockholm 32.2 skd at SD 140 per skd	4,518.0
24	**Subtotal**	**233,696.2**
25	To purchase of bell copper 38.5 skd at SD 140 per skd and 19 skd Stockholm weight at SD 135.3 per skd	8,343.0
26	To freight for copper in Nyköping 97.3 skd Stockholm weight at SD 100 per skd	9,729.0
27	To *råkoppar* from His Majesty's *avrad* copper 90.1 skd at SD 110 per skd	9,921.5
28	To copper purchase in Stockholm 61.5 skd mine weight at SD 147.7 per skd	9,123.0
29	To 0.3 skd *råkoppar* at SD 110 per skd	33.0

1 Because of rounding, and use of decimal units instead of currency extension the reader will note some minor discrepancies in the "sum column."

2 Riksarkivet, Handel och Sjöfart arkiv, file 2 # 100–04.

	Balance of Debits for April 1627 (The Copper Company)	In SD
30	To purchase ditto pro-rata	127.0
31	To purchase copper from Lars Nielson	107.0
32	To purchase copper 3.2 skd Stockholm weight at SD 138 per skd	443.0
33	To purchase of goods in Stockholm	201.0
34	To forging repair	88.0
35	To purchase goods for Arboga	243.7
36	To purchase goods for the factory	334.1
37	To remittance from Säter to Nyköping	685.5
38	To payment to Lars Larson	198.7
39	To payment to Lars Tomingson	478.7
40	To advance to Säter for charcoal	4,052.0
41	To advance for charcoal	3,359.0
42	To purchase foundry coal	610.0
43	To payment of lease for Säter	7,827.5
44	Subtotal	55,904.7
45	To spending for buildings	77,698.0
46	To purchase general inventory	1,309.3
47	To payment to the employees of Säter and the Kopparberg	6,536.9
48	To *cassa* at the Kopparberg	818.0
49	To payment to His Majesty for *råkoppar* for the mint at Nyköping 99.9 skd at SD 114.7 per skd	11,474.1
50	To payment for His Majesty the King and the *Råd Kammar* for divers ammunition	22,292.0
51	To payment for His Majesty the King for diverse ammunitio	608.0
52	To payment to the *bergsmaen* for 268.9 skd *råkoppar* which His Majesty in his mercy allows the company to purchase at SD 50 per skd	13,422.7
53	To payment of the Toll to His Majesty who graciously allows us to buy from the Kopparberg 268.9 skd at SD 60 per skd	16,107.0
54	To payment for misc.	288.0
55	To payment for construction at the mine	186.5
56	To payment for diverse expenses to the *bergsmaen*	5,612.0
57	To payment to diverse debtors	8,220.0
58	Subtotal	164,572.0
59	Total Debit	394,880.0

	Balance of Creditors for April 1627[3]	SD
1	From His Royal Majesty the King	23,727.5
2	From his Royal Majesty the King for the cassa at Säter	1,000.0
3	From the gift for Nyköping	1,000.0
4	From His Royal Majesty the King for the *cassa* of Peter von Binningen	1,000.0

3   Riksarkivet. Handel och Sjöfart arkiv file 2 #100–04.

	Balance of Creditors for April 1627[3]	SD
5	From the general participants [shareholders]	283,257.6
6	From the special general participants for buildings	9,744.8
7	From misc.	8,644.8
8	Subtotal	18,389.6
9	From interest on the special capital SD 18,389.6 for one half year at the rate of 12 percent per year	1,103.3
10	From the well born Herr, the Chancellor	3,607.8
11	From the well born Peter Kruse for his copper	255.7
12	From William Coyint, mint master for 7 skd large bar copper at SD 132.7 per skd	928.8
13	From William Coyint, mint master	4,552.3
14	From Jonas Rollang	30.9
15	From misc.	187.0
16	From diverse creditors	18,787.9
17	From the bergsmän for bought in copper	9,541.5
18	From company servants for salary	11,000.0
19	From the copper buyers at Falun salary	3,906.3
20	From provision for diverse goods	7,963.0
21	From ammunition and for shipments of copper which His Gracious Majesty will sell in Russia	4,584.9
22	For Hungarian plate which His Majesty will also sell	187.5
23	Total	395,011.6

Beginning with the debit side we once again appreciate the benefit of reviewing the balance sheets. One immediately notices that the company purchased small quantities of copper compared to 1625, at prices that no longer fit the realities of the market. The largest single purchase was from the *bergsmän* of Falun, (figure 12 line 52) 268.9 skd at SD 50 per skd plus the toll to the king (figure 12 line 53) of an additional SD 60 per skd. This adds up to a cost of SD 110 per skd mine weigh (RD 67.7 per skd mine weight), or RD 62 per skd Stockholm weight. In addition, the company purchased 241 skd at SD 127.8 per skd Stockholm weight or RD 78.7 per skd (see figure 12 line 12). The average market price in Amsterdam during 1626 was RD 62.5. The company was buying copper at a price in Sweden that would guarantee selling at a loss in Amsterdam, even before calculating freight and financing.

Turning to the credit side, we notice even more warning signs. The crown owed the company SD 23,727.5 (figure 12, Credit side line 1). Based on the king's track record, this was a high-risk debt. As in most balance sheets from this period, the shareholders' equity is listed on the credit side, instead of the modern practice of showing shareholders' equity together with the liabilities or debits. The seventeenth-century practice gave the impression that the shareholders still owed money. However, they had already paid for and received shares in the company. It also appears that the chancellor owed the company SD 3,607.8 (figure 12 Credit side line 10). This meant either that he took a loan from the company, or that he pledged to buy more shares and had not yet paid for them. Item 17 (figure 12 Credit side) was also intriguing. How could the *bergsmän* owe the company SD 9,541.5? This could only mean that the company had paid ahead of time for 191 skd of copper to the *bergsmän*, which was not yet delivered. In light of the company's notorious reputation for late payment this is unlikely. The same is true with items 18 and 19 (figure 12 Credit side). Why would salaries be carried as credit? It would mean that the company employees and the copper buyers at Falun would be paying the company to work! It appears that the author of this document deliberately shifted items from the debit side to the credit side to disguise the extent of the company's problem.

Bibliography

Archival Sources

Riksarkivet. Handel och Sjöfart arkiv, file 2 # 100–04.

Appendix D[1]

Figure 13. Copper Accounting with Erik Larsson 1627-1628 (Debit)

		Copper Company copper in Skeppund	Price in RD	Extension in RD
1		2,528.8 *Gårkoppar*	50	126,441.5
2		1,202.2 Plate	50	60,110.5
3		1,857.1 *Råkoppar*	40	74,285.8
4	Subtotal	5,588.2		
5		Avrad copper		
6		360.5 *Gårkoppar*	50	18,023.5
7		42.7 Plate	50	2,131.5
8		338.7 *Råkoppar*	40	13,548.0
9	Subtotal	742.0		
10		*Råkoppar* Falkenberg Deposit		
11		2,717.0	40	108,680.0
12	April 1627	500.0	40	20,000.0
13	Subtotal	3,217.0		
14	Shipping and entry		7,000.0	
15	Total	9,547.1		430,220.8
16	May 1627	2,535.5 *Gårkoppar*	50	126,775.0
17	August 1627	1,813.5	50	90,675.0
18	Nov. 1627	1,422.0	50	71,100.0
19	Jan. 1628	800.0	50	40,000.0
20	May 1628	525.0 *Avrad*	50	26,250.0
21	Subtotal	7,096.0		354,800.0
22	Total	16,643.1		785,020.8
23	Pro Saldo			38,460.0
	Sales Record			
24		2,528.8 *Gårkoppar*	62	156,787.8
25		1,202.2 Plate	60	72,132.0
26		1,857.1 *Råkoppar*	50	92,856.3
27	Subtotal	5,588.2		
28		360.5 *Gårkoppar*	62	22,348.6
29		42.7 Plate	60	2,557.8
30		338.8 *Råkoppar*	50	16,935.0
31	Subtotal	742.0		
32		500.0 *Gårkoppar*	50	25,000.0
33		2,717.0 *Råkoppar*	50	135,850.0
34	Subtotal	3,217.0		

1   Because of rounding, and use of decimal units instead of currency extension the reader will note some minor discrepancies in the "sum column."

		Copper Company copper in Skeppund	Price in RD	Extension in RD
35	Freight and Entry		7,000.0	
36	Total	9,547.1		531,467.4
37	May 1627	2,535.5 *Gårkoppar*	62	157,201.0
38	Aug. 1627	1,813.5	62	112,437.0
39	Nov. 1627	1,422.0	62	88,164.0
40	Jan. 1628	800.0	62	49,600.0
41	Subtotal	6,571.0		407,402.0
42	May 1628	525.0 *Avrad*	62	32,550.0
43	Plus *Avrad*	7,096.0	62	439,952.0
44	Subtotal	16,643.1		439,952.0
45	Total			RD 971,420.0

Figure 14.   Copper Accounting with Erik Larsson 1627-1628 (Credit)

1	Through the Financial Kammer	RD
2	To Livonia	26,343.0
3	To Lübeck	42,429.0
4	To Elbing	1,800.0
5	To His Majesty	29,600.0
6	Paid in November	64,629.0
7	**Subtotal**	**164,801.0**
8	The balance owed on the RD 80,000 for November	15,371.0
9	For payment on the loan of RD 200,000 at 7.5 percent	90,000.0
10	**Subtotal**	**105,371.0**
11	To Livonia for the "War State"	50,512.0
12	To Mårtin Wewitzer	6,000.0
13	For April to His Majesty	23,000.0
14	To pay the balance of the RD 50,416 for copper	22,411.0
15	For Niels (last name illegible) member of the *Råd*	759.0
16	**Subtotal**	**102,682.0**
17	Received by Conrad Falkenberg	107,250.0
18	Interest paid to the Estates General	25,256.0
19	Interest paid in Lübeck	10,238.0
20	Paid to Camerarius as the king's deputy	4,094.0
21	Freight and entry	2,540.0
22	Paid to Per Baner	520.0
23	For (name illegible) Expenses	2,540.0
24	For gunpowder and touch paper (for muskets)	14,000.0
25	Anders (Last name illegible)	30,772.0
26	Paid to Louis de Geer	46,161.0
27	Copper mint to Riga	12,000.0
28	Letter of Credit	40,000.0

29	Anders (Last name illegible)	90,000.0
30	Provision for insurance and convoy	23,000.0
31	Interest	23,170.0
32	Subtotal	431,541.0
33	Actual total	804,395.0
34	Swedish Accountant's Total	823,481.0
35	Pro Saldo	147,939.0
36		**RD 971,420.0**

We are fortunate to have a surviving balance sheet for the copper business between de Geer's consortium and the crown for the years 1627 and
1628.[2] As usual, the numbers tell us a lot about the business. First, however,
some explanation is necessary. The deposit system was a method for the
crown to mortgage copper, while retaining ownership. The balance sheet
was written from the point of view of the king. The copper was shipped by
the king to Amsterdam, so the transactions are recorded on the debit side
(see figure 13). De Geer and Larsson then made various payments to the
king and to the king's creditors. Those payments are on the credit side (see
figure 14). Line items 1 to 11 (see figure 13) represent the copper on deposit
in Amsterdam, and lines 16 to 20 represent the copper sent to the mints in
Sweden to be made into coins. During the year the crown had 9,547 skd of
copper on deposit in Amsterdam, and loans totaling 430,220.75 from the
consortium (line item 15, figure 13).

Larsson then reported to the chancellor on the state of the contract. They
had received 1,714 skd of *gårkoppar* for deposit in Amsterdam and Larsson
had instructed Trip to make payments to the armies at Riga, Livonia, and
Elbing via Lübeck. The revenue from that quantity of *gårkoppar* would be
RD 85,700 based on a mortgage of RD 50 per skd. These payments are listed
on the credit side of the balance sheet as line items 2, 3, and 4 (figure 14).
There was, however, no more copper due for mortgaging because the king
wanted the balance to go to the mint. In fact, the king was anticipating
minting 400,000 *dalers* (copper mint) to finance the armies in Prussia and
Livonia, and he would need 7,000 skd of copper for this purpose.[3] Per the
crown's instruction, between May 1627 and January 1628, de Geer and Larsson
shipped a total of 6,571 skd of *gårkoppar* plus 525 skd of *avrad* copper for a
total of 7,096 skd from the mine to the mints. This can be seen from llines

2   Riksarkivet. Leufsa arkiv, file 81 # 119, Koppar Rechnings meds Erik Larsson 1627–1628. (This
reference for figure 17 and figure 18 that follow.)
3   Riksarkivet. Leufsa arkiv, file 81 # 119, Koppar Rechnings meds Erik Larsson 1627–1628. (This
reference for figure 12 and figure 13 that follow.)

16 to 20 on the debit side of the balance sheet (figure 13). Finally, Larsson reported that the partnership was up to date with payments to the *bergsmän* at the Stora Kopparberg: "The *bergsmän* are properly paid for all copper that has been weighed in, and there is a reserve so they will have money for the market times."[4] The *bergsmän*, at least, were benefitting from the new regime.

Regarding the future, Larsson had both good news and bad for the chancellor. He wrote that in order to pay current and anticipated crown debts in Sweden and elsewhere, he and the consortium expected to need a total of 15,738 skd Stockholm weight of copper, both for mortgaging in Amsterdam and for minting. The last shipment (see line 22, figure 13) was 525 skd of *avrad* copper, listed as shipped in May 1628, at which time they had a total of 16,643 skd in storage in Amsterdam, and at the mint (line item 25, figure 13). Larsson also wrote that he was expecting additional copper to be weighed in at the mine shortly, which he thought would put the crown in a comfortable position regarding *råkoppar*.[5]

The issue of the *gårkoppar* and plate for minting was an altogether differ-ent story, because refining capacity was limited. The reader will recall that as part of this contract, Larsson and de Geer agreed to deliver 40,000 *daler* copper mint to the crown each month for payment of military expenses. If they failed to deliver, they were required to make up the difference from their own resources. When Larsson was writing to the chancellor, there were only 400 skd of copper in Säter being prepared for the mint and perhaps another 150 skd at the refining plant in Falun. In other words, they were not going to meet the monthly obligation to deliver 40,000 *dalers* copper mint to Riga and Elbing, and Larsson feared that they never meet the obligation given the limited capacity at the various mints and refining plants. Larsson appeared distraught at the situation:

> I swear to you that I am suffering. The Treasury Council is after me daily
> to give them more copper coins or pay myself for the missing coins. The
> quarterly forecasts [for output of coins] were not realistic, and if I have
> to advance the missing amount it will cause me great harm.[6]

Larsson continued in his letter that he was diligent in overseeing the mine and the processing plants, but that he could no longer trade for his own account and was suffering a loss of income on top of all the other problems.

---

4   AOSB, II, 11, 424, Letter from Erik Larsson to Axel Oxenstierna. Stockholm, November 10, 1628.
5   Ibid.
6   Ibid., 425.

There is, however, no evidence that he and de Geer were ever actually required to make up the shortfall in currency, and the king probably put the clause in the contract to focus their attention on the production issue. There is only one specific reference to a copper mint shipment to Riga: line item 27, (figure 14), on the credit side of the balance sheet showing a shipment of RD 12,000 in the form of copper mint. This was equal to 37,500 *daler* copper mint, or less than one month's requirement. In addition, line item 11 (figure 14), allocates RD 50,512 for the war in Livonia. Although not stated, this was probably also part of the obligation in copper mint. This was equal to another 157,850 *daler* copper mint, so combined, the amount shipped was 195,350 *daler* copper mint. De Geer first announced the crown's contract to Peter Trip in May 1627. The last entry on the balance sheet was for May 1628. Thus, the contract had run about one year when Larsson drew up this balance sheet. During that year the consortium had minted 195,350 *daler* copper mint, short of the 480,000 *daler* copper mint called for in the contract, but given the limits on refining capacity, it was no small feat.

The Larsson letter to the chancellor and the balance sheet allow us to trace the actual execution of the agreements. For example, in November 1627, the king reached an agreement with Larsson and de Geer that was part of the larger contract to ship 2,000 skd to Amsterdam for mortgaging.[7] The king then instructed the partners to pay the RD 80,000 to the chancellor in Elbing. This shipment is represented on the debit side of the balance sheet, as 1,857 skd (line item 3, figure 13). Part of the money that came from this shipment, RD 15,371, was still owed to the chancellor and appears on the credit side in line item 8 (figure 14).

The balance sheet also shows how the deposit system functioned. The king provided the consortium with copper as collateral; de Geer and Larsson, in turn, lent him money they borrowed from the Trip family. They then forwarded money to the Swedish armies in Livonia and Elbing, and they paid crown officials. (See payment to Ludwig Cammarius, the king's envoy in Amsterdam in line item 20, figure 14). The king also instructed them to reimburse crown employees for their expenses, such as Mårtin Wewitzer on line 12 (figure 14). They also serviced existing loans like the one mentioned in line 9 (figure 14) and made interest payments against old loans from the States General in The Hague and in Lübeck (lines 18, and 19, figure 14). Like the company before them, the partners were also paying for gunpowder and touch paper[8] on line item 24 (figure 14). In addition, they sent direct

---

7   LDGBOA, 154.
8   Touch paper was used for fuses in the matchlock muskets of the time.

payments to the king, as can be seen on lines 5 and 13 on the credit side (figure 14). The partners were functioning as part of the crown's financial bureaucracy, and with the backing of the Trips they functioned as the king's bankers. Finally, the partners acted as merchants; they chartered the freight and covered the insurance. At the same time, they were overseeing the minting of copper, which they would also send to the armies.

There is one important omission on the balance sheet; there is no mention of paying the *bergsmän*. Larsson, in his letter to the chancellor, told him that the *bergsmän* had been paid in full for all copper received. The *bergsmän* had delivered 16,643 skd Stockholm weight, the equivalent of 15,090 skd mine weight. The crown was still paying the miners SD 50 per skd so the full amount owed to the miners would be SD 754,500. There was no mention in the balance sheet of any such sum.

Figure 15.   Income Statement for the Crown for 1628

Sales in skd		Sales Price in RD per skd	Extension in RD
2889.33	*Garkoppar*	62	179,138.5
1244.91	Plate	60	74,694.6
5412.83	*Råkoppar*	50	270,641.5
Total			524,474.6
Cost of Goods Sold			
2889.33	*Gårkoppar*	50	144,466.5
1244.91	Plate	50	62,245.5
5412.88	*Råkoppar*	50	270,644.0
Total			477,356.0
Gross Profit in RD			47,118.6[9]

During 1628 and afterwards, de Geer and Larsson sold some of the copper in the deposit from the crown in Amsterdam. These transactions are recorded in lines 24 to 34 (figure 13) and the results are shown on the income statement for the crown (figure 15). The king mentioned some transactions to the chancellor in a letter at the end of 1628.[10] He complained that payment would be made by bill of exchange routed through either Conrad von Falkenberg in Amsterdam or Anders Swenson in Hamburg, the crown's banker there. The funds would not be received in Sweden until June or July 1629.[11]

9   AOSB, II, 1, 451
10   AOSB, II, 1, 451.
11   AOSB, II, 1, 451.

Bibliography

Archival Sources

Riksarkivet. Leufsa arkiv, file 81 # 119, Koppar Rechnings meds Erik Larsson 1627–1628.

Printed Primary Sources

Oxenstierna, Axel. *Rikskansleren Axel Oxenstierna skriften och brefvexling*, Series I, 16 vols. Stockholm: P.A. Norstedt & Söner, 1888–Present.
Oxenstierna, Axel. *Rikskansleren Axel Oxenstierna skriften och brefvexling*, Series II, 14 vols. Stockholm: P.A. Norstedt & Söner, 1888–Present.

Appendix E[1]

Figure 16[2]

His Magesty's Copper Accounting 1632			Debit
	Year	January	SKD
1		*Gårkoppar* received from wellborn Herr Räntekammar and Mårtin Wewitzer shipped from Nyköping and received in Amsterdam by Elias Trip in February, March, April and May received in skd	720.0
2		In March anno 1631	55.8
3		Total in skd	775.8
4		Paid out in Amsterdam in March, April and May 1631 by Elias Trip	RD
5	1630	Mayor Knipquyler	16,344.0
6		Ouirste Mitsål	6,000.0
7		Camerarius	4,000.0
8		Admiral Clerck	3,000.0
9		Ernst Ruyter	2,000.0
10		Freight and expenses	6,904.0
11		Total	38,248.0
12		October 6 months interest at 7 percent	1,338.8
13		6 months storage at RD 4	24.0
14		Paid out as specie	980.0
15	1631	April 6 months interest at 7 percent	1,420.8
16		6 months storage at RD 4	24.0
17		October 6 months interest	1,471.3
18		6 months storage	24.0
19	1632	April 6 months interest	1,523.0
20		6 months storage	24.0
21		February Transfer from E. Trip	42.0
22		City tax	78.0
23		Labor tax	17.0
24		Land tax	40.0
25		3 months storage	12.0
26		3 months interest	500.0
27		Total	45,766.8
28		Preceding November Total in RD	45,767.3
29		Commission on RD 45,767.25 at 2 percent	915.2
30		Illegible	124.5
31		Total in RD	46,807.0
32		Total in DG	117,014.8

1   Because of rounding, and use of decimal units instead of currency extension the reader will note some minor discrepancies in the "sum column."

2   Riksarkivet. Leufsta archiv, file 81 # 137–39, Con. Mat. Coperreecken.

Once again, we will rely on a balance sheet to refute the claims made in a letter. The details of the transactions that de Geer negotiated with the 720 skd of copper, that the king asked him to put on deposit in Amsterdam, are recorded in a balance sheet I came across in the de Geer family archives (*Leufsta arkiv*).[3] It is now housed in the Riksarkiv in Stockholm. As can be readily seen, the copper arrived between February and May 1630 (figure 16, lines 1 to 3 and payments to creditors began that same year. In March of the following year the crown sent an additional 55.8 skd probably to cover the interest on the first shipment.

The balance sheet shows us the mechanics of the deposit system. When the parcel arrived, the mortgaged amount was not sent back to Sweden, or to the king's army in Germany, it was distributed by Trip to a list of creditors, most of them probably in Amsterdam. On line 5 (figure 16) we see a payment to Mayor Knipquyler. We will learn later that this was an interest payment, for the crown, on a loan from the States General. On line 7 (figure 16) Trip paid Ludwig Camerarius his annual salary of RD 4,000. We encountered Admiral Clerck in the second chapter waiting in Stockholm for funds to outfit a fleet of ships. Perhaps the RD 3,000 (figure 16, line 8) was for the same purpose.

Unfortunately, we do not know the other recipients, but the pattern was clear. The crown would send copper to Amsterdam to be mortgaged, and then use the funds from the mortgage to pay creditors. Line items 18 to 25 (figure 16) were for interest and storage expenses. Unpaid interest was compounded every six months. The other issue of note was the commission on line 29 (figure 16). It is not clear who took this 2 percent commission; it was probably Trip for acting as banker on the transaction. The commission was on the entire value including the interest.

Figure 17[4]

His Majesty's Copper Accounting 1632				Credit	
	Year	Day		Amst. lbs	Total in DG
1	1632	23 April	Pieter Schlyn at DG 45.3 (or RD 49.6)	12,070.0	5,506.5
2		23	Gans van Aspers at DG 46 (or RD 50.3)	8,224.0	3,783.0
3		23	Volquin Momma at DG 46	4,484.0	2,062.0
4		11 May	Momma at DG 49 (or RD 53.6)	10,003.0	4,901.3
5		11	Larz Clockner at DG 49	5,989.0	2,934.3
6		24	Casper Engelbrecht at DG 49	5,005.0	2,452.2
7		25	Gans van Aspers at DG 49	8,000.0	3,920.0

3   LDGBOA, 196, Kontrakt med LDG. angående 720 skd gårkoppar deposition och 38,824 rdr däremot att leverera. Ulvesund, February 1, 1630.
4   Ibid.

His Majesty's Copper Accounting 1632			Credit	
Year	Day		Amst. lbs	Total in DG
8	27	Pierre Gabin at DG 51 (or RD 55.7)	49,500.0	25,245.0
9	27	Pierre Gabin at DG 50.5 (or RD 55.2	89,757.0	45,327.2
10	2 June	Casper Engelbrecht at DG 51.5 (RD 56.33)	4,001.0	2,060.3
11	17	Illegible at DG 52 (or RD 56.9)	2,847.0	1,480.0
12	17	Illegible at DG 52.5 (or RD 5;8)	4,000.0	2,100.0
13	28	Janz Courct at DG 53 (or RD 58)	2,400.0	1,272.0
14	30	Gunbert Ganternde de Worl at DG 53	2,487.0	1,318.0
15		Total	208,767.0	104,361.8
16		Preceding November total	208,767.0	104,361.8
17		Interest on the sales of Gårkoppar		12,653.0
18		Total		117,014.8

In the letter to the king which was quoted earlier, de Geer pledged to take no more profit than the interest the king paid him on the mortgage.

On the credit side we begin to detect discrepancies with de Geer's claims to the king. (The weights are Amsterdam pounds because the prices are Dutch guilder per hundredweight.) As explained in the body of chapter five, de Geer made the first sale from the inventory in April (figure 17, line 1) and the last sale was on June 30. The reader will recall that de Geer did not write to the king until August, and he worded his letters as if the transactions he described were taking place during that month. In the famous letter de Geer explained to the king that the siege of Maastricht had created the conditions for a price increase. We dispelled this "red herring" in the chapter. The siege did not begin until June 9, 1632, and the balance sheet shows that de Geer made only four small sales after that date.

De Geer wrote the first letter trumpeting his price manipulation on May 19 to Pieter Spierinck, the chancellor's financial adviser. He had made only four sales of copper from the 720 skd parcel when he wrote that letter, and the highest sale price was RD 53.9. He wrote to Spierinck that he had sold at RD 57 per skp. Probably the letter to Spierinck was a routine attempt to stay in royal favor, not to take over the copper trade in Amsterdam. It was only in August, when he realized that copper prices remained strong, that he began a serious campaign.

Line items 1 to 14 (figure 17) on the credit side are individual sales. He made the last two sales on June 28 and June 30 at DG 53 both as RD 58.3 per skd. Then he waited two months before he informed the crown that he had caused a significant copper price increase in Amsterdam. And he presented the news as if the flurry of activity coincided with his letters.

Bibliography

Archival Sources

Riksarkivet. Leufsta archiv, file 81 # 137–39, Con. Mat. Coperreecken.

Printed Primary Sources

Dahlgren, Erik Wilhelm, ed. *Louis de Geers brev och affärshandlingar 1614–1652*. Stockholm: P.A. Norstedt & Söner, 1934.

Appendix F[1]

Figure 18[2]

	Debit in SKD		RD	DG
1		Gustav Adolf king of Sweden debit	308,291.0	770,727.4
2	1318.0	Copper deposited in 1629 with Pieter Trip in May 1629 at RD 44 per skd	57,992.0	145,007.3
3	2389.0	Copper deposited from de Geer and Larsson in May 1629 at RD 55 per skd	131,395.0	328,487.3
		Additional copper deposits		
4	112.0	Summer		
5	31.5	August		
6	100.0	September		
7	100.0	From Hendrick Trip		
8	28.5	Refined copper		
9	10.0	From Larsson		
10	60.0	From de Geer		
11	442.0	Total at RD 55 per skd	24,310.0	60,733.3
12	1,565.3	From Hendrick Trip raw coper at RD 44	68,873.2	172,210.1
13		Total	282,575.6	706,439.0
14		Interest due	25,715.4	64,288.4
15		Total deposit	308,291.0	770,727.4

Figure 19

	Interest Calculation 1629 to 1634	RD per Skd	DG
1	Principal and interest due May 1630		770,727.4
2	Principal and interest due May 1631		832,385.6
3	Principal and interest due May 1632		898,976.4
4	Principal and interest due May 1633		970,894.6
5	Principal and interest due May 1634		1,048,566.1
6	Total skeppund on deposit		5,714.30
7	Redemption cost per skeppund in May 1634		183.5
8	The above in RD per skd	73.4	
9	Average cost in May 1630	49.5	
10	Difference (interest)	23.9	

1   Because of rounding, and use of decimal units instead of currency extension the reader will note some minor discrepancies in the "sum column."
2   Riksarkivet. Handel och Sjöfart arkiv, file 46 #208, Interest Calculation for the 1629 Deposit. We derived the riksdaler column from the Guilder column because that alone appears in the original document. The accountant made some minor errors in multiplication.

11	Deposit price for *gårkoppar* in May 1629	55.0
12	Redemption price for *gårkoppar* in May 1634	78.9
13	Deposit price for *råkoppar* in May 1629	44.0
14	Redemption price for *råkoppar* in May 1634	67.9

Judging the effectiveness of the deposit system is relatively easy. Let us take one deposit that was small and straightforward and calculate the cost of keeping the copper in deposit, rather than selling it outright into the market. We encountered this deposit in the Deposit System chapter. It was negotiated between Elias Trip and Conrad von Falkenberg in May of 1629 as part of a much larger deposit. The balance sheet was drawn up for Erik Larsson in 1634 because Trip formed a new consortium in May 1634 to take over the entire deposit.[3] This balance sheet was prepared for that eventuality. The parcels from line 2 and 3 (see figure 18) were already in Amsterdam at the time. The parcels in lines 4 through 12 (see figure 18) were added during the year. Line 14 (see figure 18), interest due, would have covered the interest for the first year, or up to May 1630. Therefore, we should calculate the interest from May 1630 to May 1634, when Elias Trip formed a new company.

As can be seen from line 10, in figure 19, the average interest cost was RD 23.9, which means that the cost of redemption for *gårkoppar* was now RD 78.9 (line 12, figure 19) up from RD 55 per skd in May of 1629; the cost of redemption for *råkoppar* was RD 67.9 (line 14, figure 19), up from RD 44 in May 1629. In other words, it cost the crown RD 23.9 per skp during the term of the deposit.[4] The deposit system was an innovative idea and if the crown had used it as a short-term expedient, as was originally intended, it might have worked in the crown's favor. The long-term financing of these large parcels, however, was disastrous for crown financing and threatened to ruin relations with the merchant community in Amsterdam.

Bibliography

Printed Primary Sources

AOSB, II, 11, 532.

3   AOSB, II, 11, 532.
4   The king's cost at the mine, SD 50 per skd mine weight, was equal to RD 27.7 per skd Stockholm weight. The deposit price for råkoppar in 1629 was RD 44 per skd. If we subtract the price drop of RD 23.9 we get a price at the mine of RD 20.1 per skd Stockholm weight, well below the king's cost at the mine.

Bibliography

Archival Sources

Handel och Sjöfart arkiv. Riksarkivet, Stockholm.
Kontraktsböcker, huvudserie (1617) 1619–1622. Riksarkivet, Stockholm.
Kontraksböcker, specialserie (1613) 1620–1622 (1624). Riksarkivet, Stockholm.
Leufsta arkiv. Riksarkivet, Stockholm.

On-Line Sources

Riksarkivet. Stockholm, SVAR. Royal Copybooks 1600–1632. http://www.svar.ra.se.

Printed Primary Sources

Dahlgren, Erik Wilhelm, ed. *Louis de Geers brev och affärshandlingar 1614–1652.* Stockholm: P.A. Norstedt & Söner, 1934.

Oxenstierna, Axel. *Rikskansleren Axel Oxenstierna skriften och brefvexling,* Series I, 16 vols. Stockholm: P.A. Norstedt & Söner, 1888–Present.

Oxenstierna, Axel. *Rikskansleren Axel Oxenstierna skriften och brefvexling,* Series II, 14 vols. Stockholm: P.A. Norstedt & Söner, 1888–Present.

Stiernman, Anton von, ed. *Samling utaf kongl. brev, stadgar och förordordningar i angående Sweriges Rikes,* 4 vols. Stockholm: Kongl. Tryckeriet, 1747.

Van Dillen, Johannes Gerard, ed. "Amsterdamsche Notarieele Acten Betreffende den Koperhandel en de Uitoefening van Mijnbouw en Metaalindustrie in Zweden." In *Bijdragen en mededeelingen van het Historisch Genootschap* 58. Utrecht: 1937.

Secondary Sources

Ahnlund, Nils. *Gustav Adolf the Great.* Translated by Michael Roberts. Cambridge: Cambridge University Press, 1940.

Åström, Sven-Erik. "The Swedish Economy and Sweden's Role as a Great Power 1632–1697." In *Sweden's Age of Greatness 1632–1718,* edited by Michael Roberts, 38–10. New York: Macmillan 1973.

Bonney, Richard, ed. *The Rise of the Fiscal State in Europe, c.1200–1815.* Oxford: Oxford University Press, 1999.

Boëthius, Bertil and Eli Filip Heckscher. *Svensk handelsstatistik 1637–1737*. Stockholm: Thule, 1925.

Boëthius, Bertil. *Karl IX och driftsorganisationen vid Stora Kopparberget*. Stockholm: Hugo Löjdquist, 1957.

Boëthius, Bertil. *Koppar bergslagen fram till 1570–talets genombrott, uppkomst, medeltid vasatid*. Uppsala: Almquist &Wiksells, 1965.

Brand, Hanno and Leos Muller, eds. *The Dynamics of Economic Culture in the North Sea-and Baltic Region*. Hilversum: Verloren, 2007.

Brems, Hans. "Sweden: From Great Power to Welfare State." *Journal of Economic Issues* 4, no. 2/3 (June–Sept, 1970): 1–16.

Carlos, Ann M., and Stephen Nichols. "Giants of an Earlier Capitalism: The Chartered Trading Companies as Modern Multinationals." *The Business History Review* 32, no. 1 (1958): 14–59.

Coleman, D. C., ed. *Revisions in Mercantilism*. London: Methuen & Co. Ltd, 1969.

Dahlgren, Erik Wilhelm. *Louis de Geer, 1587–1652, hans lif och verk*, 2 vols. Uppsala: Almqvist & Wiksells, 1923.

De Vries, Jan, and Ad van der Woude, eds. *The First Modern Economy, Success, Failure, and, Perseverance of the Dutch Economy, 1500–1815*. Cambridge: Cambridge University Press, 1997.

Downing, Brian M. *The Military Revolution and Political Change, the Origins of Democracy and Autocracy in Early Modern Europe*. Princeton: Princeton University Press. 1992.

Edvinsson, Rodney. "Early Modern Copper Money: Multiple Currencies and Trimetallism in Sweden 1624--1776." *European Review of Economic History*, 16, 2011, 405--429.

Edvinsson, Rodney. "International Political Economy of Early Modern Copper Mercantilism: Rent Seeking and Copper Money in Sweden 1624–1776." *Explorations in Economic History* 49, no. 3 (2012): 303–15.

Flarierski, Gregor. "Rötter: den judiska fragan i brevvaxlingen mellan Hugo Valentin och Eli Heckscher." *Historisk Tidskrift*, Series 102 (1982): 177–201.

Friedman, Milton. "Bimetallism Revisited." *The Journal of Economic Perspectives* 4, no. 4 (1990): 85–104.

Friis, Astrid. "Forbindelse mellem det europaeiske og asiatiske kobbermarked." *Scandia* XII (1939): 151–80.

Frost, Robert I. *The Northern Wars: War, State, and Society in Northeastern Europe 1558–1721*. London: Routledge, 2014.

Glamann, Kristof. *Dutch-Asiatic Trade, 1620–1740*. Copenhagen: Danish Science Press. 1958.

Glete, Jan. *War and the State in Early Modern Europe, Spain, the Dutch Republic, and Sweden as Fiscal-Military States, 1500–1660*. London: Routledge 2002.

Geyl, Pieter. *History of the Dutch Speaking Peoples, 1555–1648*. London: Phoenix, 2001.

Hallenberg, Mats and Magnus Linnarsson, eds. *Politiska rum, kontroll, konflikt och rörelse i det förmoderna Sverige 1300–1850*. Lund: Nordic Academic Press, 2014

Hallenberg, Mats. *Kungen, fogdarna och riket, lokalförvaltning och statsbyggande under tidig vasatid*. Stockholm: Brutus Östlings, 2001.

Hale, John Rigby. *Renaissance Fortification, Art or Engineering?* London: Thames and Hudson, 1977.

Hamilton, Earl J. *American Treasure and the Price Revolution in Spain, 1501–1650*. Cambridge, Ma: McGill-Queen's University Press, 1934.

Heckscher, Eli F. *An Economic History of Sweden*. Translated by Goran Ohlin. Cambridge, Ma: Havard University Press, 1968.

Heckscher, Eli Filip. "Den europeiska kopparmarknaden under 1600 talets." *Scandia* XI (1938): 215–79.

Heckscher, Eli Filip. "Kopparen under sveriges stormaktstid." *Historisk Tidskrift* I Series 57 (1937): 286–95.

Heckscher, Eli Filip. *Mercantilsm*, 2 vols. Translated by Medel Shapiro. New York: Macmillan,1962.

Heckscher, Eli Filip. *Sveriges economiska historia från Gustav Vasa*, 2 vols. Stockholm: Albert Bonniers, 1936.

Heckscher, Eli Filip. "1600-tals kopparen än en gång." *Historisk Tidskrift* II, Series 1.

Hette, Björn. "Ekonomisk historia i Sverige under femtio år; institutionell utvekling och forskningsinriktning." *Historisk Tidskift* 43 (1980): 140–75.

Hilderbrand, Karl-Gustav. *Falu stads historia 1641–1687*. Falun: Falu nya boktryckeri, 1946.

Israel, Jobathan. *Dutch Primacy in World Trade, 1641–1740*. Oxford: Clarendon Press. 1990.

Kellenbenz, Hermann, ed. *Schwerpunkte der Kupferproduktion und des Kupfer-handels in Europa 1500–1650*. Cologne: Böhlau Verlag, 1977.

Kellenbenz, Hermann. *The Rise of the European Economy, an Economic History of Continental Europe from the Fifteenth to the Eighteenth Century*. New York: Holmes and Meier 1976.

Kindleberger, Charles P. "The Economic Crisis of 1619 to 1623." *The Journal of Economic History* 51, no. 1 (March 1991): 149–75.

Klein, Peter Wolfgang. *De Trippen in de 17e Eeuw, een Studie over het Ondernemersge-drag op de Hollandse Stapelmarkt*. Rotterdam: Assen, 1965.

Kristiansson, Sture. *Falu kopparvåg 1546–1873, historiska inblickar i en institution och livet kring denna*. Filipstad: Bronells Tryckeri AB, 1993.

Kristiansson, Sture. "Kopparsmugglingen vid Stora Kopparberg 1580–1638." *Berg-slagsarchiv: årsbok för historia och kulturhistoria I bergslagen* 4 (1992): 52–64.

Kumlien, Kjell. "Staat, Kupfererzeugung und Kupferausfuhr in Schweden 1500–1650."
    In *Schwerpunkte der Kupferproduktion und des Kupferhandels in Europa 1500–1650*,
    edited by H. Kellenbenz, 241–59. Cologne: Böhlau Verlag, 1977.

Lindroth, Sven. *Gruvbrytning och kopparhantering vid Stora Kopparberg intill 1800
    talets början*, 2 vols. Uppsala: Almqvist & Wiksells, 1955.

Lesger, Clé and Leo Noordegraaf, eds. *Entrepreneurs and Entrepreneurship in Early
    Modern Times, Merchants and Industrialists within the Orbit of the Dutch Stable
    Market.* The Hague: Hollandse Historische Reeks XXIV, 1995

Lesger, Clé. *The Rise of the Amsterdam Market and Information Exchange: Merchants,
    Commercial Expansion, and Change in the Spatial Economy of the Low Countries,
    1550–1630.* Translated by J.C. Grayson. Aldershot: Ashgate, 2006.

Lindbad, Thomas. "Louis de Geer (1587–1652) Dutch Entrepreneur and the Father of
    Swedish Industry." In *Entrepreneurs and Entrepreneurship in Early Modern Times,
    Merchants and Industrialists within the Orbit of the Dutch Stable Market*, edited by
    CléLesger and Leo Noordegraaf. The Hague: Hollandse Historische Reeks XXIV, 1995.

Lunde, Henrik O. *A Warrior Dynasty, the Rise and Fall of Sweden as a Military
    Superpower, 1611–1721.* Oxford: Casemate, 2013.

Lundkvist, Sven. "The Experience of Empire: Sweden as a Great Power." In Michael
    Roberts, ed. *Sweden's Age of Greatness*, edited by Micahel Roberts, 20–57. New
    York, 1973.

Nilsson, Sven A.. "Gustav II Adolf och Axel Oxenstierna: En studie i maktdelning
    och dess alternativ." *Scandia* 62 (1966): 169–94.

Nordstrom, Byron J. "Christina (1626–1689)." In Jonathan Dewald, ed., *Europe
    1450 to 1789, Encyclopedia of the Early Modern World*, 6 vols, edited by Jonathan
    Dewald, 1, 486–87. New York: 2004.

North, Michael. *The Baltic, a History.* Translated by Kenneth Kronenberg. Cambridge,
    Ma: Harvard University Press, 2017.

Nováky, György. "Inledning." In *Louis de Geer, 1587–1652, hans lif och verk*, by Erick
    Wilhelm Dahlgren, 5–24. Malmö: facsimile edition, 2002.

Odén, Brigitta. *Kopparhandel och statsmonopol*, studier I svensk handelshistoria
    under senare 1500-talet. Stockholm: Almqvist & Wiksells, 1960.

Olsen, Albert. "Kobberpolitik I den svenske stormagtstid." *Scandia* X (1937): 38–73.

Olsen, Albert. "Kopperpolitik og kritik." *Scandia* X (1937): 295–305.

Olsen, Albert. "Professor Eli Heckscher og det japanske Kobber." *Scandia* XI (1937):
    157–59.

Oredsson, Sverker. *Gustav Adolf: Sverige och Trettioåriga kriget.* Lund: Wahlström
    & Widstrand, 1992.

Paas, Martha, George C. Schoolfield, and Roger Paas. *The Kipper und Wipper Infla-
    tion, 1619–23: An Economic History with Contemporary German Broadsheets.* New
    Haven: Yale University Press, 2012.

Parker, Geoffrey. *The Army of Flanders and the Spanish Road 1567–1659.* Cambridge: Cambridge University Press, 1974.

Parker, Geoffrey. *Europe in Crisis, 1598–1648.* Oxford: Blackwell, 1979.

Parker, Geoffrey. *Global Crisis, War, Climate Change, and Catastrophe in the Seventeenth Century.* New Haven: Yale University Press, 2014.

Parker, Geoffrey. *The Thiry Years War.* New York: Barnes and Noble, 1993.

Parrott, David. *The Business of War, Military Enterprise and Military Revolution in Early Modern Europe.* Cambridge: Cambridge University Press, 2001.

Posthumus, Nicolaas Wilhelmus. *Inquiry into the History of Prices in Holland,* 2 vols. Leiden: E.J. Brill, 1946.

Redish, Angela. *Bimetallism, an Economic and Historic Analysis.* Cambridge: Cambridge University Press, 2000.

Ringmar, Erik, *Identity, Interest and Action: A Cultural Explanation of Sweden's Intervention in the Thirty Years War,* Cambridge: Cambridge University Press. 1996.

Roberts, Michael. *Gustavus Adolphus, a History of Sweden 1611–1632,* 2 vols. London: Longmans, Green and Co., 1957.

Roberts, Michael. "Oxenstierna in Germany, 1633–1636." *Scandia* 48, no. 1 (1982): 61–105.

Roberts, Michael. *The Swedish Imperial Experience 1560–1718.* Cambridge: Cambridge University Press, 1979.

Roberts, Michael, ed. *Sweden's Age of Greatness 1632–1718.* New York: St. Martin's Press, 1973.

Rydberg, Sven. *The Great Copper Mountain, the Stora Kopparberg Story.* Hedemora: Gidlunds Publishers, 1988.

Rydberg, Sven. "Stora Kopparberget: The Great Copper Mountain." Copy of a paper presented at the Science Museum, London, October 12, 1988.

Rystad, Göran. "The King, the Nobility, and the Growth of Bureaucracy in 17th Century Sweden." In *Europe and Scandinavia, Aspects of the Process of Integration in the 17th Century,* edited by Göran Rystad, 59–70. Lund: 1983.

Rystad, Göran, and Klaus-R Böhme. *In Quest of Trade and Security: The Baltic in Power Politics, 1500–1890,* 2 vols. Lund: Lund University Press, 1994.

Safley, Thomas Max. "Bankruptcy." In *Europe 1450 to 1789, Encyclopedia of the Early Modern World,* 6 vols, edited by Jonathan Dewald, 1, 219–22. New York: 2004.

Safley, Thomas Max. "Commerce and Markets." In *Europe 1450. to 1789, Encyclopedia of the Early Modern World,* 6 vols, edited by Jonathan Dewald, 2, 11–19. New York: 2004.

Sandström, Åke. *Mellan Torneå och Amsterdam, En undersökning av Stockholms roll som förmedlare av varor i regional-och utrikeshandel 1600–1650.* Stockholm: Stockholmsmonografier, 1990.

Schumpeter, Joseph A. *The Theory of Economic Development, an inquiry into Profts, Capital, Credit, Interest, and the Business Cycle.* Translated by Redvers Opie. New Brunswick: Transaction Publishers, 2008.

Soll, Jacob. *Free Market, the History of an Idea.* New York: Basic Books, 2022.

Soll, Jacob. *The Reckoning, Financial Accountability and the Rise and Fall of Nations.* New York: Basic Books, 2014.

Soon, Arnold. "Die Merkantilistische Wirtschaftspolitik Schwedens und die baltische Städte im 17. Jahrhundert." *Jahrbücher für Geschichte Osteuropas*, Neue Folge 11, no. 2 (June, 1963): 183–222.

Stryker, Lawrence. "'Sharp Practice' Among Merchants in Seventeenth-Century Amsterdam 1620–1632." *The Journal of European Economic History* XLIII, no. 3 (2014): 131–62.

Stryker, Lawrence. "Swedish Copper and Financial Skullduggery in Amsterdam, 1610–1625" *The journal of European Economic History* LI, no. 2 (2022) 45–82.

Stryker, Lawrence. "The King's Currency: Gustav II Adolf and the Copper Standard 1619–1632." *Scandinavian Economic History Review* 65, no. 1 (2017): 52–69.

Stolpe, Sven. *Drottning Christiana.* Stockholm: A.Bonniers, 1974.

Söderberg, Tom. *Stora Kopparberg under medeltiden och Gustav Vasa.* Stockholm: Tryckt hos Victor Pettersons, 1932.

Sundberg, Ulf. "An Energy Analysis of the Production of the Great Copper Mountain of Falun during the mid 17th Century." *International Journal of Forest Engineering* III (1991): 4–16.

Svenski Biografiskt Lexikon Band 04 (1924) sida 325.

Tjaden, Anja. "The Dutch in the Baltic, 1544–1721." In *The Baltic in Power Politics 1500–1990*, vol. 1, edited by Göran Rystad, Klaus-R Böhme, and William M. Carlgren, 61–137. Lund: Lund University Press, 1994.

Thompson, Erik. "Chancellor Oxenstierna, Cardinal Richelieu, and Commerce: The Problems of Governance in Early Seventeenth-Century France and Sweden." PhD. diss., John Hopkins, 2004.

Thompson, Erik. "Swedish Variations on Dutch Commercial Institutions 1605–1655." *Scandinavian Studies* 77, no. 3 (Fall 2005): 331–42.

Timm, Albrecht. "Die Bedeutung des Mansfelder Kupfers zwischen 1500 und 1630." In *Schwerpunkte der Kupferproduktion und des Kupferhandels in Europa 1500–1650*, edited by H. Kellenbenz, 184–89. Cologne, 1977.

Utterström, Gustav. "Eli Heckscher, Bertil Boëthius och Sveriges economiska historia från Gustav Vasa." *Meddelande från institutionen för ekonomisk historia* 2 (1982): 1–33.

Van Dillen, Johannas Gerard. *Van Rijkdom en Regenten. Handboek tot de Economische en Sociale Geschiednis van Nederland tijdens de Republiek.* The Hague: Martinus Nijhoff, 1970.

Van der Muijssenberch, Winifried. "Corporate Governance, The Dutch Experience." *Transactional Law* 63 (2002–2003).

Vlachovic, Josef. "Die Kupfererzeugung und der Kupferhandel in der Slovakei vom Ende des 15. Bis zur Mitte des 17. Jahrhundert." In *Schwerpunkte der Kupferproduktion und des Kupferhandels in Europa 1500–1650*, edited by H. Kellenbenz, 148–71. Cologne, 1977.

Weibull, Curt. *Christina of Sweden*. Translated by Alan Tapsell. Stockholm: Bonnier, 1966.

Weibull, Curt. "Gutaf II Adolf." *Scandia* VI (1933).

Westermann, E. "Zur Silber-und Kupferproduktion Mitteleuropas vom 15 bis zum Frueher 17. Jahrundert." *Der Anschnitt* 38 (1986): 187–211.

Wetterberg, Gunnar. "Johan Skytte." In *Levande 1600 tal*. Stockholm: Atlantis, 2003.

Wetterberg, Gunnar. *Kansler Axel Oxenstierna*, 2 vols. Stockholm: Atlantis, 2002.

Wetterberg, Gunnar. "Louis de Geer." In *Levande 1600 tal*. Stockholm: Atlantis, 2003.

Wingquist, S. "Om det gamla koppar-compagneit och kopparmyntningen under Gustav II Adolfs tid." *Skandia* IV (1834,): 5–68.

Wittrock, Georg. *Svenska handelscompaniet och kopparhandeln under Gustav II Adolf*. Uppsala: Almqvist & Wikesell, 1919.

Wolontis, Josef. *Kopparmyntning i Sverige 1624–1714*. Helsingfors: 1936.

Yun-Casalilla, Bortolomé and Patrick K. Ó Brien, eds. *The Rise of Fiscal States, A Global History, 1500–1914*. Cambridge: Cambridge University Press, 2012.

Index

Gustav II Adolph is referenced as GA throughout the index, except for his own main entry where his name is spelled out in full.

References to illustrations are in *italics*.
References to tables are in **bold**.